The Political Economy of China

For Fan, Grace, Patrick, and Thomas

The Political Economy of China

HONGYING WANG

polity

Copyright © Hongying Wang 2025

The right of Hongying Wang to be identified as Author of this Work has been asserted in accordance with the UK Copyright, Designs and Patents Act 1988.

First published in 2025 by Polity Press

Polity Press
65 Bridge Street
Cambridge CB2 1UR, UK

Polity Press
111 River Street
Hoboken, NJ 07030, USA

All rights reserved. Except for the quotation of short passages for the purpose of criticism and review, no part of this publication may be reproduced, stored in a retrieval system or transmitted, in any form or by any means, electronic, mechanical, photocopying, recording or otherwise, without the prior permission of the publisher.

ISBN-13: 978-1-5095-3680-1 (hardback)
ISBN-13: 978-1-5095-3681-8 (paperback)

A catalogue record for this book is available from the British Library.

Library of Congress Control Number: 2024945641

Typeset in 10/13pt Swift Light
by Cheshire Typesetting Ltd, Cuddington, Cheshire
Printed and bound by CPI Group (UK) Ltd, Croydon, CR0 4YY

The publisher has used its best endeavors to ensure that the URLs for external websites referred to in this book are correct and active at the time of going to press. However, the publisher has no responsibility for the websites and can make no guarantee that a site will remain live or that the content is or will remain appropriate.

Every effort has been made to trace all copyright holders, but if any have been overlooked the publisher will be pleased to include any necessary credits in any subsequent reprint or edition.

For further information on Polity, visit our website:
politybooks.com

Contents

Figures, Tables, and Boxes	x
Acknowledgments	xii
Abbreviations	xiii
Preface	xvi
1 History: From the "Middle Kingdom" to the "Century of Humiliation"	1
2 The Enigma of the Party State	26
3 The Transformation of Rural China	52
4 The Commanding Heights of the State Sector	71
5 Private Sector Growth	91
6 China's New Proletariat	112
7 Weaving a New Social Safety Net	132
8 Money in the Chinese Economy	154
9 Macroeconomic Policy	178
10 In Search of Clear Waters and Green Mountains	196
11 Laying Eggs with Borrowed Hens	222
12 China's "Going Out" Policy	241
Conclusion	259
Glossary	275
References	283
Index	318

Detailed Contents

Figures, Tables, and Boxes	x
Acknowledgments	xii
Abbreviations	xiii
Preface	xvi

1 History: From the "Middle Kingdom" to the "Century of Humiliation"	1
"The Great Divergence"	1
Failed Reforms and Experiments	13
Conclusion	24
Questions for Discussion	25
2 The Enigma of the Party State	26
The Party	26
The State	33
Central–Local Relations	39
State–Society Relations	45
Conclusion	50
Questions for Discussion	51
3 The Transformation of Rural China	52
From Collective to Household Farming	53
The Rise and Fall of Township and Village Enterprises	57
Rural–Urban Integration	61
Political Consequences of Economic Transformation	66
Conclusion	69
Questions for Discussion	70
4 The Commanding Heights of the State Sector	71
Incremental Reform in the 1980s	72
Drastic Restructuring in the 1990s	77
Consolidating State Control in the 2000s	81

The Political Economy of State-Owned Enterprise Reform	85
Conclusion	89
Questions for Discussion	90

5 Private Sector Growth — 91

The Rise of Private Enterprises	91
State Accommodation of the Private Sector	97
The Private Sector's Embrace of the State	105
Conclusion	109
Questions for Discussion	111

6 China's New Proletariat — 112

Labor Market Development	113
Labor Conditions	119
Labor, Capital, and the State	125
Conclusion	129
Questions for Discussion	131

7 Weaving a New Social Safety Net — 132

The Pension System	133
Healthcare	138
Social Assistance	147
The Political Economy of Welfare Reform	149
Conclusion	153
Questions for Discussion	153

8 Money in the Chinese Economy — 154

The Fiscal System	154
The Financial System	161
Financial Instruments of the Developmental State	172
Conclusion	176
Questions for Discussion	177

9 Macroeconomic Policy — 178

Macroeconomic Management	179
The Central Bank	184
Economic Imbalance	190
Conclusion	195
Questions for Discussion	195

10 In Search of Clear Waters and Green Mountains	196
Environmental Degradation	197
The Political Economy of Environmental Policies	205
Environmental Issues in Chinese Foreign Relations	215
Conclusion	220
Questions for Discussion	221
11 Laying Eggs with Borrowed Hens	222
Foreign Trade	223
Foreign Direct Investment	231
Conclusion	239
Questions for Discussion	240
12 China's "Going Out" Policy	241
Outward Foreign Direct Investment	241
Development Aid	251
Conclusion	258
Questions for Discussion	258
Conclusion	259
A Chinese Development Model?	259
A Successful Model?	266
Questions for Discussion	274
Glossary	275
References	283
Index	318

Figures, Tables, and Boxes

Figures

0.1	GDP per capita in China 1978–2022	xvii
2.1	Formal and Actual Flow of Authority in China's Party State	28
2.2	CCP Membership since 2008	46
3.1	China's Urban Population 1975–2020	64
5.1	Comparing Private Enterprises and SOEs in Efficiency	97
6.1	Unemployment in China 1991–2023	118
7.1	Gini index – China 1990–2020	134
7.2	Out-of-Pocket Spending on Healthcare 2000–2021	146
9.1	Inflation, Consumer Prices 1987–2023	180
10.1	CO2 Emissions in China and the United States 1990–2020	199
10.2	Level of Water Stress in China 1980–2020	201
11.1	China's Exports of Goods and Services 1980–2020	226
11.2	FDI Inflow 1985–2021	232
12.1	Chinese Outward Foreign Direct Investment 1990–2022	248
12.2	Chinese Development Finance 2000–2021	253

Tables

1.1	A Historical Comparison of Europe and China	12
1.2	Major Dynasties in Chinese History	25

Boxes

1.1	The Pan Family	7
1.2	Excerpts from Emperor Qianlong's Letter to King George III	10
1.3	Mao's Persecution of "Capitalist Roaders"	22
2.1	The CCP's 20th National Congress	29
2.2	The Mysterious COD	32
2.3	Covid and the Surveillance State	49
3.1	The Story of Xiaogang Village	54

3.2	Huaxi – "Number One Village Under the Sky"	60
4.1	The Superiority of Gradualism?	76
4.2	Deng's Southern Tour	78
4.3	China's National Champions	83
5.1	Shazi Guazi (Fool's Sunflower Seeds)	94
5.2	The Rise and Fall of Jack Ma	104
6.1	Losing the "Iron Rice Bowl"	117
6.2	Deaths at Foxconn	123
6.3	The Gains and Limitations of the Honda Strike	129
7.1	Attacks on Doctors	142
8.1	"Soldiers of Fortune"	156
8.2	The Stock Market and the "National Team"	170
8.3	Made in China 2025	175
9.1	Inflation and Political Instability	181
9.2	Zhou Xiaochuan, the Technocratic Central Banker	187
10.1	China's "Cancer Villages"	202
10.2	The Nu River Dam Project	212
10.3	Liang Congjie and Friends of Nature	214
11.1	Ricardo's Model	223
11.2	Foreign Capital and China Unicom	239
12.1	The Poland Fiasco	250
12.2	Oil for Infrastructure and Housing	255

Acknowledgments

In writing this book, I have benefited from the help and support of many people. It is a pleasure to acknowledge Nancy Breslin, Eric Helleiner, and Thomas Hueglin for reading the manuscript and offering their feedback at different stages of the writing process.

I would also like to thank my students at the University of Waterloo, who took my course on Chinese Political Economy. They were invariably curious and enthusiastic. Keeping in mind their questions and reactions to the course materials, I have tried to approach the subjects as intuitively and explain the concepts as straightforwardly as possible.

I owe a huge debt to my editor at Polity Press, Louise Knight. When she first proposed this project to me several years ago, neither of us expected it to take such a long time to complete. Without her incredible patience and steadfast guidance, this book would not have seen the light of the day. I would also like to thank Inès Boxman and Olivia Jackson, who worked closely with Louise to keep the project on track.

Two anonymous reviewers of the manuscript offered extraordinarily detailed and thoughtful comments. I am deeply grateful to them for their collegiality and intellectual generosity. Their input has improved the book considerably, although I alone am responsible for the remaining mistakes and inaccuracies.

Last, but not least, I would like to thank my family for their understanding and support. My children, Fan and Patrick, and my mother, Grace, may well have been perplexed by how long this book project has taken, but they have put up with my slowness with good humor. My partner, Thomas, who knows what is involved in writing a book, has often reminded me not to lose my focus. I dedicate this book to these special people.

Abbreviations

ABC	Agricultural Bank of China
ACFTU	All-China Federation of Trade Unions
AFC	Asian financial crisis
AIIB	Asian Infrastructure Investment Bank
APC	Agricultural Producers' Cooperative
BOC	Bank of China
BRI	Belt and Road Initiative
BRICS	Brazil, Russia, India, China, South Africa
BVI	British Virgin Islands
CBDC	central bank digital currency
CBI	central bank independence
CBRC	China Banking Regulatory Commission
CCB	China Construction Bank
CCDI	Central Commission for Discipline Inspection
CCF	China-China-Foreign
CCP	Chinese Communist Party
CDB	China Development Bank
CHIBOR	China Interbank Offered Rate
CLAPV	Center for Legal Assistance to Pollution Victims
CM	China Model
CMS	Cooperative Medical System
CNY	Chinese yuan
COD	Central Organization Department
COE	collectively owned enterprise
COPD	chronic obstructive pulmonary disease
COVEC	China Overseas Engineering Group Co. Ltd.
CPI	consumer price index
CREA	Centre for Research on Energy and Clean Air
CSF	China Securities Finance Corporation
CSIS	Centre for Strategic and International Studies
CSRC	China Securities Regulatory Commission
DAC	Development Assistance Committee
EBF	extra-budgetary finance
EKC	Environmental Kuznets Curve

EP	export processing
EPIL	environmental public interest litigation
EU	European Union
EV	electric vehicles
FDC	funded defined contribution
FDI	foreign direct investment
FIE	foreign-invested enterprise
FON	Friends of Nature
FSDC	Financial Stability and Development Committee
FTC	foreign trade company
GATT	General Agreement on Tariffs and Trade
GDP	Gross Domestic Product
GFC	global financial crisis
GHG	greenhouse gas
GIS	Government Insurance Scheme
GLF	Great Leap Forward
GONGO	Government Organized NGO
GVC	Global value chains
HKEX	Hong Kong exchange
ICBC	Industrial and Commercial Bank of China
IEA	International Energy Agency
IMF	International Monetary Fund
IPO	initial public offering
ITO	International Trade Organization
JMC	Financial Regulatory Coordination Joint Ministerial Committee
KMT	*Kuomintang* – Chinese Nationalist Party
LGFV	local government financing vehicles
LIS	Labor Insurance Scheme
MEE	Ministry of Ecology and Environment
MIC	Made in China
MNC	multinational corporation
MOF	Ministry of Finance
MSA	medical savings account
NCMS	New Rural Cooperative Medical Scheme
NDB	New Development Bank
NDC	nationally determined contribution
NGO	non-governmental organization
NIE	newly industrialized economy
NPC	National People's Congress
NRDC	National Development and Reform Commission
NRPS	New Rural Pension Scheme
ODA	official development assistance
OECD	Organization of Economic Cooperation and Development

OFDI	outward foreign direct investment
OMO	open market operations
OOF	other official flows
PAYG	pay as you go
PBC	People's Bank of China
PLA	People's Liberation Army
PRC	People's Republic of China
PRD	Pearl River Delta
PV	photovoltaic (solar panels)
R&D	research and development
RMB	Renminbi (Chinese currency)
ROA	return on assets
ROC	Republic of China
SAFE	State Administration of Foreign Exchange
SARS	Severe Acute Respiratory Syndrome
SASAC	State-Owned Assets Supervision and Administration Commission
SEEA	System of Environmental–Economic Accounting
SEPA	State Environmental Protection Administration
SEZ	special economic zone
SHIBOR	Shanghai Interbank Offered Rate
SIE	state-invested enterprise
SOCB	state-owned commercial banks
SOE	state-owned enterprises
SP	social pension
SPA	social pooling account
SPC	Supreme People's Court
SSE	Shanghai Stock Exchange
SWF	sovereign wealth funds
SZSE	Shenzhen Stock Exchange
TMT	technology, media, and telecom
TSS	tax sharing system
TVE	township and village enterprise
UEBMI	Urban Employee Basic Medical Insurance
UMLGS	Urban Minimum Living Guarantee System
UNCCD	United Nations Convention to Combat Desertification
UNFCCC	United Nations Framework Convention on Climate Change
UNICEF	United Nations International Children's Emergency Fund
URBMI	Urban Resident Basic Medical Insurance
URPP	Urban Residents Pension Plan
URRBMI	Urban–Rural Resident Basic Medical Insurance
VAT	value-added tax
WHO	World Health Organization
WTO	World Trade Organization

Preface

As I write this preface in mid-summer 2024, most news stories discussing the Chinese economy run with gloomy headlines: "China's economy falters, raises pressure for more stimulus" (Reuters, July 15), "China's economy growing slower than expected as leaders meet for third plenum" (*Guardian*, July 15), "China's factory activity falls for third straight month" (*Financial Times*, July 31), "China May Be on a Well-Trod Path to Economic Trouble" (Bloomberg, August 3), "China's Economy Keeps Gliding on Just One Engine" (Yahoo Finance, August 4), and "Does Beijing Have Any Idea What To Do About China's Troubled Economy?" (*Forbes*, August 6).

Worryingly for China, these headlines are the tip of the iceberg. Over the last few years, the country has been experiencing significant economic challenges, including sky-rocketing local government debt, a deepening property sector crisis, massive youth unemployment, and strong pushbacks from Western countries against Chinese exports and access to technology.

For years, local governments in China, without adequate budgetary resources, have resorted to direct and indirect borrowing to build infrastructure, subsidize economic development, and provide social services. In the process, they have accumulated more and more debt. As of 2022, the explicit and implicit debt owed by local governments in China amounted to three quarters of the country's GDP, exceeding the GDP of France, Germany, and Japan combined (Mark 2024). Even more concerning is that there is no clear pathway for local governments to repay the debt.

Meanwhile, China's vast property sector, began to show signs of serious stress in 2021, when major developers ran short of cash and headed for default. Until then, real estate development and associated businesses had been a pillar of Chinese economic development, making up between 25 and 30 percent of the country's GDP. After years of continued growth, the property sector now faces a huge oversupply problem. As of early 2024, unsold housing inventory reached an estimated RMB 30 trillion (or over $4[1] trillion) (Hale and Leahy 2024). This has cast a long shadow across industries ranging from steel and cement to construction and furniture manufacturing. It also poses a threat to the stability of the financial system as local governments depend

---

[1] $ refers to US dollars throughout.

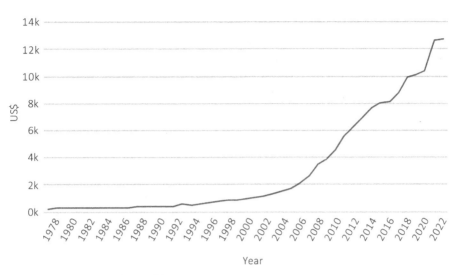

Figure 0.1 GDP per capita in China 1978–2022
Source: World Bank Group.

heavily on land development for their financial revenues and large numbers of Chinese families have their wealth invested in real estate property.

For many young people in China, the prospect of finding a satisfying job has faded significantly in the last few years. As of mid-2023, the unemployment rate for youth aged 16 to 24 reached an astonishing 21.3 percent (*Economist* 2024). This is in part due to the slowdown of economic growth. World Bank data indicate that China's GDP increased by an average of over 10 percent annually between 2000 and 2010, but that figure dropped to 6.5 percent from 2011 to 2023. Another major contributor has been the mismatch between the expectations of university-educated youth and the labor market demand, leading many graduates to choose between menial jobs and unemployment (*Economist* 2024).

These domestic economic difficulties are worsened by the external environment. Western governments have taken an increasingly tough stand against Chinese exports and access to technology. For instance, in mid-2024 the US government announced it would quadruple the tariffs on Chinese electric vehicles (EVs) sold in the American market from 25 percent to 100 percent. The European Union followed suit, though not to the same extent as the US (da Silva 2024). Meanwhile, the US government has imposed limits on the sale of semiconductor technology and equipment to China by American companies and others, severely hindering Chinese advancement in telecom, artificial intelligence, and weapon systems (Swanson 2022). Western governments, especially American policymakers, have justified these restrictions by citing concerns over China's growing dominance of key technologies in these and other areas.

These troubling trends are of course challenging for China. But situated in a broader context, they pale against the success story of its meteoric rise as an economic superpower over the last five decades. In a historical "blink of an eye," China transformed itself from one of the poorest countries in the world to a major player in the global economy and a leader in important areas of technology. This rise of a powerful and prosperous China has been the cherished dream of the Chinese people since the mid-nineteenth century.

* * *

The political slogan of the "China Dream" (*zhongguo meng*), first promoted by Xi Jinping, who became General Secretary of the Chinese Communist Party (CCP) in 2012 and President of the country the following year, has permeated the whole of Chinese society. It is the title of China's most popular singing contest (*zhongguo meng zhi sheng*) and reality talent show (*zhongguo meng xiang xiu*). It has been widely used by business groups – legitimate or fraudulent – to attract investors. The appeal of the concept is hardly surprising. As one of the oldest civilizations, China was a world leader in economic, political, and cultural development, but it lost its preeminence in modern times. For around a hundred years, between the mid-nineteenth century to the mid-twentieth century, it suffered invasion, exploitation, and humiliation in the hands of stronger foreign powers. During this "century of humiliation," millions upon millions of Chinese patriots fought to regain their nation's sovereignty, dignity, and rightful place in the world.

After the CCP took power in 1949, it created a socialist economic structure, seeking to leverage government planning and state ownership to modernize the country. During the reign of Mao Zedong that model was implemented intermittently, often interrupted by mass political campaigns that took over normal economic activities. In the end, it failed to build a strong and prosperous China worthy of its historic glory. At the time of Mao's death in 1976, the People's Republic was one of the poorest countries in the world with a GDP per capita of $165 a year. Having learned their lesson the hard way, Mao's successors gradually abandoned government planning and reduced state control of the economy. With economic liberalization, China's fortunes began to change. From 1978 to 2010, Chinese GDP grew by an astonishing average of 10 percent a year, an economic miracle unprecedented not only in China but in the history of the world. By 2010, barely three decades after beginning its economic reform, China had overtaken Japan to become the world's second largest economy (after the United States). Figure 0.1 shows this steady increase in GDP per capita in China from the late 1970s onwards.

How has China accomplished its economic miracle? What is the Chinese development model? Does the Chinese economy operate in fundamentally different ways than market economies and thus pose a danger to the existing international economic order? Scholars have debated long and hard on these questions. Drawing insights from studies by historians, economists, political scientists, sociologists, and others, this book offers students a multifaceted introduction to the politics and economics behind China's remarkable development and its rise to global prominence. Along the way, it will uncover the distinctive features of Chinese political economy, including the role of the state and its relations with various economic actors.

Chapters 1 and 2 lay the groundwork of our study, with an introduction to the history and the political system of China from the decline of the imperial Qing Dynasty in the mid-nineteenth century to the era of the People's Republic of China that began in 1949. Chapters 3, 4, and 5 examine rural economic reform, the reform of state-owned industries, and the rise of private enterprises in turn. Chapters 6 and 7 explore the transformation of the labor market and the welfare system. Chapter 8 covers the fiscal and financial systems, while Chapter 9 discusses macroeconomic management. Chapter 10 turns to the environmental challenges facing China and its response. Chapters 11 and 12 discuss China's foreign economic relations – the inflow and outflow of goods and capital – and their consequences. Chapter 13 concludes with a reflection on the concept of the "China Model" of economic development and draws together answers to some of the key questions raised throughout the book.

Each chapter features boxes that illustrate core ideas discussed in the text and concludes with questions for discussion. These are designed to encourage students to exchange ideas and to further explore the issues covered in the chapter. You can also find a glossary of key terms at the back of the book (each term is set in bold on its first occurrence in the text).

1

History: From the "Middle Kingdom" to the "Century of Humiliation"

The official narrative of contemporary Chinese economic development has a distinctively historical undertone, evoking China's newly achieved prosperity and its growing economic weight in the world as a return to the country's historical grandeur. Indeed, a rich and strong China has been the dream cherished by generations of Chinese. In this chapter we will take a whistlestop tour of China's development from the long durée of the so-called "Middle Kingdom" (*zhongguo*) to the **"century of humiliation"** and into the communist era. This historical background aims to help us understand the ambitions and the strategies of economic development in contemporary China.

Section I reflects on the relative decline of Chinese economy at a time of European ascendance with the Industrial Revolution of the eighteenth and nineteenth centuries. It presents contending perspectives on the so-called "great divergence" between China and Europe in terms of their modern economic development. Section II takes a closer look at the crises faced by China and its responses from the end of the Qing Dynasty (1644–1912) to the Communist era. It highlights the **Self-Strengthening Movement** led by Qing officials in the late nineteenth century and the modernization experiments under the Chinese Communist Party (CCP) in the mid-twentieth century and explores why, after losing its lead in the world economy in the eighteenth century, China failed to catch up with the front runners in the ensuing two centuries.

"The Great Divergence"

The Venetian merchant and traveler, Marco Polo, visited China in the thirteenth century during the Yuan Dynasty (1271–1368). This was a time of division and war in Europe, where nations, city-states, and the Catholic Church competed against each other fiercely and continuously. In contrast, China enjoyed relative peace after the conquest by the Mongols. Polo stayed in China for seventeen years and traveled extensively to different parts of the country. After returning to Italy, which was in the midst of a war between Venice and Genoa, he recorded what he had seen and experienced. His book, *A Description of the World* or *The Travels of Marco Polo*, described a China that was far ahead of Europe in its economy, technology, urban development, and bureaucratic organization (Polo 1903). For instance, he reported the wide use of coal ("black stone existing in beds in the mountains"), which was a better and less costly kind of fuel than wood, large-scale iron and salt production, exquisite quality of porcelain and silk, as well as the circulation of paper money, all of which were eye-opening for the Europeans.

Polo was particularly vivid in his description of the wealth and splendor he witnessed in China. Speaking of the palace of Kublai Khan, the Mongol emperor of China who made Beijing his capital city, Polo marveled, "This is the greatest palace that ever was ... The building is altogether so vast, so rich, and so beautiful, that no man on earth could design anything superior to it." His description of the city of Beijing was just as euphoric, stating that it "has such a multitude of houses, and such a vast population inside the walls and outside, that it seems quite past all possibility ... To the city also are brought articles of greater cost and rarity, and in greater abundance of all kinds, than to any other city in the world."

He described the "many roads and highways leading from the capital to a variety of provinces," where "the traveling messengers of the emperor would find at every 25 miles of the journey a station called a 'Horse Post-House.' At each of those stations used by the messengers, there is a large and handsome building for them to stay at, in which they find all the rooms furnished with fine beds and all other necessary articles in silk, and where they are provided with everything they can want." He concluded that this communication system "was done on the greatest scale of magnificence that ever was seen."

Polo was sent by the Great Khan to inspect the amount of his customs and revenue in various areas of the country. He was deeply impressed by the scale and wealth of Chinese cities. He noted that "the great and noble city" of Suzhou contained "merchants of great wealth and an incalculable number of people ... 6,000 bridges, all of stone, and so lofty that two ships together could pass underneath them." He praised the even grander city of Hangzhou for its size, population, lively markets, guilds of craftsmen, boats, and barges, and the "finest and largest baths in the world ...," proclaiming "the city is beyond dispute the finest and noblest in the world."

Indeed, for much of its history, traditional China was the world's largest and most advanced economy. Economic historians' meticulous research shows that from the tenth to the early fifteenth century Chinese per capita income was higher than that of Europe and that, as of 1830, the Chinese economy was still the biggest in the world, accounting for almost 33 percent of the world's GDP, while Europe made up 26.6 percent (Maddison 2007). In the later eleventh century, by using coal and coke in blast furnaces, the Chinese produced as much pig iron as the British did 700 years later. In the thirteenth century, power-driven spinning machines appeared in China, about 500 years before spinning mules appeared in England (Landes 2006). In the early fifteenth century, Ming Dynasty's Admiral Zheng He took his armada sailing through

Southeast Asia to East Africa. Chinese navigation technology then was superior to anything the Europeans would have at the time when Christopher Columbus and Vasco da Gama set off on their voyages many decades later (Wakeman 1983). In his famous 1776 treatise, *Wealth of Nations*, Adam Smith wrote that China was "a much richer country than any part of Europe."

However, underneath the appearance of continued Chinese preeminence, important changes began to take place. From the fifteenth century to the eighteenth century, Western Europe gradually overtook China in its pace of economic growth. A recent study, relying on historical data on **GDP per capita**, points more precisely to the period of seventeenth to the early eighteenth century as the start of the divergent trajectories of development in China and Europe (Broadberry et al. 2018). In time, this divergence would lead to disastrous encounters between China and European powers.

By the late eighteenth century, the Industrial Revolution had made Britain an enthusiastic and competitive international trader, seeking overseas markets for its industrial goods. Its economic expansion led it to China, the land of silk, tea, and fine porcelain – all luxury items highly desired by European consumers. However, British merchants had one big problem: while there was a lot they wanted to buy from China, the Chinese had little interest in buying anything they had to offer. They resorted to selling opium to China to pay for their purchase of Chinese goods. As the scale of the opium trade expanded, its harmful effect on the Chinese population alarmed the Qing government. It introduced an opium ban. In 1839, the court dispatched Lin Zexu, an passionate and determined patriotic official, to the southern city of Guangzhou to crack down on the opium trade. He arrested opium dealers, seized and destroyed large quantities of opium, and sought to blockade further opium smuggling. Britain retaliated swiftly, sending its naval forces to China and brought the Qing Empire to its knees. Following the **first Opium War** (1839–1842), China lost many more wars to Britain and other foreign powers, paid heavy reparations, ceded massive territories, opened its market to foreign trade, and granted extraterritoriality to foreign nationals. While the country remained formally independent, its sovereignty was in shambles.

Why did China fall so far behind Europe in its economic and technological development, despite its significant lead in previous centuries? Moreover, it was not just that its economic development was stagnant compared to that of Europe during the Industrial Revolution, but it regressed from its own past. For example, the Chinese invented the hemp-spinning machine in the fourteenth century, but it was never adapted for manufacturing cotton. Although China invented the technology for using coal and coke, it fell into disuse, reversing the progress achieved previously by the iron industry. When confronting the European invaders in the nineteenth century, the Chinese had forgotten how to use the cannons they had developed in the thirteenth century (Landes 2006).

Scholars have long puzzled over the great divergence between China and Europe in the modern era. Much of the discussion focuses on the question of why China did not experience the development of modern capitalism and the Industrial Revolution that transformed the economy of Europe. This may be a natural question to ponder, given the subsequent competition and conflict between Europe and China. However, as the historian Nathan Sivin points out, it is odd to ask "why something didn't happen in history. It is analogous to the question of why your name did not appear on page 3 of today's newspaper" (Sivin 1985, p. 6). A better way to think of the great divergence is to consider the factors that facilitated the rise of capitalism and Industrial Revolution in Europe, while China continued its own trajectory of development.

Nevertheless, there is heuristic value to the question of why capitalism and Industrial Revolution took place in Europe, while nothing comparable happened in China. When historians debate about the rise of the West in modern times, their analysis implicitly points to what was missing in China in that period (Daly 2014). In some ways, why the West and why not China are two sides of the same coin – what China got wrong is often a mirror image of what Europe got right. Three broad categories of factors have received the most attention in the literature – political system, economic and demographic conditions, and culture/mentality.

Political System

Historically, the international political systems in Europe and in China formed a sharp contrast, each with its strengths and weaknesses. In Europe, the fall of Rome in the fifth century led to the emergence of various political entities in the Middle Ages, which competed against each other for survival and dominance. The political turmoil and instability were destructive, and often hampered Europe's economic development. On the other hand, the pressure of competition paved the way for the Renaissance and the Industrial Revolution later. Indeed, some scholars contend that the constant need to prepare for war and to upgrade their military capabilities played a major role in Europe's economic and technological development (Lieberman 2009; Satia 2018).

The situation was quite the opposite in China. From the Qin Dynasty (221–206 BCE) onward, the Chinese empire maintained long periods of unity, despite intervals of division. Moreover, geographically isolated by the high plateaus and deserts in the west and the Pacific Ocean in the east, China seldom faced an existential security threat. Although the nomadic tribes of central Asia caused periodic headaches for the Chinese, they were largely able to manage these "barbarians" with a combination of appeasement and limited warfare (Rossabi 1983). The absence of constant external threat created a peaceful environment for economic development in China, but it also took away a major driving force for military and technological advancement.

There were also significant differences internally between Chinese and European political systems. In Europe, from the Middle Ages on, churches, cities, and guilds constituted alternative centers of power outside the state. European states had to contend with these and other societal forces. In comparison, the Chinese political system was dominated by a powerful bureaucratic state, which faced little competition from other organizations (Landes 2006; Qian 1985; Bodde 1991). The existence of a powerful bureaucratic state worked well for China's agricultural development. It developed large hydraulic works, maintained a public granary system to ensure imperial food supplies, provided technical advice to diffuse new seeds and crops to different areas, and settled farmers in new productive regions (Maddison 2007). But, outside agriculture, the Chinese system had its drawbacks. Two characteristics of the Chinese bureaucratic state were especially consequential.

First, unlike the rulers in Europe, Chinese emperors relied on bureaucrats rather than territorial vassals to govern the country. In China's bureaucratic state, officials recruited from the literati enjoyed the highest status. Ambitious young men typically spent years studying **Confucian** classics in preparation for the imperial examinations. By passing these examinations and becoming academic degree holders, they would gain official positions or, short of that, enter the gentry class, which assisted the government in managing local economies and communities and constituted a ready pool for future officials. Bureaucrats and members of the gentry enjoyed many benefits, such as favorable tax treatment and extra income by acting as agents for commoners in their dealings with the government. They also had opportunities to generate substantial income from landownership, commercial activities, and teaching. They and their families were exempt from many types of levies, punishments, and duties that the common people had to bear (Maddison 2007). For centuries, China's best and brightest became servants of the state and almost the entire educated population were defenders of the state orthodoxy.

This characteristic of the Chinese state features prominently in Justin Yifu Lin's answer to the so-called **Needham puzzle**. Named after the British scientist, Joseph Needham, who led a monumental study of the history of science and technology, this puzzle consists of two questions – (1) why China had been far in advance of other civilizations early on, and (2) why China had fallen behind after the seventeenth century. Lin, a prominent Chinese economist, and a former chief economist of the World Bank, distinguishes the nature of technological innovation in the pre-modern era and the modern era. He argues that pre-modern technological innovation depended on experience, where China had an advantage because of its large population. With many people experimenting with many ways of doing things, it was relatively easy to develop new and better technologies. However, modern technology is quite different; it relies on science, which requires significant investment in human capital over a long period of an individual's life. Under the political system of imperial China, the primary pathway for upward mobility was to join the imperial bureaucracy; there was little incentive for talent to flow to scientific inquiries. Thus, Lin argues, China was not able to break new grounds in modern technological innovation (Lin 1995).

A vivid case from the Ming Dynasty (1368–1644) shows how the dependence of Chinese intellectuals on the state shaped their attitude toward new scientific knowledge. In the seventeenth century, Jesuit missionaries introduced Western mathematics and mathematical astronomy to China. Chinese scholars recognized that Western mathematical models were better at explaining and predicting astronomical phenomena than the methods they were using. However, this revelation did not provide them with a fundamentally new understanding of Nature or human relations with Nature. Ironically, the encounter with European science led these scholars to rediscover the forgotten methods in Chinese history. According to Sivin, although Western scientific techniques were impressive, they did not offer the Chinese literati an alternative route to security and fame in a political system where the civil service examination was the way to advance one's status and wealth. Evaluating any innovation in the light of the official ideology they had to defend and pass on to the next generation, Chinese scholars used the new scientific knowledge not to cast off old traditions but to revive them (Sivin 1985).

A second characteristic of the Chinese bureaucratic state was its centralized control of resources and important economic activities. For example, as early as the Han Dynasty (206 BCE–220 CE), Emperor Wu decreed iron and salt production to be state monopolies. Over the centuries, the government restricted or prohibited private operations in many sectors of the economy. Furthermore, the state offered very little protection for private entrepreneurs and their property. This line of policy limited the incentives and opportunities for private entrepreneurs, whose pursuit of independent wealth and influence could have supported the development of capitalism and industrialization in China (Needham 1981; Qian 1985; Landes 2006). Indeed, Europe's transition to an industrial society benefited enormously from the emergence of a strong urban entrepreneurial elite after the Middle Ages. It's worth noting that in the early modern period of 1600–1800, Chinese agriculture was as productive as that of England. However, whereas the agrarian surplus in England enabled capitalist industrialization in the eighteenth century, no such leap took place in China. A crucial factor that led to this divergence was the weakness of urban entrepreneurs and their inability to centralize agrarian surplus and invest it in industrial innovation (Hung 2008).

To be sure, in late imperial China there were lively commercial activities in parts of the country, and a nascent entrepreneurial elite engaged in profitable long-distance trade and finance (Hamilton 2006). However, the political system kept this group small and weak. The Confucian state often took a paternalistic attitude toward class conflicts in urban China. When merchants and workers confronted each other, the government typically sided with the workers, emphasizing the employer's obligations to provide employment and livelihood for the employees. Such policies aimed to avoid conflicts, but they often increased the cost of doing business. As a result, merchants lacked the motivation to expand their commercial and manufacturing undertakings, even though the technology and labor power were available. The lack of state protection of the merchants made them especially vulnerable in times of political turmoil. During peasant uprisings, for example, the merchants often found themselves squeezed between increased taxation by the government and confiscation by the rebels, losing much of their accumulated wealth (Hung 2008).

In addition, the Chinese system was strictly hierarchical and favored the political elite over all other groups. Typically, successful entrepreneurial families would leave commerce once they had accumulated substantial wealth and try to find their way into the bureaucratic state. Many spent their resources to educate the younger generation in Confucian teaching, in preparation for the civil service examinations (Hamilton 2006). When opportunities arose, especially during government fiscal crises, some actually used their wealth to purchase official positions (Kaske 2011). Under these circumstances, China did not develop a strong urban entrepreneurial elite capable of ushering the country into industrial capitalism. One can get a glimpse of the failure by the urban entrepreneurial class to reproduce and expand itself through the case of one family from Anhui Province (see Box 1.1).

Box 1.1 The Pan Family

In the Qing Dynasty, Anhui province by the lower Yangzi River, an economically advanced region in the country, produced many successful entrepreneurs, who profited from the production of, and trade in, salt, textiles, and tea. The Pans were one of the wealthiest merchant families in Anhui in the seventeenth century. Having made a fortune in salt and condiment trade, they moved to the prosperous city of Suzhou in Jiangsu Province. But, after achieving commercial success there, the family began to shift their resources from business investment to education, building schools and hiring scholars to educate its own children. Many family members took the civil service examinations to gain entry into the bureaucratic state. After obtaining different levels of imperial degrees, they became leading members of the gentry, with some serving as high officials in the central government. The pursuit of academic status and political power led the younger generations in the family away from commerce. By the late eighteenth century, only one minor branch of the extended family remained in business (Xu 2004). This was a pattern found in many other wealthy merchant families. (Hung 2008)

Cultural Factors

Max Weber, a sociologist with a strong interest in the institutions of economic life, was a pioneer in exploring the historical origins of capitalism in Europe. His famous work on religion and economic development contends that the Protestant reformation of Christianity, especially the emergence of Calvinism, played a major role in the rise of capitalism. Protestant exaltation of thriftiness facilitated savings and investment. Its view of worldly success as signs of salvation encouraged hard work and the pursuit of economic gains. Most importantly, the emergence of Protestantism undermined the political, social, and economic institutions of Absolutist Europe (Weber 2001). On the other hand, Weber argues that Confucianism and other religions in China were conservative, upholding old and rigid social and political institutions. In particular, he points out that their low regard for commerce and merchants forged unfavorable conditions for commercial and industrial activities (Weber 1951).

Confucius (551–479 BCE) was a scholar in the Spring-and-Autumn period (770–476 BCE), which was a tumultuous era in Chinese history. As the authority of the imperial house of the Zhou Dynasty (1046–256 BCE) declined, various local nobles fought against each other and competed for supremacy. Confucius lamented the chaos of his time and longed for the order of a unified state in the past. He argued that rulers should be concerned about the welfare of the subjects and should govern by setting moral examples. Meanwhile, the people should cultivate themselves with learning and follow the ethical codes appropriate for their positions in society. That was the way to achieve harmony.

This cultural perspective is shared by many other scholars who study why capitalism, industrialization, and scientific breakthroughs eluded China (e.g. Qian 1985; Bodde 1991; Landes 2006). They contend that Confucianism stifled innovation, with its emphasis on following traditions, its nostalgic rather than forward-looking tendency, its preference for the "golden mean" over radicalism, and, above all, its demand for proper behavior stipulated by one's place in society. Confucianism, which became the official ideology as early as the Han Dynasty and became even more encompassing in the Tang Dynasty (618–906 CE), dominated China for centuries. Chinese families and society were organized according to Confucian ethics. Laws and customs based on Confucianism shaped people's lives. The civil service examination system led generation after generation of educated Chinese to immerse themselves in Confucian teachings and defend Confucian doctrines. Such a cultural milieu greatly reinforced the conservative social and political order, while thoroughly discouraging daring explorers and independent thinkers.

In post-medieval Europe, the competition for ideas – such as the intense resistance and prosecution during Reformation – created intellectual diversity and vigor, and produced a favorable environment for scientific progress. In contrast, in China the absence of religious and other alternatives to the orthodoxy of the state deprived people of an important instrument with which to challenge official values and institutions (Needham 1981; Bodde 1991).

Besides its dim view of commerce, Confucianism was unconducive to the development of industrialization because of its contempt over manual labor. The latter resulted in an unbridged gap between the intellectual elite and the artisans, which hindered progress in science. Moreover, Confucianism and other major schools of thought in China, like Legalism and Daoism, except for Mohism, had little interest in the empirical study of nature. There was no tradition of natural philosophers in China. Although the state patronized a few officially sanctioned sciences, such as astronomy and civil engineering, the prime concern of the intellectual elite was about ethics rather than nature (Needham 1981; Sivin 1985; Qian 1985; Bodde 1991).

Last, but not least, scholars blame an attitude of complacency for China's stagnation. After centuries of being at the forefront of the world economy, the "cultural triumphalism" of late imperial China meant that the Chinese were eager to show others their accomplishments but had little interest in learning from others (Landes 2006). This attitude was epitomized by Emperor Qianlong's response to the Macartney embassy in 1793. At that time, British merchants had tried to enter the Chinese market for some years and were increasingly frustrated with the highly restricted trading system in China. The Chinese government only allowed foreign merchants to trade with Chinese counterparts in the southern city of Guangzhou for a few months in a year. The British government dispatched Lord George Macartney to the Qing court to request diplomatic representation in China and more trading opportunities. Emperor Qianlong granted Lord Macartney an audience in Beijing, but thoroughly dismissed his request. He sent the British envoy back with a patronizing letter to King George III (see Box 1.2).

To understand this seemingly absurd diplomatic communique, it is worth remembering that, for centuries prior, China had been the center of the known universe (primarily of East Asia), with far greater wealth, higher levels of political and cultural sophistication, and more advanced technology than the surrounding societies (Frank 1998). The Chinese regarded the empire as civilization *per se* and all others as barbaric to various degrees, depending on their cultural distance from China. While Lord Macartney may well have thought of his visit to China as a diplomatic mission from one sovereign nation to another, Emperor Qianlong almost certainly saw it as a tributary mission of yet another barbarian tribe seeking the blessing of the Middle Kingdom, no different from the tributary missions from Korea, Japan, and Vietnam over the previous centuries.

Box 1.2 Excerpts from Emperor Qianlong's Letter to King George III

"You, O King, live beyond the confines of many seas, nevertheless, impelled by your humble desire to partake of the benefits of our civilization, you have dispatched a mission respectfully bearing your memorial. Your Envoy has crossed the seas and paid his respects at my Court on the anniversary of my birthday. To show your devotion, you have also sent offerings of your country's produce.

As to your entreaty to send one of your nationals to be accredited to my Celestial Court and to be in control of your country's trade with China, this request is contrary to all usage of my dynasty and cannot possibly be entertained . . .

. . . If I have commanded that the tribute offerings sent by you, O King, are to be accepted, this was solely in consideration for the spirit which prompted you to dispatch them from afar. Our dynasty's majestic virtue has penetrated unto every country under Heaven, and Kings of all nations have offered their costly tribute by land and sea. As your Ambassador can see for himself, we possess all things. I set no value on objects strange or ingenious, and have no use for your country's manufactures. This then is my answer to your request to appoint a representative at my Court, a request contrary to our dynastic usage, which would only result in inconvenience to yourself." (Backhouse and Bland 1914)

Economic and Demographic Conditions

In addition to the political and cultural factors, certain economic and demographic conditions shaped China's development trajectory. Economic historians agree that Chinese population and average income were both largely stable for the first millennium of the Chinese imperial state. However, around the time of the Song Dynasty (960–1279), China experienced a major economic transformation with the development of hitherto under-explored territories in the south. Before that period, the population center was in the north, where the main crops were wheat and millet. After that, three-quarters of the people settled south of the Yangzi River, where warmer weather and better irrigation led to massive rice cultivation. This resulted in a one-time improvement in agricultural productivity, which enabled denser settlement and raised living standards. As a result, the population doubled, probably from around 55 million to 100 million from the beginning to the end of the Song (Maddison 2007).

In the ensuing centuries, the Chinese population continued to grow, although there were two dramatic drops in the fourteenth and the seventeenth century, due largely to regime-change turmoil and epidemics such as the bubonic plague and smallpox. Then, the eighteenth century saw a large demographic expansion. Remarkably, the agricultural output managed to accommodate a four-fold increase in population compared with the thirteenth century, while maintaining a stable average per capita income (Maddison 2007).

As the population grew rapidly, arable land did not. Compared with that of other countries, China's arable land is severely limited by topography and climate factors. It has never been much above ten percent of its total territory, compared say with India's more than fifty percent. Labor abundance and land shortage affected pre-modern Chinese economic development in several ways. First, traditional agricultural practice involved intensive labor input and continuous land cultivation. Through heavy use of irrigation and natural fertilizers, double-cropping and intercropping, and limiting grazing livestock, Chinese agriculture was able to improve its productivity to sustain more and more people. Although the Chinese population increased more than three-fold from 1700 to 1840, much faster than that of Europe and Japan, there was no fall in per capita income (Maddison 2007). Second, given the excess supply of labor relative to land, there was little need for labor-saving innovation. This was a very different situation from that in Europe, where the relative shortage of labor and availability of capital encouraged such innovation (Frank 1998).

These two factors combined seriously limited the likelihood of an industrial revolution in China. Mark Elvin (1984) uses the concept of "high-level equilibrium trap" in his analysis, arguing that the accomplishment of extreme agricultural efficiency in traditional China led to a dead end. As peasants exploited land to the maximum, and as the population continued to grow, the agricultural surplus, per capita income, wages, and per capita demand all fell. By the late imperial period, the Chinese economy had reached an equilibrium that trapped further progress. Agriculture efficiency and land productivity could no longer be improved without major technological breakthroughs, such as steam engines and chemical fertilizers. However, given the surplus population in relation to land, there was no incentive for technological breakthroughs. Furthermore, people were living at near subsistence level, which meant there was no agricultural surplus for industrialization. Similarly, Philip Huang describes the situation as "agricultural involution" and "growth without development" (Huang 2002).

There are other economic factors that facilitated the European Industrial Revolution but were missing in late imperial China. One was the availability of cheap energy and raw materials. Historians point out that the discovery of vast and easily accessible coal deposits in England played an important role in its economic transformation. Without this geological accident, English agrarian capitalism would not have made the transition to industrial capitalism based on the production of steam engines and iron (Wrigley 1988; Freese 2003). In addition, they argue that European colonialism was another enabling factor

Table 1.1 A Historical Comparison of Europe and China

Factors	Post-medieval Europe (especially England)	Late imperial China
Political	Constant international competition for survival	Rare existential threats from neighbors
	Diverse societal power centers contending with the state	Dominance of a powerful bureaucratic state controlling the literati and discouraging private entrepreneurs
Cultural	Protestant work ethics and other schools of thought	Confucian orthodoxy, conservative and contemptuous of commerce and manual labor
	Competitive mentality	Extreme complacency
Demographic and economic	Abundant land, labor shortage	Abundant labor, land shortage
	Discovery of coal	N/A
	Resources and trade opportunities through colonialism	N/A

in its industrialization. England was able to develop its modern industry in large part because of the massive raw materials coming from English colonies in the New World (Pomeranz 2000). The colonies also provided England with a boom in international trade, which greatly improved real wages in that country (Allen 2011).

Table 1.1 recaps the historical perspectives discussed in this section. It highlights the political, cultural, economic, and demographic factors that facilitated the development of capitalism and industrialization in Europe in the eighteenth century, which were apparently weak or missing in late imperial China.

Besides the factors discussed above, scholars have identified additional conditions that may also have contributed to China's lack of indigenous industrialization and capitalism. For instance, Bodde (1991) argues that the Chinese language itself made mastering literacy difficult and Chinese rejection of quantification was detrimental to the development of science. Needham (1981) points out the absence of primogeniture (the custom for the firstborn son to inherit the family's land) prevented the accumulation of wealth and surplus necessary for investment. Deng (2002) submits that the "cult of agriculture" meant landowners were the main interest group that influenced the state, and that Chinese peasants collectively prevented the development of non-agricultural activities. It is impossible to attribute to one or two precise causes China's lag behind Europe in modern economic development. As one scholar put it, traditional Chinese society was a multifaceted equilibrium. It was a complex and interconnected network of hardware and software that shaped the historical development in China (Deng 2002).

Failed Reforms and Experiments

As the nineteenth century went on, China's relative decline accelerated. Less than fifty years after Lord Macartney's fruitless mission to the Qing court in 1793, Britain sent in its military, and soundly beat the Qing Empire in the first Opium War. The Treaty of Nanjing, signed to end the war in 1842, forced China to pay a heavy indemnity to Britain, to cede the Island of Hong Kong to the British, and to open five treaty ports to foreign trade. The second Opium War followed in 1856 and continued to 1860. This time, the French joined the British in pressing China for more concessions, including additional treaty ports, access for foreigners to interior China, legalization of opium trade, and increased Christian missionary activities in China. The Qing court also ceded the Kowloon Peninsula, across the harbor from Hong Kong, to Britain. Particularly traumatic for the Chinese was the looting and destruction by the British and the French troops of the Imperial Summer Palace – the *Yuanmingyuan* – a masterpiece of imperial gardens, combining Eastern and Western architectures. As the emperor was forced to flee Beijing, it had become crystal clear to the Chinese that China was no longer the all-powerful Middle Kingdom it had been; but rather it was entering an international system, where it had to fight hard to preserve its very survival.

Reform in the Late Qing

How to ensure China's survival in this new era? The Chinese elite were divided in their views. Some officials and scholars began to learn about the world beyond the traditional sphere around China. They were open to foreign ideas and eager to reform the old ways of doing things. One example of this was Wei Yuan, a scholar of the statecraft (*jingshi*) school, which emphasized the search for knowledge "of practical use to society." Concerned about the problems faced by China, he rejected the moralism of neo-Confucianism, which had prevailed since the Song Dynasty. Instead, he advocated Han Learning, based on interpretations of Confucianism during the Han Dynasty, which placed more emphasis on the pragmatic tasks of administration. In 1844, Wei compiled an influential book, *Illustrated Gazetteer of the Countries Overseas*, which included information about the geography, society, and technology of Western countries. Known as the "first Chinese with eyes open to the world," he advised learning from the West and using foreign techniques to contain foreigners (*yiyi zhiyi*). Although a Confucian scholar, he nevertheless came to advocate the pursuit of wealth and power (*fu qiang*) (Leonard 1984).

Others in the Qing government were slow to adjust to the new reality. The ruling Manchus came from an ethnic minority group. Conscious of their minority origins, they had gone out of their way to enforce Confucian ethics to control the largely Han Chinese population. Toward the later years of the dynasty, the Qing rulers were particularly conservative, reluctant to introduce any reform. Nor were they comfortable in granting much power to the Han Chinese officials. However, the escalating internal and external crises forced them to reconsider their position. In 1850, a massive peasant uprising, known as the Taiping Rebellion, erupted in southwestern China, where poverty, famines, and over taxation by the government led to strong anti-Manchu sentiments. Led by Hong Xiuquan (1814–1864), a self-proclaimed brother of Jesus, who had earlier in life failed repeatedly to pass the civil service examinations, the movement soon swept through much of the country. The rebels established their capital city in Nanjing and promised to overthrow the Qing dynasty, which they saw not only as immoral and corrupt, but also as totally incompetent in resisting foreign encroachment on Chinese sovereignty. In response to the double jeopardy of internal turmoil and external threat, the Manchus finally decided to accept some of the reform ideas put forth by the Han officials, and gave them the authority to experiment with those ideas.

Zeng Guofan (1811–1872) and Li Hongzhang (1823–1901) were two prominent representatives of this group of Han officials. Both men were immersed in traditional education in Confucianism, and passed the highest level of the civil service examinations. They became provincial leaders with power bases in Hunan and Anhui respectively. Zeng was given supreme command in fighting the Taiping Rebellion. He, along with Li and other provincial governors, organized regional militia to help the Qing military combat the rebels. They imported Western weapons, employed Western trainers, and collaborated with Western governments and mercenaries. After years of fighting and the loss of millions of lives, they finally crushed the rebellious movement in 1864. That experience reinforced their belief that China needed to emulate the West in creating strong military and industrial capabilities.

Zeng, Li, and other provincial leaders embarked on the so-called Self-Strengthening Movement (*ziqiang yundong*), also known as the Westernization Movement (*yangwu yundong*) from the 1860s to the 1890s. During the first stage of the movement (1861–1872), the reformers focused on gathering information and building a modern military. They organized the translation of Western works and created foreign language schools to train Chinese diplomats. They imported Western firearms and machines, and constructed arsenals and shipyards. They also invited foreign advisors and even hired Westerners to run the newly established customs service of China. Eager to encourage the learning of Western knowledge, Li recommended adding a new subject to the imperial examination on Western science and technology, but his proposal was rejected by the Qing court (Chu and Liu 1994).

The next stage of the movement (1872–1885) expanded the focus from the military to industrial development. New enterprises were established under the model of "government supervision and merchant operation (*guandu shangban*)." For instance, Li started a joint-stock steamship line and a coal mine, using Western engineers and equipment. There were also textiles mills, telegraph companies, iron and steel complexes, and railways. However, as joint government–private enterprises, they were plagued by problems such as nepotism, corruption, monopoly, and poor management. During this period, the reformers continued their efforts in military modernization. They sent young cadets to European countries to be educated in modern military strategy.

The third and final stage of the Self-Strengthening Movement (1885–1895) involved greater coordination of the modernization of the military and the pursuit of industrial development. In the military realm, the reformers strengthened the army in addition to the navy, creating new army academies. On the industrial front, enterprises gained greater freedom from government intervention. In addition to the heavy industries, investment went into the light industries as well. However, all of this was too little and too late. In the Sino-Japanese war of 1894–1895, Japan triumphed over China, thanks to its naval advantage. Li went to the Japanese city of Shimonoseki to negotiate peace. His counterpart, Ito Hirobumi, one of the founding fathers of modern Japan asked, "Ten years ago I talked with you about reform. Why is it that up to now not a single thing has been changed or reformed?" Li replied with embarrassment, "Affairs in my country have been so confined by tradition that I could not accomplish what I desired . . . I am ashamed of having excessive wishes and lacking the power to fulfill them" (Fairbank 1986, p. 119).

As a result of losing the war to Japan, China paid heavy reparations and handed over Taiwan to the Japanese in 1895. This was a particularly humiliating defeat because, historically, the Chinese saw Japan as a "younger brother." Now the table was turned; Japan had joined the ranks of major powers encroaching upon China. In response to this extraordinary national humiliation, twelve hundred classical scholars, assembled in Beijing for the imperial examination in 1895, signed a long memorial to the throne. Drafted by the famous reformer, Kang Youwei, the memorial demanded policy change beyond the adoption of Western technologies. In particular, it called for the creation of parliaments to strengthen the bond between the ruler and the people. In 1898, the young Emperor Guanxu officially took over the reign, while his aunt, the Dowager Cixi, receded into the background. Advised by Kang and other radical reformers, Guanxu issued about forty decrees in one hundred days. These sought to modernize the Chinese state, including its administration and laws, as well as the economic and military systems.

The conservatives led by Cixi saw these reforms as a mortal threat to their power and interests. They staged a coup, put the emperor under house arrest, and executed his reformist advisors. The abrupt end of the Hundred Days' Reform made it clear that a top-down approach to change the status quo was futile.

The Boxer Rebellion of 1899 was another outburst of popular frustration with China's suffering from foreign invasion and exploitation. The rebels, known as the Boxers because of their training in Chinese boxing, vowed to "support the Qing and wipe out the foreigners (*fuqing mieyang*)." They broke into the cities of Beijing and Tianjin, fighting legation guards, and killing foreigners. Allied foreign forces retaliated and looted Beijing. In 1901, Li signed the Boxer Protocol with eleven foreign powers, which involved executing ten high officials and punishing many others, enlarging and fortifying the legation quarters in Beijing, destroying 25 Chinese forts, and having China pay the equivalent of $330 million in indemnity over the next thirty-nine years. Under internal and external pressure, the Qing dynasty stumbled on for another decade. In 1911 a series of mutinies and rebellions finally overthrew the regime, marking an end to over two millennia of imperial rule of China.

Just as scholars have debated why capitalism and industrialization developed in Europe but not in China, they have examined the question of why late imperial China was not able to modernize quickly, as Japan did in the second half of the nineteenth century. Some of them point to problems within China, while others blame Western imperialism, noting that China's greater profile subjected it to more extensive Western incursion than Japan. In recent decades, most analysts have come to conclude that China's failure was a result of both internal weakness and foreign invasion. The debate has shifted to the question of the relative weight of the two (Moulder 1976; Pong 2003).

A key internal difference between nineteenth-century China and Japan was their respective political systems before the arrival of Western powers. Although the Chinese empire experienced periods of division from time to time, it was characterized by an impressive degree of unity and centralized power. This was certainly the case for the Ming and the Qing Dynasties. As discussed earlier, the lack of competition hindered innovation and economic development. By comparison, the Japanese system was more fragmented. From the twelfth to the mid-nineteenth century, the emperor of Japan was the country's ruler only in name. The actual power of administration was in the hands of the *shogun* (military general). But even the *shogunate* had control mostly in the realm of national security and foreign affairs. Within the country, feudal lords, known as daimyos, controlled various domains. In this sense, the political system of Japan was similar to that of Europe. The relative autonomy of the domains and the competition among them meant that there was far more dynamism in Japan than in China. During the late

Tokugawa Shongunate (1603–1868), some domain officials embraced mercantilism, placing great emphasis on commerce as a way of generating financial resources to serve state interests. Even before the American naval ships led by Commodore Matthew Perry landed in Japan in 1853, threatening to use force to open the island country to trade, reformist officials in some regions had begun their own self-strengthening policies, by learning from Western knowledge of shipbuilding and steel manufacturing (Sagers 2006). Following Perry's threatening visit, regional leaders became increasingly impatient with the shogun's inability to protect Japan from Western powers. In 1868, forces from the southwestern domains of Japan overthrew the Tokugawa Shogunate and restored the imperial system. In the name of the young Emperor, Meiji, they eagerly and quickly transformed Japan into an industrialized country in the next three decades.

Another important distinction between China and Japan was their attitude toward learning and borrowing. As mentioned earlier, China had been the center of East Asia for centuries, and had developed a culture of complacency. The elite's pride in Chinese values and institutions was accompanied by persistent prejudice against other societies and their ways of doing things. China's defeat in the hands of Western powers (and later of Japan) convinced officials and scholars that it was necessary to adopt Western military and industrial equipment and technologies. However, it did not persuade them to change the traditional political system and the Confucian rules and norms. Even the leaders of the Self-Strengthening Movement insisted on having "Chinese learning as substance and Western learning for application (*zhongxue weiti, xixue weiyong*)." By contrast, Japan had a long history of importing foreign ideas and practices. In the 600s and 700s, for example, Japan borrowed heavily from Chinese and Korean cultures. Japanese thinkers did not view Confucian culture as Chinese or Korean, but universal, and thus not a threat to Japan's identity or pride. Similarly, Meiji era reformers learned from the West, as they now saw Western ideas as representing the highest level of civilization. Just like in earlier times, they were able to separate powerful ideas from their geographic origins. In contrast to the Chinese elite, they did not see a Western v. Japanese confrontation. Under this cosmopolitan chauvinism, cross-cultural borrowing was highly compatible with improving Japan's position in the world (Ravina 2017). In contrast to the Self-Strengtheners in China, the Japanese not only imported Western machinery and technology, but they also imitated Western institutions (Westney 1987). Most importantly, they adopted elements of Western democratic politics, including constitutional monarchy, greater equality among different social economic classes, and basic rights for the citizens. The sense of ownership gave ordinary people the motivation to build a strong nation together.

The 1911 revolution ended the Qing Dynasty and led to the establishment of the Republic of China in 1912, with Sun Yat-sen, a revolutionary leader, as its first provisional President. This created high hopes among the Chinese for national rejuvenation. However, in the following decades, China was almost constantly mired in civil wars and foreign invasion. First came the era of warlords (1916–1927), when military strongmen controlled different areas of China and fought each other for resources and influence. This period of continued crises saw the establishment of two political parties – the Nationalist Party (*Kuomintang* or KMT) in 1919 and the Chinese Communist Party (CCP) in 1921. Both parties shared a desire to unify the country and to free it from foreign bullying, but they held very different visions for China. The KMT was keen to preserve the property and privileges of landowners and private businesses, whereas the CCP sought to create a communist society where the state owns the means of production, such as land and capital, and socio-economic inequality is eliminated.

In the early 1920s, the KMT and the CCP collaborated in a joint military expedition to defeat the warlords and unify the country. After Sun, who had founded the KMT, died in 1925, Chiang Kai-shek took full control of the KMT. A military strongman with a fascist orientation, Chiang saw the Communist Party as a dangerous political and ideological rival and tried to crush it. In 1927 the KMT's purge of the CCP led to the death of hundreds of thousands of people across the country. Shortly thereafter, the KMT managed to establish a national government in Nanjing, which exercised nominal control of most of the country. Although some of the warlords retained strong local influence, it was the CCP that continued to be a main challenger for the KMT regime. Chiang launched several military campaigns against the CCP's Red Army, but a small number of Communist solders escaped by taking a Long March to the northwestern region of the country. For about a decade (1928–1937), under the rule of the KMT, large areas of China experienced a short period of modern economic development. Benefiting especially from the nascent financial infrastructure in coastal cities, China's overall industrial output grew by double digits annually from 1912 to 1936 (Ma 2008).

But soon, Sino-Japanese war broke out. In 1931, Japan took *de facto* control of China's northeastern provinces. In 1937 it launched a full-scale invasion of China, capturing major cities such as Shanghai and Beijing, forcing the KMT government to retreat to Chongqing in the southwestern province of Sichuan. For the following eight years, over twenty million Chinese died in the war. The northeastern provinces experienced some industrial and transportation development under Japanese rule. But the country as a whole was too wartorn to sustain normal economic activities. No sooner had the war with Japan ended in 1945, did the KMT and the CCP plunge into yet another civil war. In 1949 the communists, led by Mao Zedong, finally defeated the Nationalists and proclaimed the establishment of the People's Republic of China (PRC). For the first time in over a hundred years (since the first Opium War of 1839–1842), peace and unity resumed in China. The new CCP government was determined to put an end to the poverty, underdevelopment, and indignity that had plagued China in the "century of humiliation."

Mao's Revolution

In the early years of the PRC, the new government rushed to put an end to the economic chaos left by the Nationalist regime. It not only cleaned up the city streets, but also rid them of beggars, prostitutes, and criminals. It abolished foreign concessions, repaired public works, and set out to spread literacy. Most importantly, it tamed the hyperinflation under the old regime. After the war with Japan ended, the economy under the KMT suffered an enduring shortage of goods and runaway inflation. In 1948, after repeated failures to control prices, Chiang's government introduced a "currency reform," forcing all holdings of specie and foreign currencies to be converted into the new "gold yuan." But, in only six months, prices rapidly rose again by 85,000 times! When the CCP came to power, it took over the banking system and controlled all credit. Nationwide trading associations were set up to manage the supply of major commodities. People got paid in baskets of basic goods. With these measures, the new government reduced inflation to about fifteen percent a year (Fairbank and Goldman 2006, p. 348). These accomplishments won immediate public support for the new regime.

In rural China, economic restructuring came quickly. In June 1950 the central government issued a Land Reform Law, fulfilling a promise the CCP had made to millions of peasants during the revolution to encourage them to join the communist forces. In fact, land reform began even before 1949 in areas controlled by the CCP. From 1950 to 1953, about 300 million peasants who had little or no land became small landowners. Governmental work teams entered the villages and organized the peasants to attack the landlords. They confiscated land from the latter and redistributed it to the poor. In this process, struggle sessions and executions of the rich brought an atmosphere of terror, and an estimated several million people lost their lives (Fairbank and Goldman 2006, p. 350).

However, private land ownership did not last long. Soon after the peasants acquired their own land, the government called for agricultural collectivization. First, CCP local organizations pressured peasants to organize themselves into mutual-aid groups. In the next few years, they were told to form Agricultural Producers' Cooperatives (APCs), where they pooled their land, animals, and equipment, and gained a return according to their contribution. Almost immediately thereafter, they were pushed to enroll in higher-level APCs, where all the members worked for wages, regardless of their input to the means of production. By the end of 1956, this process was completed across China. The CCP leadership believed that collective farming would increase productivity, lead to greater equality among the peasants, and – most importantly – enable the government to control agricultural revenue to support the country's industrialization.

In urban China, the government took a somewhat more gradual approach to economic transformation. New to the cities and unfamiliar with modern industries, the CCP was eager to keep in place many capitalist entrepreneurs and even former KMT officials, so that they could continue to run the urban centers until new personnel could be trained to take over. From the Party's point of view, there were two types of capitalists – **comprador bourgeoisie** (merchants in the importing and exporting business, collaborating with foreign imperialists in exploiting China) and **national bourgeoisie** (indigenous industrial capitalists, interested in building up the national economy). The government purged the former right away and cooperated with the latter in running the urban economy, but that cooperation declined quickly. Using accusations of bribery, tax evasion, theft of state assets, cheating in labor or materials, and stealing state economic intelligence, the CCP significantly weakened private businesses. In 1949 the private sector accounted for more than half of the industry, but it dwindled to less than twenty percent in 1957 (Fairbank and Goldman 2006, p. 358).

Learning from the Soviet Union, the CCP government launched the first five-year plan of national economic development in 1953. The plan included 156 major industrial projects supported by Soviet aid. Roughly 10,000 Soviet experts descended on China and 25,000 Chinese trainees went to the Soviet Union. Following the Soviet model of industrialization, Chinese economic planners emphasized investment in heavy industries. All the Soviet-aided projects were large scale, capital intensive, and located in inland China. On paper, Chinese economy was doing well. During the first five-year plan, national income grew by an average of 8.9 percent yearly (Fairbank and Goldman 2006, p. 358).

As impressive as these achievements were, Mao was impatient. He began to contemplate more radical methods for economic development. Mao's mentality was profoundly shaped by the recent revolutionary experience. Although poorly equipped compared with the Nationalist forces, which had the backing of the United States, the CCP triumphed in the end because of its superior discipline, morale, and organization. That made Mao a firm believer in the power of the human spirit. He harbored the romantic notion that an inspired population could accomplish anything. In 1958 he launched a campaign called the "Great Leap Forward (GLF)." Seeking to industrialize China quickly, the government proclaimed the ambitious goal of surpassing Britain's steel production in fifteen years and catching up with America's in two decades.

In this context, rural APCs were forcefully expanded to much larger people's **communes**. From 1957 to 1958, 130 million family farms folded into 26,000 people's communes. With an average size of 6,700 workers working together, these communes were semi-military units that abolished family life and material incentives (Maddison 2007, p. 19). Whole regiments of farmers engaged in backbreaking labor around the clock, building dikes, digging irrigation channels, and making steel in backyard furnaces. With red flags flying high, they marched around in military formation, chanted revolutionary slogans, and threw themselves enthusiastically into a heroic battle to industrialize the country.

This ill-fated campaign did not generate the desired development outcomes. Per capita agricultural output in 1961 was 31 percent lower than in 1957. The output of much of the industrial production was useless. With peasants taken away from farming and unable to harvest the crops, agricultural output suffered. But local officials, seeking their own political advancement, reported unprecedented harvests to higher levels of government offices. State quotas for grain procurement rose accordingly, far exceeding the actual production yields. Peasants lost their basic food provision to fulfill the quotas while government-procured grain rotted in warehouses. In one of the worst man-made disasters and the largest famine in world history, between 25 and 36 million Chinese lost their lives (Yang 2012). The tragic human costs of this campaign undermined Chinese peasants' faith in collective institutions. Two decades later, the scar of this disaster served as a strong motivation for rural de-collectivization in the economic reform era (Yang 1996).

In the aftermath of the GLF, Mao retreated from the frontline of governing the country. Liu Shaoqi and Deng Xiaoping, veteran revolutionaries with a pragmatic orientation, stepped forward to try to lead the country out of the economic disaster. Their new economic policies adopted material incentives to improve productivity. In rural China, the communes that had sprung up during the GLF remained in place, but actual farm management moved downward to the production teams. Whereas communes were made up of thousands of households, production teams typically had dozens of families. In addition, individual households were allowed to work on small family plots and to sell their products in free markets. Agricultural output began to recover in 1962 and continued to increase in the following years. In the cities, the government placed a new emphasis on enterprise "profitability." Factory managers were given more decision-making autonomy and workers received bonuses for good performance. China's industrial production grew by eleven percent per year from 1963 to 1965, and industrial labor productivity rose by 1.5 percent annually (Meisner 1999, p. 266).

But, before long, China was engulfed in political turmoil again. In 1966, Mao launched the "Great Proletarian Cultural Revolution" (Cultural Revolution). This was a bold attempt by Mao to carry out a permanent revolution against established institutions, which he worried were losing vigor and ideological purity. It was also a shrewd move, for Mao to regain the political power he lost after the humiliating failure of the GLF (see Box 1.3). Radicals led by Mao's wife, Jiang Qing (no doubt with Mao's approval), purged large numbers of state

Box 1.3 Mao's Persecution of "Capitalist Roaders"

Liu Shaoqi joined the communist revolution early and worked closely with Mao from 1922 on. While Mao was the romantic visionary, Liu was a meticulous organizer on the ground. He spent many years leading the labor movement among China's urban industrial workers. He was also a Party theoretician well-versed in Marxist and Leninist works. He wrote a booklet – "How to Be a Good Communist" – in 1939, which became the standard textbook for Party followers. After the CCP's victory, he became one of the top leaders of the newly created PRC. Following the disastrous GLF, Liu succeeded Mao as the chairman of the state (equivalent of the president). The new economic policies he supported led to a successful economic recovery. As Liu's prestige rose, Mao began to see him as a threat to his own political power. At the start of the Cultural Revolution in 1966, he labelled Liu a "capitalist roader" and a traitor to the revolution. Liu was stripped of his official positions and kicked out of the Party. The Red Guards – young rebels claiming to defend Chairman Mao – attacked him and his family members. Tortured and denied medical care, Liu died in prison in 1969, far away from Beijing.

Deng Xiaoping joined the Communist revolution in the 1920s, while he was still a teenager studying in France. He became a major military and political leader in the CCP's march to power. He played an important part in the CCP's major military operations, including the Long March (1934–1935), the fight against the Japanese (1937–1945), and the battles against the KMT (1946–1949). In the 1950s, he was the CCP's General Secretary and a Vice Premier of the State Council. After the GLF, he worked closely with Liu Shaoqi in implementing the new economic policies. Like Liu, he became a target of Mao's political persecution. The Red Guards imprisoned his oldest son, Deng Pufang, who jumped or was thrown out of the window of a four-story building and became paraplegic. Deng and his family were later exiled to the rural area of Jiangxi province, where he was put to hard physical labor. Toward the end of his life, Mao tried to reestablish unity and stability in the country. He reinstated Deng to run the government from 1974 to 1975. However, in a short time, Mao became paranoid that Deng was going to stop the Cultural Revolution altogether. Once again, he removed Deng from power.

officials, veteran revolutionaries, and professionals such as scholars, writers, artists, teachers, and doctors. Nationwide political struggles interrupted the normal operations of government agencies, enterprises, universities, schools, hospitals, and other urban organizations. Ordinary citizens turned against each other, with family members and neighbors spying on each other and accusing each other of political crimes. Violence broke out among different groups, each proclaiming loyalty to Mao. The most radical stage of the Cultural Revolution lasted from 1966 to 1973, at times bordering on coup d'état and civil war.

After the death of Mao in September 1976, Hua Guofeng took over the country as Mao's chosen successor, becoming the chairman of the CCP and the Premier of the State Council. In October of the same year, Hua ordered the arrest of the radical faction led by Jiang Qing – known as the Gang of Four. At this point, the CCP regime had fallen into a profound legitimacy crisis. Almost three decades of revolutionary experiments had failed to bring about significant economic progress. People's living standards had improved little. China's relative standing in the world economy was low. A rich and strong China remained a distant dream.

Hua was keenly aware of the urgency to develop the country's economy. Combining socialist planning with a willingness to join the international economy, he embarked on a ten-year plan – dubbed by some as the "Great Leap Outward." The plan was ambitious, involving 120 large and mostly heavy-industry projects, including ten new oil fields, thirty large power plants, and five new ports. However, the plan quickly collapsed under its own weight, undermining Hua's credibility as a leader. In less than five years, Hua was removed from his positions as Chairman of the CCP and Premier of China. Deng replaced him as the new leader of the country.

In retrospect, the fall of Hua and the rise of Deng was to be expected. Until the end of Mao's reign, Hua was a little-known political figure. Having worked primarily at the provincial level, he did not have a strong power base in Beijing. In contrast, Deng had held high positions in the Party, the government, and the military for decades. Not only did he have a proven record of getting things done, which even Mao had grudgingly admitted, but he also had developed a wide and deep network of powerful supporters in all branches of the state. Waiting in the wings after Mao's death, he soon gained the posts of Vice-chairman of the CCP Central Committee, Vice-chairman of the Military Commission, and Chief of the General Staff of the People's Liberation Army. Even before Hua officially stepped down in 1981, the political elite in China already turned to Deng as the *de facto* new head of the government.

One of Deng's best-known sayings – "it does not matter if a cat is white or black, if it can catch mice, it is a good cat" – epitomizes his down-to-earth pragmatism. When he assumed China's leadership in the post-Mao era, he had no blueprint for China's future. He was prepared to try different ways to develop and modernize the country. He and his reformist colleagues adopted the approach of "**crossing the river by groping the stones.**"

Deng was far from the only one who recognized the disastrous experiments led by Mao, most notably the GLF and the Cultural Revolution. There was a consensus among the top officials that the CCP had failed to bring the fruits of socialism to the Chinese people and the regime was faced with a serious legitimacy crisis. However, how to reform the economic system was a matter of opinion. Another veteran revolutionary, almost as well-respected as Deng, was Chen Yun. An economist by training, Chen played an important part in the initial economic achievements of the CCP, including the rapid defeat of inflation following the communist takeover of the country in the late 1940s and the success of the first five-year plan in the 1950s. Chen championed a return to the model of planned economy of the 1950s borrowed from the Soviet Union. But Deng was skeptical. He saw planned economy as rigid and had a more positive view of market mechanisms, believing they would provide incentives and information, both crucial for economic development. The early years of the reform era – from the late 1970s onwards – were full of uncertainties as to which direction China was moving toward – a better planned economy or a marketized economy. The policy debate was accompanied by a power struggle in the Chinese leadership circles (Fewsmith 2016). Ultimately, Deng's vision won out. In 1993, the CCP adopted a "Decision on Issues Concerning the Establishment of a Socialist Market Economic Structure," officially endorsing the abolishment of the planning system in favor of the establishment of a modern market system.

Conclusion

Prior to the eighteenth century, China was ahead of most other parts of the world in terms of economic and technological development. After the Industrial Revolution in Europe, the Middle Kingdom lost its relative superiority. From the mid-nineteenth century on, China suffered one military defeat after another in the hands of Western imperialist powers and Japan. It lost vast territories and large amounts of wealth, with its national sovereignty in tatters. Recognizing the dire situation faced by the nation, reformers and revolutionaries sought to modernize the country's economy and strengthen its military power. From the Self-Strengthening Movement in the Qing Dynasty to the GLF under the communist regime, successive Chinese governments carried out a myriad of experiments to achieve those goals. However, political, socio-economic, and cultural obstacles hindered their efforts. By the end of the Maoist era in the mid-1970s, China was still a long way from being a rich and strong nation. A new generation of CCP leaders was determined to bring about change.

Table 1.2 Major Dynasties in Chinese History

Dynasty	Period	Emperors and other individuals mentioned
Zhou Dynasty	1046–256 BCE	
Spring and Autumn	770–476 BCE	Confucius
Warring States	475–221 BCE	
Qin	221–206 BCE	
Han	206 BCE–220 CE	Emperor Wu
Six Dynasties	220–589	
Sui	581–618	
Tang	618–906	
Five Dynasties	907–960	
Song	960–1279	
Yuan	1279–1368	Kublai Khan, Marco Polo
Ming	1368–1644	Zheng He
Qing	1644–1912	Lin Zexu, Wei Yuan, Hong Xiuquan, Zeng Guofan, Li Hongzhang, Kang Youwei, Dowager Cixi, Emperor Guangxu

Questions for Discussion

1. How might the concept of the "century of humiliation" affect the CCP's legitimacy in the eyes of the Chinese public?

2. Why did China fail to modernize itself in the nineteenth century, when Japan managed to do so?

3. What's your understanding of the principle of "Chinese learning as substance and Western learning for application"?

2

The Enigma of the Party State

A fundamental premise of the study of political economy is the connection between politics and the economy. On the one hand, political factors shape economic activities. On the other, economic phenomena have political consequences. Before exploring the politics of contemporary Chinese economic development, this chapter introduces China's political system, highlighting the most relevant political institutions and processes for the country's economic governance.

China has a unitary state. Like other unitary states, such as Japan, the United Kingdom, and France, policymaking is concentrated in the central government. Regional governments are primarily enforcers of unified national rules. This is distinctive from countries with a federal system, where political power is shared by the central government and regional governments. In those countries, including Germany, the United States, and Canada, the Constitution guarantees regional governments' authority in making their own laws in a range of policy areas. In addition, China has a one-Party political system. The Chinese Communist Party (CCP) has been the ruling Party since the beginning of the People's Republic of China (PRC). We will examine how the CCP dominates the organs of the government throughout the country and explore the interactions between the national government and regional (provincial, municipal, and county) governments. Although China's economic governance has been through cycles of centralization and decentralization, there has been little change in the centralized nature of political power. Finally, we turn to the relationship between state and society in contemporary China. Contrary to the conventional expectation that economic modernization leads to political democratization, China's one-party authoritarian system has persisted, despite economic sea change. Indeed, the CCP has tightened its grip on Chinese society in recent years.

The Party

Founded by a handful of revolutionaries in 1921, the CCP led a successful social revolution in the ensuing years. The Party's role in bringing unity and dignity to China, along with its powerful portrayal of itself as the savior of the country after a hundred years of humiliation, provided it with a great deal of political legitimacy. In the early years of the PRC, the vast majority of the Chinese people genuinely supported the Party and its leaders. However, a series of policy mistakes and the brutal political oppression of large numbers of people in the following decades, especially the Great Leap Forward (GLF) and the Cultural Revolution, badly tarnished the image of the CCP. By the time of Mao's death in 1976, serious challenges faced the Party. A quarter of a century of CCP rule had hardly improved the living standards of the population, while millions had lost their lives in various political campaigns. When Mao's successors took over the country, they were deeply cognizant of the urgent need to modernize the country and to rehabilitate the Party's legitimacy through economic development. Since then the CCP has had extraordinary success in turning its fate around. Today, it is the second largest political Party in the world (after the Bharatiya Janata Party in India) – with a membership of nearly 99 million as of 2024. It also has the dubious honor of being the Party that has been in power continuously for the longest time in history – 75 years as of 2024.

Superficially, China looks like that of many other countries in its political structure; it has a legislative body, an executive branch, and a judicial system. But, unlike most other countries, China's state organs are under the control of the CCP. From the national to the regional levels of government, a Party apparatus runs parallel with the state apparatus. At each level, the Party acts as the decision-maker, whereas the state organs are tasked with implementing those decisions. In addition, Party committees or Party groups are embedded inside the state organs to ensure they follow the leadership of the Party. The overwhelming and enduring dominance of the CCP of the state organs has given rise the concept of a "**Party state**" (Wright 2015).

Unlike political parties in democratic countries, the CCP is a Leninist Party. As such, it is committed to the organizational principle of "democratic centralism," with a clear emphasis on "centralism." This principle, shared by other Leninist parties, stipulates organizational unity like that of the military. According to the CCP constitution, Party members must obey the decisions of Party organizations, and lower levels must obey the orders of higher levels of Party organizations. At the apex of this hierarchical system are the CCP National Congress and its Central Committee. Below the national level, there are regional Party congresses and committees.

In theory, Party members elect delegates to the Party congress at all levels, and the delegates in turn elect members of the Party committee. The CCP National Congress meets every five years to deal with major policy decisions of the Party, amend the Party constitution as necessary, and elect the Central Committee as well as the Central Commission for Discipline Inspection (CCDI). Members of the Central Committee elect members of the **Political bureau (Politburo)** and the Politburo's standing committee. The Central Committee meets at least once a year, convened by the Politburo, to hear the Politburo's report regarding its ongoing work. Year round, when the Central Committee is not in session, the Politburo exercises its power on its behalf. The Central Committee's secretariat, headed by the Party's General Secretary, carries out the daily administrative tasks of the Central Committee. The General Secretary is also the convener of the Politburo and its standing committee.

Such a framework gives the impression that the ultimate power within the CCP lies with its members. They are the ones who choose their leaders and – presumably – remove the leaders who have lost the confidence of the members. But the reality is starkly different. Contrary to the formal procedure specified in the CCP's constitution, personnel matters are decided by top-down selections rather than bottom-up elections. Members of the outgoing Politburo standing committee are critical in selecting the next generation of CCP leaders, including candidates for the Politburo. This behind-the-door process often involves intense political negotiations and power struggles. The CCP's Central Organization Department (COD) plays an important role in identifying and vetting delegates to the National Congress and candidates for the new Central Committee to ensure only loyalists are selected. As Figure 2.1 shows, the actual authority and power within the Party flows in the opposite direction from the formal electoral process. Moreover, policymaking power is highly concentrated at the top of the Party. The small number of people that make up the Politburo, especially its standing committee, are the key decision-makers for the Party and the country. The annual meetings of the

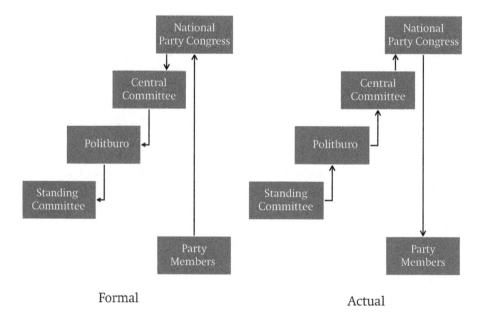

Figure 2.1 Formal and Actual Flow of Authority in China's Party State

CCP Central Committee and the meetings of the CCP National Congress that take place every five years largely serve to rubber-stamp the policies set by the Politburo.

It is difficult to exaggerate the degree of power concentration in a country of 1.4 billion people, where a handful of men (all 24 members of the current Politburo are male and there has never been a woman on the standing committee of the Politburo) monopolize the making of the most important decisions for the population. What makes the situation even more extreme is the fact that at various times in the history of the PRC one man has risen above the entire Party establishment and gained near absolute power. This was the case of Mao Zedong, who was the Party's chairman from 1949 until his death in 1976. It was also true of Deng Xiaoping – to a somewhat lesser extent – after he assumed power in 1978. Although Deng never took the formal title of Party chairman, he was known to all as China's "paramount leader." Since Xi Jinping became the Party's General Secretary in 2012, he has established himself as the new strong man. A decade into his tenure, he successfully extended his rule for another five years, with further extension likely into the foreseeable future (see Box 2.1). Many observers have compared him to Mao and even labelled him as China's new emperor.

Box 2.1 The CCP's 20th National Congress

In October 2022, the CCP held its 20th National Congress. The election of the delegates to the Congress began almost a year earlier, in November 2021. As usual, the "election" was a formality; the candidates were selected by the COD following the direction of the Politburo's standing committee. To avoid any mishaps, the Party kept a watchful eye on any potential dissent. In May 2022 the CCP General Office issued regulations forbidding any negative political comments or discussions of the Party's policies ahead of the Party's National Congress, warning that violations of the regulations would be dealt with severely. Just days before the opening of the Party Congress, a physicist and democracy activist named Peng Lifa hung a banner on a bridge in Beijing, criticizing the CCP for mishandling the Covid pandemic and for violating human rights, and condemning Xi for his cult of personality and ambition for lifelong leadership. The police immediately arrested Peng and removed the banner. The government censored all online images and discussions of the protest. When the 2,296 delegates finally gathered in Beijing for the Congress, they unanimously elected the 69-year-old Xi the Party General Secretary for a third term, violating the informal retirement age of 68 and breaking the convention of two-term limit for the Party's leader. The 20th National Congress sent unmistakable signals to the world about just how much power Xi had consolidated in his hands.

However, the centralization of power in the Chinese political system does not mean unity or coherence. Under the Maoist regime, frequent political campaigns and dramatic power struggles at the political apex reflected profound internal division of the CCP. The division was often rooted in ideological differences, factional interests, and/or bureaucratic competition. The stakes were high. Those on the losing side were not only kicked out of their official positions and jobs, but they and their families were subject to harsh punishment, ranging from public humiliation, hard labor, and imprisonment to murder. As mentioned in Chapter 1, in the aftermath of Mao's disastrous experiment with the GLF, Liu Shaoqi and Deng Xiaoping introduced new economic policies based on material incentives and revived China's economy. Mao perceived his erstwhile comrades as ideologically deviant and politically threatening to his own status. Liu and Deng and their families met with cruel punishment. A similar fate fell on many other veteran Party leaders who were on the wrong side of intra-party struggles. For example, Peng Dehuai was one of ten marshals of the People's Republic recognized for their extraordinary military leadership. He was responsible for many of the communist victories against the KMT forces during the civil war. He also led China's effort to aid the North Koreans during the Korean War. However, his fortune turned after he criticized Mao's GLF campaign. He was forced to criticize himself in front of other Party leaders, lost his position as the defense minister, and put in jail, where he died after years of torture.

In the post-Mao era, intra-Party conflicts have continued. But, unlike their predecessors, the losers rarely end up in jail or have their families persecuted. For instance, Deng and his supporters pushed aside Hua Guofeng, Mao's loyal successor, to make way for their economic reform. Hua lost the position of Premier of the State Council in 1980 and that of Party chairman in 1981, but he remained a member of the CCP's Central Committee for many years thereafter, until his retirement in 2002. As noted in Chapter 1, early in the reform period, there were intense disagreements among China's leaders as to the direction the country should take to modernize its economy. Deng succeeded in outmaneuvering Chen Yun, a veteran of the CCP and a renowned economic policy expert, who championed a return to planned economy rather than a move toward a market economy. Although Chen and his allies lost their policy influence, they were not purged politically. In fact, Chen continued to be widely respected as a Party elder. Nor was his family marginalized. Later, his son, Chen Yuan, would become a powerful figure in the Chinese financial bureaucracy.

There are, however, a few cases where political struggles at the top level have led to rather dire outcomes for the losing side. In spring 1989, a massive student-led demonstration took place in Beijing. Thousands of students occupied Tiananmen Square, the highly symbolic and most prominent public space in China. Supported by workers and other citizens, the students protested rising corruption in the Party and the government and growing inequality in Chinese society. They demanded freedom of speech, freedom of the press, greater accountability of the government, and better social protection for people whose welfare was hurt by the rapid economic change. Within the CCP leadership, reformers led by General Secretary Zhao Ziyang were sympathetic toward the students, while the conservatives felt threatened by the public criticisms and were determined to put down the movement. In the end, the conservatives won the battle and forced Zhao out. He was put under house arrest for the rest of his life. Another high-stake political contest took place in the early 2010s. Bo Xilai, son of an influential Party elder, was a charismatic and ambitious rising star in the CCP. From 1993 to 2012, he built an impressive resume as an innovative and effective mayor of Dalian City, governor of Liaoning Province, Minister of Commerce, and the CCP Secretary of Chongqing, a provincial-level city of thirty million people. In the leadup to the CCP's 17th National Congress in 2012, when the current Party leadership was to step down, Bo launched a vigorous bid for the top position in the Party, but ultimately lost to Xi. His political opponents accused him of corruption, abuse of power, and other serious crimes. He – along with his wife – was sentenced to life imprisonment.

CCP has developed a wide range of instruments to govern China. One of these instruments is the control of personnel. The Party's COD plays a vital role in this area. Not only does it wield enormous influence in selecting members of the CCP Central Committee and the delegates to the Party's National Congress, but it also has broad power on the personnel matters at various levels of the government and in almost all the major organizations in the country, the vast majority of which are led by members of the CCP (see Box 2.2). It keeps Party members' dossier, evaluates their performance, and recommends or vetoes the selection of individuals for important appointments in the Chinese nomenklatura system (Burns 2019). The control of Party members and of key officials throughout the country ensures the Party's political power and policy influence.

Alongside personnel control, the Party uses a variety of other means to ensure loyalty and compliance on the part of its members and the general public. CCP's Department of Propaganda is in charge of ideological indoctrination. Its routine tasks include disseminating the Party's policy, guiding and monitoring media content and cultural activities, and censoring any undesirable information and dissenting voices. The Department of United Front Work engages with and seeks to coopt non-communist groups at home and abroad, including the so-called democratic parties in China, influential individuals in minority ethnic groups and religious organizations, compatriots in Hong Kong, Macao and Taiwan, and overseas Chinese communities. The International Department works on creating and maintaining good relations with all types of political parties in other countries to promote the CCP's

Box 2.2 The Mysterious COD

"Just imagine a single body in the US that oversaw the appointment of the entire US cabinet, state governors and their deputies, the mayors of major cities, the heads of all federal regulatory agencies and the justices on the Supreme Court. In addition, the same body would also clear the appointments of the chief executives of GE, Wal-Mart, Exxon Mobil and about fifty of the remaining largest US companies; the editors of the *New York Times*, the *Wall Street Journal*, and the *Washington Post*; the bosses of the TV networks and cable stations; the presidents of Yale and Harvard and other big universities; and the heads of think tanks like the Brookings Institution and the Heritage Foundation. Not only that, the vetting process would take place behind closed doors, and the appointments announced without any accompanying explanation about the basis on which they were made. This body goes by the rather spooky name of the Central Organization Department." (McGregor 2010)

foreign-policy goals. The Committee of Political and Legal Affairs coordinates the policing and the judicial organs to ensure law enforcement follows the Party's priorities at any given time. The Committee of Financial and Economic Affairs leads and supervises the economic work of both the CCP and the State Council. Headed by the General Secretary of the CCP, it is the center of financial and economic policymaking for the entire country.

Besides the Central Committee, the CCDI is another powerful organization in the CCP. Standing outside the Party Central Committee, it acts as a watchdog and an important enforcer of the Party's internal regulations. For much of the CCP's history, the CCDI (and its predecessors) has been given the task of uncovering violations of Party rules to ensure Party unity and the authority of the Party Central Committee (Li 2016). Since the mid-1990s, fighting corruption has been a major part of the Commission's workload. This is because the transition from a planned economy to a market economy has created new opportunities for officials to turn their political resources into economic gains. As corruption runs rampant, it poses a serious threat to the Party's legitimacy. Under Xi's rule, anti-corruption campaigns have become a constant state. On the one hand, they are designed to make the Party state more effective in governing the country, to pacify the public's discontent toward government officials, and to improve the CCP's image among the public. On the other hand, they have provided a lethal weapon for Xi to fight his political enemies within the Party and centralize power in his own hands (Carothers and Zhang 2023). In this process, CCDI has gained significant coercive power in investigating and punishing Party officials (Li 2019). In 2022, a deputy secretary of CCDI stated that 207,000 party officials had received some form of punishment in the decade since Xi took power in 2012 (AP 2022).

From its birth, the CCP declared itself to be the vanguard of the proletariat, representing the interests of the workers and the peasants. This claim remained in place throughout the Maoist era. In the reform era that began in the late 1970s, however, the Party has gradually redefined itself and diversified its membership. Besides workers and peasants, it now recruits members from a wide variety of backgrounds, who can contribute to the country's economic development and the stability of the Party's rule. At the start of the post-Mao reform era, there was a new emphasis on education. In 1978 only 12.8 percent of the Party members had high school or better education; two decades later, in 1997 the number had risen to 43.4 percent. By then, 92 percent of Central Committee members had at least some college education (Dickson 2000, p. 523). In the early twenty-first century, the CCP opened its door to private entrepreneurs.

Besides the CCP, China has eight so-called democratic parties, such as the Revolutionary Committee of the Chinese Kuomintang, China Democratic League, and China National Democratic Construction Association. These are not independent political entities; they are all sanctioned and financed by the CCP. Totally dependent on the ruling Party and with memberships ranging from 3000 to 280,000, they merely serve to create a façade of political pluralism. As the Chinese constitution states explicitly, "The system of the multi-Party cooperation and political consultation led by the Communist Party of China will exist and develop for a long time to come."

The State

While the CCP – as the ruling Party – is the ultimate policymaker in China, it uses a parallel state apparatus to implement its policies. The main components of the state apparatus are the **National People's Congress** (NPC), the State Council, the Supreme People's Court (SPC) and the Supreme People's Precuratory. Nominally, they resemble the legislative, executive, and judicial organs found in most other countries in the world. However, their operations are guided and controlled by the CCP.

According to the Chinese constitution, the NPC is "the highest organ of state power." It has the authority to make and amend national laws, including the constitution. Subnational people's congresses exercise similar legislative authority locally. However, in reality, the NPC and its lower-level counterparts largely rubber stamp CCP's policies. Comprised of Party-vetted representatives of different social groups, they exist largely to provide the appearance of democratic representation and participation. For a brief period following its establishment in 1954, the NPC served as a forum for policy review, where the deputies brought forth public concerns and where Party and state officials admitted their mistakes. During this time of relative political liberalization, the CCP even launched a "Hundred Flowers" campaign, encouraging people to express their (critical) views on the Party and its policies. But soon the leadership found the criticisms to be too threatening and brought an end to the campaign. In the remaining years of the Maoist era, the NPC largely stopped functioning; it did not even meet at all from 1965 to 1975.

After the Cultural Revolution, the CCP rehabilitated the NPC as the nation's legislature. Having experienced the political and economic chaos associated with Mao's whimsical personal commands, the new leaders of China turned to the use of law to govern the country. Law-making was a major first step in that direction. The NPC set up numerous working groups and hired an expanding professional legislative staff. The Standing Committee of the NPC oversaw the making of numerous new legal codes in a short time. The CCP ensured that the NPC carried out its legislative work strictly according to its will by its pre-approval of draft laws, the involvement of the Central Political–Legal Leading Group, COD's control of key appointments, and the Party's role in setting of NPC meeting agendas and the tone of legislative debates (Tanner 2019).

According to Kevin O'Brien, the Chinese national legislature offers a window of three pathways explored by Chinese reformers since the end of the Qing Dynasty to make China a strong and prosperous nation – liberalization, rationalization, and inclusion (O'Brien 2008, pp. 4–6). In the reform era, the NPC has primarily served as an instrument of rationalization and inclusion. Besides its legislative activities, which aim to bring about a more orderly political system and a more efficient government, it has made its membership more representative of different social groups. In contrast to the Maoist era, CCP in the reform era has allowed people that used to be defined as "enemies" or suspects, such as business entrepreneurs, intellectuals, and individuals with overseas connections, to participate in the political life of the country. In this atmosphere, the NPC has provided a venue for broader policy consultation and sometimes even oversight of government behavior. By enlarging the "united front," it hopes to enhance the legitimacy of the CCP regime.

However, the country as a whole and the NPC in particular have not seen much political liberalization. From time to time, heated debates on controversial issues took place in the NPC. Most notably, in spring 1992, one-third of the NPC members voted against the Resolution on the Development of the Three Gorges Project, an ambitious electric power project in an ecologically sensitive section of the Yangtze River. The deputies also sometimes cast dissenting votes on important appointments at the highest level of the government. These changes notwithstanding, the NPC has had little meaningful policy impact. For example, considerable opposition in the NPC did not stop the launch of the Three Gorges Project because the CCP leadership at that time was determined to make it happen. NPC deputies' opposition to the candidacy of Party-approved individuals has hardly ever prevented any of them from taking up official positions.

The executive branch of the Chinese state apparatus is headed by the State Council, led by the Premier. Under the State Council are commissions, ministries, offices, and bureaus that manage the routine tasks of governing a country. Examples include the Ministries of Foreign Affairs, Defense, Natural Resources, Finance, Commerce, Education, and Justice, the National Development and Reform Commission, the National Health Commission, the National Audit Office, the **People's Bank of China**, and the State Taxation Administration.

The structure of the state apparatus, the number of ministries and commissions, and their responsibilities have evolved over time. According to a study in 2020, there had been thirteen rounds of major institutional reforms in the previous seven decades, including six before the beginning of the reform era and seven since then. The creation, elimination, and reshuffling of the bureaucracies led to wide fluctuations of the number of organs of the State Council, ranging from a low of 32 during the Cultural Revolution to a high of 100 at the beginning of the reform era (Ma and Christensen 2020).

A major impetus of state restructuring in the reform era has been China's economic transformation. For example, the State Planning Commission was a pillar of the planned economy. Modeled after the Soviet Gosplan, it was in charge of making five-year plans and annual plans, and – along with other government agencies – of implementing the plans through administrative means. Such plans set a myriad of mandatory production targets and directed state-managed resources accordingly, including raw materials, equipment, and credit. They also fixed prices and foreign-trade quotas. With the decline of old-style economic planning, the Commission evolved. It was renamed the State Development Planning Commission in 1998 and then the National Development and Reform Commission (NDRC) in 2003. Unlike its predecessors, the NDRC does not micromanage production targets and resource allocation, except for a small number of large-scale key investment projects. Instead, it focuses on the overall balance of the country's economy, its long-term development strategy and optimal structuring. Rather than a planner, the NDRC engages in strategic policy coordination across different actors and regions, resource mobilization to support the country's industrial policy, and macroeconomic control to ensure economic stability (Heilmann and Melton 2013).

The impact of market transition on state restructuring was especially salient in the 1990s. Unlike the 1980s, when the State Council reorganized itself in order to streamline the ministries and downsize the staff, the restructuring in the following decade aimed to transform the functions of the state organs, change their relationship with the industries, and create a government compatible with a socialist market economy. An important goal of the administrative reforms in 1993 and 1998 was to separate the government from state-owned enterprises (SOEs). Many industrial ministries were abolished. Two of these – the Ministry of Light Industry and the Ministry of Textile Industry – were turned into the China National Light Industry Council and the China National Textile Council. In contrast to the industrial ministries, these trade associations do not direct industrial enterprises but mediate between the enterprises and the government. Meanwhile, the Ministry of Aeronautics and Astronautics morphed into the China Aeronautics and Space Corporation (Ngok and Zhu 2007, p. 226). Another goal of the administrative reforms was to enhance the government's capacity for macroeconomic management. The State Council strengthened ministries and commissions dealing with macro-control, such as the Ministry of Finance and the People's Bank of China, as well as the State Development and Planning Commission mentioned above (Ngok and Zhu 2007, p. 227).

As China's economy became increasingly marketized, it was urgent to develop policies and programs to handle new problems such as unemployment and the need for social welfare reform. A new Ministry of Labor and Social Security was established, replacing the old Ministry of Labor, emphasizing the role of the government in social security provision. Likewise, the newly marketized economy saw a rise in speculation, the making and trading of counterfeit goods, and poor quality control of production. The government enhanced The State Taxation Administration, the State Administration for Industry and Commerce, and the State Bureau of Quality and Technical Supervision (Ngok and Zhu p. 228). In 2023, yet another round of reorganization of government ministries involved an overhaul of the financial regulatory agencies, an enhancement of the science and technology bureaucracies, and the establishment of a new National Data Bureau. These reforms are responses to the changing domestic and international environment and reflect the growing importance of data in economic development and political control.

While the reform of the Chinese state apparatus has been stimulated by the economic reform, it in turn has had profound implications for the economy. Some scholars optimistically describe the administrative reforms as having turned the former "positive state" to a "regulatory state." In a positive state, the government controls the economy through direct intervention, command, and enterprise ownership. In a regulatory state, the government uses indirect macroeconomic levers to regulate the market. It also invests in infrastructure and provides public goods to promote economic development (e.g. Yang 2004; Bach et al. 2006). Others are more skeptical in their assessments. They do not see the creation of new regulatory state agencies as a sign of convergence with the Western model of a regulatory state, where the agencies act as arms-length regulators of the market. They point out that the Chinese government continues to own large companies in strategic industries and exercise strong influence over them. Furthermore, many of the newly created regulatory agencies have weak authority in the Party-state bureaucracy (e.g. Pearson 2005; Hsueh 2011). In their view, the CCP's determination to maintain its neo-authoritarian rule constitutes an insurmountable obstacle for the healthy function of a market economy (Pei 2006).

Besides the legislative and the executive branches, the judicial branch is another component of the Chinese state. The Cultural Revolution attacked almost all the established state institutions. It halted the work of the judicial organs such as the police, the procuratorates (offices of the prosecutors) and the courts. Under a red terror, the fragile legal framework created after 1949 collapsed. In the late 1970s, the CCP decided to restore the judicial system as part of the larger project of building a socialist legal system. In 1999, for the first time in the history of the People's Republic, the Chinese constitutional amendments explicitly called for "the socialist state of rule of law." Two driving forces were behind this development. First, the reformist leaders, many of whom had suffered political purges by Mao and extra-judicial violence at the hands of the Red Guards, were eager to bring some degree of institutionalization to the political life in the country. This would provide predictability in their own careers and re-build the badly damaged legitimacy of the CCP regime. Second, the reformers believed that China must have a modern legal system to facilitate its transition to a market economy and to interact with the international economy. Marketization and internationalization were necessary conditions for China's economic modernization, which was in turn essential for the continuation of the CCP regime (Potter 2004; Peerenboom 2006).

The courts are an important part of the judicial system. Once rehabilitated, they expanded rapidly in the 1980s and the 1990s. By 1997 the employees in the various courts exceeded 290,000 (Zhang 2003, p. 70). However, the large size of the court personnel did not translate into high-quality judicial work. For years there was a shortage of qualified professionals. Judges were often military veterans with little legal education, or cadres previously involved in political and legal work in other organizations. There was little internal distinction among all types of workers in the court system. Judges not only adjudicated court cases, but also executed the court orders and managed internal court affairs. Indeed, anyone employed in a court who handled some paperwork would be called a judge (Zhang 2003, p. 78). In 1999, the SPC issued a blueprint of legal reform, seeking to improve the judicial structure. It stipulated that judges would be carefully selected from the existing stock of judicial tribunals and lawyers with established good performance and that judicial personnel unable to meet the standard would have to leave their posts (Zhang 2003, p. 72). In 2015, the SPC launched another round of reform, including a judge quota system, attempting to build up a leaner but more qualified elite of professional judges. When the reform was completed in 2017, the number of judges dropped from 210,000 to 120,000 (He 2021, p. 54).

An even greater challenge for the Chinese court system than personnel is the lack of judicial independence. In a political system where all organizations fall under the leadership of the CCP, the courts are no exception. Scholars argue that Chinese courts and their judges are constrained by several types of embeddedness, including political, administrative, social, and economic (Ng and He 2017). Political embeddedness refers to the overwhelming influence of the Party's priority on the court's judicial work. Preserving social stability has been a perennial preoccupation of the CCP. Judges must keep that consideration in mind when they adjudicate lawsuits ranging from unpaid wages to housing demolition, and from rape to divorce cases, lest grievances lead to petitions and protests. Administrative embeddedness involves the internal and external hierarchy that limits the judges' autonomy. Within the courts, administrative ranks trump legal expertise, and cases are reviewed by adjudicative committees led by senior judges to ensure correct outcomes. External to the courts, Party and government officials often pressure the judges to support their policies regardless of the law. Under the individual case supervision system, the procuracy and people's congress can challenge court decisions (Peerenboom 2006). Social embeddedness describes restraints on the judges imposed by their personal and social ties while economic embeddedness refers to the fiscal dependence of courts on local governments.

In 2014, the CPC adopted a "Decision to Strengthen the Rule of Law," which sought to address some of these limitations on the autonomy of Chinese courts. A major reform measure was the introduction of a judges' "responsibility system," which aims to "let the adjudicator judge but hold those who adjudicate responsible." A key to understanding the reform lies in the differentiation of what the Party considers to be legitimate and illegitimate influences on judges. While the new system has indeed reduced the influence on courts rooted in social embeddedness, which the Party views as illegitimate, it has not changed other types of embeddedness. Indeed, Party-sanctioned legitimate influences have even been reinforced (He 2021). In cases of administrative litigations, where citizens sue government officials, there has been no increase in civil actors' probability of winning since the reform. Moreover, when politically powerful actors are the defendants, citizens are significantly more likely to lose, suggesting the persistent political influence on the courts (Zhou et al. 2021).

A quarter of a century ago, a prominent scholar on Chinese laws labelled the Chinese legal system as a "bird in a cage" (Lubman 1999). That observation remains valid today. In fact, the cage has become even more confining in recent years. In some areas, there have been obvious signs of the retreat of the law. For example, the Party has turned to use extralegal means to deal with its policy priorities, including the massive detainment and "re-education" of Muslims in Xinjiang, and the harassment and arrests of activist lawyers. The

Central–Local Relations

China is territorially the third largest country in the world, after Russia and Canada. The east–west span of the country is wide enough for five time zones (although there is only one official time zone as dictated by the government). North–south-wise, there are multiple temperature zones – equatorial, tropical, sub-tropical, warm-temperate, temperate, and cold-temperate. The vast territories of contemporary China are divided into 34 provincial-level units, including twenty-three provinces (including Taiwan, which the Chinese government insists is a province of China, even though it has been *de facto* separated from mainland China since 1949), five autonomous regions where large groups of ethnic minorities congregate, four centrally-controlled major cities, including Beijing, the country's capital, Tianjin, Shanghai, and Chongqing, and two special administrative regions – Hong Kong and Macao (see map on next page). Under these provincial-level governments are over 2,800 counties and cities. Below them are many more townships and districts.

Despite China's unitary political system, the national government faces challenges in effectively controlling all parts of the country. This is perhaps not surprising, given the country's continental size. During the imperial dynasties, the proverb "the sky is high, and the emperor is far away" highlighted the limited reach of the court beyond the capital city. With the modernization of transportation and communication technologies, the national government is more capable of gathering information, transmitting its directives, and monitoring policy implementation throughout the country. But local officials have their own concerns and interests, and they have to work within their varying local conditions. Oftentimes they find ways to bend the policies of the central government to suit their concerns and interests and to deal with their specific conditions. The Party state has regularly criticized the phenomenon of *shangyou zhengce, xiayou duice* (the upper levels have policies, and the lower levels have counter-policies). But local officials have shown seemingly endless ingenuity in manipulating or evading the orders coming from above.

The CCP has developed a crisscrossing network of authority relationships in its attempt to govern the vast country. In Chinese bureaucratic parlance, the two major types of authority relationships are known as **tiaotiao** (strips) and **kuaikuai** (pieces). When *tiaotiao* is the dominant line of command, government agencies prioritize guidance from their counterparts at higher levels. When *kuaikuai* is the dominant line, government agencies first and foremost follow the order from local Party and government leaders. Historically, periods of centralization are often characterized by a shift toward more *tiaotiao*-based

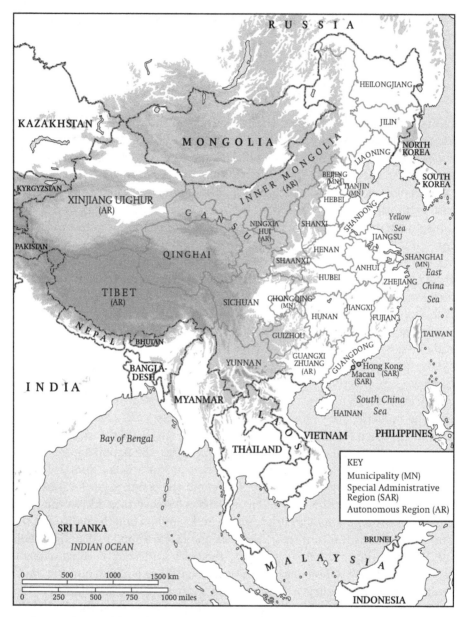

Provinces and Provincial-Level Administrative Units in China

authority and periods of decentralization typically see the expansion of *kuai-kuai*-based authority (Mertha 2005). The cleavages in this institutional matrix render the exercise of actual authority highly fragmented. Scholars have coined the phrase "**fragmented authoritarianism**" to capture this feature of the Chinese political system (Lieberthal and Oksenberg 1988).

In its long history, China often experienced centrifugal tendencies. Political division, military infighting, and the collapse of the central government engulfed the country from time to time. The fear of losing control has been a perennial preoccupation of Chinese rulers. At the same time, national leaders recognize that a highly centralized political system has costs and drawbacks. They continuously seek to balance between central control and local discretion. The relationship between the national and the sub-national governments periodically goes through cycles of decentralization and re-centralization, known as *fang* (letting loose) and *shou* (tightening up).

After the founding of the People's Republic, the CCP built a system that centralized all forms of power – political, economic, and social. This was a reaction to the country's sorry state from the mid-nineteenth to the mid-twentieth century, when reformers and revolutionaries lamented China's weakness and often attributed it to the lack of a strong central government. In the early twentieth century the founding father of modern China, Sun Yat-sen, often reminded his fellow countrymen and women that foreigners ridiculed the Chinese as a "a sheet of loose sand." Both his KMT and the opposing CCP aspired to create a strong and united China.

The new communist regime began with a high level of central political, economic and social control. But economic centralization soon began to fluctuate. In the early 1950s, China adopted the Soviet model of a centrally planned economy. Beijing imposed direct administrative control over local governments through the physical planning of production, centralized allocation of materials, and budgetary control of revenue and expenditure. The number of central government-controlled enterprises grew from 2,800 in 1953 to 9,300 in 1957. The items in material allocation under central planning increased from 55 in 1952 to 231 in 1957 (Qian and Weingast 1996).

But before long this model ran into difficulties. Central planners had a hard time gathering accurate information about local conditions. Moreover, local governments lacked incentives to cooperate with the center on large industrial projects. In an internal speech to high Party officials in 1956, Mao suggested granting more power to local governments, pointing out that decentralization was ultimately in order to enhance the center's power and that weakening local power would not serve the center well. In the next few years, the government transferred many SOEs to local governments, moved economic planning from a national to a regional level, and granted more tax revenue to local governments. However, such decentralization quickly led to a loss of coordination among regions, resulting in duplication of economic activities and inefficiency. Recentralization followed in the late 1950s and early 1960s.

Starting from the early 1960s, Chinese policymakers became increasingly concerned about the country's external environment. As early as 1962, Party leaders discussed contingent plans to move industries from coastal cities to inland areas in case of a military attack by the KMT forces in Taiwan. After the US government increased American military involvement in Vietnam in 1964, Mao instigated an ambitious campaign to create a whole new industrial system in central and western China – the so-called "Third Front" campaign. Beijing mobilized massive investments in large industrial complexes and transportation networks in mountainous areas in land-locked provinces. The goal was to ensure that in case of war, China would be able to supply its needs and produce military equipment to defend itself (Naughton 1988).

In the early 1970s, the government introduced another round of economic decentralization, setting development targets for local governments and encouraging the latter to achieve regional self-sufficiency. Similar to the first round of decentralization, the outcome was unsatisfactory and led to centralization again in the mid-1970s.

With the onset of the economic reforms in the late 1970s, a new process of economic decentralization got under way. Unlike in the past, decentralization after the late 1970s went hand-in-hand with the marketization of the economy. Scholars point out that Deng Xiaoping and his reform-minded allies understood the difficulty in breaking away from the old model of economic development. Many powerful groups had vested interest in the planned socialist economy and would resist the dismantling of that system. They developed a shrewd strategy to garner political support for their reform agenda, which included making particularistic contracts with provincial governments that allowed the latter more autonomy in economic decision-making and greater claims on the fruits of increased local productivity (Shirk 1993).

Another feature of the new economic decentralization had to do with the changing shape of the Chinese economy. Market reforms opened the door for new economic actors and dynamics. In the 1980s, **township and village enterprises** (TVEs) sprang up in the rural areas, whereas the urban centers saw the growth of private entrepreneurs. Meanwhile, coastal cities welcomed foreign capital to set up operations. Moreover, the state sector that made up the core of Chinese industry became bifurcated. While the government continued to assign production targets to the SOEs and supplied them with resources according to the plan, it allowed the SOEs to use their extra capacity to make goods and sell supplies in the marketplace. This dual-track system effectively encouraged economic growth outside the plan (Naughton 1995). In this context, the nature of central–local relationship was transformed. In the previous cycles of centralization and decentralization, the focus was on the administrative control of enterprises and production planning. Now, under a partially marketized economy, where more and more enterprises were non-state owned and more and more goods were no longer subject to government planning, the main issues for inter-governmental balance turned to investment activities, tax policies, bank credits, and interregional trade policies (Huang 1996).

Compared with the Maoist era, the reform era has seen the central government delegating more authority, especially in the economic realm. However, the cycles of *fang* and *shou* have continued. After wide-ranging decentralization from the late 1970s to the mid-1990s, the national government recentralized power in many areas. In the early 1990s Chinese policymakers decided that **fiscal decentralization** of the previous years had seriously weakened the national government's capacity to fund its priorities and to redistribute resources across different regions. In 1994, it changed its taxation system and drastically increased Beijing's share of fiscal revenue at the expense of the local governments (Zhang 1999). At the end of the 1990s, the People's Bank of China – the country's central bank – was reorganized, replacing the provincial branches with nine regional ones cutting across administrative boundaries. This restructuring aimed to reduce the local influence on bank lending that had led to too many non-performing loans and macroeconomic instability (Wang 1999). Since Xi became the CCP leader in 2012, the national government has taken considerable power of environmental policymaking, implementation, and oversight out of the hands of local governments. It believed that local governments' lax attitude toward environmental protection was responsible for the country's worsening environmental problems and that more central control would improve the situation (Kostka and Nahm 2017). A major theme underlying re-centralization in various policy areas is combating "local protectionism," which distorts national laws and regulations to suit the interests of local officials and undermines the creation of an efficient, integrated national economy (Mertha 2005).

In contrast to the swinging pendulum in economic governance, central control over local governments in the political realm has changed little throughout the history of the PRC. An important instrument used by Beijing has been personnel control. The national government has always monopolized the appointment and promotion of provincial level leaders, even during periods of economic decentralization. For instance, in the early 1980s the central government reduced its direct management of lower-level officials, reducing the number of cadres subject to direct COD appointment or removal from about 13,000 to 7,000. But, at the same time, the center developed new rules to regulate those appointments and to monitor cadre performance. The net result was actually a modest increase in the center's capacity for personnel management (Huang 1996).

The CCP has used its control of personnel to implement its policies across the country. Officials with political ambitions are closely attuned to every twist and turn in the directives of the Party state. They are highly motivated to demonstrate their devotion to the latest priority of the leaders. During the Maoist era, when the Chairman aspired to keep the revolution going, officials around the country enthusiastically involved themselves in various political campaigns and ideological indoctrination of the population. In the reform era, when the Party shifted its priority to economic development, officials at all levels of the government tried to maximize the GDP in their jurisdictions. Abundant research shows provincial leaders' career advancement to be closely tied to their performance in generating economic growth and/or revenue (Maskin et al. 2000; Li and Zhou 2005; Shih et al. 2012). During the Covid pandemic, which began in early 2020, the Party again put its personnel control to effective use. At the beginning of the crisis, most local officials hesitated to impose lockdowns for fear that such drastic measures would hinder economic growth in their regions. However, when national leaders warned that officials who failed to control the spread of Covid would be removed from office, many of them quickly implemented lockdowns, supporting the new priority of the Party state.

However, local governments are not passive and powerless. Many of the provinces are as big as mid-sized European countries. For example, Guangdong, Shandong, and Henan provinces each has a much larger population than Germany. In 2021, Guangdong's nominal GDP was the equivalent of Australia's, while Jiangsu's was about the same as that of Portugal. Some of the provinces have rich natural resources (e.g. coal in Shanxi and iron in Liaoning), while others occupy strategic locations (e.g. Hainan by the South China Sea and Fujian across a strait from Taiwan). Some have great wealth and vibrant cultural institutions (e.g. Beijing and Shanghai) while others are vital to national security and unity (Xinjiang and Tibet). The national government depends on the active cooperation of local governments for economic development and political stability. Thus, the relationship between the center and local governments consists not only of control, but also bargaining and reciprocity (Zheng 2007).

Local governments are notorious for lobbying higher-level governments for resources, favorable policies, and greater discretion. Many provincial and even sub-provincial governments have liaison offices in Beijing. Like mini-embassies, they collect information, build networks, and promote their local interests in the capital city. In the early 2000s, their expansion and shady dealings led the central government to close many of them and to require financial auditing of the remaining offices. At various times during the reform era, local governments have fiercely competed for central government designation of their areas as special development zones or experiment zones, which come with political as well as material support for economic liberalization and innovation (Yang 2012).

Compared with pre-modern China, the People's Republic has had a strong national government. Local autonomy rises and falls largely according to the will of the national leadership. Different regions seek special treatment from the central government, but they do not band together and demand overall decentralization of power, let alone constitutionally guaranteed division of power, which is the hallmark of a federal system. In fact, the atomistic nature of their deals with the center often serves to strengthen the center. Furthermore, the ability of various local governments to carry out policy experiments provides a valuable mechanism for the national government to test different models of governance, which have facilitated policy breakthroughs and corrections (Heilmann 2008; Ang 2018). Overall, the management of central–local relations has been firmly in the hands of the central Party state. Even during periods of considerable decentralization of economic policymaking power from the 1980s to the early 1990s, there was never any real danger of the country disintegrating, as was the case with the collapse of the Soviet Union.

State–Society Relations

State–society relations refer to the relations between the government and the people. In an ideal democratic political system, people elect the government, and the government is accountable to the people. Citizens enjoy constitutional protection of their civil and political liberties. Under an authoritarian regime, ordinary folks have little say in choosing their government or shaping its policies. They also lack basic political freedoms, such as freedom of speech, the press, and association. State–society relations under the CCP's one-Party rule fall squarely in the latter category. In fact, China during the Maoist era had a totalitarian regime, where the state's control of society was total (e.g. Schwartz 1960).

Since the beginning of economic reform in the late 1970s, the Chinese state has retreated from direct control of the economy in many areas. China's turn toward a more marketized economy prompted some scholars and policymakers to expect a more pluralistic political system to emerge. They argued the old political regime would be undermined by the contradiction between economic dynamism and political immobility. Their view drew inspiration from the influential modernization theory, which suggests that as countries become industrialized, wealthier, more urbanized, and people become better educated, they will more likely develop a democratic political system (e.g. Lipset 1960; Przeworski and Limongi 1997). Their optimism was bolstered by the experience of Taiwan and South Korea (hereafter Korea), where rapid economic development from the 1950s on led to strong democratic movements and – finally in the 1980s – an end to the authoritarian regime in each country. However, the reality in China has turned out very differently. After over four decades of impressive economic development, the CCP's monopoly of political power has not weakened. In some ways, the Party state is now even

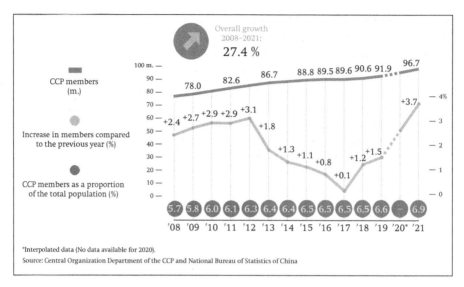

Figure 2.2 CCP Membership since 2008
Source: MERICS.

more dominant over Chinese society than in the recent past. Figure 2.2 shows the steady increase of CCP membership alongside China's economic growth.

The highly restricted political participation in China provides an illustration. In democratic societies, election is a major form of political participation. Citizens get to choose their government from competing political parties and candidates. While elections also exist in China, they are largely performative. As discussed earlier in this chapter, delegates to the CCP congress and deputies of the NPC are selected through a top-down process. The only elections that give people some meaningful choices are limited to the local communities.

The first experiment with local elections began in the 1980s in Guangxi, one of the poorest provinces in the country. The Party state allowed the peasants to elect the villagers' committees as a way of filling the governance vacuum created by the recent dismantling of the communes, which had been one of the main administrative organizations in rural China from the 1950s to the 1980s. The practice gradually expanded to other regions. It became enshrined in law in 1998, when the NPC promulgated the Organic Law on Village Self-Governance. Villagers' committees are responsible for administering tax collection and budgets, ensuring public order, providing public goods and services, and – until 2015 – enforcing the unpopular family planning policy of the state. While these committees are theoretically accountable to the villagers, they are also subject to the monitoring and intervention by local Party committees, to ensure they do not deviate from the CCP's leadership. Many of the committee members are CCP members or are recruited by the

Party once they become committee members (Pastor and Tan 2000; O'Brien and Han 2009).

In a parallel development, economic reform in urban China led to a gradual decline of the so-called **work units (*danwei*)**. These were ubiquitous economic production units as well as social control organizations; they provided city residents with employment and welfare under the planned economy. To fill the gap left by the disappearance of work units, the government encouraged community (*shequ*) development. It expanded the role of community resident committees and allowed new organizations, such as homeowners' associations, to play a role in self-governance (Derleth and Koldyk 2004). In some areas, city dwellers are given the opportunity to elect members of the committees and associations, although the process often involves the Party's vetting of the candidates. In other areas, the members are still appointed. In any case, they must operate under the guidance and supervision of local government authorities and Party committees. Like the villagers' committees, they are assistants to the Party state. Their existence and operations have not changed the old model of state-dominated governance (Wu et al. 2018).

If election is a main form of *sanctioned* political participation, protest is an archetypical type of *unsanctioned* political activities in China. The most consequential political protest in the reform era was almost certainly the **Tiananmen movement** in the spring of 1989. As described in Chapter 1, university students, supported by workers and ordinary citizens, gathered in Beijing and other cities to criticize the corruption in the Party and the government and demand freedom and democracy. After weeks of standstill, the government imposed martial law in the capital and ultimately sent in the military, killing hundreds of people, if not more, and jailing thousands. The bloody crackdown of this movement showed the Chinese public the heavy price of expressing political dissent. Meanwhile, the CCP adopted a mentality of being under permanent siege from enemies at home colluding with enemies abroad. In the decades since, the Party state has adopted increasingly sophisticated strategies to combat any potential threat to its power (Schell 1995; Nathan 2019).

Since the 1990s, China has seen many more protests. Instead of the central government and the CCP regime, they have mainly targeted local governments, corrupt officials, and greedy corporations. The issues in contention are typically about narrow material interests, such as inadequate compensation for land appropriation and illegal collection of levies in the rural areas, and unpaid wages and worker lay-offs in the cities (O'Brien and Li 2006; Cai 2002). In the twenty-first century, environmental concerns have become a growing source of open public discontent (Steinhardt and Wu 2016). Unlike its response to the 1989 Tiananmen uprising, the central government has largely avoided direct intervention, leaving it to sub-national governments to deal with these contentious events. Local officials have sometimes resorted to coercive suppression, but often they have sought to compromise with the protestors to "buy" peace (Chen 2012).

The relative aloofness of the central government does not mean a lack of concern. In fact, national leaders are obsessed with containing social upheavals. They have steadily expanded the security apparatus around the country and made *weiwen* (maintaining stability) an important criterion for evaluating cadre performance (Wang and Minzner 2015). Under Xi, the CCP has stepped up from maintaining stability to consolidating state security. The state has ruthlessly cracked down on advocates for greater political freedom, human rights lawyers, and non-government organizations with mass mobilization capacities and/or close ties with overseas groups (Zhu and Lu 2022). The political space for dissent has become narrower than at any time since the late 1970s.

From its beginning, the PRC has been a surveillance state. During the Maoist era, the CCP used local Party branches and networks of activists to monitor the citizens. People often spied on each other and reported politically incorrect words and deeds to the authorities. In recent years, the Party state has adopted digital technologies to enhance its surveillance capacity. As of 2022, China was estimated to have half of the world's nearly one billion surveillance cameras, keeping a close watch on its population of 1.4 billion. An investigative report by the *New York Times* finds that the police strategically place these cameras to maximize the collection of facial recognition data. These data are fed to powerful analytical softwares, which can tell someone's race, gender, and if they are wearing glasses or masks. An enormous amount of such data is stored on government servers. One document from Fujian Province indicates that the police estimated that there were 2.5 billion facial images stored at any given time (Qian et al. 2022).

Cameras are but one of many instruments used for surveillance. With growing access to the massive amounts of data generated from e-commerce, online banking, mobile phone tracking, social media, and other digital flows, and with ever improving artificial intelligence (AI) technology, the Chinese state is more and more efficient in targeting potential threats to the social, economic, and political order. Digital technology, which was once the promise of freer flow of information and ideas, has become yet another tool to strengthen the authoritarian regime in China (Xiao 2019). The recent Covid 19 pandemic has given another opportunity to the CCP to augment the surveillance state (see Box 2.3).

Until recently, economic growth was a top priority for the CCP because it provided an important basis for the country's political stability. Following the crackdown of the 1989 student movement, the Party state made an implicit social contract with the Chinese people – in exchange for their support of the CCP's monopoly of political power and forbearance of their lack of civil and political rights they would enjoy continued improvement in their living

Box 2.3 Covid and the Surveillance State

Following the outbreak of the Covid 19 pandemic in early 2020, all levels of Chinese government greatly intensified the use of digital technology to track and control the population. To trace exposure to the coronavirus and minimize the spread of Covid, citizens were required to install on their phones a health code app. The red code and the green code respectively indicated the presence and absence of possible exposure to the virus. Without a green code, individuals could not leave their homes, let alone go on trips. With its ability to monitor the citizens and to restrict their movements, the app quickly became a political control mechanism for the Party state. In late 2021, Xie Yang, a human rights lawyer, tried to visit the mother of a political dissident in Shanghai. The police warned him against it, but he embarked on the trip anyway. To his surprise, his health code suddenly turned red even though he had been in Changsha, a city with no Covid cases for weeks. Airport security stopped him and tried to put him in quarantine. Mr. Xie told reporters that "The Chinese Communist Party has found the best model for controlling people." In early 2022, he was detained by the police, who accused him of inciting subversion and provoking trouble (Buckley et al. 2022). Although the public health threat of Covid-19 has subsided, some of the new mechanisms of social control introduced during the pandemic, such as biometric surveillance tools, have stayed. (Miao forthcoming)

standards. Empirical research shows that economic development resulted in citizens' high satisfaction with government performance, and the latter in turn led to high trust in government institutions (Wang, 2005). In other words, China's rapid and sustained economic growth during the reform era has given the CCP regime important performance legitimacy.

However, lately significant changes inside and outside China have reshaped the Party state's orientation. First, after decades of continued rapid expansion, the Chinese economy has slowed down. According to the IMF, China's annual GDP growth rate declined from 10.6 percent in 2010 to three percent in 2022. Second, having exhausted its advantage in cheap labor and simple manufacturing, China needs intensive technological upgrading to reach the next stage of economic development. While Chinese leaders clearly recognize the imperative, they face major obstacles in meeting that challenge. On the one hand, the Party state remains determined to maintain its control of the country's economy. This means continued restrictions on the private sector and on dynamic competition in strategic industries, thus limiting domestic innovation. On the other hand, China's relations with the United States and its allies have deteriorated significantly during the Xi era. Not only is the Chinese government confronted with greater hostility in its attempts to increase its international influence, Western initiatives of de-coupling and de-risking, vis-à-vis the Chinese economy, have made it increasingly difficult for China to access advanced technologies abroad. Under these new circumstances, the CCP has steadily broadened its policy priority since the mid-2010s. While economic growth remains a major policy goal, other objectives have risen high on the agenda, including equitable distribution of wealth, green development, technological independence, and national security. Under the concept of "holistic national security concept" (*zongti guojia anquanguan*) set forth by Xi in 2014, the Chinese government increasingly seeks to balance economic growth with these other considerations. There is evidence that security, as it is defined by the CCP, has become a central concern, so much so that the Chinese government has shown a willingness to pursue it at the cost of slower economic development.

Conclusion

China's political system is complex, enigmatic, and evolving. An outstanding feature of Chinese politics is the enduring dominance of the CCP. For over seven decades, it has been the single political party ruling China. As researchers have pointed out, a secret of the CCP's longevity lies in its extraordinary adaptiveness (Shambaugh 2008). After the Cultural Revolution, when its claim to be the Party that had made China stand up began to lose its luster, it repositioned itself as the Party that would make China rich. The remarkable economic development achieved by the Chinese under the CCP regime has given the latter an important new source of legitimacy. In this process, the CCP has reinvented itself in many ways. Ideologically, it has made socialist market economy a new framework that can accommodate diverse economic actors and has even allowed capitalists to join the Party. Organizationally, the national government has gone through multiple rounds of re-structuring while Beijing has frequently adjusted its relations with the local authorities to balance political control and economic development.

However, the CCP's adaptiveness has its limits. State–society relations have changed little throughout the history of the PRC. Quite contrary to political theories of democratization and to the experiences of other developing countries, China has achieved remarkable economic development but has not seen a movement toward greater political freedom. A democratic political system is still a long way away. In fact, during the Xi era in the last decade, the Party state has tightened its political control of the Chinese society in many ways. The space for political participation by the citizens has shrunk from what it had been in the recent past. Moreover, taking advantage of the advancement of technology, the CCP has turned China into the world's largest surveillance and police state. Meanwhile, the Party state remains committed to growing the Chinese economy, if for no other reason than to maintain political stability and to prolong the rule of the CCP regime.

With this political context and the historical background set in the last chapter, we are now ready to explore the major issues in contemporary Chinese political economy. In the next chapter, we will examine the progress and problems of economic development in rural China.

Questions for Discussion

1. What is the secret of the CCP's longevity as China's ruling party?

2. Is a federal system more appropriate for governing a country as large and diverse as China?

3. How does the Chinese political system of the Xi Jinping era resemble and differ from that of the Mao Zedong era?

3

The Transformation of Rural China

Until the twentieth century, China was largely an agrarian society. Vast territories of the country were rural, and the overwhelming majority of the Chinese people were peasants. Although a communist party is theoretically a party of urban industrial workers, the Chinese Communist Party (CCP) from its early days was made up mostly by peasants. The so-called communist revolution that created the People's Republic in 1949 was primarily a peasant revolution. During the Maoist era, despite the government's priority of industrialization, urbanization remained quite limited. In fact, China became deurbanized from the 1950s to the 1970s. In 1978, on the eve of the reform era, the level of urbanization in China was only 17.9 percent, well below the 31 percent average of all developing countries (Naughton 2006, pp. 126–127). In the reform era, urbanization has resumed and accelerated, but rural areas remain a central component of contemporary Chinese political economy. According to World Bank's data, as of 2022 rural population still accounted for 36 percent of the total population in China.

Rural villages pioneered China's economic reform shortly after the death of Mao Zedong in 1976. The emergence and rapid development of household farming led to the demise of the people's commune and the end of collective agriculture. The rise of the so-called township and village enterprises (TVEs) ushered in a golden era of rural industrialization from the 1980s to the mid-1990s. Over time, as large numbers of peasants were freed from the land and farming, they became migrant workers, who staffed the assembly lines in coastal industrial centers and took up the hardest jobs in urban China, ranging from construction workers to domestic caregivers. Since the beginning of the twenty-first century rapid urbanization has turned villages into towns and expanded existing cities into rural areas. In this chapter, we trace the major contours of the transformation of rural China, how rural China fits in the overall transition of the Chinese economy, and the political consequences of economic change in the rural areas.

52

From Collective to Household Farming

Upon its ascendance to power, the CCP immediately redistributed land from the rich landlords to the poor peasants. Following the land reform, driven by its communist ideology and by its eagerness to industrialize the country quickly, the CCP introduced agricultural collectivization. In a few years, peasants were organized into agricultural producers' cooperatives (APCs). Research shows that this initial process of agricultural collectivization went relatively smoothly, and agricultural output increased from 1952 to 1958. However, the situation changed when the APCs were aggregated into much larger communes during the Great Leap Forward (GLF) in the late 1950s. In 1959, the grain output dropped by fifteen percent; in 1960 and 1961 it reached only about seventy percent of the 1958 level (Lin 1990, p. 1229).

A major factor undermining the productivity of communes was the incentive problem. A commune consisted of thousands of households and was divided into brigades, and the brigades were in turn sub-divided into production teams, each composed of dozens of households. Peasants followed their job assignments and earned work points, which would be converted into payments in the form of grains with a small amount of cash. However, the value of each work point depended on the net output of the entire commune. Even if some commune members were totally unproductive, the value of their work points would decline by a fraction of a percent. Therefore, individuals were not motivated to work hard. Moreover, supervision was difficult given the size of the commune. The weakness of internal drive and external pressure made shirking the norm (Perkins and Yusuf 1984).

In the early 1960s, in their effort to revive the economy after the GLF, Chinese policymakers made the production team the basic unit in agricultural production, while communes and brigades managed non-agricultural activities, such as industrial development and social service provision. This move ameliorated the incentive problem somewhat. However, agricultural output did not regain the growth rate of the pre-GLF period. Justin Yifu Lin argues that this was because the compulsory nature of commune membership was unchanged. From 1962 to 1978, there was no sign that peasants could withdraw freely from a production team. Using game theory, Lin explains that the right for members to leave the collective was essential for the would-be shirkers to rethink their position: if they performed poorly, it would lead the more productive peasants to leave and the collective to collapse, leaving them worse off. Without that threat, shirking could continue, resulting in continued low productivity (Lin 1990).

From the mid-1950s to the mid-1970s, rural income stagnated. The living standard for most peasants was scarcely above subsistence. Nor did rural China provide abundant food and raw materials for the rest of the country as the Party had hoped. Despite the government's "grain first" agricultural policy, grain output barely increased faster than population growth. Other crops, such as cotton and oil seeds, fared even worse. This resulted in severe shortages of agricultural products in urban China, forcing the government to resort to rationing. City residents were given coupons for meager portions of rice, flour, meat, cloth, and oil.

As mentioned in Chapter 1, in the early 1960s Liu Shaoqi and Deng Xiaoping stepped in to deal with the disastrous consequences of the GLF. They introduced new economic policies to revive the economy, including allowing household farming and limited market exchanges. Later, these liberalization measures were put to an end as Liu and Deng fell victim to Mao's political persecution. But that brief period of experiments left a useful legacy. In the late 1970s, household farming re-appeared in parts of China. It brought dramatic improvement in productivity and new hopes for a better life (see Box 3.1). News about such practices inspired some reformist local and provincial leaders. Most notably, Wan Li, the CCP leader in Anhui Province, and Zhao Ziyang, his counterpart in Sichuan Province, supported the expansion of household farming in their regions. In a short time, the so-called "**household responsibility system**" or "household contracting" spread across the country.

Box 3.1 The Story of Xiaogang Village

Before the reform era, *Xiaogang* Village in eastern Anhui province was a very poor community in one of China's poorest counties. Under collective agriculture, the peasants had no incentive to work hard. They even lacked the time to farm because of mandatory political studies. Each year, many villagers roamed the countryside to beg for food. During periods of famine, families boiled tree leaves, bark, and any edible wild plants to feed themselves. In 1978, Anhui experienced a major drought. Starvation threatened villagers imminently. In desperation, eighteen farmers – including cadres of the production team – secretly divided up the collective land and contracted plots to individual households for cultivation. The households agreed that once they delivered the full quota of grain to the state and to the commune, they could keep whatever remained. In the political context of that time, this was a highly risky and dangerous scheme. The experiment may not work, and/ or it could be reported to the authorities as a major offense against existing rules. The farmers promised each other that if things went south, the cadres would be willing to go to prison and die, and other commune members would bring up their children for them. Fortunately, the experiment turned out to be successful. In 1979, *Xiaogang* reaped a bumper harvest, producing six times the grain of the previous year. (Zhang 2012)

Initially, peasant households were given contracts for one year. Soon, the contracts were extended to three, five, and even fifteen years. Households were expected to fulfill the production quota specified in the contracts and would be free to consume or sell the residual of their harvests. The new system gave the peasants strong incentives to improve their productivity and led to dramatic increases in agricultural output. From 1979 to 1984 grain production grew by 4.9 percent annually and the overall agricultural output rose by an average of 7.6 percent each year in gross value (Brandt et al. 2002). In 1985, China became a net grain exporter for the first time since the GLF. In 1983 the Chinese government officially abolished the communes. Their administrative functions were taken over by newly established township governments. Brigades and teams were dissolved, and the village (typically the size of the former brigade) became the basic unit of rural communities.

What explains rural de-collectivization from the late 1970s to the early 1980s? One perspective attributes a vital role to the national leaders, who realized that the old model of collective farming was bankrupt and were ready for alternative methods of organizing agricultural production (Shirk 1993; Vogel 2011). Another perspective highlights the role of local governments and communities in carrying out various experiments in the reform process, but they emphasize that it was "experimentation under hierarchy" (Heilmann 2008) or "directed improvisation" (Ang 2018). A third view sees de-collectivization as a revolution from below. It portrays de-collectivization as a largely spontaneous and disorganized movement coming from peasant initiatives, which was powerful enough to overcome official opposition (Kelliher 1992; Zhou 1996). A fourth explanation argues that reform-minded regional leaders were key to the pace of de-collectivization. It points out that while peasants in many parts of the country were eager to adopt household farming, they were only able to proceed in those areas where provincial Party secretaries were supportive, such as Sichuan under Zhao Ziyang and Anhui under Wan Li (Chung 2000).

The household responsibility system was extraordinarily successful in boosting agricultural production. However, once the new incentives were in place, further growth became more difficult. From 1985 to 1994, the increase in grain output was only 0.9 percent annually (Brandt et al. 2002). In some provinces, agricultural production actually contracted. A variety of factors undermined agricultural growth after the mid-1980s, including the growing opportunities for off-farm work, the lowering of state procurement prices for quota commodities, the rise of input prices, and the corrupt behavior of local officials who delayed and reduced cash payment to the peasants for their grains (Oi 1999; Walter 2006).

Another important but controversial factor behind the slowing down of agricultural productivity growth was land tenure. Under the household responsibility system, land still belonged to the villages and was reallocated among households from time to time. The reallocation was typically made administratively by the villagers' committee according to the changes in labor availability and productivity. Some scholars argue that given the limited length of tenure and the constraints on their rights to decide how to use the land, including whether they could rent the land to others, households were hesitant to invest in the land and maintain its productivity (Prosterman et al. 1996). But other researchers find that there was a great deal of heterogeneity in land reallocation among different villages. In some villages, peasants held relatively long tenure and had considerable autonomy in deciding the use of the land. In some other villages, the opposite was the case. Overall, they believe rural land management system only had a modest impact on investment in the land and on production (Brandt et al. 2002). In any case, in 1993 the Chinese government decided that new land contracts would be for thirty years and for marginal land (land of lower quality or inconveniently located) the lease rights could be as long as fifty years. It also granted peasants more autonomy in how to use their land productively.

For the Chinese government, food security has always been a strategic priority. It issued a white paper in 1996, setting the goal of 95 percent self-sufficiency for grains, including rice, wheat, and corn. Over the years, the Chinese government has gradually increased agricultural subsidies. In 1996, subsidies accounted for about one percent of the gross farm receipts. In 2018, it reached 14.3% (OECD n.d.). With considerable support from the government, Chinese agriculture has produced roughly equal amounts of grains as China's consumption. This is no small accomplishment given the dramatic increase in food consumption in the country. In 1975, on the eve of Mao's death, Chinese consumed 125 million metric tons of grain. By 2018, the figure had gone up to 420 million tons (CSIS n.d.).

It is worth noting that on a per hectare basis, by the end of the 1990s China had achieved yields higher than the world average. In wheat production, it exceeded yields in the United States. However, China's labor intensity was 150 times that of the US level. Moreover, Chinese fertilizer consumption per unit of land was three times the world's average (Naughton 2006). There is an obvious parallel between contemporary Chinese agriculture and the historical tradition of extreme labor intensity and maximal land productivity. This is perhaps inevitable given the factor endowment of the country. While China has about twenty percent of the world's population, it has only less than nine percent of the world's arable land.

Similar to other modernizing countries, agriculture in China has been a shrinking portion of the overall economy. According to World Bank's data, agriculture, forestry, and finishing accounted for thirty percent of Chinese GDP in 1979 at the beginning of the reform era. It has declined to seven percent in 2022. Even for the rural areas, where household farming kick-started the era of economic reform, it was the growth of rural industry that soon became the main engine of economic takeoff.

The Rise and Fall of Township and Village Enterprises

For centuries, Chinese peasants engaged in small-scale industrial activities alongside farming. They made silk, wove cotton, and produced ceramics. They traded these and other items in the marketplace. The communist regime put an end to these traditional industrial operations, in order to give priority to grain production in rural China. It also abolished the rural marketplace. During the GLF in the late 1950s and the Cultural Revolution from the mid-1960s to the mid-1970s, communes and brigades engaged in some industrial activities. Unlike traditional rural industry, which mainly involved household-based handicrafts, the new rural industrialization focused on making steel and supplying producers' goods for agriculture. It was capital intensive, replicating the heavy industry-oriented development strategy promoted by the state. However, it made only a limited contribution to the local economy and failed to absorb large numbers of rural workers (Naughton 2006).

The adoption of household farming from the late 1970s onwards opened opportunities for a market-based rural industry. As peasants gained control over their agricultural output beyond the state quota, they needed industrial enterprises to process these products for consumption and for sale. That created a strong demand for rural industry. At the same time, the end of collective farming meant that households with surplus labor could now free some family members to engage in non-agricultural activities. This supply of cheap labor further promoted rural industry.

Another favorable condition emerged with the onset of enterprise reform in urban China, a subject we will discuss in detail in the next chapter. In the early and mid-1980s, the Chinese state relaxed its control of the urban economy. It gave permission for non-state-owned producers to fill some gaps in the supply of consumer goods. TVEs provided much-needed small merchandise, ranging from buttons to shoes and from cigarette lighters to umbrellas. The government also began to allow some cooperation between the state-owned enterprises (SOEs) and other types of enterprises. Some TVEs took contract work from the SOEs in some industries. In this process, many TVEs prospered, making profits as high as thirty to forty percent. Until the mid-1990s, rural China experienced a golden era of TVE development (Naughton 2006).

TVEs provided new employment opportunities for millions of peasants. Growing numbers of peasants attracted by jobs in rural industry left farming or became part-time farmers. Some even bought grain from the marketplace to meet state-mandated grain production quotas, while they worked off the land (Oi 1999). In 1983, TVE workers on average accounted for 9.4 percent of all rural laborers. A decade later, the figure rose to 27.8 percent. The weight of TVEs rose steadily in the rural economy. In 1983 they accounted for 24.7 percent of the total rural output. In 1992, this figure climbed to 66 percent (Zweig 1997, p. 23). Rural industry contributed much of the increasing income for rural households. By 1987 more of total rural income had come from rural industry than from agriculture (Oi 1999, p. 1).

The rise of TVEs not only changed the structure of the rural economy, it also profoundly affected the entire Chinese economy. From the late 1970s to the mid-1990s, TVEs were the most dynamic sector of the Chinese economy. Their value-added rose from six percent of the GDP in 1978 to 26 percent in 1996 (Naughton 2018, p. 310). They brought competition to the SOEs in many areas, not only in under-supplied consumer goods, but also in growing industries such as construction and construction materials production (Naughton 1995, pp. 150–151). From 1985 to 1996, the share of TVEs in gross industrial output expanded from 14.6% to 27.8%, whereas that of SOEs shrank from 65% to 28.5% (Jefferson and Rawski 1999, p. 27). In foreign trade, TVEs performed especially well, as their operations were more in line with the actual market conditions than those of the SOEs (Perotti et al. 1999). The rise of rural industry forced the entire Chinese economy to become more efficient.

The successful development of China's TVEs poses an interesting puzzle. Economic historians and theorists of economic institutions generally agree that market competition and secure property rights are important conditions for economic development (North and Thomas 1973; North 1990). When post-Soviet Russia and the former communist countries of Eastern Europe invited Western advisors to guide them in their economic reform in early 1990s, they were told that to jump-start their economy, which had suffered from gross inefficiency for decades, they needed to immediately put in place a capitalist market system. In a very short time, they implemented drastic measures of price liberalization and enterprise privatization. On the contrary, the Chinese government did not implement such institutional reform. From the late 1970s to the mid-1990s, the state only gradually reduced its price control over goods and services, and there was hardly any privatization of state-owned assets (Weber 2021). How did the rural industry take off while the state continued to dominate the economy?

Researchers argue that contrary to conventional wisdom, Chinese rural industry took off not despite of but because of the prominent role of the state. According to Jean Oi (1999), the local state played a pivotal role in enabling the early development of rural industry. The abandonment of collective farming transferred the ownership of agricultural harvest from the brigades to individual households. Village governments, which succeeded the old brigades, had lost their traditional revenue. In addition, in the 1980s the central government decided to reduce its investment in rural infrastructure, shifting that burden to the local governments. As village leaders desperately looked for new sources of revenue, rural industry appeared to be a highly attractive candidate. Townships and counties also developed a strong interest in developing rural industry. Unlike villages, they did not lose revenue because of agricultural de-collectivization. Rather, they were motivated by the fiscal reform, which was mentioned in Chapter 2 and will be discussed in greater detail in Chapter 8, that gave them new claims to the economic surplus generated in their jurisdictions (Oi 1999).

Local governments in China not only had the incentives to develop TVEs, but they were also well-equipped to do so. Unlike in many other developing countries with a weak or even failing state apparatus, the Chinese Party state is well-organized and highly efficacious. Once local Party and government officials saw the benefit of TVEs, they used their authority and resources to protect and promote the latter. The county issued licenses, offered tax breaks, certified products, granted loan deferments, and provided information and technology to the TVEs. The township and the village gave contracts to the TVEs, secured credit, guaranteed loans, supplied materials, made production decisions, and repaid debts for the enterprises in trouble. In this type of "state corporatism," local governments worked like a large multilevel corporation, pooling risks and sharing profits (Oi 1999). Comparative research of TVEs and SOEs shows that although TVEs were disadvantaged in the areas of technologies, labor skills, access to loans from state-owned banks, and official channels of material distribution, they were more competitive than the SOEs because of the hard budget constraints they faced (the state did not bail them out endlessly), the pressure of market competition, the relative freedom from the burden of full employment and generous welfare for the employees, small size, and more flexibility (Perotti et al. 1999).

Across the country, different models of TVEs emerged. The best-known models in the 1980s and early 1990s were the Sunan model, the Pearl River Delta model, and the Wenzhou model. The Sunan model came out of the experience of TVEs in southern Jiangsu Province. It was characterized by collective ownership and direct local state involvement in rural industrial development (Ma and Fan 1994). *Huaxi* Village in Jiangyin County is a famous (or notorious) illustration of this model (see Box 3.2). The Pearl River Delta model was based on the experience of TVEs in Guangdong, a province situated next to Hong Kong, which China lost to Britain in the nineteenth century and stayed a British colony until 1997. Its economic development benefited from the abundant investment from overseas Chinese who had ancestral roots in the region. It was the host of several **special economic zones** designed to spearhead China's open policy toward the outside world (Johnson 1992). The Wenzhou model was developed in a mountainous area of Zhejiang Province, which had limited arable land but a strong tradition of entrepreneurship. This model was characterized by the prominence of *de facto* private enterprises, many of which pretended to be TVEs to take advantage of the protection and services provided by the local government (Parris 1993).

After the mid-1990s, TVEs declined steadily. An important cause was that the economic environment for the TVEs had become more competitive. Greater liberalization took place throughout the national economy after the

> ## Box 3.2 Huaxi – "Number One Village Under the Sky"
>
> Founded in 1961, *Huaxi* was similarly poor as other Chinese villages (called brigades under the collective farming regime) at that time, with a per capita annual income of less than twenty yuan (or less than $7 at the exchange rate then). The CCP secretary of the village, Wu Renbao, quietly led the villagers to create some small mills and hardware factories in the 1960s. Once economic reform began in the late 1970s, *Huaxi* further promoted its local industries. However, unlike TVEs in many other areas, it preserved the socialist principles of collective ownership and shared prosperity. In the 1990s, thanks to Wu's political leadership and business acumen, *Huaxi* successfully developed a variety of businesses, including iron and steel, textile and apparel, and real estate and tourism. By the early twenty-first century, the *Huaxi* Group had over one hundred companies. The villagers continued to work together and were all shareholders of the companies. All the families had luxury cars and villa-style residences. The collective paid for the children's education and people's healthcare and other welfare benefits. In 2004, the average annual salary of the villagers was 122,600 yuan ($25,200). While *Huaxi* became known as China's richest village, profiting from the market economic reform in the country, its village song proclaimed that "The sky of *Huaxi* is the sky of communism. The land of *Huaxi* is the land of socialism" (Watts 2005). In recent years, the fortune of *Huaxi* has declined, due to a host of factors, including the passing of Mr. Wu, the overcapacity of iron and steel production in China, and the difficulty of transitioning to new industries. (Chen 2021)

early 1990s and increased market integration across the regions. This meant there were fewer niche opportunities for the TVEs. The end of the shortage economy in China and the rising demand for high-quality products by the end-users also made it hard for many TVEs to survive, given their relative disadvantage in technologies and access to bank loans. The old models of TVEs ran into serious difficulties. For example, the Sunan model relied on collective ownership and direct local governments involvement in business management. TVEs of this kind could not keep up with their competitors when market mechanisms took on a major role in allocating the input and output of production (Wei 2002). The Wenzhou model featured family-based private entrepreneurship. When such TVEs sought to expand their reach and/ or to improve their products, their capacity was limited by the kinship and local networks they were locked into (Wei et al. 2007).

Some TVEs were converted to joint-stock cooperatives owned by the workers. Some became **joint ventures** between the local government and new private managers, where the government retained some ownership but left the operation in the hands of private operators. In other cases, the local government sold TVEs to the managers (Naughton 2006, pp. 291–292). The restructuring of TVEs has not been monolithic but rather shows multiple trajectories. Some of them have been replaced by domestic private enterprises while others have been taken over by SOEs or foreign-invested enterprises (Yuan et al. 2014).

Rural–Urban Integration

A prominent feature of contemporary Chinese political economy is the systematic separation of the rural and the urban. Since the early years of the People's Republic, the CCP has adopted different mechanisms to govern the economy and the people in rural and urban areas. Despite the CCP's ideological and rhetoric commitment to egalitarianism, the Party state has always treated the rural areas less favorably than the urban areas.

During the Maoist era, collective agriculture meant that rural land was under collective ownership. Peasants worked in production teams, brigades, and communes, primarily growing grains for the country. They supplied their own food and had limited welfare benefits provided by the local agricultural surplus. In urban China, the state owned all the means of production, including land. Almost all working-age people worked in *danwei* (work units), which included most organizations, ranging from government bureaucracies to SOEs, from schools to universities, and from banks to hospitals. They were guaranteed access to food and basic consumer goods. Through their *danwei*, urbanites enjoyed welfare benefits provided by the state, including pension, healthcare, and social assistance. Such a system was based on exploiting the rural population and reflected China's strategy of industrialization without urbanization or "industrialization on the cheap" (Chan 2010).

The privileges of urban life made cities attractive. However, the Party state did not want rural Chinese to migrate to the urban centers because that would undermine its development strategy. In 1951, the government introduced a household registration system – known as the **hukou** system – to monitor the population and control their mobility. It was first put in place in the cities, but later covered both the urban and the rural households. People were expected to live where they were registered. In the aftermath of the GLF, the widespread famine in Chinese villages drove many peasants to the cities to find ways to survive. But the cities were short on food supply as well. The government implemented food rationing in urban areas. Only registered urban residents had state-guaranteed food supply, forcing non-residents to return to the countryside. It was then that the government hardened the use of *hukou* to ban rural-to-urban migration. After the GLF, household registration became strictly enforced as a caste-like system, sealing the divide of Chinese citizens into first-class urbanites and second-class peasants (Cheng and Selden 1994; Wang 2005). With almost no chance to change one's *hukou* status, Chinese citizens were locked into a "birth-ascribed stratification system" (Potter 1983). One's *hukou* status – agricultural or non-agricultural – not only determined where an individual lived, but also everything else that shaped her life's chances (Solinger 1993).

Rural–Urban Migration

The onset of economic reform in the late 1970s brought greater physical, economic, and social mobility to China. Growing numbers of peasants, freed from farming and farmland, began to look for economic opportunities in the cities. In the mid-1980s the government allowed people with rural registration status to work in some jobs in the cities on a temporary basis, provided they obtained their own food in the marketplace and did not require state-provided services and benefits. Many peasants became contract workers in urban enterprises. Some set up their own small businesses peddling goods and services. Over the next few decades, large numbers of migrant workers formed a **"floating population,"** working in the cities without the urban *hukou* and the urban services and welfare attached to that status.

In the 1980s, most migrant workers moved to other areas in their own province. But in the 1990s, inter-provincial migration surged and overtook intra-provincial migration. These long-distance migrants were especially concentrated in the Pearl River Delta in southern China. In 2000, Guangdong had a "floating population" of 21 million, which was 25 percent of its population. A secondary destination for migrant workers was the Lower Yangtze River Delta in eastern China, including Jiangsu, Zhejiang, and Shanghai. In 2000, it recorded fifteen million migrants, which amounted to eleven percent of the region's total population (Naughton 2006, p. 130).

In the twenty-first century, rural-to-urban migration continued to expand, with the number of migrant workers reaching 296 million at the end of 2022. Several new patterns of the more recent migration set it apart from the 1990s (Liang et al. 2014). First, the importance of interprovincial migration has declined relative to intra-provincial migration. From 2000 to 2010, interprovincial migration dropped from 54 percent of the total migration to fifty percent. The rise of (or return to) intra-provincial migration indicates more economic opportunities locally. Second, among long-distance migrant workers, the most popular destination has shifted from the Pearl River Delta to the Lower Yangtze River Delta. This reflects the better working and living conditions in the latter region. Third, more long-distance migration workers have returned to their home provinces than in the previous decades. This is likely the result of more favorable agricultural policies introduced by the government in the 2000s, including the elimination of agricultural taxes, increased subsidies for grain production, greater state investment in developing the inland provinces, and policies by migrant-sending provinces to attract migrants back home. In addition, the global financial crisis in 2008 led to a downturn of Chinese exports, thus reducing the labor demand in export-oriented coastal cities. Finally, over the longer-term, foreign-invested enterprises have gradually moved to inland China, where the cost of operations is lower than in coastal provinces. This has created employment opportunities for migrant workers in their home provinces.

Working the assembly lines, constructing roads and airports, and building skyscrapers, migrant workers have contributed mightily to urban economic development in the last few decades. Furthermore, they have become the backbone of services in Chinese cities, ranging from taxis to e-commerce delivery and from domestic help to garbage collection. Urban life would literally come to a halt without migrant workers. During the recent Covid pandemic, when Chinese cities were locked down, many migrants lost their factory jobs and small business operations in the urban areas, but those employed in the gig economy played a major role in filling online orders of food and other essential items for people trapped in their homes.

While rural-to-urban migration is a common phenomenon in many developing countries, it has several distinctive features in China. First, it has taken place after several decades of strict separation between the rural and the urban areas. This has made it difficult for both the migrants and the urban residents to adjust to their close co-existence. Cultural clashes have plagued their relationship. Second, the massive scale of the migration in contemporary China is unprecedented in world history. It has been exceptionally challenging to manage this magnitude of population movement. Third and most significant, despite the growing porousness in the rural–urban divide, the *hukou* system has been slow to change. In its shadow, the vast majority of migrant workers and their families can only be temporary residents in the cities. This strategy of "incomplete urbanization" takes advantage of migrants' economic contribution, while denying them the benefits and welfare associated with "urbanized" status (Chan 2010).

Just as rural-to-urban migration has been a major driving force of the economic development of Chinese cities, it has also reshaped rural China and the lives of those left behind, not always in a beneficial way. One example of this is that rural women who have remained in the villages have taken on more family responsibilities, including providing care for the young and the old and agricultural production. Moreover, separation from their spouses has made them more vulnerable (Wu and Ye 2016). Meanwhile, there is evidence that the elderly relatives of migrant workers face higher risks and less family support than before. Their network of safety has been significantly weakened (He and Ye 2014). The literature is mixed on how rural children have been influenced by the absence of their migrant parents. Some researchers argue that the left-behind children have suffered from increased workloads, inadequate tutoring and supervision, and the lack of parental affection (Ye and Lu 2011). But others disagree. For instance, a large-scale survey shows that on a series of health, nutrition, and education indicators, migrants' children left in the villages perform as well as or better than children living with both parents. On the other hand, this study finds that both groups of children fare poorly on most of these indicators by international standards. It suggests that rural Chinese children, regardless of their parents' migration status, need more resources and care (Zhou et al. 2015).

On the positive side, rural Chinese have flexibility in making decisions about migration, and their decisions evolve across different stages of life (Ye 2018). After years of work in the cities, more and more migrant workers have returned to their regions and even their native villages. They come back with new skills and knowledge, network connections, the spirit of entrepreneurship, and accumulated savings. These are valuable resources for rural economic development. Research shows that returning migrants are more likely to start businesses than other peasants, playing an active role in stimulating economic growth in their home regions (Ma 2002; Démurger and Xu 2011).

Urbanization

Besides peasants' migration to cities, another major path of rural–urban integration has been urbanization, i.e. the transformation of villages to towns and the expansion of Chinese cities into rural areas. As noted at the beginning of this chapter, urbanization has progressed significantly in the reform era. According to World Bank's data, urban population rose from eighteen percent of the total population in 1978 to 64 percent in 2020 (see Figure 3.1). In this

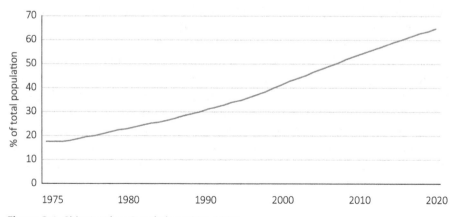

Figure 3.1 China's Urban Population 1975–2020
Source: World Bank Group.

process, large areas of rural land have been transformed into industrial or real-estate development sites, lost to agriculture and to the peasants. For example, from 1998 to 2017, urban built-up area expanded from 21,379.6 square km to 55,155.5 square km, while the annual expropriation of land for urban construction increased from 515.5 square km to 1, 934.4 square km (Zhang 2020). In fact, the growth of land acquired for urbanization has been faster than the increase of urban population, raising questions of land-use inefficiency and environmental degradation (Wang et al. 2015).

Land has been a highly contentious issue in China's urbanization process. As noted earlier, unlike in urban areas, where land and other means of production belong to the state, rural land belongs to the collectives. Beginning in the 1990s, local governments began to obsess with acquiring rural land and selling or leasing land rights to industrial and urban commercial developers. This was in large part driven by their financial needs. In 1994, after years of generously sharing fiscal power with the regions, Beijing tightened its control of taxation. With most tax revenue centralized in the hands of the national government, local governments were badly underfunded. However, the latter were still responsible for economic development and public and social service provision in their jurisdictions. Local officials had to look for new ways of financing their mandates. They turned to converting agricultural land for industrial and commercial development (Lichtenberg and Ding 2009; Hsing 2010). Since then, land conversion and transactions have been a major source of local governments' finance. Typically, they expropriate land from the peasants at low prices (often based on the value of the agricultural output of the land in recent years) and then sell the land-use rights to various industrial or commercial developers at much higher prices. They also collect land and property-related taxes. These practices have grown over time. In 2012 the combined revenue from selling land-use rights and collecting land-related taxes accounted for 27 percent of total fiscal revenue for all local governments; this figure rose to 38 percent in 2021 (Huang 2023).

The acceleration of urbanization reduced farmland as well as the agricultural labor force. A sensational book by an American environmental analyst, Lester Brown – *Who Will Feed China?* – predicted that industrialization in China would make it a large importer of food and drive up the world food price and that China's land scarcity would be the world's land scarcity (Brown 1995). The Chinese government became more aware of the danger that farmland loss would threaten the food security of the country. Shortly thereafter, it announced a "red line" of keeping 1.8 billion mu (120 million hectares) of arable land for farming. This policy has been firmly in place since then. It prohibits the converting of farmland into urban land unless an equal amount of unused land is turned into farmland (Liu and Zhou 2021). Local governments have strategically managed to keep their quota of farmland, while continuing to expropriate rural land from the peasants. Between 1990 and 2008 about

88 million peasants became landless, and scholars expect another fifty million to lose their land by 2030 (Sargeson 2013, p. 1068). The peasants whose lives are interrupted and forever changed by the expropriation of their land are nevertheless excluded from the decision-making process. Nor are they adequately compensated for the loss of their traditional livelihood. Forced to relocate from their villages to densely populated apartment blocks in peri-urban areas, they face great uncertainties and serious challenges. Few of them have adequate resources to survive long-term the costly urban lifestyle. They also lack the skills to pursue employment in non-agricultural sectors. Many of them experience significant social and cultural discrimination by their urban neighbors, whom they now live next to but have almost nothing in common with (Zhang 2020).

Political Consequences of Economic Transformation

The economic transformation of rural China has had profound political consequences. In this section, we focus on two issues – governance reform and contentious politics. Under a marketized economy, the Maoist rural organizational apparatus dissolved and was replaced by new forms of rural governance. While economic reform has improved the lives of many in rural China, it has also caused new problems and challenges. Peasant grievances have given rise to different forms of struggles and resistance, which have in turn generated strong reactions from the government.

From the late 1970s to the early 1980s, as collective agriculture gave way to household farming, communes, brigades, and production teams were dismantled. This meant that the traditional governance structure was no longer in place. In some areas, community-minded peasants created villagers' committees to fill the governance gap. These committees were called "leadership groups for village public security" or "village management committees." In 1982, the new Chinese constitution – the fourth in the history of the People's Republic, following those of 1954, 1975, and 1978 – described villagers' committees as elected mass organizations of self-government. For the reformists in the Chinese government, represented by Peng Zhen (head of the National People's Congress and a veteran revolutionary), village self-governance promised to give peasants a sense of ownership and to remove incompetent and corrupt local cadres, thus consolidating the CCP regime in the context of post-socialist rural economy.

Have village elections brought about democratic governance in rural China? Scholars and election observers alike find that the elections of village heads are fair and competitive in most places most of the time. However, the ultimate authority in the villages typically lies with the CCP secretaries, who are not elected but appointed by higher levels of Party organizations. In any case, village leaders – elected or appointed – operate at the bottom of a hierarchical administrative system. Township and county governments influence their decisions in one way or another, making it difficult for them to govern according to the will of the villagers (O'Brien and Han 2009).

Besides the transformation from collective to household farming, TVE restructuring and urbanization have also had an impact on rural governance. The decline of TVEs after the mid-1990s deprived village cadres of resources and diminished their redistributive capacity. They began to call for private enterprises to return to collective ownership (Chen 2016). Meanwhile, the acceleration of urbanization from the 1990s on means more and more rural communities lost their land. Village leaders proved to be ineffective in protecting the interests of the peasants because they lacked the incentives and the capacity to do so (Cai 2003). In the twenty-first century, new models of economic organization have appeared, with the potential for ensuring the peasants their share in the collectively owned rural assets.

In 2003, the Chinese government called for a revival of collective economic organization in rural China. Inland provinces have seen the rise of new agricultural collectivism and the emergence of shareholding land cooperatives. In coastal provinces many TVEs have turned into cooperatives of shareholding economy. Peasants have become shareholders of collectively owned land and enterprises. Some researchers argue this economic restructuring can make village governance more democratic because it shifts the control of collective assets from the cadres to the villagers, thus giving the latter a voice in decision-making (Chen 2016). Others argue that shareholding does not necessarily serve as a weapon of the weak since a small number of elites continue to control the collectives and use them as vehicles to enhance their own interests and wealth (Kan 2019).

While the experimentation in rural governance has produced uncertain outcomes, there has been a clear trend toward greater contestation in rural politics. In the 1990s peasant grievances centered around the financial extraction by the local governments. In response to the recentralization of taxation power after 1994, local officials intensified the imposition of fees and levies on the peasants. These heavy financial burdens combined with the lack of transparency and accountability angered the peasants. They organized opposition by clans, secret societies, and unregistered mass organizations. Sometimes they coordinated protests across provinces. In some areas, peasants even formed paramilitary forces and killed local cadres (Walker 2006).

This trend generated grave concerns in Beijing. Worried about the deteriorating relationship between the Party state and the rural population, the Chinese government issued laws and regulations to reduce the burdens on the peasants. However, the situation did not improve because the underlying fiscal pressure on the local governments remained unaddressed (Bernstein and Lu 2003). As local officials continued their financial squeeze of the peasants, the latter used the rules and policies of the central government to justify their riots against the exploitation. This type of defiance carried out in the name of the government's own established principles came to be known as **"rightful resistance"** (O'Brien and Li 2006). Similar to James Scott's concept of "everyday resistance," "rightful resistance" is a form of rebellion that seems prudent in that it does not openly challenge the ruler. It employs official rhetoric against the corrupt and oppressive behavior of local cadres.

In the early 2000s, the Chinese government introduced a tax-for-fee reform, which eliminated all local fees and replaced them with a single agricultural tax. Soon afterwards, the Hu Jintao-Wen Jiabao administration abolished the agricultural tax. This was part of the CCP's campaign of "constructing a new socialist countryside" to address the economic and governance problems in rural China. The campaign sought to achieve many objectives, such as agricultural modernization linked to ecological sustainability, improved public services, including healthcare, education, and social assistance, tidying up the villages, relocating peasants to new villages or urban areas, and expanding vocational training for the peasants. Different locales experimented with their own models along the lines of some of these objectives (Ahlers and Schubert 2013). However, very quickly the campaign turned to demolition and renovation that served the urbanization project, featuring a neoliberal emphasis on profits and capital accumulation at the expense of public services and community protection (Looney 2015).

Unlike their "rightful resistance" against local government financial exploitation earlier, in their more recent struggles against land loss the peasants have not been able to take advantage of the divided priorities within the Party state. The project of rural–urban integration has been promoted by Beijing as well as the local governments. From the perspective of the Party state, urbanization must proceed to achieve development and modernization. It is a necessary process of turning rural land and housing from dead capital into valuable marketable assets. Selling, leasing, building and rebuilding on previously agricultural land creates economic development. To deal with peasant resistance, local governments have tried to absorb the opponents to land expropriation into a formal channel of bargaining. They offer incorporation of rural residents into urban citizenship in exchange for the latter's land. In doing so, they have depoliticized the resistance to land expropriation and divided the opposition (Chuang 2014). This strategy has succeeded to some degree, but it has not prevented violent conflicts from happening. The unfair monetary deal compounded by displacement, unemployment, and an uncertain future for the peasants leads periodically to petitions, protests, and riots (Lin et al. 2018). According to a survey by Landesa Rural Development Institute, in 2010, conflicts over land use accounted for 65 percent of the 187,000 "mass incidents" in China (Zhao and Xie 2022). These collective actions are often violently suppressed by the government. As one scholar put it, "the violence of land expropriation in China constitutes urban development" (Sargeson 2013, p. 1066).

Conclusion

In this chapter we have traced the major contours of the economic changes in rural China. In the reform era, the Chinese countryside has undergone rapid and profound transformations – the transition from collective agriculture to household farming, the rise and fall of TVEs, and the partial rural–urban integration through peasant migration to Chinese cities and through accelerated urbanization. These changes have literally changed the landscape of China and have been a major contributor to the impressive economic growth of the country.

Many factors underly the successful development of China's rural economy in recent decades. The recovery and expansion of agricultural production after the Cultural Revolution was largely the result of giving material incentives to the farmers and liberalizing the market for agricultural products. The takeoff of rural industry from the 1980s to the mid-1990s was enabled by the local state, whose fiscal motivations and organizational capabilities made them effective supporters of TVEs. Market forces and state intervention co-existed in creating the initial economic miracle in rural China.

Since the 1990s, the development of the Chinese countryside has become increasingly linked to Chinese cities. Economic liberalization in urban China has created a huge demand for migrant workers from the rural areas. These migrant workers have played a significant part in building up the urban economy, while also contributing to rural development with their capital, skills, and entrepreneurship. More recently, rural China has been swept up by the urbanization push by the Chinese state. Local governments – pressed by fiscal shortfalls and tempted by the opportunities to profit from land transactions – have gone all out to expropriate rural land, turning it to industrial and commercial development. As was the case earlier in the reform era, market forces and state intervention are jointly reshaping the rural economy of China.

The economic change in rural China has been accompanied by political transformation. The emergence of elected villagers' committees after de-collectivization granted peasants limited self-governance, but state power has remained deep-seated through the reach of the CCP to the village level and the influence of local governments at the township and county levels. Moreover, tension between the rural population and the Chinese state has grown since the 1990s, first over the heavy financial burden imposed by the local government on the peasants and then over the exploitative land expropriation in the process of urbanization. In addition, environmental issues have become a growing focus of peasant protests, a subject we will discuss later in Chapter 10.

The economic growth in rural China over the last four decades has no doubt reduced poverty and improved the living standards of Chinese peasants. However, the well-being of many of them has been undermined by the lingering institutional barrier between rural and urban China. The persistence of the *hukou* system traps migrant workers in the status of second-class citizens in their own country. The separate land ownerships in rural and urban China have enabled local governments to exploit the farmers in the urbanization process, depriving them of their traditional way of life and robbing them of their rights. Critics argue that the economic success of China has given rise to "gangster capitalism," where the ruling CCP and its hangers-on have enriched themselves by plundering the public, including hundreds of millions of Chinese peasants. In a global context, the contentious politics in rural China is part of a broader movement against the violence and power of the market and against an urban-centered model of development (Walker 2006).

Questions for Discussion

1. Why has the Chinese government used the *hukou* system to keep rural and urban areas separated for so long?

2. How has rural China contributed to the Chinese economic miracle?

3. Who have been the winners and losers of China's urbanization process?

4

The Commanding Heights of the State Sector

The core of the Chinese economy lies in its industries. During the era of Mao Zedong (1949–1976), the state owned and managed almost all of Chinese industries. As of 1978, state-owned enterprises (SOEs) produced 77 percent of China's industrial output, with collective enterprises and township and ownership and village enterprises (TVEs) contributing fourteen percent and nine percent respectively (Naughton 2018, p. 343). For decades the SOEs operated inefficiently, and turned out products that were often of poor quality. The achievements of rural reform in the late 1970s and early 1980s encouraged the post-Mao leaders of China to make similar changes in the urban areas and its industrial economy.

The restructuring of Chinese industries progressed much more gradually than the rural reform. Throughout the 1980s, the government introduced material incentives and market mechanisms but refrained from privatizing the SOEs. Although new non-state actors entered some of the industries and made them increasingly competitive, the state sector retained the same scale as before, thanks to the continued protection and subsidies by the government. It was only in the late 1990s that the urban reform took a more radical turn. The government ditched many inefficient small and medium-sized SOEs, leaving them to sink or swim on their own in the marketplace. Its focus turned to supporting the large SOEs in strategic industries. These privileged large SOEs not only have survived, but they have also grown in scale. However, many of them remain inefficient, due to the lack of market discipline and hard budget constraints. From the standpoint of economic efficiency, there is a clear imperative for greater liberalization of the state sector. But, so far, efforts in this direction have been half-hearted and periodically reversed.

The transformation of the urban industrial economy has been protracted and complicated because SOEs play a special role in the national economy. They are not only economic actors but have important social and political missions. Early in the reform era, they were critical in keeping urban unemployment under control and avoiding social instability. Later, they became a main vehicle used by the government to direct economic development. In addition, state ownership of industrial assets is an important source of the Party state's power. Although Chinese leaders often speak of the need to improve economic efficiency through deepening market-oriented reforms, they are determined to maintain the Party state's control of the "commanding heights" of the nation's economy – strategic industries, such as energy, resources, and infrastructure. In the third decade of the twenty-first century, the simultaneous pursuit of national economic development and state control of the economy remains a central and unresolvable dilemma for China. In this chapter, we trace the evolution of the state sector since the 1980s and analyze the political economy of SOE reform.

Incremental Reform in the 1980s

From the beginning of its rule the Chinese Communist Party (CCP) set an ambitious goal to build China into a modern industrialized nation so that it would never again be subject to the bullying of other powers. At first China emulated the experience of the Soviet Union and adopted a strategy of "big push industrialization." The government mobilized resources from around the country to support industrial development, especially heavy industries. It also delinked the Chinese economy from the capitalist world economy (Naughton 2018, p. 65). This strategy was a major departure from China's tradition of household industry. It also went against China's natural endowment. Heavy industries, such as metallurgy, machinery, power generation, and chemical products, are capital intensive. China had abundant labor but scarce capital.

Initially, China received much-needed financial and technological assistance from the Soviet Union. But, in the late 1950s and early 1960s, the friendly relationship between the two communist countries ended because of their ideological disagreements and conflicting national interests. Thereafter, China continued to pursue industrialization through other means. It experimented with import substitution, replacing imported goods with domestic products, thus promoting indigenous industrial development. In the early 1970s, the hostile relations between the People's Republic and the United States, going back to the civil war between the CCP and the Kuomintang, began to thaw. After President Richard Nixon's visit to Beijing in 1972, a rapprochement between the two countries opened the door for China to secure some economic and technological assistance from Western countries.

China's big push industrialization produced mixed results. From 1952 to 1978, industrial output increased by an average of 11.5 percent annually, and the share to industry in the country's GDP rose from eighteen percent to 44 percent (Naughton 2018, p. 67). The heavy industrial base developed in those years laid a useful foundation for future economic development (Marquis and Qiao 2022). But this strategy of industrialization distorted the economy in ways that were both inefficient and unfair.

The inefficiency came in part from its mismatch with China's comparative advantage, as noted above. It also was rooted in the nature of the Chinese economic system. Under China's command economy, SOEs did not act as economic actors as understood in a typical market economy. Rather, they were bureaucratic agencies of the state. Managers did not make decisions regarding production, investment, or wages. Their mission was to follow the plan of the government. The State Planning Commission (SPC) and its subsidiaries played a key role in setting production targets for and allocating materials to the enterprises, and the latter carried out their assignments accordingly. The prices set by the government made the SOEs profitable, and the SOEs in turn submitted all their profits to the government.

Within the SOEs, there was little differentiation in the status or earnings among the workers. Instead of material incentives, the CCP relied on ideological indoctrination to motivate the workers to be productive. Like other urban *danwei*, SOEs were total institutions. In addition to turning out products, they were expected to provide life-time employment and comprehensive welfare for the workers, including pension, healthcare, childcare, and housing. They were also tasked with monitoring and controlling the thoughts and actions of the workers and their families, making sure they were loyal to the CCP and followed government policies (Walder 1986; Frazier 2002; Bian 1994).

The big push industrialization came at a huge cost to the rural economy. For years, the economic planners set the prices of agricultural products low and those for industrial output high, using this "price scissor" as a mechanism to squeeze agriculture to subsidize industrialization. The SOEs were highly profitable. In 1978, their profits were fourteen percent of the country's GDP (Naughton 2018, p. 352). Meanwhile, hundreds of millions of Chinese peasants lived in poverty. In addition, the concentrated investments in heavy industries meant light industries, such as textile, apparels, and food processing, were left behind seriously. The result was chronic consumer goods shortages. Service industries were similarly neglected. From the 1950s to the 1970s, people's living conditions improved little, even in the urban areas. In any case, by the end of Mao's reign, China's development strategy had clearly failed to achieve the results hoped for by the CCP. In fact, China had fallen far behind its East Asian neighbors – Japan, Korea, Singapore, Taiwan, and Hong Kong. The latter had chosen very different paths of economic development from China's – capitalistic, prioritizing light industries, and integrating with the world economy. Their success offered an appealing model for Chinese reformers (Naughton 2018, pp. 68–69).

The first phase of urban industrial reform began in the early 1980s. By then, Zhao Ziyang, who had successfully encouraged household farming in Sichuan Province in the late 1970s, had become the Premier of the State Council. With Deng Xiaoping's backing, he took charge of the country's economic restructuring. A first step of SOE reform was to turn them from bureaucratic units into economic actors. To do so, it was necessary to provide the SOEs with autonomy and material incentives and to allow the planned economy to be supplemented by a market economy.

Beginning in the late 1970s and early 1980s, the government introduced a policy of "*fangquan rangli* (releasing authority and sharing benefits)." The government delegated some decision-making authority to SOE managers and allowed the SOEs to retain some of their profits. As in the past, the SOEs still had to follow government planning in their production. But, after they fulfilled their production quota, they could use their remaining capacity to make products for the "grey market" that had emerged in the margins of the urban economy. Over time, the SPC reduced the scope of its mandatory economic plan, allowing more goods to be produced and exchanged in the marketplace. After the mid-1980s, many SOEs adopted a "contract management responsibility system." They negotiated with the government on profit targets and profit delivery to the state. In exchange for fulfilling the contracts, the SOEs gained extensive autonomy and retained substantial excess profits (Nolan and Wang 1999). This was the dual-track system mentioned in Chapter 2.

Under the dual-track system, the SOEs operated both under the planned economy and in the marketplace. Their input and output were priced differently depending on where their transactions took place. Within the planned economy, raw materials, production equipment, and final products were priced by administrative means. Outside the plan, their prices were determined by market supply and demand. As SOEs bought and sold more and more materials and products outside the plan, they became increasingly responsive to market signals (Jefferson and Rawski, 1994). At the same time, the dual pricing system created ample opportunities for arbitrage. Many government officials and otherwise well-connected actors enriched themselves by utilizing these opportunities (Hao and Johnston 1995).

Not all the SOEs fared equally well under the new circumstances (Xie and Wu 2008; Chan and Unger 2009). Some enterprises took advantage of the new business opportunities and became profitable. Their employees received increased bonuses and generous welfare benefits. But other SOEs were less adaptive. Not only did they fail to make profits, but their survival became dependent on government subsidies. In the 1980s, three-quarters of the SOEs owned by local governments were making a loss. Over time, the government became less willing and able to support those enterprises. As enterprises faced a hardening of the **"soft budget constraint"** (the elastic allocation of fiscal resources to bail out the enterprises), they increasingly turned to banks and other sources for funds, including their retained profits. In the late 1980s, "self-raised funds" accounted for over two-fifths of the fixed investment of SOEs (Nolan and Wang 1999). The employees of the uncompetitive enterprises lost their bonuses and some of them were even furloughed. The socialist ideal of equality among the workers began to crumble.

Alongside the reform within the SOEs, an even more powerful force was reshaping the state sector of the Chinese economy – the entry of other types of enterprises. The first wave was made up mostly by collectively owned enterprises, including TVEs that sprang up in rural China in the 1980s. Unlike the SOEs, they did not have the financial backing of the national government. At the same time, they also did not shoulder the burden of providing socialist welfare for their employees. Born to compete in the emerging marketplace, they were nimble and flexible. Sometimes working with SOEs and sometimes challenging them, the TVEs brought unprecedented dynamism to Chinese industry. The non-state enterprises changed the environment in which SOEs operated and had a profound impact on their performance. Research reveals that in the 1980s the state industry was least profitable in provinces where the output of non-state industry (mostly TVEs) grew the fastest. It also shows that the total-factor productivity in state industry was associated with large shares of non-state industrial output. This means that the non-state sector encouraged greater efficiency in the state sector even as it squeezed the latter's profit (Singh et al. 1993).

In the 1980s, the government also allowed "household businesses," small businesses run by entrepreneurial individuals or families, to operate in Chinese cities. Some of them later grew to be larger-scaled private enterprises, which became the most dynamic and innovative components of the Chinese economy, a point we will discuss in detail in the next chapter. Around the same time, the Chinese government began to open the country to welcome **foreign direct investment** (FDI) to a few special economic zones (SEZs) created near Hong Kong and Taiwan. Later, foreign-invested enterprises (FIEs) spread to many more Chinese cities, bringing capital, technology, and access to global trade networks. FDI has made a significant contribution to Chinese economic development, a subject we will focus on in Chapter 11. For Chinese SOEs, FIEs represented both opportunities (e.g. through joint ventures and other forms of cooperation) and challenges (e.g. by increased competition). Overall, FDI had a positive effect on the industrial reform in China in the early years (Chen et al. 1995).

The industrial reform through the 1980s improved the performance of the SOEs in many ways. Their output, exports, and total-factor productivity all increased. They also grew more innovative. The exposure to market forces led to gains in both static and dynamic efficiency. The former is achieved by refining existing products, processes, or capabilities. The latter typically comes from the development of new products, processes, and capabilities (Jefferson and Rawski 1994). Nevertheless, the SOEs as a group were not as productive as non-state-owned enterprises. The latter steadily reduced the shares of the SOEs in Chinese industry. From 1978 to 1992, the proportion of industrial output produced by SOEs dropped from 78 percent to 48 percent (Nolan and Wang 1999). As a leading economist puts it, China's industrial economy grew "out of the plan" (Naughton 1995).

The early stage of industrial reform in China was a study in contrast with the experience of post-Soviet Russia and the former socialist countries in Eastern Europe in the late 1980s and early 1990s. The latter pursued a "**shock therapy**," privatizing their SOEs and removing administrative control of prices rapidly. In China, there was no privatization of the state sector and the government took an incremental approach to price liberalization, first allowing for a dual price system and then gradually moving to market pricing for more and more goods and services. The slow and deliberate pace of China's reform created opportunities for new economic actors while leaving the SOEs and their employees largely untouched (Weber 2021). Although the competition from non-state enterprises squeezed the profits of many SOEs, government protection prevented them from going out of business right away. Scholars have described this stage of Chinese reform as "reform without losers" (Lau et al. 2000).

Box 4.1 The Superiority of Gradualism?

China's gradualist economic reform brought steady economic growth early on and won praises from many observers. According to a report published in 1998 by the Federal Reserve Bank of San Francisco, since the launch of economic reform in the late 1970s, China's per capita income had more than quadrupled. In contrast, since Russia began its rapid "big bang" reform in 1992, its per capita income had declined by twenty to forty percent (depending on the estimated size of the black-market economy). The apparent success of the Chinese reform led some to argue that Russia should have adopted China's strategy. However, as this report went on to point out, the comparison of China with Russia was misleading because of the vastly different political and economic context in each country (Kasa 1998). Moreover, gradualism was not unproblematic. The slow and partial reform allowed for short-term economic growth, but it also created distortions in the economy and trapped China's transition. Indeed, the winners of a semi-reformed economy turned out to be formidable obstacles for further economic and political liberalization. In the early twenty-first century, it became clear that Chinese economic institutions, such as regulatory framework, capital markets, and legal system, functioned less well than those in Eastern European transition countries and other large developing countries. (Pei 2006)

Drastic Restructuring in the 1990s

As the 1980s went on, problems associated with the gradualist reform in urban China became salient. First of all, as the government adopted limited price liberalization, it brought periodic inflation. Although the situation was much less dramatic than in countries that went through "shock therapy", it nevertheless caused growing public resentment. Given the history of hyper-inflation in the 1940s that shook the KMT regime, the CCP leadership was particularly sensitive to the potential political consequences of price increases. Second, the partial liberalization of the economy benefited some groups in the country much more than others. This new inequality was jarring for many people in China, who had recently lived under a largely egalitarian regime (except the rural–urban divide) and were angry to see some individuals and families becoming ostentatiously wealthy. But more troubling was the fact that many of the newly rich gained their wealth through personal and political connections. SOE managers, for instance, as well as other well-connected individuals exploited the opportunities for arbitrage under the dual price system. Families and friends of government officials used their political power to obtain commercial gains, e.g. by obtaining import permits and land-use rights controlled by the state (Hao and Johnston 1995). Meanwhile, the CCP's slow pace of political liberalization was frustrating for those who dreamed of greater freedom of speech and press and more diverse voices in the public space. The government's periodic campaigns against "spiritual pollution" and "bourgeois liberalization" led to the purge of prominent theorists, authors, and artists, dampening the enthusiasm and optimism of the intellectuals (Gold 1984; Sullivan 1988).

Public discontent culminated in the Tiananmen movement in spring 1989, which met with the government's brutal suppression. The CCP tightened its political control and became ever more vigilant toward any signs of political dissent. Chinese economic reform also slowed down to a crawl as intense debate and power struggle continued among the Party elite. The conservatives saw the protests as a dire warning of the threat of excessive liberalization. Their concern was augmented by the collapse of the Soviet Union two years later. From their point of view, the downfall of the Soviet regime was the result of Mikhail Gorbachev's badly managed economic and political reform, which opened the door to corrosive Western influence. It was the kind of "peaceful evolution" advocated by the US government since John Foster Dulles was Secretary of State. In contrast, Deng and his allies drew a different lesson from the Soviet experience. While they were also resolved to avoid a peaceful evolution in China, they argued that the collapse of the Soviet Union was due to its poor economic performance. For the communist regime to survive and thrive in China, it needed to succeed in economic development, which in turn required further market reform. In the end, Deng prevailed over the conservatives by staging a dramatic tour of several southern cities in 1992, using his personal charisma and authority to push the CCP back to the path of economic reform (see Box 4.2).

Box 4.2 Deng's Southern Tour

Deng stepped down from his last official post – chairman of the CCP Military Commission – in November 1989. His position had been weakened because the Tiananmen movement emboldened the anti-reformists in the CCP. Concerned about the loss of momentum of the economic reform he had initiated and continued to believe in, he came out of retirement in early 1992. From January 17 to February 20, accompanied by his daughter, he traveled to the southern cities of Guangzhou, Shenzhen, Zhuhai, and Shanghai, areas of or near the special economic zones at the forefront of economic reform. Along the way, he praised economic reform and criticized its opponents. Deng was hoping to use his personal appeal, his veteran leader's status, and his prestige as the architect of China's reform program to break the ideological impasse in the CCP and mobilize public support for continued economic liberalization.

But his chance of success was not preordained. During his trip, Hong Kong's news media published timely reports, whereas a few regional media outlets in Shenzhen and Shanghai carried photos and summaries of his speeches. But the official media in Beijing, controlled by the anti-reform faction in the CCP, kept silent. It was only at the end of March that China Central Television Station broadcasted a documentary that informed the public of the tour. Around the same time, other CCP mouthpieces finally caught up with the two-month-old news and aired Deng's call for further economic reform. The delayed media coverage and endorsement of Deng's reformist message was a telling sign of the intense struggle behind the scenes between the two factions in the CCP. (Zhao 1993)

In November 1993, the Third Plenum of the 14th CCP Congress adopted the historical Decision on Issues Concerning the Establishment of a Socialist Market Economic Structure. Until then, a heated ideological debate had been going on for some time as to how much socialism could accommodate a market economy. With its official endorsement of market economy – albeit a socialist one – the CCP implemented further industrial reform, including clearly delineating property rights, clarifying the rights and responsibilities of different actors, and separating enterprises from the government. The goal was to turn the SOEs into modern enterprises.

An important milestone came in 1994, when the newly legislated Company Law went into effect. It created a common legal framework for companies of all types of ownership. Among other things, this law served as a tool for restructuring the state sector (Clarke 2007). Under its framework, many SOEs gradually became corporatized. The larger ones turned themselves into joint stock companies, resembling public companies in the West, with large pools of assets and tradeable equity interests. The smaller ones transitioned to limited liability companies, which in principle are similar to private companies in the West, with a limited number of shareholders.

The corporatization of SOEs was a slow process. It took almost two decades after the making of the Company Law for eighty percent of the SOEs to be corporatized in 2013 (Naughton 2018, p. 346). In theory, corporatization makes SOE managers more autonomous and more profit-driven. They are now only accountable to the board of directors and not to a host of bureaucracies. Their mission is to make the company as profitable as possible. Although the implementation of corporatization has often been superficial, it has brought about sufficient change in corporate governance (how the company is directed and controlled) to improve the performance of many SOEs (Aivazian et al. 2005).

Corporatization also opened new channels for SOEs to raise capital besides bank loans; they could now engage in public listing on the stock market. For instance, from the late 1990s to the early 2000s large SOEs in multiple sectors, including oil, gas, and telecom got listed on the stock exchanges at home, in Hong Kong, New York, and elsewhere. In addition, corporatization created a path toward privatization of the SOEs. As the shareholders of the companies become diversified, the Chinese state could choose to reduce its holdings and increase the private ownership in these companies.

Despite the progress in SOE restructuring, the state sector as a whole was losing ground to other types of enterprises. In the mid-1990s, over sixty percent of the 11,000 largest SOEs were loss-making (Brødsgaard and Li 2013). As subsidies for the SOEs ate up more and more of the government budget, the CCP decided to take more radical measures of reform. In 1997 the 15th CCP Congress officially adopted a policy of "*zhuada fangxiao* (**grasping the big and letting go the small**)." The government cut loose the smaller SOEs and focused its attention and resources on improving the financial condition and business performance of the big SOEs. The largest SOEs operating in strategic industries not only survived but they became more profitable thanks to enhanced corporate governance and to government protection. Meanwhile, many smaller SOEs shut down or became privatized. The number of SOEs decreased from 120,000 in the mid-1990s to about 34,000 in 2003 (Naughton 2018, p. 344).

The bifurcation of the state sector actually began well before the official abandonment of the smaller SOEs. For years, large SOEs had enjoyed more state support and protection than their smaller counterparts. Their share of gross output value rose from 32 percent in 1980 to sixty percent in 1994. In the mid-1990s, the 500 largest SOEs accounted for 37 percent of total assets,

46 percent of sales value, and 63 percent of total profits (Nolan and Wang 1999). These large SOEs were the backbone of China's strategic industries. These included natural monopoly industries, such as those in energy resources and basic raw materials, "pillar" industries, such as petrochemicals, heavy machinery, and automobiles, and industries related to national defense. The Chinese government was keen to keep the largest SOEs afloat and under its control. On the other hand, huge numbers of small and medium-sized SOEs produced mostly downstream products. They operated in sectors that became highly competitive with the entry of TVEs and FIEs. The government had neither the interest nor the resources to continue to support them all. Increasingly, they were contracted out, leased, sold, or allowed to go bankrupt.

Before *zhuada fangxiao*, the state sector was a gigantic financial burden for the country. In the late 1990s, China's banking system had become technically insolvent in large part because of the non-performing loans they had made to the SOEs. In the end, state-owned banks had to write off 1.4 trillion yuan in bad loans (Brødsgaard and Li 2013). With *zhuada fangxiao*, the government abdicated from its traditional commitment to the workers. The closing of thousands of struggling small and medium SOEs led to massive unemployment. From 1998 to 2002, over 25 million workers were officially laid off (Giles et al. 2006). The newly unemployed and their families struggled to eke out a living in the margins of the fast-changing urban economy, a topic we will return to in Chapter 6.

The economic restructuring of the state sector was accompanied by the restructuring of the Chinese government. As discussed in Chapter 2, throughout the 1980s and 1990s, the Chinese government introduced several rounds of administrative reform, aimed at streamlining the state bureaucracy and making it more compatible with a more marketized economy. Many line industries were abolished, with their coordination functions transferred to various industry associations. The most dramatic downsizing of the central government took place in the 1998 State Council reform under Premier Zhu Rongji, a no-nonsense technocrat determined to push for economic liberalization. The total personnel of the comprehensive economic agencies dropped by 41 percent from 1,768 to 1,040. The all-powerful SPC lost the authority to "draw up and implement industrial policy" (Chen and Naughton 2016).

Some observers contend that the restructuring of the Chinese government marks the transformation from a command-and-control state to a "regulatory state" (Yang 2004). As noted in Chapter 2, in a command-and-control state (or positive state), the government directly plans and manages the economy, whereas in a regulatory state the government makes the rules to govern the market and ensures a level playing field, but otherwise leaves autonomous economic actors to operate on their own. Other observers disagree. They argue that although China created a host of new regulatory agencies, the new regulators were not given independence. The National Development and

Reform Commission (NDRC), which succeeded the SPC, continued to wield enormous power over government investment, industry licensing, and price setting. Furthermore, the CCP Central Committee remained the ultimate arbiter when it came to major economic decisions (Pearson 2005; Breslin 2012).

Regardless of the long-term impact of government restructuring on the role of the state in the economy, the gradual elimination of the industrial ministries weakened the chains of command from the government to the enterprises. In this context, enterprises accelerated the development of linkages among themselves. In the 1990s, a major trend in the state sector was the formation of enterprise groups. With state encouragement, many enterprises formerly overseen by the same ministry organized themselves into a group, although some of them went outside the traditional administrative boundaries and aligned with other enterprises. Typically clustered around a central firm called the group company, these enterprises were connected with each other through a variety of ties, including financial, personnel, trade, joint production, and collective lobbying. Some of these enterprise groups grew to be the largest corporations in the country. The emergence of the enterprise groups enhanced the autonomy of the managers from the government in their routine business operations. However, the state and the managers shared a common interest in making the SOEs more competitive and profitable (Nolan and Wang 1999; Keister 2000).

Consolidating State Control in the 2000s

In contrast to the 1990s, when SOE reform reduced state ownership and control, in the 2000s the pace of the market-oriented reform has slowed down and even been reversed in many areas. SOEs or state-controlled enterprises have become more profitable, gained greater shares of the market at home and abroad, and come under more government intervention. A prominent economist describes this phenomenon as "the state strikes back" (Lardy 2019).

The loss of reform momentum began around 2003, when Hu Jintao and Wen Jiabao replaced Jiang Zemin and Zhu Rongji as CCP General Secretary and State Council Premier respectively. Several factors were likely to have contributed to this change. First, compared with the 1990s, the government fiscal condition had improved significantly. The fiscal reform in 1994 (to be discussed in Chapter 8) and the shedding of large numbers of smaller SOEs meant there was far less financial pressure on the government to deepen liberalization to improve efficiency. Second, a major impetus for the drastic restructuring of the state sector in the 1990s was China's desire to join the World Trade Organization (WTO). To gain WTO membership, the Chinese government had to cut back the role of the state in the economy, including subsidies for SOEs that could not compete in the marketplace. Once China made its way into the WTO in 2001, this external driver for reform quickly diminished. Finally, as the remaining SOEs became consolidated and profitable, their political influence grew. Many of them were closely intertwined with elite families in the CCP. Their economic and political resources enabled them to effectively advocate the preservation of their privileged position.

In 2003, the Chinese government created the State-owned Assets Supervision and Administration Commission (SASAC). Working under the State Council and ultimately accountable to the CCP Central Committee, SASAC is the institutional embodiment of the Party state's rights and responsibilities as the owner of the state sector. Its mission is to preserve and increase the value of state-owned assets. Central SASAC supervises the largest and most important SOEs under the jurisdiction of the central government. It appoints many senior executives of those enterprises, evaluates their performance, manages their wages, guides the restructuring of those enterprises, and decides whether to approve their investment overseas. Regional SASACs perform the same functions vis-à-vis SOEs controlled by provincial and municipal governments (SASAC n.d.).

In the years following the creation of SASAC, the government gradually clarified the scope of its jurisdiction. In 2006 the government's guidelines stipulated that large SOEs in defense, electricity, petroleum, telecommunications, coal, civil aviation, and shipping would be under SASAC supervision. In 2007 shipbuilding, metal work, and construction were added to SASAC's list (Brødsgaard and Li 2013). SASAC has adopted an "expand or perish" approach to mold SOEs into **national champions** (see Box 4.3). It makes it clear to companies that they would either become the dominant players in their sectors (e.g. become one of the top three companies) or be taken over. This has led to the consolidation of nearly 200 original SASAC enterprises into fewer than one hundred in 2020. While the number of SASAC companies may be small, they each have multiple layers of subsidiaries and affiliated enterprises. They are the core of vertically integrated corporate groups, which in turn are linked to other business groups and to governmental organs and state institutions (Lin and Milhaupt 2013).

The global financial crisis (GFC) of 2008 further reversed the market-oriented reform of the 1990s. In response to the crisis, the Chinese government launched a gigantic fiscal stimulus program, hoping to counter the effects of a worldwide economic recession. It injected four trillion yuan (or $586 billion) into the Chinese economy. The funds went primarily to infrastructure development, an area dominated by large state companies. Taking advantage of the financial windfall, the state sector expanded quickly. At the same time, small and medium enterprises in the non-state sector were hard hit by the shrinking export market for downstream products. Their situation was not helped by the banking sector's continued discrimination against private companies. The disparity between different companies led to increased

> ## Box 4.3 China's National Champions
>
> National champions are large companies aided and protected by the state, which dominate one or more sectors of the national economy and compete effectively on the international stage. Long before China, European countries, Japan, and Korea developed their own national champions, such as British Steel, Volkswagen, Mitsubishi, and Daewoo. But the Chinese state has gone much further than these predecessors in its use of governmental policy and resources to support large state-controlled businesses. In the twenty-first century, Chinese national champions have gained increasing international visibility. In 2000, Fortune Global 500 included only nine Chinese companies on the list of the world's largest firms by revenue. By 2024 the number has risen to 128, including three in the top ten – State Grid Corporation (3rd), Sinopec Group (5th), and China National Petroleum Corp (6th). These and many other Chinese SOEs, have become the largest multinational corporations in the world, including giant financial institutions such as the Industrial and Commercial Bank of China (22nd) and China Construction Bank (30th), infrastructure builders such as China State Construction Engineering (14th) and China Railway Engineering Group (35th), and telecommunication companies such as China Mobile Communications (55th) and China Post Group (83rd). (*Fortune* 2024)

acquisitions of private enterprises by SOEs. Moreover, state-owned companies expanded to new fields and competed with private and foreign businesses in non-strategic industries such as real estate and food processing. Critics called attention to the phenomenon of "*guojin mintui* (the advancement of the state, and the retreat of the private)," warning about its dampening effect on market competition (Yu 2014).

On the surface, many of the large SOEs have been highly profitable. However, a deeper look reveals their profitability is largely a function of favorable state policies. The Chinese government has often granted land for SOEs to use at no cost or low cost. It has also kept the prices for SOEs low in their purchase of nationally owned natural resources, including oil, natural gas, and coal. In addition, state-owned banks habitually provide SOEs with cheap credit. Finally, the government has injected significant amounts of subsidies into its favored SOEs. Without the implicit and explicit support from the government, the SOEs would have been far less profitable. In fact, research shows that between 2001 and 2009, when the benefits derived from state policies were deducted from the nominal profits, Chinese SOEs were in fact loss-making every year except two (Brødsgaard and Li 2013).

Around 2013 the reform of the state sector took yet another turn, when the CCP issued a document indicating that it would encourage an increase of "mixed ownership" of enterprises. The main idea was to let more private capital join state capital and operate in previously restricted industries. This was a response to the declining profitability of the SOEs in the preceding years. In theory, bringing more private capital and recruiting managerial talent from non-state enterprises could make the SOEs more efficient and competitive. The government has applied this reform differently to various kinds of SOEs. The primary targets of the reform have been enterprises operating in fully competitive industries, such as building materials, real estate, and the manufacturing of electronic products. There is a great deal of flexibility as to how dominant state ownership is in these enterprises, ranging from absolute majority to minority. The main concern is to increase the returns on assets. For enterprises in pillar industries related to national security and the lifeline of the national economy, such as energy, telecommunications, steel, and electrical machinery, the government seeks to preserve controlling stakes by the state. The goal is to improve enterprise performance, while also realizing strategic development objectives. For enterprises in public goods provision, such as food storage, railways, and military supplies, the reform involves allowing non-state capital to participate through licensing only and preserving absolute state control. The goal is to introduce market mechanisms to cut costs and improve quality (Beck 2023).

In this context, it is useful to note that the meaning of SOEs has been modified over time. In 2008, the National People's Congress, China's legislature, passed the Law on the State-Owned Assets of Enterprises, delegating to "state-invested enterprises" (SIEs) the responsibility of managing state-owned assets. SIEs do not only include wholly state-owned enterprises and companies, but also state-controlled and state-invested shareholding companies. A recent study reports that the portion of state-controlled companies that have mixed ownership rose from 54 percent in 2012 to seventy percent in 2020 (Beck 2023, p. 270).

However, this apparent encouragement of private actors' participation in SOEs does not mean a departure from the government's control of the state sector. Some of the seemingly private investment funds are in fact controlled and guided by the government. They provide an indirect, wealth-management type of instrument for the state to influence the enterprises (Naughton 2016 a; Pan et al. 2021). Moreover, alongside the encouragement of mixed ownership, the CCP has strengthened its position in all types of enterprises. The Party's role in corporate governance has been institutionalized by company charters, which grant Party groups and Party committees a great deal of power in business decision-making, and by the cross-appointments between Party organs and the company board. The strong influence of the Party dims the prospect of improved business performance expected from ownership reform (Beck and Brødsgaard 2022).

The Political Economy of State-Owned Enterprise Reform

When the post-Mao Chinese leaders decided that the old socialist model had failed to turn the country into a modern industrialized power, they were clearer about what to abandon than what to adopt. A popular metaphor describes Chinese reform as "crossing the river by groping the stones." While policymakers allowed rural reform to proceed relatively quickly, they were much more cautious about transforming the urban industries. This is because unlike agriculture, industry was central to Chinese economy; radical changes could result in disasters with serious consequences for the country. For instance, drastic enterprises restructuring would result in massive unemployment and create major public discontent. Rapid price liberalization would increase the prices for energy and raw materials and destabilize industrial production. A dramatic reduction in industrial output would in turn decrease government revenue and weaken its ability to carry out development policies and manage crises. Thus, rather than following the "big bang" approach, China's SOE reform has taken a long and zig-zagging path, often with two steps forward and one step back.

What should the relationship be between the Party state and the state sector? This has been a central question confronted by China throughout the reform era. Soon after urban economic reform began in the mid-1980s, Premier Zhao pushed for the separation of the government from the SOEs (*zhengqi fenkai*). He believed that to improve economic efficiency it was imperative to remove the Party and the government from the operations of the SOEs and to transfer the decision-making authority to professional managers. But his political downfall during the Tiananmen crisis cut short his brand of enterprise reform. In particular, his attempts to reduce the role of the CCP in SOEs were discredited. However, his successors continued to look for ways to balance the pursuit of efficiency and the preservation of control of the state sector. On the one hand, they reduced the direct involvement of government agencies in running the SOEs, for example, by abolishing industrial ministries in the late 1990s and setting up SASAC in 2003. On the other hand, the CCP has found other methods to maintain and even strengthen its control of the state sector, especially the largest SOEs (Li, C. 2016).

The most important method used by the CCP to keep its grip on the state sector is the enterprise *nomenklatura* system. A legacy of the planned economy, such a system establishes lists of leading personnel positions and appoints individuals to fill those positions. The Party's Central Organization Department appoints and evaluates the occupants of the most senior positions in the largest SOEs, which are designated as "important backbone state-owned companies." These include Party committee secretary, general manager, and chair of the board of directors. They are given the equivalent rank of a vice-minister. SASAC appoints and evaluates the vice executives of these enterprises and the top managers of other SOEs within its jurisdiction (Leutert 2018).

Although the government has habitually called for the professionalization of enterprise managers, the recruitment rules and practice have departed little from the Maoist criteria of being "red and expert," i.e. politically loyal and technically capable. Recent research on the managerial elite of Chinese central SOEs shows that while education and industry-specific knowledge are important criteria for recruitment and promotion, loyalty to the CCP is an essential condition. In fact, the CEOs of virtually all the SASAC-controlled SOEs and the top one hundred listed SOEs are CCP members (Lin 2017). This is corroborated by research on the corporate elite of Chinese state-owned oil giants, which finds that while they are committed to the commercial values and interests of their companies, they remain firmly tied to the state apparatus and faithful to the CCP's values and priorities (De Graaff 2014). Likewise, a study of central SOE leaders from 2003 to 2017 finds that individuals who lead well-performing firms and have strong political connections are more likely to stay longer in office (Leutert and Vortherms 2021).

Besides personnel, the government through SASAC has the power to approve or block other important decisions for the largest SOEs, from remuneration and fringe benefits for the top executives to listing the companies in domestic and foreign stock markets. In operational terms, CCP units in SOEs have the final say over a wide range of matters, including long- and middle-term strategic and restructuring plans, annual productivity plan, financing, budget, and extra-budget capital. Such a system fuses economic and administrative power and mixes business with politics. Moreover, the CCP's Central Commission for Discipline Inspection (CCDI) wields considerable power through its authority to investigate and punish inappropriate behavior by enterprise leaders. CCDI's official website lists 615 cases of central-level officials as being under investigation for corruption since 2013. Many of them are leaders of large SOE groups, including PetroChina, China Southern Airlines, China Resources, First Auto Works, and Sinopec (CCDI n.d.). As scholars and commentators have pointed out, the anti-corruption campaign of the Xi era has been highly political, more about eliminating political rivals and ensuring compliance than ridding the system of unethical behavior. It has served as a formidable instrument of control and intimidation (Brown 2018).

Ideologically, the Party state has long adhered to the cardinal principle of CCP leadership in every area of the country's governance. Despite their divergent views on specific economic policies, various factions among the political elite share a consensus on one thing, i.e. China does not accept a fully marketized economy and that the state sector must always play a "leading role" in the economy. The policy debates since the 1970s have not been about if the state should intervene in the economy, but about what kind of state intervention would be the best. This fundamental belief in the role of the state in the national economy sets the boundaries for the twists and turns of state sector reform (Eaton 2016). Moreover, recent research finds that ordinary Chinese citizens are quite positive toward the ideas of state ownership and interventionist regulations. There is a broad agreement between the government and the citizens on the economic functions the state ought to perform, including ownership of lifeline industries, intervening in markets to ward off economic crises, and assisting domestic firms in global competition (Eaton and Hasmath 2021).

Besides ideology, the Party state's determination to control the state sector, especially the largest SOEs in key industries, is also based on practical economic calculations. Chinese policymakers have studied the experience of industrialized countries and concluded that large corporations play a vital role in advancing the national economy. Furthermore, they infer from their observations that the state often uses policy tools to nurture these corporations. They believe that the world's leading corporations have not naturally emerged from the marketplace but have developed through extensive government support (Nolan and Wang 1999; Keister 2000; Li, C. 2016). If China wants to climb up the international economic hierarchy, its government must use its policy tools to cultivate large Chinese corporations. In addition, the resources of the state sector are essential for the Party. Controlling the key assets in the economy is as important as controlling the military in order to maintain the CCP's authoritarian rule (Eaton 2016, p. 110).

It is ironic that even when promoting market-oriented reforms of the SOEs, the state plays a central role. About a decade ago, the Chinese economy was plagued by industrial over-production. In 2015 the Chinese government launched a "supply-side" structural reform. It involved the forceful closing down of many so-called "zombie enterprises," mostly SOEs that produced items with little demand in the marketplace and operated at a loss. On the surface of it, this was a step in economic liberalization. But the method of reform was heavily statist. The NDRC selected the poor performing enterprises for closure. Higher-level authorities pressured lower-level governments to stop subsidizing loss-making companies in their areas (Naughton 2016a). Around the same time, the government also led a large-scale consolidation of SOEs, merging less efficient enterprises with better performing ones (Leutert 2016).

Despite state dominance, the SOEs are not merely passive receivers of orders from the government. Large SOEs possess enormous economic resources and play an important role in implementing the Party's policies. For instance, in the last decade SOEs have been major participants in Xi's **Belt and Road Initiative** (BRI), an ambitious economic and strategic project seeking to use outward investment to connect China with other countries on multiple continents. As of October 2018, Chinese SOEs accounted for about half of BRI projects by number and more than seventy percent by project value (Dossani et al. 2020).

The national champions also tend to have strong political connections, which enable them to influence policymaking to serve their own interest. A case in point is the State Grid Corporation of China. Established in the early 2000s as one of eleven companies that broke the monopoly of the power industry by the State Power Corporation of China, it quickly became an advocate for the development of ultra-high-voltage transmission networks across the country. This was a controversial and highly risky approach to solve the power shortage problem faced by China then, but would give a chance for State Grid to outcompete other companies in the power sector. The company's entrepreneurial leader mobilized financial, technical, and political capital to sell this plan to the government. In the end, policymakers accepted the plan and the ensuing ultra-high-voltage projects helped turn State Grid into the largest utility company in the world and a global leader in ultra-high-voltage technology (Xu 2018).

Moreover, since the 2000s the Chinese government has encouraged SOEs to "go out" and make investments overseas. Many of China's national champions have established presence abroad. Their overseas operations have often evaded the close supervision of China's regulatory apparatuses because the latter are fragmented and limited in their international reach. This trend is illustrated by reports that prominent SOEs, including China National Petroleum Company and China Power Investment Corporation, have at times ignored government guidelines and undermined Chinese foreign policy (Norris 2016; Jones and Zou 2017).

In some ways, the Party state's control of the state sector has paid significant dividends. The Chinese government has often relied on SOEs as crucial instruments for its industrial policy. In the early part of the twenty-first century, under its Medium-and-Long-Term Program of Science and Technology, Beijing funded sixteen megaprojects to boost indigenous innovation. Large, centrally controlled SOEs were by far the most important players. Of these sixteen megaprojects, fifteen were run by central government ministries or enterprises (Chen and Naughton 2016). In addition, SOEs have been helpful tools for the government in dealing with economic crises. In the aftermath of the GFC, the government used large SOEs to quickly channel its stimulus investments to counter the downward economic pressure brought by the global recession. In 2015, when the stock market in China faced a nose-dive, SOEs answered the call to hold, and even buy back, their over-valued shares, thus bailing out the stock market (Li et al. 2022).

But, in other ways, state control of much of China's industry has had detrimental consequences for the country's economic development. The CCP's monitoring and control of the SOEs has had a corrosive effect on corporate governance, weakening managerial incentives, and hindering corporate transparency. This has facilitated insider control, economic corruption, and the illicit grab of state assets by the well-connected (Beck and Brødsgaard

2022). Furthermore, the protection and financial support given to the state sector has been a drag on China's economic growth. Restricting the entry of private enterprises into strategic sectors and limiting private enterprises' access to bank credit have artificially propped up SOEs, but have hampered the most dynamic economic actors. The IMF reports in 2020 that about a quarter (by assets) or over a third (by number) of SOEs incur losses, many of which are nonviable (IMF 2020). Nevertheless, the state sector has continued to soak up large portions of the financial resources of the country. According to one estimate, the crowding out of private investment by the inefficient SOEs reduces China's growth by 1.6 to 2.0 percentage points annually (Lardy 2019).

Conclusion

During the Maoist era, SOEs were the mainstay of China's planned economy and of Chinese industry. Since then, the state sector has undergone continuous changes, from the incremental reform of the 1980s to the drastic restructuring in the 1990s, and from a retreat of the state in the late twentieth century to the return of the state in the early twenty-first century. Compared with the beginning of the reform era, Chinese urban economic landscape has become much more diverse. The weight of SOEs in the national economy has decreased greatly thanks to the rise of other types of enterprises. The state sector's share of the overall national industry dwindled from four-fifths in 1978 to one-fifth in 2015 (Lardy 2019, p. 333). Furthermore, the SOEs themselves have changed in important ways, including their operating principles, investment sources, corporate governance, and international reach. They have been transformed from bureaucratic organizations to modern corporations. On the other hand, the state sector has maintained many traditional characteristics, including their nomenklatura system, the omni-presence of Party units, and their role in the government's industrial policy. Through the largest SOEs, the state has retained firm control of the strategic industries and thus the commanding heights of the Chinese economy.

A broader question underlying state sector reform lies in the relationship between the state and the economy. Although the CCP has explicitly embraced the notion of a socialist market economy since the early 1990s, the exact meaning of the term remains uncertain. Chinese leaders insist that socialism requires public ownership of the means of production and a state capable of shaping the national economy. At the same time, they recognize that material incentives and market competition are necessary to deliver economic efficiency. The twists and turns of SOE reform can be seen as an ongoing effort to get the right balance between maintaining sufficient state control of the economy and taking advantage of market forces for economic development.

The pendulum swung in the direction of marketization from the 1980s to the 1990s, but back toward statism in the twenty-first century.

Scholars have debated vigorously how to characterize the relationship between the state and the economy in China. Many use the term "state capitalism" or "Party-state capitalism" to capture the complexity. On the one hand, the Party state dominates the economy. On the other hand, the Chinese economy has become significantly marketized outside the strategic industries. Indeed, even the SOEs themselves have adopted many features of for-profit commercial entities (e.g. Naughton and Tsai 2015; Eaton 2016; Pearson et al. 2023). Others describe China as a "**developmental state**," a model exemplified by several of its East Asian neighbors. Similar to Japan, Korea, and Taiwan, the Chinese government has been development-oriented. It has adopted incentive structures and made institutional adjustments to serve the priority of growing the national economy (Knight 2014).

While it is debatable which of these two labels gets closer to the reality of China, both recognize the central role of the state in Chinese economic development. In recent years, dominance of the state sector of Chinese industry has only become more salient. However, despite the impressive size of China's largest SOEs, the overall efficiency and productivity of the state sector are inferior to private enterprises. From an economic perspective, there is no doubt that further expanding the private sector will be highly beneficial to China. But the Chinese government has been relentless in preserving and supporting state control of the strategic industries. In contrast, its policy toward private enterprises remains ambivalent. In the next chapter we turn our attention to the rise of the private sector and the limitations of its growth in contemporary China.

Questions for Discussion

1. What are the benefits and costs of the incremental reform of China's SOEs?

2. How do twenty-first century SOEs in China differ from SOEs of the Maoist era?

3. What are the main means used by the Party state to control China's strategic industries?

5

Private Sector Growth

In the last chapter we saw how the Chinese state has played a central role in shaping China's economic development since the founding of the People's Republic. Even during the post-1978 reform era, government has continued to control the commanding heights of the Chinese economy through the largest state-owned enterprises (SOEs). This has led many observers to describe the Chinese model of development in recent decades as "state capitalism," "Party state capitalism," or "developmental state." However, the salient presence of the state should not overshadow the critical contribution of the private sector to China's economic development.

From the beginning of the reform era, Chinese policymakers recognized that to achieve faster economic development than in the past they had to incentivize individuals and enterprises, and that would require secure private property rights. However, the Chinese government refrained from privatizing the SOEs. Instead, it kept the state sector by and large intact but allowed other types of enterprises to operate and gradually grow from the margins of the national economy. Over time, a private sector has formed and expanded, while the state sector has shrunk in relative terms.

This chapter examines the rise of the private sector and private entrepreneurs in urban China. We then analyze the intricate relationship between the Party state and the capitalists in China's nominally socialist system. The Chinese Communist Party (CCP) needs the economic dynamism of private entrepreneurship, but it is also determined to ensure the private sector does not threaten the Party's power and legitimacy. Under the banner of "Socialism with Chinese characteristics," it has tried to balance accommodating the private enterprises and limiting their economic and political influence. Meanwhile, the private entrepreneurs have been eager to work with the CCP. Rather than becoming a force for democratization, they have embraced the one-party regime.

The Rise of Private Enterprises

In the early years of its rule, the CCP purged the comprador bourgeoisie, capitalists who worked for foreign interests, but it tolerated the national bourgeoisie, defined as patriotic indigenous entrepreneurs. The latter continued to

91

operate their businesses, so that they could provide much-needed industrial goods and services in a war-torn country. But, in a few years, the official policy changed. With the so-called "socialist transformation of private industry and commerce" in the mid-1950s, all private businesses were nationalized, and private entrepreneurs were eliminated as a social economic class. For the next two decades, the urban economy came under complete public ownership. The most important components were SOEs, which monopolized heavy and light industries. At the same time, a small number of collectively owned enterprises (COEs) operated in the periphery, providing employment opportunities for the disabled and for some young people who had earlier been sent to rural areas for re-education and later returned to the cities. It was only in the late 1970s that non-public enterprises (non-SOEs and non-COEs) re-emerged, including private enterprises.

Before discussing the development of the private sector, it is useful to clarify several overlapping concepts. Two concepts often used in the Chinese discourse are public (*gongyou*) and non-public (*fei gongyou*) economic sectors. SOEs and COEs fall into the former category, whereas the latter category includes individual enterprises, private companies, and foreign invested enterprises (FIEs). Some businesses are of mixed ownership, involving public and non-public economic components. To make things even more complicated, in the early years of the reform era, when private enterprises were subject to discrimination, many entrepreneurs registered their businesses as COEs or FIEs to gain support from local governments (in the case of fake COEs) or to benefit from favorable tax policies (in the case of fake FIEs). Scholars agree that the official statistics based on enterprise registration may well underestimate the number of private enterprises in China (Tsai 2007; Haggard and Huang 2008; Lardy 2014). Still, many studies use the official registration statistics to measure the private sector in the Chinese economy for the lack of a viable alternative.

The evolution of the private sector can be divided into three stages. The first stage, from the late 1970s to the late 1980s, was a period of steady liberalization. Soon after the Cultural Revolution, the Chinese government began to allow private farming plots, family businesses, and peddling, which had been previously prohibited as "tails of capitalism." In 1979, Beijing issued a policy encouraging rebuilding and developing the individual economy as a necessary supplement to the socialist economy. In this context, individually owned businesses (*geti hu*) flourished in rural and urban China. They provided products (such as fruits, vegetables, poultry, and sea food) and services (e.g. restaurants and repair shops) that had been in short supply under the planned economy. In 1982 the CCP's 12th National Congress called for multiple forms of economy to develop, encouraging individual enterprises to supplement the publicly owned economy. Later that year, the National People's Congress (NPC) wrote this into Article 11 of the country's new constitution.

By law, individual enterprises could not hire more than seven workers. This figure was apparently based on an example used by Karl Marx in *Das Kapital* to illustrate the capitalist production process. In that example, Marx referred to eight or more employees of a private enterprise. Chinese officials thus concluded that the hiring of more than eight people was a sign of exploitation. But many of the individual enterprises soon grew beyond that scope (see Box 5.1). In 1988, the government issued a Provisional Act of Private Enterprises of the People's Republic of China, which defined private enterprises as profit-making economic units established or controlled by natural persons and using more than seven employees. In the same year, the Chinese government amended the 1982 constitution, adding private enterprises to individual enterprises in Article 11. The revised article stated that the state allows a private economy to exist and grow within legal stipulations, that the private economy is a supplement to the socialist public economy, and that the state protects the lawful rights and interests of the private economy while it also guides, supervises, and regulates the latter. This was a major departure from the CCP's previous ideological doctrines.

The crackdown of the Tiananmen protest in 1989 interrupted China's economic liberalization, including the development of the private sector. In fact, the presence of private entrepreneurs among the protestors in some urban areas alarmed the CCP, deepening its distrust of this group. In the next couple of years, the Chinese government launched a systematic assault against the private sector. It was not until Deng Xiaoping's famed southern tour in early 1992 that the situation changed. Deng's call for renewed economic reform ushered in the second stage of private sector development. The CCP's 14th National Congress noted that while the public economy continued to be the mainstream, the individual economy, private economy, and foreign invested economy, would be supplements to the mainstream. In 1993 the State Council especially encouraged the growth of individual, private, and shareholding enterprises in regions with poor and backward collective economies. It urged an end to the discrimination against individual and private economies. This was a sensible strategy, given the potential for private enterprises to provide much-needed development and employment in those regions.

As reform of the state sector accelerated after the mid-1990s, it created more space for the expansion of the non-state sector. With the decision by the 15th CCP National Congress in 1997 to "grasp the big" and "let go the small" SOEs, the Chinese government redefined the individual economy and private economy as "important components of the socialist market economy." This represented a more favorable view of the private sector than the previous label of "supplements" to the publicly owned economy. The new designation was reflected in another amendment of Article 11 of the constitution in 1999. The revised constitution reiterated state guarantee of the legal rights and

Box 5.1 Shazi Guazi (Fool's Sunflower Seeds)

Nian Guangjiu was born in 1937 in a rural village in Anhui Province in eastern China. War and famine forced his family to flee to the town of Wuhu. His father, who sold fruits on the streets to support the family, died when Nian was a teenager. He inherited the trade and became a hawker at a young age. Under the Maoist regime, he continued to peddle fish and chestnuts, despite government prohibition against such "tails of capitalism." He was imprisoned briefly twice for "speculation." In 1972, he learned to roast sunflower seeds, a popular snack, and began to sell them secretly. Because his sunflower seeds were big, tasty, and inexpensive, he became known as a foolish businessman. In 1979, he registered the trademark of "Shazi Guazi (Fool's Sunflower Seeds)."

Over time, Nian expanded his makeshift stall into a workshop that employed more than one hundred workers. Some skeptics accused him of anti-socialist labor practice, triggering a national debate over whether an individual employing so many workers was guilty of "exploitation." His case reached China's top leaders. Deng Xiaoping expressed his view at a high-level meeting in October 1984: "The emergence of privately hired labor was quite shocking a while back. Everybody was very worried about it. In my opinion, that problem can be set aside for a couple of years . . . If you put the man who makes Fool's Sunflower Seeds out of business, it will make many people anxious, and that won't do anybody any good. What is there to be afraid of if we let him go on selling his seeds for a while? Will that hurt socialism?" (Li 2023). Nian's success turned him into one of China's first millionaires, but it also made him a target of jealousy and ideological dogmatization. In 1987 he came under investigation for possible economic crimes. In 1991 he was handed a three-year prison term. When Deng took his famous southern tour in 1992, he again mentioned Nian's case, suggesting that "Many people felt uncomfortable with this man who had made a profit of one million yuan. They called for action to be taken against him. I said that no action should be taken . . . if we don't handle them properly, our policies could easily be undermined, and overall reform affected. The basic policies for urban and rural reform must be kept stable for a long time to come" (Li 2023). In the aftermath of Deng's speech, Nian was declared innocent. Fool's Sunflower Seeds have been one of the best-known stories of private enterprises in reform era China.

interests of individual enterprises and private enterprises, even though it did not specify the protection of property rights.

In 2004, the NPC amended the country's constitution again. It expanded property protection beyond the protection of income and possessions and included the protection of the means of production. The wording of "owner-ship rights"[1] was replaced by "property rights." This was a significant step in improving the security of private businesses. In 2007, the NPC promulgated the Property Rights Law, making explicit the protection of private property rights and providing a more solid legal foundation of the private economy.

Ironically, around that same time as it consolidated the legal framework for protecting private property in the 2000s, the Chinese government began to change its policy toward private enterprises. In this third and most recent stage of private sector evolution, the Party state has partially reversed its reduction of the state sector and has instead turned to strengthen the remaining SOEs. As noted in the last chapter, following the 2008 global financial crisis (GFC), the bulk of the government's stimulus program went to the state sector, with only limited benefits to the private sector. State-controlled banks continued to favor SOEs over private enterprises in their lending. That resulted in the phenomenon of *guojin mintui* discussed in the previous chapter.

Soon after Xi Jinping's ascendence to the leader's position in 2012, the CCP signaled a readiness for further liberalization of the economy. In November 2013 the Third Plenum of the 18th Party congress declared that "The market must become the decisive force in the allocation of resources." However, that rhetoric did not translate into policy. To the contrary, during the Xi era the Chinese government has enhanced state industrial policy and pro-moted the SOEs harder than in the recent past. State-dominated banks have expanded their lending to the SOEs, further squeezing the private enterprises. For many years, thanks to their superior efficiency, private industrial firms grew faster than the SOEs despite unfavorable conditions. But the deterio-ration of their operating environment has reached such a level that since 2017 they have been surpassed by the growth of state industrial firms (Lardy 2019).

Recent trends notwithstanding, the private sector in China has come a long way since the beginning of the reform era. According to official statistics, as of 2023 there were over 52 million registered nonstate enterprises, including individual enterprises, private enterprises, limited liability companies, and joint stock companies not controlled by the state, accounting for more than 92 percent of all enterprises in the country (Zhao 2023). According to the *People's Daily*, the CCP's mouthpiece newspaper, the private sector is now responsible for over fifty percent of the tax revenue, over sixty percent of the country's GDP, over seventy percent of the technological innovations, and over eighty percent of urban employment (Wang 2023).

The role of the private sector in providing employment opportunities in contemporary China could not be overstated. Its contribution in this regard was made especially salient after the mid-1990s, when the drastic restructur-ing of the state sector led to the closing of many small to medium-sized SOEs. The traumatic downsize of the urban workforce was ameliorated by the absorption of large numbers of the newly unemployed SOE workers by private enterprises. In 1995 the state sector had 112.6 million workers, but by 2003 that number had fallen to 68.8 million. In the same period, employees of individual and private enterprises rose from 55.7 million to 89.5 million (Kanamori and Zhao 2004). In fact, the overall employment increase in China since 1978 has been due entirely to the expansion of the private sector (Lardy 2014).

Finally, the private sector has been an increasingly important player in Chinese exports and overseas investment. In 1995 SOEs contributed two-thirds of Chinese exports, but by 2013 their share had dropped to below five percent. In that year, private enterprises took up nearly 48 percent of the country's exports (Brandt and Lim 2020). In 2023, the private sector accounted for 66.4 percent of China's exports of its own brands of products (Ministry of Finance 2024). Meanwhile, private businesses have also become major actors in China's outward foreign direct investment (OFDI). As of 2017 about seventy percent of new Chinese OFDI came from private firms. In that year, non-state investors (including private investors) surpassed SOEs in their share of China OFDI stock, accounting for almost 51 percent of the total (Molnar et al. 2021).

The growth of the private sector is all the more remarkable when one considers the relatively unfavorable environment it finds in China. Compared with the SOEs, private enterprises face many more challenges, which we will examine later in the chapter. The steady growth of their output has largely resulted from their superior performance rather than financial input. As market actors, they have to compete to survive. Thus, they tend to be much more innovative and efficient than the SOEs (Haggard and Huang 2008; Lardy 2014). An oft-used matrix to measure how efficiently businesses use their assets to generate profits is "return on assets (ROA)," calculated by dividing a company's net income by the average balance of its total assets. As Figure 5.1 shows, the ROA of the private enterprise has been consistently higher than that of the SOEs, and the divergence has become more salient since 2008. The latter is likely due to the government's intensified support of the state sector after the GFC. The squeeze of credit on the private enterprises may well have forced them to become even more efficient.

In addition to their direct contribution to China's economic development, private businesses have been a crucial factor in the marketization of the national economy. Their very existence has increased competition among all types of Chinese enterprises. This has indirectly improved the efficiency of other economic actors, including the SOEs, COEs, and the FIEs. Moreover, the rise of the private sector has reshaped Chinese economic institutions even as the private sector itself has been shaped by those institutions. The next two sections analyze the political economy of the interactions between the Chinese Party state and private entrepreneurs.

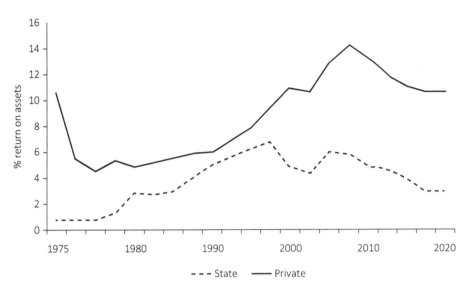

Figure 5.1 Comparing Private Enterprises and SOEs in Efficiency
Source: Lardy, N. (2019). *The State Strikes Back: The End of Economic Reform in China?* Washington DC: Peterson Institute for International Economics. Used with permission.

State Accommodation of the Private Sector

Throughout the Maoist years, capitalists of the pre-1949 era were frequent targets for political persecution. The Five Anti campaign of 1952 attacked the urban capital class in the name of acting against bribery, tax evasion, theft of state assets, shoddy work and the use of inferior materials, and stealing of state economic information. From 1953 to 1956, the socialist transformation campaign led to the nationalization of all private enterprises in urban China. It also aimed to transform the old capitalists who lived off exploitation into self-supporting laborers. Later, individuals with a capitalist background were repeatedly struggled against; many were beaten to death or committed suicide during the Cultural Revolution. In the post-Mao era, the CCP gradually reversed its radical anti-capitalist position. However, the Party state did not turn to wholeheartedly welcoming private enterprises and private entrepreneurs. Its approach has been one of passive accommodation rather than active support.

For decades, while using private enterprises to promote economic efficiency, the Chinese government nonetheless preserved the strategic and most profitable industries as the turf of SOEs. Since the mid-2000s, the government has made multiple gestures toward creating a level playing field for all types of enterprises. In 2005 the State Council issued 36 Articles guiding and supporting non-state-owned enterprises. The document formally permitted private enterprises to enter a wide range of industries that had previously been exclusively controlled by SOEs, including natural monopolies such as electric power, telecom, railway, aviation, and petroleum industries, infrastructure and public services such as urban water and heat supply, public transit, waste management, and even financial service and defense technology. In 2010 the State Council promulgated another set of policies, known as the new 36 Articles, aimed to improve private enterprises' access to resources and markets, ensure fair regulations, and protect their property and rights. In 2019 and 2023 the Chinese government issued more guidelines to combat the persistent biases against private enterprises and to reiterate the importance of the private economy to the overall economic development of the nation.

While the official policies have lowered the *de jure* barriers for non-state actors to enter economic sectors traditionally dominated by SOEs, in practice private enterprises continue to encounter many types of informal barriers that make it difficult for them to operate and succeed in those sectors. For instance, they face much greater difficulties than the SOEs in securing raw materials, land, energy, and other items that are still, at least partially, subject to government allocation. Government agencies tend to award large procurement contracts to SOEs rather than private businesses. And local authorities habitually discriminate against private enterprises in issuing permits and enforcing rules and regulations (Yuan 2023).

The most debilitating informal barrier is access to financing. The private sector in China has struggled with this problem since the beginning. A study of private entrepreneurs in 1996–1997 found that 88 percent of them had never borrowed from a formal financial institution (Tsai 2009). A nationwide survey in 2000 asked private entrepreneurs the degree of difficulty in obtaining bank loans, using a scale between one to five, with one being the easiest access, and five the most difficult. The percentages of entrepreneurs choosing four and five are 32.13 and 31.19 percent. In other words, about two-thirds of those surveyed reported very difficult access to bank loans (Bai et al. 2006). A cross-country comparison of eighty-one countries in 2000 indicated that private businesses in China were among the most constrained in the world in terms of their access to capital (Batra et al. 2003). As of the end of 2016, only eleven percent of the loans made by Chinese banks went to the private sector, while 83 percent went to SOEs (Lardy 2019).

One reason for their poor access to formal financing is the severe information asymmetry between banks and private businesses. Without reliable information about the assets, profitability and operations of the private enterprises, banks are reluctant to lend to them. But, even more importantly, this is due to the lack of strong protection of private property. Chinese law did not offer protection of property rights until 2004. Even since then, private businesses have remained vulnerable to willful exploitation and expropriation, making them less attractive to lenders. An analysis of firm-level data from 1997 to 2006 highlights two widespread types of payments private enterprises are compelled to make – public relations fees (*yingchou*) and forced apportionment of funds (*tanpai*). While such payments constitute a heavy burden for many private entrepreneurs, they are especially onerous in sectors that rely on scarce and less mobile resources controlled by the government (Zhu and Wu 2014). For entrepreneurs, such levies lead to uncertainties about expected returns on their investment and discourage them from creating private businesses. Research shows that the more local governments derive revenue from discretionary charges, the less likely it is for private entrepreneurs to choose to set up operations in their jurisdictions (Minard 2015). In any case, given the Party state's preferential policy toward SOEs, banks are seldom willing to lend to private enterprises.

This situation has forced private businesses to resort to other sources of financing, sometimes legally and often illegally. Many private entrepreneurs borrow from relatives, friends, and others in their personal networks. This makes family and friendship ties very important for entrepreneurship. Indeed, research shows that entrepreneurial activities and the weight of private enterprises in the economy are positively related to the density of clans, indicating that clans help private entrepreneurs overcome financing constraints. However, even as clans have facilitated the growth of the private sector in the absence of a well-developed financial system, dependence on the clans deters private businesses from growing into large firms (Zhang 2020). Other methods include trade credit, rotating credit associations, pawnshops, and pyramid investment associations, which are similar to Ponzi schemes (Tsai 2009).

According to some observers, the private sector fared reasonably well in the 1980s, but their access to the financial institutions worsened after that. Two national surveys – conducted in 1993 and 2002 respectively – show a decline in the private enterprises' dependence on formal financing and an increase in their use of informal financing from the 1980s to the 1990s (Huang 2010). Others take a different view, noting that later in the 1990s the emergence of urban credit cooperatives improved the financing opportunities for non-state actors; they supplied eighty percent of the credit flow to private enterprises. After 1998 these credit cooperatives became city commercial banks and continued to lend to the private sector. Meanwhile, the development of stock markets in China has also made more credit available to the private sector through non-bank financial institutions. The abolishment of the quota system for listing on the stock markets in 2000 further leveled the playing field, resulting in a decline of SOEs to just under half of the listed firms by 2010 (Lardy 2014, p. 113). However, the share of private sector has declined in Chinese stock markets since 2021. It accounted for over 55 percent of the total capitalization of the top one hundred listed companies in mid-2021, but that number shrank to 39 percent in mid-2023 (Huang and Veron 2024).

Overall, the challenging situation for private enterprises has not fundamentally improved. They still face many obstacles in accessing the formal financial system. This problem has no doubt been a serious impediment for the development of the private sector in China. Moreover, since Chinese investment began to flow overseas in the early 2000s, private companies have sought to join the action alongside the SOEs. However, the limited external sources of financing have hindered their efforts. For example, researchers using firm-level data from Zhejiang Province find that financial constraints have had a major negative impact on firms' engagement in OFDI. They argue that without better access to financing, many productive and competitive private enterprises are likely to be shut out of opportunities for overseas investment (Wang et al. 2013).

Alongside its mixed attitude toward private enterprises, the CCP has been ambivalent toward private businesspeople. In the 1980s the policymakers tolerated individual and private enterprise owners, hoping they would help promote market-oriented economic reforms. At the same time, they harbored strong suspicions about the latter's loyalty to the CCP and to the socialist cause. As noted before, the support by some of the private entrepreneurs for the student protests in 1989 deepened the distrust and hostility of the conservatives in the CCP toward them. Indeed, the government dealt with private entrepreneurs involved in the Tiananmen movement much more harshly than the students, subjecting them to long prison sentences, or worse.

After the mid-1990s, state sector reform resulted in the privatization of many small and medium-sized SOEs. This created a new class of private entrepreneurs – former managers of SOEs who became their owners after privatization. Many of these **"red capitalists"** were already members of the CCP (Dickson 2003). Their presence among the ranks of private businesspeople redefined this social economic class and improved its status. By the early twenty-first century, the CCP had become comfortable enough to open its membership to private entrepreneurs of all stripes, even though it still screened who would be allowed to play political roles. In 2001 Party General Secretary Jiang Zemin took a bold step by proclaiming that "private entrepreneurs are now one of the new social classes, and they make great contributions to socialist society through their honest labor and lawful operation . . ." In 2002 the CCP officially adopted Jiang's theory of **"Three Represents** (*sange daibiao*)," portraying the Party as representing advanced productive forces, advanced culture, and the fundamental interests of the majority of the Chinese people. As part of the "advanced productive forces," private entrepreneurs were now to be welcomed into the Party.

From the perspective of the Party state, this was a good strategy for two reasons. On the one hand, the private sector had proven itself to be highly efficient and made a vital contribution to the country's economic success. To sustain economic development and thus the legitimacy of the CCP regime, it was necessary to cooperate with private entrepreneurs. On the other hand, by co-opting the capitalists, the CCP could give them a stake in the Party. It also enabled the Party to better monitor them and prevent them from organizing themselves independently. As of 2006, about one-third of China's private entrepreneurs were CCP members, including former SOE managers who were Party members before they joined the private sector (Dickson 2007).

State accommodation of the private sector has been uneven across regions. In some areas, the local government has gone further in cooperating with private enterprises than in other areas. Private entrepreneurs use informal financing, such as shadow banking, to start and sustain their businesses, and in so doing they pose some risks for the formal financial system. Informal financial intermediaries often violate the official interest rate policy. They may outcompete the state-owned local banks in savings mobilization and facilitate the flow of bank funds into the private sector. Their unregulated lending activities may also contribute to local financial crises. The Chinese government has launched numerous campaigns against the informal financial system, but it has not been able to eliminate the latter because many local officials collaborate with private entrepreneurs in keeping the system alive. Indeed, in localities where de-collectivization started early, state officials tend to be more tolerant of informal finance. In contrast, in areas heavily populated by SOEs, the local government is typically more zealous in complying with the financial rectification and in curtailing the informal financial activities essential for private enterprises (Tsai 2009).

Variation also exists in the same region. A detailed study of Zhejiang province, where private entrepreneurship has led the rest of the country, offers a good illustration of the complexity of the situation. In the 1940s the communist cadres in Zhejiang fell into two groups: those who came to Zhejiang from the revolutionary bases in the north ("southbound cadres") and the local guerrilla fighters. After the revolution, a power struggle ensued, in which local guerrilla fighters were marginalized by the southbound cadres, who had powerful patrons at the provincial and national levels. Thus, the guerrilla cadres, who were important in running the local governments, faced political insecurity and were often the victims of political campaigns. To ensure their political survival, the guerrilla cadres worked hard to win popular support by looking after local economic interests. A kind of mutual protection and support system emerged between the local political elites and potential private entrepreneurs. Research shows that in counties run by local guerrilla cadres the private sector was more effectively protected from the radical policy of the national government after 1949 than in counties controlled by southbound cadres. In the long run, the former performed better in economic development than the latter (Zhang and Liu 2013).

The Party state's half-hearted accommodation of the private economy can be explained on ideological, economic, and political grounds. Early in the reform process, the CCP proclaimed "four cardinal principles" – upholding the socialist path, upholding the people's democratic dictatorship, upholding the leadership of the CCP, and upholding Marxism–Leninism and Mao Zedong Thought. In his speech to the 12th CCP National Congress in 1982, Deng made it clear that the Party "must integrate the universal truth of Marxism with the concrete realities of China and blaze a path of our own and build a Socialism with Chinese Characteristics" (Deng 1991). While eager to use the private entrepreneurs to achieve economic growth, Chinese policymakers have been unwilling to go beyond these ideological boundaries.

Economically, government officials at every level have vested interests in protecting the state sector even as they recognize the superior economic performance of private enterprises. SOEs tend to be large employers and important revenue contributors to the state. Owned by the state, they have a tradition of working closely with the government to achieve economic targets set by the national and the local authorities. The rise of private enterprises threatens SOEs' profitability, and even viability. Moreover, many officials view the competition between private enterprises and SOEs as unfair to the SOEs because, unlike private businesses, the SOEs carry the heavy burden of providing employment and traditional socialist welfare for their employees. They are thus justified in providing more support for the SOEs than the private enterprises.

In addition, the CCP is wary of the political consequences of a strong private economic sector. Historical and comparative research suggests a close relationship between the growth of a capitalist class (the bourgeoisie) and democratic politics. As Barrington Moore (1993) famously put it – based on his study of European history – "no bourgeoisie, no democracy." More recent experience also suggests that a rising urban middle class, including private entrepreneurs, plays an important role in political democratization (Huntington 1993). Although private businesses have largely been compliant and cooperative with the Party state (as discussed in the next section), the government has remained highly vigilant against any potential political threat coming from the private sector.

The ambivalence of the Party state toward the private sector has taken a turn for the worse during the Xi era. This has gone hand-in-hand with the entrenchment of Party state capitalism covered in the last chapter. A great sense of insecurity has driven the CCP to tighten its control of the economy in recent years, including a stronger presence in the private economy. According to the Party's own report, by the end of 2017 CCP cells had been set up in 1.88 million nonstate firms, or over 73 percent of all nonstate firms. For many private owners, this has intensified anxiety about the potential state intervention in their business management (Pearson et al. 2023).

Moreover, since the mid-2010s, the Party state has developed and deployed new financial instruments to interfere with the private economy. In 2014, the State Council called for professionally managed private equity funds to make equity investments on behalf of the state (Chen and Rithmire 2020). As noted in Chapter 4, early in the Xi era, the government introduced mixed-ownership reform allowing non-state capital to be invested in SOEs. Another component of the reform, known as reverse mixed ownership reform, encourages state investment in the private sector. Indeed, various funds owned and guided by the state have taken up minority shares of non-state-owned enterprises. This has been a particularly prominent trend in strategic industries, including private high-tech companies (Beck 2023).

Finally, in the last few years, the Party state has stepped up its assault on the private sector to tackle seemingly random policy concerns of the day. For instance, in 2021 the government abruptly imposed new rules requiring private tutoring services to register as non-profit organizations and barring them from making profits. The official rationale was to reduce the financial burden for the students and their parents. China's biggest publicly listed education companies like *Xindongfang* (New Orient Education and Technology) lost large chunks of their value (Stevenson 2021). Likewise, Beijing has periodically cracked down on the gaming industry, largely the domain of private tech companies such as Tencent and NetEase. The stated goals include protecting minors and reducing addiction among game players. The new regulations wiped out trillions of dollars in value for some of the best-known private companies in 2021, and tens of billions of dollars in 2023 (V. Wang 2024). Even prominent leaders of the private sector, who have enjoyed political support from the government, have fallen on hard times (see Box 5.2).

The CCP's rigid lockdown of the country during the Covid pandemic brought another blow to the private sector. With business opportunities gone overnight, private enterprises nevertheless had little support from the state; many went bankrupt. Since the end of the lockdown policy in early 2023, the so-called "debt triangle" has hit private enterprises especially hard. When delayed and partial payment lead businesses to owe money to each other, government organizations and SOEs tend to withhold payments to the private companies most often. The overall slowness of economic recovery and persistent difficulty in accessing credit have worsened their plight. The loss of confidence on the part of private entrepreneurs has been manifested by a decline of private investment in 2023 (Huang and Lovely 2023). Meanwhile, many wealthy individuals have sought to take their money out of the country, ushering in a wave of capital flight (*Economist* 2023).

Suspicions of private businesses' loyalty and fears of their subversion of its monopoly of power led the Chinese government to adopt a rather unusual policy combination – suppressing local capital and favoring foreign capital. The reformers embraced foreign direct investment (FDI) early on. Chinese policy toward multinational corporations (MNCs) has been far more welcoming than in other East Asian countries at comparable stages of economic development. During its economic takeoff, Taiwan's FDI peaked in the 1960s at around three percent of the gross capital formation. In Korea, the FDI's

Box 5.2 The Rise and Fall of Jack Ma

Jack Ma (or Ma Yun) has been one of China's best-known billionaire private entrepreneurs in the reform era. A slight man, about five feet tall, he was born in 1964 and grew up in an ordinary family in the city of Hangzhou. It took him three attempts to pass the national college entrance exam. After graduating from university, he worked as a teacher for a while. In 1995, he created an internet start-up, China Pages, developing web pages for businesses. In 1999 he and a group of friends launched Alibaba, an Internet platform that connected Chinese goods suppliers with buyers in China and abroad. Later, Alibaba began to provide payment and financial services to its hundreds of millions of users. In 2014, Alibaba was listed on the New York Stock Exchange for $25 billion, the single largest initial public offering (IPO) until then. In the same year, Ma reached the top of Hurun's list of China's richest individuals. Rubbing shoulders with political leaders and business tycoons at home and abroad, Ma even accompanied President Xi Jinping on his visit to the United States in 2015.

But Ma's fortune took a sudden turn when he publicly challenged the Party's policy. In the previous few years, Internet finance had expanded rapidly. Ant Group, formerly a subsidiary of Alibaba that provided payment and financial services for the company's clients, developed into a separate but affiliated financial firm with about one billion customers in China. It planned an IPO in 2020 to raise an unprecedented $34 billion in the capital market. The Chinese government expressed concern about the possible negative implications of Internet finance for traditional banks and for the country's financial stability. It issued new regulations on Internet finance and planned for more. In October, at a high-profile business conference, Ma openly criticized the state regulators for their attempt to rein in fintech companies like Ant. The reaction from the Party was swift and devastating. The IPO of Ant Group was suspended, and Ma largely disappeared from the public. A former official in Hangzhou, who had interacted with Alibaba for years, commented that "As a private entrepreneur it's very important to find the right degree of publicity and Ma hasn't yet mastered this" (McMorrow and Yu 2021). In 2021, the government handed Alibaba a heavy fine of RMB 18.2 billion (or $2.8 billion) for abusing its market dominance. Ma has since turned to philanthropy and kept a low profile.

role was even more limited. Even after some FDI liberalization in the 1980s and 1990s, its share of gross capital formation was less than half of Taiwan's, at around 1.2 percent. In contrast, the figure for China in the 1990s was more than fifteen percent (Haggard and Huang 2008, p. 369). This bias became especially salient in the decade after the political turmoil of 1989. Although the domestic private sector created far more jobs than FIEs, bank lending to FIEs was many times (ten times in 1994 and twice in 2002) that of the credits extended to Chinese private enterprises (Huang 2003).

The different approaches by China and by other East Asian societies to domestic private entrepreneurs and foreign capital has deep roots in their different political systems. Like China, both Korea and Taiwan were ruled by authoritarian governments during their economic takeoff years, from the 1960s to the 1980s. However, in neither of them did the state have the kind of complete control economically and politically as the CCP has had in China. Despite their authoritarian government, Korea and Taiwan had their economy largely privately owned rather than state-owned. Moreover, there was competition within the ruling political elite in Korea and Taiwan; different factions wooed businesses for support. In contrast, the Chinese state owns the country's largest enterprises. Moreover, the Chinese elite is relatively coherent and largely insulated from social influence (Haggard and Huang 2008). China's favorable policy toward FDI at the expense of domestic capital was made possible by a combination of these factors. It has in turn strengthened the political control of the CCP even further (Gallagher 2002).

The Private Sector's Embrace of the State

The rise of the private sector in China has created many entrepreneurs with considerable economic resources. But, so far, they have not become a force challenging the political power of the Party state. In fact, studies show that most of the newly minted capitalists have worked closely with the government. They have embraced the state rather than rejected it, or even kept a distance from it. This is not to suggest that private entrepreneurs are always satisfied with the government's policies, which often discriminate against them in favor of the SOEs; they are not. But they have largely chosen to address their grievances by working with the CCP regime.

In the early years of the reform era, Chinese law specified that individual enterprises could not hire more than seven employees. The owners of larger private businesses "camouflaged" themselves as COEs to work around this rule. As of 1985 ten million of the twelve million TVEs were completely and manifestly private enterprises (Huang 2008, p. xiv). A 1988 survey conducted in Wenzhou, an entrepreneurial city in Zhejiang Province, identified "45,000 privately owned firms of various forms under the banner of collective enterprises, but only ten registered private enterprises" (Chen 2007, p. 57). Even later – well into the 1990s – long after the law allowed for larger private enterprises, many of them maintained the façade of TVEs, which made them seem part of the socialist system. Estimates of privately owned COEs range from one-third nationally to as high as ninety percent in some localities" (Tsai 2005, p. 1136).

This practice, which came to be known as **"wearing a red hat,"** not only allowed private businesses to grow, despite the restrictive laws, but it also facilitated their financing under difficult circumstances. When the government first permitted private enterprises to form, the registration of such companies required far more capital than many aspiring private entrepreneurs had. To overcome this challenge, they teamed up with local governments; they either borrowed money from the latter or paid them fees to register the enterprises as COEs (Tsai 2007; Nee and Opper 2012).

In addition, assuming the status of COEs offered private enterprises a certain level of protection from the grabbing hand of the government. Local officials often treated private enterprises as easy targets of exploitation through expropriation of their property, imposition of arbitrary fees and charges, and selective enforcement of rules and regulations. Wearing a red hat was one way in which private businesses tried to shield themselves from predatory government actions. Being registered as COE also gained some advantages for private enterprises, including favorable tax treatment and preferential access to bank credit. This pattern existed in both urban and rural China (Ahlstrom and Bruton 2001; Tsai 2007).

As noted earlier, the CCP began to accept entrepreneurs as members in the early twenty-first century. The following years saw a rapid increase of Party members among private businesspeople. Research shows that CCP membership of private business owners enhances the social status of their enterprises, which in turn offers better protection of their property rights and access to bank loans (Bai et al. 2006). Many private entrepreneurs have actively sought involvement in state institutions. The most politically ambitious among them find their way into the People's Congress and the People's Political Consultative Conferences at the national and the local levels. Getting a seat at these institutions helps them build networks and develop political capital, which they then use to protect their property and advance their business interests (Hou 2019).

Private business owners have also shown their loyalty to and support of the government through charitable contribution. Smaller enterprises tend to contribute to local causes, such as constructing public facilities for the community or financing the schools in their areas. Larger enterprises typically donate significant funds to national as well as local public causes. They include poverty relief projects backed by the government, education programs, and hospitals. Media attention to such charitable activities gives private entrepreneurs visibility. Equally importantly, their generosity seems to enhance their reputation with the government and generate better business outcomes. According to an analysis of survey data from 3,837 private enterprises in 31 provinces of China in 2006, there is a significant positive relationship between philanthropical donation and enterprise profitability. Companies that make more charitable donations are likely to make more money. This pattern is particularly strong in provinces with relatively weak legal institutions, which suggests that philanthropy serves to protect private businesses where law falls short in doing so (Su and He 2010). Another study finds private entrepreneurs are more likely to donate to anti-poverty programs organized by the government if they have enjoyed access to preferential loans from state-owned banks when they first began their businesses. This suggests that they provide assistance to the government in return for preferential treatments in the past and in expectation of such treatment in the future. This phenomenon has been especially salient among small firms and firms in regulated industries (Long and Yang 2016).

Besides wearing a red hat, becoming CCP members, getting involved in state institutions, and practicing charity, another way for private entrepreneurs to embrace the Party state is to provide direct financial benefits to local government organizations and officials. Through share-holding or profit-sharing, private business owners give a stake in their enterprises to local cadres or their units. They also employ key officials or their relatives without asking them to do much actual work but use them to improve the status and political connections of the enterprises (Ahlstrom and Bruton 2001). The line between such practices and bribery is often blurred. Some scholars argue that the rise of the private sector in China's transitional economy has contributed to an increase of bribery in the twenty-first century, even as other forms of corruption, such as embezzlement and misappropriation of public funds, have declined as a result of administrative reform (Ko and Weng 2012).

In industrialized societies, businesses typically form associations to handle government relations. These associations lobby for policies in their favor or support political candidates sympathetic to their concerns. In China, private entrepreneurs also have established their own associations. The Self-Employed Laborers' Association is made up of small business owners. The Private Entrepreneurs' Association represents larger private enterprises. The Industrial and Commercial Federation is the organization for the largest private enterprises. Some scholars argue that these associations provide a rare channel to voice private sector's concern to government agencies (Ahstrom and Bruton 2001). Others do not see them as having any meaningful impact. One study finds that businesses (including private enterprises) do not often rely on associations to exercise influence or solve problems; when they do, the outcomes are seldom successful. Direct contact between companies and government agencies is more prevalent and effective than working through associations (Kennedy 2008). Another study, which focuses specifically on environmental policy enforcement, reveals that larger enterprises tend to lobby the government directly to protect their business interests, while smaller enterprises rely more on business associations. The effectiveness of the associations is limited and depends heavily on the support of large enterprises (Li and Zhan 2023).

It is important to remember that business associations, like other government sanctioned social organizations in China, are "**Janus-faced**." They are not only vehicles for the expression of business interests but are also "transmission belts" for the Party state to communicate its will to the entrepreneurs (Pearson 1994). Indeed, survey research finds that private businesspeople do not necessarily believe that their associations should be representing the members' views. Similar to the officials surveyed, they are roughly equally split between those arguing that business associations should speak for their members and those contending that the associations should ensure Party leadership over the private sector. Moreover, in regions with higher levels of economic development and greater degrees of privatization, entrepreneurs are more likely to think that business associations should represent the government's point of view (Dickson 2003). This means that contrary to conventional wisdom, economic development and privatization have apparently led to increased embeddedness of the capitalists in the state, not greater autonomy from the state.

Why has the development of an economically dynamic private sector not led to a more democratic political system in China? Many scholars attribute the resilience of the CCP regime to its extraordinary adaptiveness to new circumstances (Nathan 2003; Shambaugh 2008). When the Party realized the utility of private enterprises, it did not hesitate to reinterpret socialism to permit them to develop. The Party state's governance of the private sector has been characterized by an evolution marked by "rule ambiguities," which have created opportunities for entrepreneurs (Atherton and Newman 2016). Government officials have repeatedly tolerated the rule-avoiding and rule-bending behavior of the private entrepreneurs in exchange for their economic contribution. Local state agents, in particular, often intentionally deviate from existing rules when they have convergent interests with local businesspeople, e.g. in promoting local industry, increasing local revenue, and attracting external investment. In such an environment, private businesses have been largely content enough not to seek more radical political change (Tsai 2007). In addition, the CCP's decision to admit private entrepreneurs as its members was an extraordinary step for a Leninist system. In doing so, it morphed from an exclusionary to an inclusionary system (Dickson 2003).

Others cite the fragmented nature of social groups – including the bourgeoisie – in explaining the lack of democratic movement in China (Wright 2010). While it is tempting to view the private sector as monolithic and to assume all private business owners will favor "democratic" advocacy mechanisms, neither describes the situation in China. Survey research shows that Chinese entrepreneurs have not formed a unified new class. They are highly diverse in their pre-reform experiences, employment background, social networks, and local political conditions. Their priorities also differ according to the sectors in which they operate, the scale of their businesses, and their political networks.

Consequently, they do not constitute a unified social class. They do not necessarily have the same attitude toward democratic politics, either. Many of them hold an elitist perspective, favoring their own participation in the political system but not that of others. A significant portion of entrepreneurs agree with the government's point of view on a range of political, economic, and social issues, so much so that they are among the Party's most important bases of support (Dickson 2007).

Earlier studies of the private sector show that despite some common economic interests, e.g. regarding fair competition, taxes, and access to credit, private businesses in China lack the unity for collective action (Dickson 2005; Tsai 2007). More often than not, they engage in divergent and subtle activities to cope with the institutional challenges they face. Their attitudes toward the government can be classified as being avoidant, grudgingly acceptant, loyally acceptant, and assertive. Besides the minority in the "assertive" category, most private entrepreneurs do not speak critically about the government or its policies. Instead they try to protect their interests through quiet interactions with officials and government agencies or by bending the rules in their operations (Pearson 1997; Tsai 2007).

More recent research sheds additional light on a particular group of private enterprises – "mafia-like business systems," which are large private conglomerate firms that have similar organizational features and practices as organized crime syndicates in a market economy. They have complex and obfuscating structures and plunder state and social resources. They collaborate with members of the political elite in pursuit of short-term gains, often engaging in extortion and shadowy manipulation of the financial system. Not all the large private enterprises are mafia-like, but this particular enterprise type occupies an important space in government–business relations. Unlike other private enterprises, their relationship with the Party state is not only of mutual cooptation, but "mutual endangerment," where each side holds the other hostage with incriminating information, leading to major scandals (Rithmire and Chen 2021). Since the mid-2010s, a number of high-profile tycoons have disappeared, been jailed, or become fugitives overseas, while their political patrons have suffered embarrassing downfalls. This type of private entrepreneur clearly has little interest in promoting a democratic political system.

Conclusion

Although the private sector is a relatively new component of the Chinese economy, it has been the most dynamic force driving China's economic growth in the reform era. Its rise would not have been possible without the permission of the Party state. However, it is undeniable that the Chinese government has persistently favored the SOEs and discriminated against private businesses. The latter face high barriers of entry into strategic and profitable industries and are restricted in their access to formal financing. They are also vulnerable to the predatory behavior of government agencies and officials. Despite these challenges, private entrepreneurs have worked closely with the Party state. Refraining from political advocacy and relying on informal institutions, ranging from collaboration with local officials to mutual endangerment with the political elite, they have managed to survive under the CCP regime and even become a major pillar of the national economy.

Thus far, the state has grudgingly accommodated the private sector and the private sector has supported the CCP for instrumental reasons. The two have formed a symbiotic relationship that has given each side what it seeks. Private enterprises have contributed significantly to Chinese economic development, boosting the Party state's legitimacy and helping enrich the political elite along the way. The government's tolerance of institution-bending strategies of the private entrepreneurs has given the latter opportunities to grow their businesses despite considerable risks and uncertainties. This has resulted in a rather strange situation: while the Chinese government proclaims the socialist nature of the Chinese economy, the private sector has come to account for two-thirds of the country's GDP; while the private entrepreneurs practice the logic of capitalism and purse profits, one-third of them are members of the Communist Party.

How sustainable is this formula of mutual accommodation in the long term? Individual entrepreneurs can create and utilize political capital to protect and promote their own interests. But on a macro level, this strategy does not help build a reliable system of the rule of law. The particularistic transactions between businesses and government officials encourage bribery and promote corruption among bureaucrats (Kanamori and Zhao 2004). In some areas, the quid-pro-quo is so blatant that election of members of local people's congress has become a commercial matter; private entrepreneurs pay to secure political positions (Zhang 2017). From the Party state's standpoint, reaching out to private capitalists, the very elements in society it previously persecuted, has led to their successful cooptation in the short run. But, in the future, this can undermine the organizational competence of the Leninist system and ultimately result in its collapse (Dickson 2003). The recent surge of mafia-like businesses indicates that the seemingly cozy relationships between the Party state and big private companies can be quite precarious and are potentially quick to turn acrimonious. They can lead to political scandals, financial instability, capital flight, and defection, thus undermining the CCP regime (Ruthmire and Chen 2021).

Questions for Discussion

1. Why has the Chinese government been more favorably inclined toward foreign capital than domestic private capital?

2. How have private enterprises contributed to China's economic success in the reform era?

3. Is the Chinese bourgeoisie a major force for political democratization?

6

China's New Proletariat

Young women nimbly assembling electronic products by fast-moving conveyer belts and young men welding metal frames atop rising skyscrapers are familiar sights in contemporary Chinese cities. These images vividly illustrate the tremendous contribution labor has made to China's economic success in the post-Mao era. The hardworking and disciplined Chinese workers have not only modernized China's own economy, but they have made their country the world's factory, supplying large portions of manufactured goods – e.g. garments, footwear, electric cars and mobile phones – consumed around the globe.

From the late 1970s to the mid-2010s, China enjoyed a labor advantage rarely seen in human history. To some degree, it was a matter of demographic luck; a rapid increase of working-age population in this period led to a declining **dependence ratio** – the ratio of the very old and the very young to the working-age population. But a far more important factor was policy change. Economic liberalization in the reform era, particularly the emergence of a labor market, freed the labor force previously controlled by economic planning and made it much more productive than ever before. However, the labor force that has made China an economic powerhouse has not uniformly benefited from the economic reform. China's transition from a traditional socialist economy toward a marketized one has been a mixed blessing for rural and urban laborers. For many competitive individuals, it has opened opportunities to improve their living standards, but for the less fortunate ones it has worsened their insecurity.

This chapter begins with a brief examination of the emergence and evolution of the labor market. It then discusses the labor conditions of migrant workers and former state-owned enterprise (SOE) workers, two groups of people profoundly affected by the economic reform. We will see that many members of the working class, whom the Chinese Communist Party (CCP) used to call the "masters of the country," have become the new proletarians. To explain this ironic phenomenon, the next section explores the relationship among labor, capital, and the state. The chapter will conclude with a short discussion of the challenges for improving China's labor condition in the coming years.

Labor Market Development

To provide a context for understanding the emergence of the labor market and its significance for China's economic growth in the reform era, it is helpful to recall briefly how labor was managed in the Maoist period. From the mid-1950s to the late 1970s, the Chinese state controlled all factors of production – land, labor, and capital. Under a system of central planning, labor was not a commodity traded in the marketplace, but a resource directed by state command. There were no market signals for the supply and demand of labor, and the pricing of labor (wages) was set by fiat.

In rural China, peasants were organized into teams, brigades, and communes. They worked collectively to fulfill the production quotas set by the government. In some areas, peasants also built irrigation projects and engaged in small-scale industries. They earned work points according to the tasks they accomplished and the days they worked. At the end of the year, when the total income of the collective was calculated, individuals would get their share based on the work points they had earned. The difference in their income – mostly grains and a little cash – was insignificant. Such a system provided no material incentives for individuals to work harder and produce more output than anyone else. Moreover, peasants were completely bound to their collectives, with no freedom to leave or to engage in alternative economic activities.

Urban workers were predominantly employed by SOEs, while a small minority worked in collectively owned enterprises (COEs). Like other state-run entities, such as government bureaucracies and service organizations (e.g. schools and hospitals), enterprises did not have the authority to hire or fire employees, nor did employees have the choice as to whether or where to work. The wages for factory workers and technicians followed an eight-level scale (Schran 1974). Administrative and managerial staff in government bureaucracies and service organizations were remunerated according to a hierarchy of ranks, which was modified over the years but remained largely disconnected from individual productivity (Chew 1990). The differentiation in income for all types of employees was narrow, more a reflection of individuals' status in the system than their labor output. Unlike their rural counterparts, urban employees enjoyed a range of social welfare, including pension, healthcare, childcare, and housing provided by their work units (*danwei*).

Moreover, during the era of planned economy, the government used the household registration – *hukou* – system to keep the rural and the urban populations separated and frozen in place. There was almost no labor mobility between the countryside and the cities after the Great Leap Forward in 1958. An exception was the so-called "sent-down youth movement," which sent approximately seventeen million young urbanites to rural China from 1968 to 1980. This was not a voluntary movement by the participants, but a political campaign launched by Mao, who sought to bridge the rural–urban divide and to have privileged urban youth "re-educated" by the peasants (Honig and Zhao 2019). There was also very little mobility within the rural and the urban areas. Most people worked in one place throughout their careers.

Although the planned economy had some success in industrializing China by concentrating national resources on the development of heavy industries, the strict control of the workforce and the lack of material incentives for workers severely stifled labor productivity. After the late 1970s, economic reform gradually reduced the role of government planning in allocating the factors of production, including labor. Over time, a labor market emerged and developed in China. As a result, large numbers of people have been free to move to different locations in search of desirable jobs. Moreover, wages are no longer determined by administrative fiat, but are shaped by such things as the demand and supply of labor, workers' skills and education, and their productivity. It is worth noting, however, that the *hukou* system still exists to this day. Although it has become less rigid and more porous, it continues to influence people's employment opportunities and living conditions.

Labor market reform began first in rural China. As household farming replaced collective agriculture in the late 1970s and early 1980s, peasants' income became closely linked to their productivity, motivating farmers to maximize their output. Economists calculate that the adoption of the household responsibility system raised agricultural output and in doing so contributed 0.43 percentage points to the annual GDP growth between 1978 and 2004 (Brandt et al. 2008, p. 686). Moreover, as households became more efficient in farming, fewer hands were needed to work in the fields. Some members took up new activities in commerce or industry. In 1979, 91 percent of rural labor was in agriculture. In 2003, it had dropped down to 61 percent. From 1978 to 2005, the non-agricultural workforce in rural China grew from 28 million to 188 million, including 145 million employed in township and village enterprises (TVEs) (Cai et al. 2008, p. 190). The employees holding off-farm jobs created most of the increase in rural incomes in the late 1980s and 1990s (Rozelle, 1996).

While some peasants took up non-agricultural work in the rural areas, others went farther, into the cities, to find better-paying jobs. Nationwide, agriculture's share of total employment dropped by more than half between 1978 and 2004, from 69 to 32 percent (Brandt et al. 2008, p. 683). The reallocation of rural labor from agriculture to industrial and commercial activities provided 1.02 percentage points in annual GDP growth during the same period, a much bigger contribution than the 0.43 percent due to improved agricultural productivity cited above. The combination of the two made up 1.45 percentage points of the GDP or 20.83 percent of 8.16 percent total GDP growth (Brandt et al. 2008, p. 686).

Following the successful rural reform, the CCP turned to economic restructuring in urban China, including changing the management of labor. Without abolishing the old socialist system of lifetime employment, the government began to allow enterprises to hire some workers by contract. In 1986 the State Council issued "Temporary Regulations on the Use of Labor Contracts in State-Run Enterprises," formalizing the nascent labor market taking shape in Chinese industries. In 1985 contract workers accounted for four percent of the total enterprise employees. The proportion grew to thirteen percent in 1990 and 39 percent in 1995. By 1997 a hundred million workers had signed labor contracts with their employers (Cai et al. 2008, p. 172). The use of labor contracts increased the freedom for employers to recruit workers and brought competition among potential employees. It is worth noting that managers had greater freedom to hire than to fire workers because the government was eager to minimize unemployment for the sake of social stability. In time, urban China developed a diversified labor-allocation system, which included not only job assignments by the government, but also spontaneous hiring by enterprises, and self-employment under the general guidance of the state plan (Cai et al. 2008, p. 172).

Just as household farming increased agricultural productivity and shifted rural labor from agriculture to non-agricultural activities, enterprise reform led to a major relocation of workers from SOEs to other more productive types of enterprises. From 1978 to 2004 the state sector's share of non-agricultural employment decreased drastically from 52 percent to thirteen percent (Brandt et al. 2008, p. 683). The transfer of labor from the state to the nonstate sector contributed 1.77 percentage points of the annual GDP growth in that period, which was even more significant than the contribution of a transfer of labor from agricultural to non-agricultural activities noted above (Brandt et al. 2008, p. 687).

Besides labor allocation, wages also came under greater market influence. In the mid-1980s, enterprises replaced their fixed wage system set by the government with a new floating system. Under the new system, an SOE's total wage bill – along with its profit remittances to the government – was linked to its economic performance in the previous three years. Factories that performed well were allowed to distribute small amounts of bonuses to the workers as rewards. Over time, workers' wages and benefits became more closely associated with the profitability of their enterprises. This had consequences for employers and the workers. Employers increasingly had to compete for the best employees available. The competition was intensified by the rise of non-state enterprises, which did not have to follow wage regulations and could offer better pay to their recruits. For employees, earnings were increasingly tied to productivity rather than seniority. As productivity is often connected with education, the return to education rose dramatically, while the return to experience fell (Meng 2012). After the mid-1990s, the return to schooling grew quickly in China and eventually reached levels comparable to other developing countries (Cai et al. 2008).

The formation of a nationwide labor market in China has been made possible by the relaxation of the rural–urban divide in the reform era. As the demand for labor in urban areas grows, especially in the labor-intensive export sectors, the Chinese government has modified the *hukou* system to allow the surplus rural labor to fill the job vacancies in the cities. From 1990 to 2009, the number of rural migrant workers in Chinese cities skyrocketed from 25 million to 145 million. By 2022 the number approached 300 million.

However, the *hukou* system has not disappeared; it continues to segment the labor market. Rural migrants have been routinely exploited and discriminated against in urban China. Some local governments exclude migrants from specific occupations in order to reserve the better-paying and less dangerous jobs for those with urban *hukou* status. Some impose high fees, for example for identification and certification documents, on migrants entering the city. Migrant workers who manage to find jobs are often poorly paid. Studies of workers' wages from the mid-1990s to the mid-2000s show that migrants earned much less than local workers in the same occupations. In the mid-1990s, for example, the hourly wage of rural migrants in Shanghai was only fifty percent that of local employees. According to these studies, much of this difference cannot be explained by observable differences in the personal characteristics of the two groups (Knight and Song 1999; Meng and Zhang 2001). For years, wage increases for migrant workers have been as little as half the rate for other workers (Huang and Tao 2010). Migrants are also deprived of the same levels of social welfare benefits such as pension, healthcare, unemployment insurance, and various social services as those available to urban residents. This means that employers save considerable non-wage costs when they employ migrant workers.

China's labor-driven economic development has not only been made possible by its population dividend and the development of a labor market. It has also been facilitated by the international environment. When Chinese reform began in the late 1970s, Asia's newly industrialized economies, especially Hong Kong and Taiwan, happened to have reached a critical point. Having successfully grown their economies by exporting labor-intensive products, they were losing international competitiveness because of rising labor costs. The opening of China, with its much cheaper labor, provided manufacturers from those economies a second chance. Beijing's designation of four special economic zones (SEZs) in Guangdong and Fujian, two provinces next to Hong Kong and Taiwan respectively, made it convenient for them to relocate their labor-intensive manufacturing. Attracted by the geographic proximity as well as the family and cultural ties with those two coastal Chinese regions, Hong Kong and Taiwan entrepreneurs rushed to the SEZs. Combining their technical know-how and international business connections with the low labor cost in China, they quickly achieved new business success. In doing so, they also provided China an opportunity to use its labor pool to launch its economic takeoff. In the following years, multinational corporations from beyond Hong Kong and Taiwan also shifted large portions of their production to China, selling their products not only to the Chinese market but also to the rest of the world. The "made-in-China" label soon became ubiquitous in every corner of the globe.

While labor market reform has boosted Chinese economic growth considerably, it has also resulted in a troubling new phenomenon that the CCP regime used to describe as a problem only under capitalism – unemployment. Industrial economic restructuring exposed many SOEs to unprecedented competition from TVEs, foreign-invested enterprises, and private businesses. Large numbers of them suffered chronic financial losses. By the late 1990s, the government decided to abandon the smaller ones to concentrate on supporting the largest SOEs in strategic industries. Tens of millions of workers lost their jobs, which they had counted on for life as **"iron rice bowls"** (see Box 6.1).

Box 6.1 Losing the "Iron Rice Bowl"

In the spring of 2023, a TV series entitled "The Long Season" became a blockbuster in China. On the surface, this is a suspense drama, but its appeal lies in its powerful portrayal of the impact of economic reform in the 1990s on SOE workers and their families. The main protagonists are former employees of a state-owned steel factory in northeastern China. Large SOEs like their factory used to employ tens of thousands of workers and provide them and their families with everything, down to soda in the summer and warmer jackets in the winter. There was no competition on the job, and every worker was guaranteed employment for life. But pressure was building up as the steel factory lost ground because of its inefficiency and went bankrupt in 1998. The story focuses on several middle-aged workers after they were laid off. One of them not only became poor, but also lost his son and sick wife; he tried to commit suicide. Another opened an illegal beauty clinic and was beaten up after a botched procedure. And a third became an escort in a bar. The former security chief of the steel factory relied on scalping car licenses to make a living. As the show vividly reveals, with the SOE reform intensifying in the late 1990s, workers and their families paid a heavy price. Dignity, marriages, and lives were lost.

At first, their employers put them on furlough (*xiagang*) without officially dismissing them from the SOE. The government established a one-time special program to help them find reemployment and provided up to three years of financial aid, including subsidies, pension and healthcare benefits. But many of the laid-off workers – especially the older ones – failed to find new jobs and later officially entered the ranks of the unemployed. In the following years,

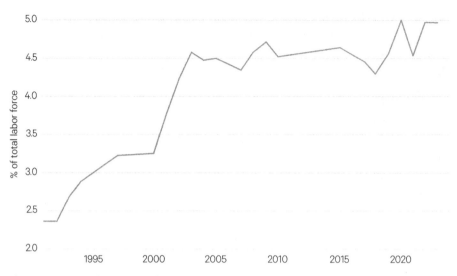

Figure 6.1 Unemployment in China 1991–2023
Source: International Labor Organization.

the number of unemployed workers rose steadily in China. Figure 6.1 shows the official statistics reported by the Chinese government and international organizations. The actual situation was much worse.

The importance of labor in China's economic success was especially salient in the first twenty-five years of the reform era. This was a time when the composition of trade shifted significantly toward China's comparative advantage – abundant supply of labor relative to its endowment of land and capital. According to Chinese customs statistics, this period saw a decline in the country's net exports of land-intensive bulk commodities, such as grains, oilseeds, and sugar crops, and a rise in exports of higher-valued, more labor-intensive products, such as horticultural and animal goods (including aquatic products) (Anderson et al. 2004).

In time, Chinese exports have evolved from simple low-end products to more sophisticated higher-end products. However, labor has remained a key to China's economic growth. The electronics industry offers a good illustration. Since 2005, China has been the world's largest exporter of electronics, such as portable computers, mobile phones, LCD screens, and various computer and phone accessories. However, its competitiveness in this industry has not been in the making of high value-added parts and components, most of which it imports from suppliers in Japan, Korea, Taiwan, and Germany. Instead, China's input has been primarily the labor required to assemble the components, which constitutes only a small share of the value of the final products. In the year 2003, China exported $142 billion in electronic and information technology products, which contained $127 billion of parts and components. In other words, China's net exports of electronic and information industry products only amounted to $15 billion (Branstetter and Lardy 2008, p. 662). Around 2010, a study by the Personal Computing Industry Centre indicated that each iPad sold in America cost $275, but the value of the actual work performed in China was only $10 (*Economist* 2012).

Until the early twenty-first century, Chinese policymakers consciously sought to maintain China's comparative advantage in labor. Many of China's R&D resources were used to develop ways of adapting and utilizing foreign technologies to a more labor-intensive setting (Hu and Jefferson 2008). But in recent years the rising labor cost and the aging of the Chinese population have steadily reduced the affordable labor pool, challenging the country to seek new comparative advantages to keep its economy competitive.

Labor Conditions

The emergence of a labor market has allowed a massive transfer of labor force from farming to non-agricultural sectors and from SOEs to non-state enterprises. Economic liberalization has also greatly improved labor productivity. In a sharp departure from the focus on capital-intensive industries during the Maoist, China has ripped great benefits from its abundant supply of labor. Herein lies a crucial factor in China's rapid growth and soaring competitiveness in the world economy (Lin 2011). However, all is not well on the labor front. Distortions remain in the labor market, preventing it from reaching its full potential in maximizing economic efficiency. For example, administrative barriers, especially the *hukou* system, continue to segregate the labor market and hinder labor mobility. Moreover, there are serious social and ethical problems in China's management of its labor force. While Chinese workers have created an economic miracle for the country, many of them have been kept in relative poverty, facing harsh conditions and unfair treatment.

Two groups of workers have borne the brunt of the assault on labor in the reform era – the migrant workers from rural China and former SOE workers, who have lost their jobs during the state sector restructuring. They are the new Chinese proletariat. But before we proceed to examine their experience, it is useful to clarify which migrant workers we include in this discussion.

Migrant workers make up a large portion of the labor force that has modernized China. For the first two decades of the reform era, researchers estimate, there were more than ten million people joining the urban population every year (Zhang and Song 2003). The vast majority of the migrants went from inland provinces in central and western China to coastal cities in eastern China. Sichuan, Henan, Anhui, Hunan, and Jiangxi were the largest sources of migrant workers, while Guangdong, Shanghai, Zhejiang, Fujian, and Beijing were the most popular destinations. In the early 2010s, migrant workers numbered 250 million in total, accounting for 72 percent of China's urban workforce of 347 million (Lee 2016). In 2022, they were nearly 300 million strong.

But migrant workers are not a monolithic group. Most peasants who work in Chinese cities are treated by their employers and local governments as temporary workers, even after they have spent many years working in the cities. In contrast to these **temporary migrants** are "**permanent migrants**" who are granted local *hukou* and thus become full-fledged local citizens. They tend to be individuals with high levels of education and specialized skills, whose migration is sponsored by the state. Compared with the temporary migrants, they have far superior human capital attributes and mobility resources. Indeed, comparative research on these two types of migrants and native urbanites shows that permanent migrants are the most privileged of the three groups, followed by the natives, with temporary migrants at the bottom of the hierarchy (Fan 2002).

In this chapter we focus on the temporary migrants. They do the low-paying, back-breaking, and/or dangerous jobs unwanted by the urbanites. Jobs with the highest concentration of migrant workers are manufacturing, construction, food service, retail, delivery, and sanitation. Before the late 1990s, while urban Chinese workers held stable jobs in SOEs, temporary migrant workers filled the more volatile contractual jobs or worked in the informal economy. In later years, these rural migrants were joined by some former SOE workers, who had lost their jobs in the state sector. However, temporary migrants have remained the main workforce in the most unprotected and difficult occupations. Now as then, migrant workers toil for long hours, often in unsafe environments with dust, toxic substances, noise, and poor ventilation.

Migrant workers dream of upward mobility in the city. However, because of their low level of education, they have found it almost impossible to enter higher-skilled and higher-paid jobs. According to the 2000 census, local residents were much more likely to be in white-collar jobs (38.8 percent) than migrants (12.5 percent). This gap was especially salient in high-skill sectors, such as finance and education (Cai et al. 2008, p. 193). Another study around that time finds that rural migrants concentrated heavily in self-employment (57 percent) and the private wage-earning sector (36 percent) while urban residents were overwhelmingly employed in the public sector (71 percent). The latter group had more education (by almost four years) and earned higher incomes (Démurger et al. 2009). Furthermore, the children of migrant workers have not been able to move up the socio-economic ladder. Although they arrived in the cities at a young age, or were born in the cities, they are held back by their poor education experience. Without urban *hukou* status and well-educated parents, they are either stuck at the bottom of public schools or relegated to the dilapidated migrant schools that charge higher tuition and offer sub-standard education. The educational institutions in urban China reproduce and reinforce the second-class citizenship of migrants (Xiong 2015; Friedman 2022).

As noted in the previous section, in China's segregated labor market, migrants are paid much lower wages than the locals. To make things worse, migrant workers are routinely subject to delayed wage payment. Many employers use this as a tactic to prevent the migrant workers from leaving freely. Moreover, they often fail to pay the premiums required for the social insurance programs for the migrant workers. A 2003 study on rural migrants in Shanghai shows that only fourteen percent of the 4,714 migrants surveyed had health insurance and only ten percent had pension plans. In contrast, 79 percent and 91 percent of local employees had health insurance and pension plans (Feng, Zuo, and Ruan 2002). Another survey in 2012 finds that among formal sector workers 95 percent had health insurance and ninety percent were enrolled in pension programs, but among informal sector workers (mostly migrant workers) the figures were just 58 percent and 47 percent respectively (Jiang et al. 2018, p. 346). There has been progress in the social protection of migrant workers, but the gap with the urban residents is still glaring.

The pandemic of Covid-19 upended life for the entire population. However, it had a particularly devastating effect on migrant workers. Researchers estimate that at least thirty to fifty million migrants lost their jobs in late March 2020, far more than the urban residents. An online survey indicates that more than ninety percent of workers with rural *hukou* could not find work as of late February, more than double the 42 percent of those with urban *hukou*. In addition, despite their dire needs, migrant workers did not have the same safety net as the urban workers. In more ways than one, the pandemic exacerbated the inequalities between groups divided by their *hukou* status (Che et al. 2020).

Life beyond work is also harsh for many migrant workers. They are the builders of the cities but struggle to find affordable and safe housing for themselves. About two-thirds of the migrants shelter in the private rental sector in the receiving cities. Without urban *hukou*, they cannot access government housing assistance reserved for local *hukou* holders, e.g. Economic Housing, Cheap Rented Housing, Public Rented Housing, Limited Priced Housing, Common Rights Housing, and Housing Purchase Subsidies. Meanwhile, commercial apartments on the market are priced well beyond the reach of most migrants. The rent-affordability stress (rent-to-income ratio) exacerbates the inequality between migrants and locals (Liu et al. 2020).

Migrants tend to concentrate in poorly built structures in the peri-urban areas. These structures are often unsafe, unsightly, and in violation of regulations. Local governments used to tolerate the existence of such "grey space," which was technically illegal, because they depended on the migrant workers for infrastructure development, construction, and services needed by the local economy. However, around the mid-2010s, the national government adopted a National New-Type Urbanization Plan (2014–2020), which encouraged the expansion of small cities but restricted the growth of large cities. Mega-cities, such as Beijing, Shanghai, and Tianjin, imposed stricter control over the "grey space," including migrant villages. In the name of safety, high-quality economic growth, and national pride, they began to expel dwellers and small business operators in that space. A dramatic escalation of this process happened in Beijing in late 2017. In November, a fire broke out in Xinjian Village, an area inhibited mostly by migrants, killing nineteen people. In the following days and weeks, city officials implemented a mass eviction program targeting migrants, whom they referred to as the "low-end population" (*diduan renkou*). They demolished many structures housing migrant workers and their families and forced many of their small businesses to close. The misery of the young and the old, who suddenly lost their shelter in the winter, generated widespread anger and sympathy but did not change the government's policy (Morris 2022).

As second-class citizens in the cities, migrants from the rural areas are not only subject to government policy discrimination, but also suffer from stigmatization and humiliation by urban residents. There is a common perception among the urbanites that migrants are ignorant, uncivilized, and crime prone (Solinger 1999; L. Zhang 2002; Ngai 2005). Besides their cultural biases, urban Chinese, especially laid-off SOE workers, view migrants as a threat to them in the job market. The multitude of everyday stress casts a shadow on the migrants, leading to widespread mental health problems (Wong et al. 2007; Zhan 2011; Zhou and Cheung 2017).

One can get a glimpse of the condition of migrant laborers in contemporary China through the widely reported experience of workers in Foxconn factories. Founded in Taiwan in 1974, Foxconn Technology Group (formerly known as Hon Hai Precision Industry) began to invest in mainland China in 1988 to take advantage of the cheap labor there. Operating factories in China with 20,000 to 400,000 workers each, Foxconn has become the world's largest contract manufacturer of electronics, making half of the world's electronics for companies such as Dell, Compact, Apple, Huawei, and Xiaomi. Foxconn workers typically work for eighty hours each week, more than doubling the limit of 36 hours set by the Chinese Labor Law. On the factory floor, workers execute their assigned tasks with high speed and high precision all day. Managers use a stopwatch to measure workers' capacity and maximize their workload. According to a report in 2016, in Foxconn's factory in Zhengzhou city in central China, about 350,000 workers assemble, test, and package iPhones – up to 350 a minute (Barboza 2016). On the shift, the workers perform monotonous and repetitive motions under intense psychological and physical stress. Off the shift, they are all housed in factory-provided dormitories, where they are isolated from friends and social networks, and constantly subject to the surveillance of their supervisors (Ngai and Chan 2012). These conditions led to serious damage to the physical and mental health of the employees (see Box 6.2).

Box 6.2 Deaths at Foxconn

In 2010 the international community was shocked by media reports of eighteen attempted suicides by young migrant workers at Foxconn facilities in China. The first death came in January. A nineteen-year-old worker apparently jumped from a high floor of the factory's dormitory. The police ruled it to be suicide. The worker's family, including his sister, who also worked at Foxconn, said he hated the job – an eleven-hour overnight shift, seven nights a week – which involved forging plastic and metal into electronics parts amid fumes and dust. His pay stub showed that he had worked 286 hours in the month before he died, including 112 hours of overtime. For all his labor, including the overtime pay, he earned the equivalent of $1 an hour. More deaths followed under similar scenarios (Barboza 2010). A worker's blog then said it all – "Perhaps for the Foxconn employees and employees like us, the use of death is to testify that we were ever alive at all, and that while we lived, we had only despair" (cited in Chan et al. 2020, p. 9).

In response to the strong public condemnation, Foxconn took some superficial measures, including setting up nets around the dormitories to prevent disgruntled workers from jumping to their death, establishing a company phone helpline, and raising workers' pay (while raising their work quota even more). The number of suicides fell, and media attention moved elsewhere, but the stress and misery for Foxconn's workers and the millions of other migrant workers in similar facilities has not changed fundamentally since then.

The bleak condition of temporary migrant workers is in large part related to their vulnerable existence in Chinese cities without local *hukou*. However, *hukou* alone is not sufficient to guarantee decent living. In the late 1990s, more than thirty million SOE employees, who were officially registered urban residents, were laid off or forced to retire early. Like rural migrants, they were not highly educated and had trouble finding new jobs, many of which require specialized skills. Moreover, mostly middle-aged and having spent years in inefficient state-run *danwei*, these former SOE workers were less prepared than young rural migrants for the demanding jobs in the private sector. Those who could not compete simply dropped out of the labor market altogether.

Compared with its attitude toward rural migrants, the CCP has shown greater concern over the hardship for the workers laid off by the SOEs. Following the labor retrenchment in the state sector in 1990s, there was widespread labor unrest across different regions in China (Cai 2002; Hurst 2004). The Chinese government developed various programs to assist their transition out of the SOEs. Local authorities tried to keep certain categories of jobs away from rural migrants. Many cities rolled out so-called "Re-employment Projects," for the newly unemployed workers. But these efforts were undermined by a scarcity of funds, corruption among local cadres and managers, who siphoned off funds and opportunities from the intended recipients, and a serious undersupply of employment opportunities in the economy. The government set out to create some safety nets for the former SOE workers, including basic livelihood allowance, unemployment insurance, and a minimum cost of living guarantee, which will be discussed in more detail in Chapter 7. However, these programs failed to achieve their declared goals, leaving many laid-off workers in a state of misery and helplessness (Solinger 2002).

Some researchers have used the concept of "precarization" to capture the labor conditions for migrant workers and laid-off SOE workers. They argue that the **precariat** now stands beneath the "proletariat" in Chinese cities. Compared with the proletariat, who are exploited by capital in the labor market, the precariat is even worse off, as they try to eke out an unstable living in unregulated sectors, oscillating between exploitation and exclusion (Lee 2016; Hillenbrand 2023). Others have used the term "marginalization" to describe the living experience of migrant workers (Wong et al. 2007).

The precarization and marginalization of migrant workers and laid-off SOE workers is closely related to their involvement in the informal labor market (Cai et al. 2008; Kuruvilla et al. 2017). Informality in this context consists of two dimensions – working without a written labor contract and employment without social insurance, such as pensions, health insurance, and unemployment benefits (Lee 2016). In fact, working without a contract, especially a long-term contract, often leads to poor social insurance coverage. Research shows that migrant workers are much more likely to gain social insurance when they move from having a short-term contract or no contract to having a long-term contract, while losing a long-term contract reduces the likelihood of having social insurance (Gao et al. 2012).

The size of the precariate is considerable. Data collected through nationally representative surveys of workers from 2014 to 2018 show that among the employed workers, 23.3 percent are in the formal sector and 76.7 percent are in the informal sector (Lin et al. 2023). This new group of vulnerable workers does not only include temporary migrants, but also SOE employees. Even in the most classical state-owned industries, such as oil and automobile, SOEs have been restructured into a smaller "core" of permanent employees and a larger "non-core" of informal workers (Lin 2017; Zhang 2017). Nevertheless, migrant workers have made up the majority of the informal sector workforce. According to a 2014 survey by China's National Bureau of Statistics, 62 percent of the country's 274 million migrant workers lacked labor contracts. This was much higher than the 26.3 percent of local resident workers who worked without formal contracts (Lee 2016). Survey data from 2014 to 2018 suggest that most employees in the low-tier informal sector are rural *hukou* holders, including 95 percent of the self-employed and 79 percent of the wage-employed. They also indicate that less than a quarter of the workers in the formal sector are migrants from rural China (Lin et al. 2023).

The fast-growing Internet-based gig economy in urban China has further increased the prominence of precarious employment in the labor market. For example, the drivers for ride-hailing services (e.g. *Didi Chuxing*, similar to Uber) and the delivery people for online shopping platforms (e.g. Alibaba, similar to Amazon), find themselves working under informal contracts, irregular working hours, low wages, delayed payment, and high risks. Many of these gig workers are migrants, whose rural *hukou* status and low education level limit their employment opportunities in the formal sector. They provide a willing workforce that enables the platform economy to thrive. At the same time, they are stuck in a hyper-exploitative and precarious existence, trading their physical and mental health for the (false) promise of a better future for themselves and their children (Zhou 2022).

In sum, life has not been easy for many workers in China, especially for migrant workers from the rural areas and former SOE employees who lost their jobs during the restructuring of the state sector. With the majority working in informal employment, they have formed a new class of precariate in Chinese cities. The poor working and living conditions for these workers have been public knowledge for years and have generated a great deal of public sympathy. Yet the situation has not improved. Why? To answer this question, we need to understand the relationship between labor, capital, and the state.

Labor, Capital, and the State

During the Maoist era, China's elite SOE workers were "masters of the nation" and enjoyed the security of life-time employment and state-provided welfare. Much has changed since the heydays of the "proletariat dictatorship." Labor market liberalization has made supply and demand key to the allocation of labor. In China's large labor pool, this has given tremendous power to employers over employees in all types of enterprises – state, collective, private, and foreign. In its pursuit of rapid economic growth, the CCP has aligned itself with capital, often sacrificing the interests of the working class to serve its own agenda and the needs of business owners.

In Chapter 4 we examined the process of SOE reform. Through the 1980s, the change was gradual, making it a process "without losers." In the late 1990s, intensified state sector restructuring resulted in massive layoffs of SOE workers. In Chapter 5 we discussed the changing relationship between the CCP and the private enterprises. Although the party state remains suspicious of the new capitalists, it has formed a mutually accommodating relationship with the latter, whose innovation and productiveness have been crucial to the country's economic success.

The CCP's embrace of foreign capital has had a major impact on China's labor market. As noted in the last chapter, contemporary Chinese policymakers opened the country to foreign direct investment (FDI) before they allowed the development of a healthy domestic private sector. The arrival of foreign investors brought competitive pressure to Chinese regions, enterprises, and workers. In the SEZs, where foreign invested enterprises (FIEs) were first allowed to operate, they were given considerable flexibility and autonomy in hiring and firing workers as they saw fit. This had a strong impact on Chinese enterprises in general. To compete against FIEs, other types of enterprises, including SOEs, began to emulate the latter's practices, chipping away the traditional job security for the workers. The presence of FDI provided the "laboratories for change," which led to a labor market empowering the employers and weakening the working class (Gallagher 2007).

Rhetorically, the Party has consistently emphasized the importance of protecting workers' rights and ensuring their well-being. Indeed, the Chinese state has made laws and regulations along these lines. In 1994 the National People's Congress passed the Labor Law. On the one hand, it permitted no-fault dismissal of workers, to facilitate the process of economic restructuring, especially SOE restructuring that was getting underway in a serious manner. On the other hand, it established a unified legal framework across all types of enterprises for labor relations and for safeguarding workers' rights. On paper, Chinese Labor Law offers strong protection of the workers. It stipulates a host of labor rights, including equal rights to obtain employment, the right to rest days and holidays, the right to a safe workplace environment, the right to receive social insurance and welfare, the right to bring labor disputes for resolution, the right to a minimum wage, and the right to "equal pay for equal work." It sets a maximum of eight-hour work days and forty-hour work weeks. It specifies overtime wages and limits the amount of overtime per day and per month (Cai et al. 2008).

Since the 1990s, the Labor Law has been augmented by more specific laws regarding labor contracts, labor dispute mediation and arbitration, employment promotion, and anti-discrimination. In fact, the legal framework for labor protection in China espouses such a high standard that according to an OECD report in 2008, China ranked second on employment protection across ten major developing economies and it exceeded the OECD average substantially (Lee 2016, p. 320). More recently, the Chinese government has passed new laws to restrain the informalization in the labor market and to strengthen the social safety net for workers in precarious situations (Gallagher and Dong 2017).

However, the high standards set in the national laws are often poorly implemented on the ground. An important factor undermining labor policy consistency and effectiveness lies in the different priorities of the central and the local governments. Following the beginning of the reform, Beijing devolved power and responsibilities to local authorities and encouraged them to develop their economies. Since then, a top priority for the local cadres has been to boost local GDP growth, employment, and tax revenue. In contrast, the central government has more encompassing concerns, including maintaining social stability and its own political legitimacy. Although economic development serves these goals in the long run, the pursuit of efficiency and profits in the short run often comes with wage suppression and workforce reduction, leading to tension and protests. From time to time, the center may be eager to give in to workers' demands to avoid social upheavals, but local officials may be more concerned about pleasing investors and maintaining GDP growth, thus unwilling to accommodate labor. Moreover, the laws passed by the national legislature are often ambiguous, allowing flexibility for local enforcement (Gallagher and Dong 2017). Researchers find that the application of the labor laws varies across the country, depending on local circumstances (Lee 2016, p. 320). The same pattern exists in the implementation of workers' pension schemes, with many local governments failing to carry out the stipulations made by the central government (Frazier 2017).

Ultimately, the weakness of labor's rights in China is rooted in the lack of genuine representation of the working class in the political process. From its own revolutionary history, the CCP knows well that political mobilization of the masses can be a dangerous threat to the ruling elite. Since the beginning of the People's Republic, the government has used officially sanctioned mass organizations to "represent" social groups such as workers, business entrepreneurs, women, and youth, while strictly prohibiting the existence of alternative associations outside the Party state's control. The **All-China Federation of Trade Unions** (ACFTU) is the official mass organization for Chinese labor. Its dual identity includes being an instrument of the Party state and serving the interest of the workers. By its own description, it is "a bridge and link between the party and the workers" and its number one mission is following "the party's basic theory, basic line, basic program and labor movement policies, and focusing on the overall work of the Party and the country . . ." (ACFTU n.d.).

Throughout the 1980s and 1990s, the shrinkage of the state sector resulted in its membership decline. Furthermore, staffed by Party appointed officials, the ACFTU closely followed the government's new reformist policy, including the state strategy of attracting foreign investment and promoting labor market liberalization. It lost credibility in the eyes of the workers because it always sided with the management and the government during labor disputes (Taylor and Li, 2007). More recently, the ACFTU has grown again, largely as a result of the top-down directives by the CCP leadership. In 2022, the membership reached close to 300 million, almost quadrupling from 87 million in 1999. Meanwhile, the ACFTU has regained some trust of the workers by advocating for them within the Party-controlled framework. For example, ACFTU played a crucial role in getting the Labor Contract Law passed by the national legislature in 2008 and in having the law revised and strengthened in 2012 (Lee 2016; Chou 2018). It has also tried to improve the function of workplace union organizations and to develop new collective wage consultation tactics to enhance workers' welfare (Brown and Cao 2023).

Nevertheless, the ACFTU – like the other labor-focused bureaucracy, the Labor Ministry (and its successors, the Ministry of Labor and Social Security, and then the Ministry of Human Resources and Social Security) – is a relatively weak player in the Party state apparatus. Its bureaucratic ranking is much lower than the economic agencies, such as the National Development and Reform Commission (and its predecessors), the Ministry of Finance, the Ministry of Commerce (and its predecessors), and the People's Bank of China. The latter bureaucracies are powerful and preoccupied with China's GDP growth. They tend to favor market-friendly policies and are keen to maintain China's cheap labor-based export competitiveness for as long as possible. When push comes to shove, their policy preferences often carry the day, defeating alternatives that aim to improve the living standards of the working class (Remington 2018).

The CCP has always forbidden workers from organizing themselves outside the ACFTU system. Its vigilance against independent trade unions was intensified by several political crises in the late 1980s and early 1990s, including the collapse of the communist regimes in Eastern Europe and the Soviet Union, and the Tiananmen movement in China in 1989. In each of the crises, workers organized outside the traditional state-led system and mounted serious political challenges to the government (Chan 1993). Having learned those lessons, the CCP has adopted increasingly repressive strategies against mass organization among Chinese workers. In contemporary China's political environment, labor organizers actually counsel and train workers *not to* organize at all because doing so invites repression. Instead, they encourage workers to engage in small-scale activism to modestly improve their working and living circumstances (Fu 2018).

The lack of independent unions has not only deprived Chinese workers of representation in the national policymaking process, but it has also kept them powerless when it comes to negotiating for better treatment by their employers and the local governments (see Box 6.3). Without their own unions, the workers face insurmountable obstacles to collective action. Their petitions, protests, and even riots, are scattered and often uncoordinated (Chen 2003; Pringle 2011). The state sees these activities as a "fire-alarm" mechanism, which calls attention to egregious labor violations (Gallagher 2014). Sometimes these actions result in government sanctions against certain abusive practices by the employers. They may even lead to new legislation for more stringent labor protection. However, without the ability to organize and mobilize as a

Box 6.3 The Gains and Limitations of the Honda Strike

Honda, the Japanese auto maker, set up a wholly foreign-owned factory in Foshan, Guangdong Province, in 2007, one of its several investment projects in China. The Foshan factory specialized in making transmissions. It employed a relatively well-educated workforce made up of twenty percent formal employees and eighty percent student interns from technical schools. In 2010 a strike broke out in the factory, involving about 1,800 workers, who demanded a wage increase and democratic reform of the union. The latter demand came from the workers' view that the union did not represent them but instead always backed the management in labor disputes. During the strike, the management rejected the workers' demands. Rather than supporting the workers, the local government dispatched the riot police and local branches of the ACFTU sent their members to threaten and suppress the labor activists at Honda. In the end, because the production of transmissions was central to Honda's overall operations in China and because the skilled workers in this factory could not be easily replaced, the management agreed to the workers' demand for a wage increase. However, it refused to make meaningful changes to workers' representation. Furthermore, once the strike was over, the government tightened its control over media reporting on strikes and further restricted civil society actors who supported the Honda workers. (Chan and Hui 2012)

collective, the atomized individual workers are unable to gain much ground vis-à-vis the capital-state alliance (Xu 2013; Lee 2016).

To summarize, the plight of Chinese workers, especially migrant workers from rural China and laid-off SOE workers, is well-known. The government has adopted high labor standards in its legislation. However, its prioritization of economic growth for most of the reform era overlaps with the interests of capital in the pursuit of efficiency and profits, including foreign capital. Consequently, it has often been unwilling to defend the well-being of labor if it increases the cost of business operations or undermines the confidence of investors. Local governments often act as a partner of the employers who violate labor rights. The power imbalance among labor, capital and the state is so lopsided that short of a fundamental political change in China the precarious existence of Chinese workers is unlikely to improve.

Conclusion

China's economic miracle has benefited significantly from its abundant supply of labor. However, this advantage has plateaued with its working-age population already reaching its peak in 2014. In recent years, Chinese population growth has slowed dramatically, shrinking by 0.2% for the first time in 2023 and again, by 0.3%, in 2024 (National Statistics Bureau of China 2024). Going forward, the greater demand than supply of labor will likely accelerate wage growth, especially at the lower end of the market, cutting into profit margins. There could be a silver lining in this development. While labor shortages and wage increases have slowed down the economic growth in China, they may strengthen the bargaining position of the workers and better their working and living conditions.

Another potential source of labor condition improvement lies in the generational transition of migrant workers. As the original migrant workers retire from their jobs, a new generation has taken their place in the Chinese labor market. These younger migrants tend to be better educated than their parents and more familiar with modern technology, including information technology. They are more class- and rights-conscious than the older generation, and more capable of mobilizing for collective action (Zhang 2015). One sign of their political efficacy is the rise of organized strikes by migrant workers in FIEs and other forms of labor activism (Chan and Hui 2012; Gallagher 2014; Thomson 2023).

But not everyone buys this empowerment thesis. Some scholars argue that optimism based on demographics and generational change neglects China's institutional and political–economic conditions. The latter have remained largely unimproved and have even deteriorated. For instance, the predatory urbanization process has led more and more rural families to lose their land. Land dispossession, in turn, has deprived migrant workers of their most important means of social reproduction and long-term security (child-rearing and schooling, healthcare, marriage, permanent housing, subsistence during unemployment, and retirement). This has exacerbated the vulnerability of the migrant workers (Chuang 2015). Scholars also point out that just because younger migrants are more tech-savvy and more engaged in social media, it does not mean they are more capable of collective action. Over the long run, their activism does not compare favorably with that of the older generation (Lee 2016). In the meantime, employers have been increasing their organizational and political capacities much faster than the workers (Pringle 2011).

In the next chapter, we turn our attention to another consequence of labor market development in China – the remaking of the welfare state in the reform era. As market forces assumed growing influence on the lives of workers and their families, the old socialist welfare system was eroded and finally collapsed. How has the Chinese state tried to rebuild a new safety net for its citizens?

Questions for Discussion

1. What role has China's labor force played in the country's economic miracle?

2. Have Chinese workers been given a fair share of China's economic success?

3. Why do Chinese labor laws not provide strong protection of labor rights in China?

7

Weaving a New Social Safety Net

Like pre-industrial countries in other parts of the world, in traditional China families and local communities looked after the poor, the sick, and the elderly. With the arrival of the communist regime, the family and community-based welfare system gave way to a socialist welfare state. From the 1950s to the late 1970s, urban Chinese received generous benefits provided by the government, whose budget was primarily funded by the revenue collected from state-owned industries. Meanwhile, rural residents developed a form of cooperative welfare based on collective agriculture. With the onset of market-oriented reform in the late 1970s, the ideological orientation of the Party state shifted from socialism and a concern about equality toward neoliberalism and a focus on efficiency. At the same time, the decline of state-owned industries and the end of collective agriculture chipped away at the economic and institutional foundations of the socialist welfare system.

As the Chinese government reduces its responsibilities for taking care of large portions of population in time of unemployment, old age, disability, sickness, and poverty, more and more citizens have had to fend for themselves in these situations. In modern capitalist countries, the state has instituted various welfare programs to protect the population against such adversities. In fact, many scholars view the modern welfare state as a byproduct of capitalist industrialization and – more recently – globalization (Pampel and Williamson 1989; Garrett 1998). But in the initial phase of China's turn toward a capitalist style market economy, the government concentrated almost exclusively on economic growth, neglecting the new insecurity and vulnerability of the citizens. Only since the turn of the century has the Party state begun to weave an increasingly inclusive social safety net for the population. It has made important strides in developing a welfare system compatible with a market economy. It has mobilized considerable resources to improve the protection of the population against the risks in the marketplace. But major gaps remain.

This chapter explores how the welfare system in China has evolved in the reform era, and how it has been shaped by the changing priorities and capabilities of the Chinese state. We single out three different areas of welfare reform for scrutiny – pension, healthcare, and social assistance. We will trace the historical legacy of the socialist welfare state and then discuss the major changes during the reform era. The final section provides an analysis of the political economy of welfare reform in contemporary China.

The Pension System

In the early years of the People's Republic of China, the Chinese government made industrialization a top economic priority. Accordingly, it adopted a welfare policy heavily in favor of the cities. In 1951, the government issued **Regulations on Labor Insurance**, which established a welfare system for workers in urban enterprises, mostly state-owned enterprises (SOEs). Pensions were a main component of this system. Premised on lifetime employment, the plan began to pay a pension to male workers at the age of sixty and to female workers at the age of fifty or fifty-five. The pension benefit was typically fifty to seventy percent of the standard wage, depending on the number of years pensioners had been in employment. Funding of the pension came from enterprise contributions set at three percent of the total wage bill. The trade unions administered the pension scheme under their umbrella organization, the All-China Federation of Trade Unions. During the Cultural Revolution (1966–1976), when the trade unions were suspended, enterprises paid pensions to the retirees out of their current revenue. After the Cultural Revolution, individual enterprises continued this practice. Since the SOEs remitted their profits to the government and received their budgets from the government, the financial responsibility for their workers' pension lay ultimately with the Chinese state (Whiteford 2003; Frazier 2004).

Besides enterprises, large numbers of urbanites worked in the government and in public service organizations (*shiye danwei*), such as schools, universities, hospitals, research institutes, and media organizations. They had the most generous pension plans, which were fully financed by the government. Retired government employees' pension included all their basic wage and seniority wage, while retirees of public service organizations received fifty to ninety percent of their basic wage (Whiteford 2003).

In contrast to their urban compatriots, Chinese peasants had no pension per se. They relied heavily on family members for old-age care, carrying on a time-honored tradition based on the Confucian notion of filial piety. The only exception was a category of people called the "Three Withouts" (without children, family, or resources), for whom the state provided very modest support in the form of "Five Guarantees" (guarantees of food, clothing, housing, medical care, and burial expenses) (Williamson et al. 2017).

Beginning in the late 1970s, economic liberalization eroded the socialist welfare system, creating rising inequality and insecurity among the population. The Gini Index is frequently used to measure inequality, where 100 means one person has all the wealth of a society and 0 means everyone has

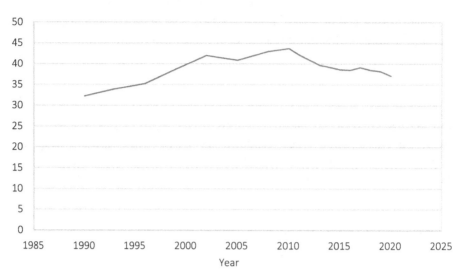

Figure 7.1 Gini Index – China 1990–2020
Source: World Bank Group.

an equal amount of wealth. As Figure 7.1 shows, China's Gini co-efficient rose steadily from 1990 on, peaking at 43.7 in 2010 before it began to decline. This was much higher than the figures for many other countries in that year. It may not be surprising that China had developed greater inequality than countries characterized by community-oriented ideologies, such as Sweden (27.7) and Japan (32.1). But it is quite remarkable that the Gini co-efficient of China exceeded that of strongly individualistic and market-driven economies, such as the United Kingdom (33.7) and the United States (40) (World Bank n.d.).

It has taken decades for the government to create a welfare system, including a new pension system. Like the Maoist era, the reformed pension system provides different levels of benefits for different groups of people. The urban–rural divide remains salient, while the urban population is differentiated by occupations and employers.

In the initial stage of industrial restructuring, the state sector gradually lost its traditional standing. The profits and market shares of the SOEs dwindled as they struggled to keep up with the newly formed competitive non-state business entities. Compared with the collective, private, and foreign-invested enterprises, the SOEs had an obvious disadvantage – the burden of providing generous welfare for their employees, including guaranteed pensions. The welfare responsibilities eroded the competitiveness of the SOEs, while their lack of competitiveness in turn decreased their capacity to sustain the traditional welfare for their employees. Many SOEs routinely had to delay pension payments (Liu and Sun 2016).

From the mid-1980s on, the government established Social Insurance Agencies to replace individual enterprises as pension administrators.

Employees were required to contribute up to three percent of their basic wages to the pension funds operated by the agencies, and employers were asked to pay fifteen percent of their pre-tax wages bill into the pension funds. By the early 1990s, such agencies had been set up nationwide, providing pensions for most of the SOE workers and some collectively owned enterprise (COE) workers. In this process, workers' pension became socialized, ceasing to be the sole responsibility of individual enterprises (Whiteford 2003).

In 1991, the State Council issued a Resolution on the Reform of the Pension System for Enterprise Workers. It was designed to cover workers of all types of enterprises in the country under one system built on two pillars. The first pillar was a defined-benefit portion of the pension based on the pay-as-you-go (PAYG) principle, where current contributions by the employees are used to pay for current benefits of the retirees. The second pillar was a defined-contribution portion, relying on mandatory individual savings, where workers build up their own retirement accounts that will make payments to them in the future. Both pillars were financed by the contributions of the employer and employees, with the employer paying twenty percent of the total payroll and employees, eight percent of their wages (Liu and Sun 2016). Since 2019, the government reduced the employer's share to 16 percent. Some provinces with large numbers of migrant workers, such as Zhejiang and Guangdong, have further lowered that figure to fourteen percent (Zou et al. 2023).

A major challenge in urban pension reform has been the fragmentation and inequality of the new pension program. Enterprises with younger workers are reluctant to meet their pension contribution requirements, while those struggling to compete in the marketplace are unable to contribute much to the pool. Moreover, although pension reform is a national initiative, the pension programs pool funds locally. Before the late 1990s, pooling happened at the level of cities and counties. With roughly 2,000 social pools across different cities and counties, the pension system was highly fragmented and uneven. Many of the pension pools had difficulty collecting adequate funds to meet the payout of benefits. Local governments were reluctant to push the enterprises too hard to meet their pension contribution target because they were fearful of the departure of the profitable companies and the collapse of the unprofitable ones. In either scenario, local economic development and tax revenue would suffer. On the other hand, the central government was not in a strong position to help because the fiscal system decentralization from the 1980s to the mid-1990s had greatly reduced Beijing's financial capacity to subsidize the pension programs (Frazier 2004). As a result, economically prosperous areas with profitable enterprises could provide good retirement benefit, but in poorer areas, pension pools suffered prolonged deficits. This led to considerable regional variation and inequality.

As SOE reform accelerated in the late 1990s and large numbers of workers lost their jobs, the need for a robust pension program became more urgent.

In 2000, Beijing established a National Social Security Fund to centralize the pension system. However, as the national government was still not ready to invest substantial financial resources, the Fund turned out to be merely a mechanism to subsidize deficit-ridden provinces, which in turn redistributed the subsidies to their cities and countries (Frazier 2004).

While that was a step forward in addressing the problem of inequality, it fell far short of establishing a truly national pension program. Over the years, the central government has encouraged local programs to expand the pooling of their funds to the provincial level with the ultimate goal of establishing a national program. But progress has been slow. Since the late 1990s, urban pension plan pools have been set up at the prefecture-city level – above counties and cities but below provinces (Zou et al. 2023).

In contrast to enterprise workers, who saw their welfare undermined soon after the launch of economic liberalization, government employees and employees of public service organizations have kept their benefits more-or-less intact. Their pension programs have largely maintained the main characteristics of the old socialist model. Until 2015, the pension program for these people was a PAYG system, fully funded by the government's general budget without individual contribution. Retired civil servants received a pension that included their basic wage as well as seniority wage and a portion of their position and post wages. Retirees from public service organizations received most of their basic wage and position wage according to the length of their working years (Whiteford 2003). For instance, the pension benefit would be at least eighty percent of the income before retirement year when public sector employees had worked for more than twenty years (Wang and Huang 2023).

In rural China, peasants remained pension-less until the 1990s, just as they had been during the era of Mao. In 1991, the Chinese government introduced a Basic Plan for Old Age Social Insurance in the Countryside. It called for individuals to contribute to their pension funds according to their financial capacity, supplemented by contribution from their employers (e.g. township and village enterprises). With both types of contribution set low, the payment received by people from age sixty on was meager (Whiteford 2003). Because the pension relied heavily on individual contribution, its payout was highly unequal. Furthermore, many rural residents profoundly distrusted the plan and refused to participate in it, which ultimately led to its failure (Liu and Sun 2016).

The situation began to improve in the early 2000s under the new government of Hu Jintao and Wen Jiabao. Having spent many years working in the less developed regions of the country, Hu and Wen showed a greater sensitivity toward the rising inequality in China, including the rural–urban disparity. In this regard, they were quite different from their predecessors, Jiang Zeming and Zhu Rongji, both of whom had built their careers in Shanghai and focused their attention on coastal urban development. Soon after the Hu-Wen administration took over, Beijing initiated a host of favorable policies toward the rural population. In 2002, the central government introduced the tax-for-fee reform, doing away with the myriads of levies on rural residents in favor of a single agricultural tax. A few years later, the government abolished the agricultural tax as well.

In this more sympathetic policy context, the government launched a New Rural Pension Scheme (NRPS) in 2009. It combined a non-contributory social pension component (SP) and a "voluntary" funded defined contribution (FDC) component. The individual contributions were set between 100 yuan and 500 yuan (or roughly $13 and $70) a year. The government was to subsidize each participant by at least 30 yuan (or around $4) per year (Wang and Huang 2023). Under this new scheme all rural residents reaching retirement age were eligible for benefits, even if they never contributed to the scheme. The government was fully responsible for the SP benefit, which was set at 55 yuan per month (or about $8) (Wang and Huang 2023). Moreover, this payment was conditional on the retirees' adult children's "voluntary" enrollment in and contribution to the FDC component. As more and more younger adults migrate to the cities, they have few incentives to contribute to the FDC if they do not have parents that could benefit from the modest SP (Williamson et al. 2017).

Soon after the introduction of NRPS, the government set out to improve the inclusiveness of urban pensions programs. In 2011, it expanded pension coverage beyond employees in the formal sector to include those working in the informal sector and those without employment. The new system, the Urban Residents Pension Plan (URPP), is similar to the NRPS in its provisions. In 2014, the State Council decided to merge the URPP and the NRPS into a unified basic pension insurance plan covering both rural residents and urban residents outside the formal sector. Unlike existing pension plans, it is disconnected from wages, contributions, and a working career. It is "universal" in its applicability and is heavily subsidized by different levels of governments. However, the benefit is quite low. At the time, the minimum payment was set at 55 yuan ($8) per month, although local authorities could supplement it according to the local cost of living. A study in 2016 reported that the actual amount paid to pensioners varied significantly across regions, from 540 yuan ($75) in Shanghai to 84 yuan ($12) in Kunming (Liu and Sun 2016). Despite the rising cost of living, the benefits have grown slowly and continue to fall far short. In 2024, the Chinese government announced that it would raise the basic pension for urban and rural residents from RMB 103 ($14) to RMB 123 ($17) a month. The extremely low level of basic pension has generated widespread ridicule by the public.

Another step taken by the government in integrating the pension system began in 2015, when it ended the wholly state-funded government pension plan enjoyed by employees of government and public service organizations.

Around forty million people in that most privileged category were brought under the same pension rules as the enterprise plans. Like enterprise workers, they must now contribute to their pension funds. This has been a major move toward eliminating the dual pension system in urban China (Liu and Sun 2016). However, to compensate for the reduced level of benefits for these retirees, government sectors and public institutions are required to set up an occupational annuity for their employees as well as an individual account with a twelve percent contribution rate. This leaves them still more privileged than other urban employees (Zhu and Walker 2018; Wang and Huang 2023).

Pension reform in China has come a long way, but the system is still highly problematic. Two challenges are particularly noteworthy – inequality and unsustainability. First, the evolving pension system has kept the discriminatory feature of the Maoist era, favoring the urbanites over the rural population, and privileging public sector employees over enterprise workers. That inequality has reinforced the stratification of market competition. Rural migrants working in Chinese cities were excluded from the early pension plans for urban enterprise workers, as were informal employees and the unemployed among urban residents. Even retirees covered by the pension plans fared very differently because those plans were based on jobs, performance, and earnings. Individuals with better education, more stable jobs, and higher salaries were entitled to more generous benefits than others. Men typically did much better than women (Zhu and Walker 2018). The more recent policy initiatives offer a basic pension to rural residents and urban residents outside the formal sector, aiming to universalize old age protection. The state has also increased its subsidies for pension plans. However, significant inequality remains between urban and rural residents, and between different types of urbanites. Moreover, the local pooling of funds means continued disparities between regions depending on their economic development (Liu and Sun 2016; Zhu and Walker 2018).

In addition, China's population is aging fast. Researchers argue that without increasing the current retirement age – sixty for males, fifty for female workers, and 55 for female government officials – the pension programs will have huge debt accumulation, which will put high pressure on the general government budget (Zuo et al. 2023). In late 2024, the Chinese government announced that it would gradually increase the retirement age for workers over a period of 15 years. Whether that scheme will fix the pension problem remains to be seen.

Healthcare

For the first three decades under the Chinese Communist Party (CCP), China was a relatively poor country, with its GDP per capita peaking at merely $272 in 1979 according to the World Bank. But the country's health-related indicators showed remarkable progress regardless. From 1952 to 1982, China's infant mortality fell from 200 to 34 per 1,000 live births, and life expectancy increased from about 35 to 68 years (Blumenthal and Hsiao 2005). This was in no small part attributable to the government's inclusive and effective health programs. Indeed, during the Maoist era, the CCP made healthcare the poster child of its ideological commitment to communism and egalitarianism. Relying on the resources and the infrastructure of a planned economy, the state ensured that the entire population had access to basic healthcare.

China's accomplishment attracted international admiration. In 1982 the World Health Organization (WHO) held a seminar in Yexian County, Shandong Province, on China's successful experience with primary healthcare. Many participants praised the Chinese model. In his speech, the executive director of UNICEF commented on how Chinese people's "health conditions have improved spectacularly" in the previous thirty years, pointing out that given its low per capita income level, China had achieved fifteen extra years in life expectancy and avoided the death of four million babies under one year old annually. He suggested four factors that contributed to China's astonishing record. The first was a "'national political will,' a serious commitment at the highest level in government to the "social goal of health for all." The second was the adoption of a primary healthcare approach, which China started to use in the 1950s through mass health campaigns and refined social organization of cost-effective medicine, alongside minimally adequate food, shelter, and clothing. Third, the expansion of literacy and education was tremendously helpful. The fourth ingredient of success was a healthcare system based on primary care principles and widespread participation by the people (WHO 1983). In addition, China developed a public health system that was highly effective in controlling infectious diseases through immunization programs and other public health measures. By the 1980s, China was becoming like developed countries in the West in that infectious diseases were giving way to chronic diseases (e.g. heart disease, cancer, and stroke) as leading causes of illness and death (Blumenthal and Hsiao 2005).

The overall achievement of the Maoist healthcare system should not blind us to the inequality between urban and rural China. Rural and urban areas had distinctive models, due to the government's urban bias. In Chinese cities, private practice of medicine and private ownership of health facilities were abolished by the CCP soon after it took power. The new government owned, funded, and operated all the hospitals. Physicians became government employees. Urban Chinese had two types of health insurance programs. The **Government Insurance Scheme** (GIS), funded by government budget, covered employees of the government and of public service organizations. The GIS also provided healthcare for retirees of those work units, as well as students and disabled veterans. The **Labor Insurance Scheme** (LIS), funded by the enterprises, covered SOE employees, retirees, and their dependents (Liu 2002).

In rural China, collective agriculture gave rise to a **Cooperative Medical System** (CMS). The CMS was funded by peasants' premium contributions, the village Collective Welfare Fund, and subsidies from higher levels of government. The system consisted of health centers at the brigade and commune levels. Among the peasants, there were rural health workers, known as "**barefoot doctors**," who had rudimentary medical training and often worked part-time in agriculture and part-time in providing basic healthcare. They often used a combination of Western and traditional Chinese medicine to treat minor medical problems. They also carried out public health services, such as infectious disease control and mother and child wellness (Fang 2012). By the end of the 1970s, the CMS covered more than ninety percent of the rural population (Blumenthal and Hsiao 2005). Sicker patients needing more sophisticated medical treatment would be transferred to county hospitals. This multi-tier system improved the rural population's health, although the medical service was far less abundant and sophisticated than what was available in urban centers.

Similar to the pension system, the healthcare system built under a planned economy became unsustainable with the unfolding of economic reform after the late 1970s. The changing ownership structure of the economy and the trend of marketization undermined the financing of the public health insurance system and eroded the infrastructure of the health delivery system. In the rural areas, the collapse of collective agriculture in the late 1970s and early 1980s led to a drastic decline of the CMS. From 1976 to 1990, the rural population covered by insurance nose-dived from 92.6 percent to 6.1 percent. Without insurance, rural residents were no longer able to pool their risks of healthcare expenses. Out-of-pocket payment for medical expenses brought financial ruin to many households. In the early 1990s, thirty to fifty percent of rural families lived below the poverty line as a result of illness. With the disappearance of the CMS, barefoot doctors who previously played a major role in healthcare delivery stopped functioning. Some of them became fee-charging private healthcare providers, whereas others ceased to practice medicine. The lack of funding and the diminished healthcare services worsened the health of the rural population. Some poor rural areas saw an increase in infant mortality and a return of infectious diseases, such as schistosomiasis, a devastating disease caused by parasitic worms, which had been nearly eradicated under the CMS (Blumental and Hsiao 2005).

In the urban areas, economic restructuring, beginning in the 1980s, ended traditional insurance schemes tied to the *danwei*. In their place, the government introduced city-based social health insurance schemes. This shift had little impact on the former GIS members but diminished the benefits for enterprise workers previously covered by the LIS. In any case, the new social insurance schemes only applied to about half of the urban population and excluded workers' dependents and migrant workers. Meanwhile, the delivery of healthcare in urban China changed radically, as state-owned hospitals confronted the steady reduction of state support. Like its approach to SOE reform, starting from the mid-1980s, the government was eager to shed its financial obligations for funding state-owned hospitals and to incentivize the latter to be more efficient. Without privatizing the hospitals, the government nonetheless pushed them to generate revenue for themselves in the marketplace. In this new policy environment, hospitals quickly reinvented themselves as commercial actors seeking to maximize their profits. Since the government set a ceiling for the fees for medical services, they resorted to conducting expensive tests and prescribing high-priced drugs to boost their income. These measures brought handsome profits to the hospitals and enriched the pharmaceutical companies. They also led to a rapid rise in medical costs, making healthcare more and more unaffordable for ordinary people (Blumenthal and Hsiao 2005; Ma et al. 2008).

A 2001 survey of residents in three representative Chinese provinces found that half of the respondents had foregone healthcare in the previous twelve months because of its cost (Blumenthal and Hsiao 2005). In the early 2000s, across the country the problems of "*kanbing nan*" (difficult to see a doctor) and "*kanbing gui*" (expensive to see a doctor) became a source of public anger (Yip and Hsiao 2005). In rural areas, poverty caused by medical expenses contributed to growing riots (Blumenthal and Hsiao 2005). In urban areas, frustrations with the cost of medical services, deep distrust in the profit-making orientation of hospitals, and disappointment with the poor outcomes of treatment led some patients and their families to harass and even violently attack doctors and nurses (see Box 7.1). The rise of medical disturbance (*yi'nao*) caught the attention of the Party state, which responded by criminalizing it without tackling the roots of the problem in the healthcare system (Huang 2020).

The deterioration of healthcare was closely associated with the dramatic reduction of government funding and the uneven distribution of resources among different regions. In 1978, central government contributed 32 percent of the national healthcare spending. By 1999, that had shrunk by more than half to only fifteen percent. To compensate for the decline of budgetary spending on healthcare, the government turned to social insurance programs. In 1998, the government introduced Urban Employee Basic Medical Insurance (UEBMI). It became the main health insurance scheme for urban enterprise workers. Funding for the program primarily comes from payroll taxes paid by both employers (six percent) and employees (two percent). The employer's contributions are divided into two parts – seventy percent going into a social pooling account (SPA), and thirty percent into individual medical savings accounts (MSAs). The employees' contributions go to their MSAs. The MSAs

Box 7.1 Attacks on Doctors

On a September morning in 2011, a man stormed into Tongren Hospital in Beijing and viciously attacked 43-year-old Dr. Xu Wen of the Ear Nose and Throat (ENT) department. Xu lay in a pool of blood with her forearms, forehead, neck, back, and left leg slashed to the bones. The attacker was Wang Baoming, a former patient Dr. Xu had treated for throat cancer. In 2006 Wang went to Tongren Hospital to seek help from Dr. Xu, a well-known ENT expert with training in the United States. He checked into the hospital ten days earlier to line up for an operation by the doctor. When he finally got operated on, he and his family were dissatisfied with the outcome. They believed that the doctor failed to remove the tumor thoroughly, which led to more operations later, with many side effects, including disfiguring and disability. The medical expenses, plus the loss of his livelihood, added to Wang's depression. After complaining to various authorities without avail, in 2008 Wang sued the hospital and demanded financial compensation. Three years passed and his case was going nowhere. Finally, Wang took matters into his own hands (Bai 2011). Similar incidents have happened in many parts of the country, so much so that in 2013 the government issued guidelines for hospitals to put in place security guards at a rate of one for each twenty beds. In 2014, the prominent British medical journal, the *Lancet*, published an editorial pointing out that while patients in other countries also complain about doctors, China stood out – "for a third of doctors to have experienced conflict and thousands to have been injured, the scale, frequency, and viciousness of attacks have shocked the world." (Lancet 2014)

are used to cover initial healthcare expenses up to ten percent of a worker's annual wages. The SPA, administered by the local government, is primarily used for catastrophic illness, covering the medical expenses totaling between ten and 400 percent of the wages. Employers may also offer workers the option of purchasing additional insurance to cover healthcare costs exceeding 400 percent of their wages. The implementation of UEBMI encountered similar problems as the enterprise pension scheme discussed earlier. Employers did not always comply with the state mandates, claiming they could not afford the contributions (Blumenthal and Hsiao 2005).

SARS

From late 2002 to early 2003, the outbreak and spread of the Severe Acute Respiratory Syndrome (SARS) threw China into a public health crisis. As the mysterious disease swept across the country, thousands of people fell seriously ill, and hundreds died. People panicked and began to lose trust in the government. The international community criticized China's slow response to SARS. The national leadership, which at first neglected the situation, soon realized that this was a crisis that threatened the Chinese population, the economy, China's international standing, and potentially the legitimacy of the CCP. The government hurried to focus its attention and resources on combating the pandemic and finally brought an end to the crisis in the summer of 2003.

SARS exposed the fragile state of China's healthcare system, including its diminished capacity to deal with public health crises. The government's initial failure to contain the infection resulted from the breakdown of the old health system without building a new one. Gone was the centralized information gathering and decision-making hierarchy of the Maoist era. Government funding for healthcare and public health initiatives had drastically declined. The well-developed network of community health services had disappeared. For-profit hospitals had little interest in preventive care and instead concentrated on curative care. Above all, the central government subordinated the healthcare of the population to the imperative of economic development (Schwartz and Evans 2007).

The lessons of SARS accelerated the CCP's efforts to improve the funding and coordination of healthcare. In 2003, after years of neglect of the rural population, Beijing officially launched the New Rural Cooperative Medical Scheme (NCMS). The NCMS is a community-based rural health insurance system financed by individual contributions and subsidies from the local and central governments. Almost all the rural residents joined the program in a few years, but the pooling of risks was localized. Four years later, the government started pilots of Urban Resident Basic Medical Insurance (URBMI) targeting urban Chinese without a stable income or employment, such as children, students, the elderly, the disabled, and other jobless individuals. Unlike UEBMI mentioned above, which is mandatory and based on employment, NCMS and URBMI are voluntary programs that provide coverage for large portions of the population previously excluded from health insurance.

Like the pension programs, health insurance programs pool risks and resources locally, with NCMS at the county level, whereas URBMI and UEBMI are at the prefecture-city level. This limited pooling rendered the insurance programs fragile. In 2009, the government took a step towards ameliorating the problem by merging NCMS and URBMI into the Urban–Rural Resident Basic Medical Insurance (URRBMI) program. Researchers argue that this integration has expanded the risk pool and improved the resilience of the insurance programs. It has also improved rural residents' access to health services and reduced regional equity in healthcare (Li et al. 2023).

Despite the progress, the national health insurance system remains highly fragmented and uneven. The multiple kinds of health insurance schemes differ considerably in terms of their sources of funding and in the costs and benefits for their members. Funding for UEBMI comes mainly from payroll taxes whereas the URRBMI relies heavily on government subsidies. They have different premium levels and reimbursement rates. Migrant workers who work in the cities but still hold rural *hukou* get very limited coverage if they need medical care where they work. Moreover, significant variation persists among regions because the insurance programs depend heavily on local funding and local governments' ability to invest in healthcare in turn depends on their fiscal capacity. All else being equal, the economically well-to-do counties and cities can invest more resources in their schemes than those in worse economic shape.

In 2009 the Chinese government issued an important document – "Opinions on Deepening Health System Reform," which proclaimed the goal of establishing an equitable and effective health system for all by 2020. In the following years, the government significantly increased spending on healthcare. From 2009 to 2013, the amount doubled from $79.4 billion to $157.6 billion. Almost half of the funds (46.4 percent) went into health insurance schemes and medical assistance funds (Meng et al. 2015). There has been steady progress toward the goal of universal coverage. The proportion of the population covered by the three social health insurance schemes rose from fifteen percent in 2000 to more than 97 percent in 2015. The benefits of the schemes also improved (Li and Fu 2017).

In 2018 the government created the National Healthcare Security Administration to administer both UEBMI and URRBMI. The new bureaucracy is also responsible for running the Medical Assistance program, which provides health security for low-income households, and for deciding on pricing and overseeing drug procurement (Yi et al. 2019). In 2016 the Chinese government announced a "Healthy China 2030" blueprint. Unlike past guidelines or plans for healthcare reform, the blueprint pays attention to a broad range of factors that affect population health, such as lifestyle, air quality, and food security (Li and Fu 2017).

Covid-19

China's response to the recent Covid-19 pandemic has shown both the strengths and the weaknesses of the Chinese healthcare system. In late 2019, doctors in the central city of Wuhan came across patients with an unfamiliar type of pneumonia. They tried to sound the alarm of a potentially new and serious virus, but were ignored. Indeed, officials suppressed the circulation of the information, punishing whistle blowers for "spreading rumor" and banning media reports on the subject. The mishandling of the outbreak wasted valuable time to understand and contain the emerging threat to public health. The initial official response to Covid was not surprising. In China's hierarchical political system, local officials are reluctant to report bad news to their superiors. They routinely cover up problems in their jurisdictions. Moreover, even after SARS, the Chinese government still placed greater value on economic growth and social stability than public health. Cadres' knee jerk reaction to a new virus was to contain the information for fear of its economic damage and negative political consequences.

In late January 2020, when it became clear that the situation had gotten out of hand and could no longer be denied, Beijing took drastic measures. It closed China's borders to travelers and imposed a total lockdown of Wuhan and other areas in the country to curtail the spread of the virus. Makeshift hospitals sprang up and began to operate in record time to isolate and treat Covid patients. By April 2020, when the rest of the world struggled to deal with rising numbers of people falling ill and dying from the disease, China began to reopen most of the cities and restart their economic activities. In the following two and a half years, the CCP adopted a dynamic zero-Covid (*dongtai qingling*) strategy. Using electronic technology as well as human networks, the authorities aggressively traced contacts among people, isolated individuals who may have been exposed to the virus, and severely restricted movement in and out of areas of potential contagion. They also carried out frequent mass testing of the virus among the population. As of November 2022, China recorded only about 6,000 Covid deaths among 1.4 billion people, a sharp contrast with the United States, which recorded more than a million deaths in a population of 330 million (National Public Radio 2022). The extremely low official number was likely due to China's definition of Covid death, which was much narrower than the reporting system in most other countries. It only included deaths in hospital and only those resulting from pneumonia or respiratory failure directly caused by the coronavirus. Deaths of patients with pre-existing illnesses, of people outside hospital, including many who could not get to a doctor because of lockdowns, were not counted. After the initial crisis was over, the CCP proudly proclaimed victory over the pandemic and touted the superiority of China's political system in managing public health crises.

However, the Chinese population paid a heavy price for this "victory." While the draconian control over the population may well have limited the spread of Covid, it seriously reduced people's access to medical care of all kinds. For example, people suffering from heart attacks and strokes could not get to the hospital. Those needing chemotherapy or dialysis had to stop their treatment. A study of healthcare utilization in China finds that it declined significantly following the outbreak of the pandemic. During and after the Chinese New Year in 2020, total healthcare expenditure and utilization declined by 37.8 percent and 40.8 percent respectively from the same period in 2019 before the pandemic (Zhang et al. 2020). The lockdowns also brought significant mental health inflictions on massive numbers of people. Moreover, when the government finally changed its policy and relaxed control in late 2022, in part due to public protests, there was an explosion of Covid cases, which

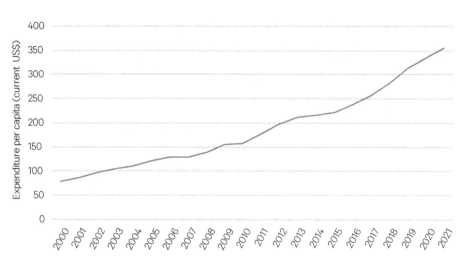

Figure 7.2 Out-of-Pocket Spending on Healthcare 2000–2021
Source: World Health Organization.

overwhelmed the hospitals. Researchers estimate that in the first two months following the new policy, eighty to ninety percent of the population became infected and that 1.2 million to 1.7 million people died from Covid (Glanz et al. 2023).

Although the Chinese government has become more attentive to healthcare in the twenty-first century, its focus on economic development still keeps it from putting more resources into the healthcare system. According to the World Bank, as of 2020 health expenditure in China was only 5.6 percent of the GDP, up from 4.2 percent in 2010. That is not only below OECD countries, where the average figure was fourteen percent in 2020, it also falls behind some developing countries, such as Brazil (above ten percent) and South Africa (8.6 percent). As a result, the out-of-pocket spending on healthcare by Chinese citizens has continuously increased (see Figure 7.2). Following the Covid pandemic, the health insurance costs rose dramatically just as many people lost their jobs or saw their income slashed because of the economic downturn. The government refused to step in to help reduce the costs. As a result, in 2022 alone nineteen million subscribers dropped out of their insurance programs (Yu 2023).

In addition, in the Chinese system community healthcare facilities have long been inadequately funded and poorly staffed. Most of the people do not trust those facilities. This results in an overcrowding of the major hospitals and prevents the grassroots health providers from acting as effective public-health monitors and medical-care providers. These and other gaps in the Chinese healthcare system exposed by the Covid pandemic indicate that China has a long way to go in reforming its health system (Xing and Zhang 2021). Transparent and effective communication, greater attention to public health, a multi-tiered delivery system, and a more balanced allocation of resources among community healthcare and hospital care should all be priorities.

Social Assistance

Social assistance refers to government-provided aid for the poverty-stricken among the population. It is typically a means-tested scheme; to qualify individuals or families have to demonstrate that they have no income or very low income. It can take the form of cash transfer or in-kind help, such as food, clothing, housing, and medical services. Unlike pension and healthcare, social assistance was only a marginal component of the pre-reform welfare system in China. It included the Five-Guarantees program for the Three-Withouts individuals in the rural areas and assistance for special categories of people in the cities, such as disabled veterans, orphans, discharged criminals, and returning overseas Chinese. As of 1992, only 190,000 people (0.06 percent of the urban population) received assistance. The total cost was 87.4 million yuan (just over $10 million) (Leung 2006).

The intensification of SOE reform in the late 1990s saw millions of SOE workers losing their jobs. Families of unemployed workers fell into poverty and became the new urban underclass. This was a major embarrassment for the CCP, which had been founded as the party of the workers and the peasants of China. Shanghai, China's biggest SOE center, took the lead in tackling this problem. In 1993, the Shanghai municipal government initiated an Urban Minimum Living Guarantee System (UMLGS), known as **dibao** (short for *zuidi shenghuo baozhang* in Chinese), to provide a safety net for the urban poor. In the following years, programs like this spread to other Chinese cities. By the end of the 1990s, almost all the urban areas had developed social assistance schemes. As of 2016, *dibao* covered 14.8 million urban residents (Yang et al. 2020).

In the following years, the benefits provided by the UMLGS differed widely across regions. Research suggests that the most important factor behind the variation in benefits was not the cost of living in different cities. Instead, it was a function of the financial capacity of the local governments. Initially, local governments were responsible for all the expenditure of *dibao*. Later, the central government assumed more responsibilities for funding *dibao*. Its financial commitment increased substantially from 26 percent of the total expenditure in 1999 to 61 percent in 2003 (Leung 2006). However, even under cost-sharing with the central government, local government finance remained crucial. Wealthier municipalities were able to set higher poverty lines for *dibao* eligibility than poorer cities. They also saw higher participation rates in the program. The recipients of assistance in poor cities fared much worse than their counterparts in well-to-do areas (Guo Y. et al. 2022).

Like the urban areas, rural China also experienced unprecedented inequality with the onset of market reform, with some groups falling into poverty without a safety net. This led to growing dissatisfaction and contributed to the rising social unrests in the 1990s. In response, the government began to introduce social assistance that applied to a broader range of people than the original Three-Withouts group in the mid-1990s. Due to limited funding, *dibao* took longer to develop in the rural areas than in the cities. It was not until 2007 that such a program was comprehensively implemented. As of 2016, it covered 45.8 million rural beneficiaries (Gao et al. 2019).

Similar to the urban program, rural *dibao* was administered locally. Benefit thresholds were set at the county level within the budgets determined by the provincial government. Decisions on applications for assistance were made at the town level, based on the recommendation of the villagers' committees. Due to the different methods for establishing *dibao* eligibility, and the different priorities of the local governments, there was considerable variation in the distribution of social assistance benefits from one county to the next.

Over time, the government expanded social assistance coverage and raised the level of benefits. One study finds that from December 2010 to September 2016 the average threshold set by counties rose by over ninety percent in urban areas and by 150 percent in rural areas (Li and Walker 2021). But, even with the increases, the *dibao* benefits still fell behind the rising cost of living and only reached the minimal international standard. Thus, the poverty reduction effect was very limited (Gao 2013). The inadequacy of the program was especially salient for rural residents. Research shows that while in the urban areas *dibao* participation was associated with an increase in education spending, rural recipients of social assistance had to prioritize healthcare and food, unable to increase their education spending (Wang et al. 2019; Yi et al. 2019). This suggests that *dibao* did little to help rural children to improve their future prospect in the labor market.

The gap between rural and urban social assistance reinforces the privilege of city residents. In the last decade, the Chinese government has taken some steps in addressing this issue. In 2014 the State Council unified *dibao* administration across the country. The process of integration moved faster in areas with stronger economic growth, a smaller share of rural population and *dibao* recipients, and decreasing caseloads (Xu and Yu 2019). According to the Chinese Ministry of Civil Affairs, at the end of 2023, the combined social assistance program covered over forty million recipients. The integration has led to a convergence of the funding and operation of the rural and the urban schemes, but not equality in benefits. In 2014, the average benefit level for rural recipients was about half the level for urban recipients (Gao 2017). Since then, the central authorities have encouraged local governments to narrow the gap between the urban and rural social assistance standards. Some regions, such as Shanghai, Beijing, Chongqing, and Guangdong, have increased the benefits of rural *dibao* at a faster rate than the urban *dibao* to gradually equalize the programs. But many other regions continue to provide better benefits for the urban poor.

As social assistance expands and progresses, another issue that has caught the attention of the government is the inefficient targeting of the programs. For instance, one estimate for 2009 suggests that as many as 89 percent of the people eligible for *dibao* did not receive the benefits (known as exclusion errors), while as many as 86 percent of those who received the benefits were ineligible for the social assistance scheme (known as inclusion errors) (Golan et al. 2014). After 2008, the Ministry of Civil Affairs – the government agency in charge of social welfare – issued new rules on assessing applicants' income and needs. The government created a national registry of people in poverty and an oversight system with regular inspections of local poverty alleviation decisions to ensure accurate identification of the poor. The eligibility test of *dibao* expanded beyond income, to include an asset test. Government departments have since established a crosscheck mechanism to verify applicants' eligibility. Townships (rural) or subdistricts (urban) now directly process applications, removing the role of villagers' or residents' committees in the process. Studies show that this has drastically reduced the inclusion errors, but the problem of exclusion errors remains, as local cadres are more eager to avoid the potential political risks of providing benefits to the undeserved than to ensure adequate help for the poor (Li and Walker 2021).

Like other means-tested welfare programs, *dibao* comes with stringent conditions and social stigma. Applicants have to reveal detailed personal information to the authorities and their life is scrutinized by fellow citizens. For example, eating in restaurants, wearing jewelry, and owning pets, are all considered unacceptable. Such a system subjects *dibao* recipients to social isolation and psychological damage (Leung 2006; Huo and Lin 2019). According to the Chinese constitution, amended in 2004, citizens are entitled to receive social assistance to maintain a basic living standard. Indeed, government pronouncements stipulate that providing such assistance is a responsibility of the state. However, empirical investigation finds that the idea of social rights has not been fully established in practice. The view of social assistance as charity remains strong. Under the philanthropic framework, recipients of social assistance are in a weak and passive position vis-à-vis the government. They are expected to feel deeply grateful for the handout given by the state. This has been the dominant theme in Chinese social welfare discourse (Zhang 2019).

The Political Economy of Welfare Reform

Welfare reform in China has been driven and shaped by a combination of political and economic forces. The old socialist welfare state was an integral part of a planned economy and reflected the CCP's early political commitment to the ideal of an egalitarian society (despite the reality of urban–rural inequality). With the start of economic reform in the late 1970s, the Party state began to look to market forces to achieve economic modernization. For the sake of incentivizing economic actors, Chinese policymakers became more tolerant of inequality. In the mid-1980s, Chinese leader, Deng Xiaoping, famously declared that some people and regions should be allowed to "get rich first" (*xian fu qilai*). As discussed in the last chapter, a labor market developed under the reform program made labor allocation more efficient and the labor force more productive. At the same time, it resulted in growing inequality between the winners and the losers in market competition.

In mature capitalist economies, the state uses welfare programs to protect the workers against market risks and ensure a basic level of living standard for all. But as a newcomer to a market economy, China did not immediately create a market-compatible welfare system to replace the crumbling old socialist welfare state (Cai et al. 2008). The overall policy of neglect reflected "a naive faith in the market" (Saich 2017). Although Beijing encouraged local governments to carry out diverse policy experiments with pension, unemployment, housing, healthcare, education, social assistance, and other welfare schemes, its *laissez fair* attitude meant there was a lack of coherent and reliable social policies, leaving many people in precarious conditions.

China's abandonment of socialist values and focus on economic growth developed in parallel with the global triumph of the neoliberal orthodoxy, which began in the 1980s with the Thatcher government in the UK and the Reagan administration in the US. In fact, international influence had a prominent impact on the evolution of the Chinese welfare system. For instance, the World Bank was deeply involved in advising the Chinese government on pension reform, pushing a strongly pro-market agenda. The pension schemes that emerged in urban China were income-centered and financed by contributions by employers and employees, very much in line with the mainstream trend of global pension reforms promoted by the World Bank. Although the individual accounts turned out to be underfunded and fragmented, the neoliberal model remained influential (Hu 2012; Liu and Sun 2016).

From the late 1990s on, new political and economic realities prompted the CCP to reconsider its approach to social welfare. On the political front, as Chinese society became increasingly stratified and the broken welfare system failed to compensate for the losers in market competition, social tension was on the rise. Desperate situations, such as those resulting from the loss of livelihood and from the astronomical medical bills, led to growing discontent. SOE workers were particularly disheartened and outraged, feeling betrayed by the government. In their eyes the CCP had broken a social contract with the working class (Frazier 2004; Hurst 2009). Public grievances produced protests and riots – labelled "mass incidents (*quntixing shijian*)" by the government – threatening political stability and even the legitimacy of the CCP. In this context, the Chinese government began to change the "efficiency first and equity second" approach (Ngok and Huang 2014). By the early 2000s, it was clear to the new Hu-Wen administration that it was politically imperative to address issues of equity and livelihood in addition to economic development. They championed a more people-oriented (*yi ren wei ben*) development approach, including better social protection of the population.

On the economic front, after years of fiscal decentralization designed to encourage local economic development, the central government reversed the course in the mid-1990s. A major reform in 1994 recentralized taxation power in the hands of the national government, a subject we will discuss in detail in the next chapter. This allowed Beijing to increase its revenue in the following years and enabled it to spend more financial resources on its policy priorities. Driven by the political necessity to maintain social stability, the central authorities rapidly increased investment in pension, healthcare, and social assistance programs. They made special transfer payments to local governments earmarked for public services. Alongside funds transfers, they reintroduced binding targets in welfare provision to hold local cadres accountable.

There are ongoing debates as to whether welfare reform will lead to greater equality and social justice in China. Some signs are promising. As discussed in this chapter, welfare programs, such as pension, healthcare, and social assistance, have come to cover more and more people. In addition, the extent of regressivity that grants privileged groups more benefits has decreased over time. A study of three waves of national household income survey finds that in 1988 social benefits increased rich households' relative income by 46 percentage points (from 198 to 244 percent of the median income). That figure was smaller in 1995 (39 percentage points) and dropped even further in 2002 (to thirteen percentage points) (Gao 2010, p. 14). On the other hand, the level of protection provided by these social programs is very low. The system so far is marked by moderate universalism, with wide coverage, but meager benefits for the majority of the participants. Furthermore, the regressive nature (despite the decreasing degree of regressivity) of many of these social programs reinforces the inequality caused by social, economic, and regional segmentation.

Scholars of comparative welfare systems note that capitalist democracies vary in the kinds of welfare state they give rise to. In his classical study, Gosta Esping-Andersen identifies three types of welfare regimes (Esping-Andersen 1990). A liberal regime, such as the one in the United States, is characterized by modest, means-tested assistance for low-income groups. It otherwise relies largely on market solutions for social problems, with the government subsidizing private welfare schemes. A conservative or corporatist regime, which is represented by Germany, encourages family-based assistance. State assistance supplements aid by family members. Moreover, the welfare benefits differ according to the recipients' social economic class, preserving the existing hierarchy. A social democratic regime, which prevails in the Scandinavian countries, follows the principles of universalism and de-commodification. Social rights and services apply to all, independent of one's market participation, and citizens enjoy high-standard equality rather than merely having their minimal needs met. The case of China does not neatly fit into any of these types. However, it clearly contains strong elements of the first two. The differentiated pension and healthcare benefits for people of different social economic status and the status-preserving tendency of these programs are consistent with the conservative or corporatist system. The minimalist and means-tested nature of its social assistance programs is typical of a liberal welfare system.

Will China develop an inclusive national social citizenship? Two formidable political obstacles make that prospect unlikely any time soon. First, the CCP runs a paternalistic state, which views welfare as a gift given to the people by the government. From this perspective, the benefits people derive from welfare programs reflect the Party state's generosity, not their inherent rights as citizens. Solinger (2014) delineates three types of motivations of state-provided welfare: (1) assistance to the needy based on the principle of the rights of the individual or social citizenship rights, (2) protection and benefits aiming to enhance the productivity of the nation, and (3) subsidies to pacify popular antagonism and silence unwelcome demands. The Chinese government has primarily used welfare to help placate the poor. Its provision of welfare is not so much associated with the hardship of groups as it is with the degree of disturbance created by them (Solinger 2014). More recently, it has moved toward using welfare to enhance the human capital pool of the country. There is no indication that the government is interested in a welfare policy based on the notion of citizenship alone (Saich 2017).

Second, the political system in China is highly fragmented, and that has a profound impact on the welfare system. As we have seen in the cases of pension, healthcare, and social assistance, Chinese welfare programs assign unequal benefits along *hukou* lines, by occupation, by employment status and so on. Furthermore, the complex relationship between the central government and local governments and the important role given to local governments in welfare provision have made it difficult for a national welfare regime to develop. Different regions vary in their resources. Local officials face competing priorities, e.g. between promoting GDP growth and preserving social stability, and between pleasing the central government and rewarding their local supporters. Regional authorities often take advantage of the vagueness of Beijing's directives and develop their own welfare programs to suit their preferences and local conditions. Such disparities have resulted in so-called "local welfare states" and distinct "welfare regions" (Ngok and Huang 2014).

Conclusion

The Chinese welfare state has evolved through the history of the People's Republic. In the reform era, the country moved from a centrally planned economy to a decentralized and increasingly market-oriented economy. At the same time, the CCP turned away from the core beliefs of communism and embraced the tenets of neoliberalism. These changes eroded the economic and institutional foundations of the socialist welfare system. For the first two decades of the reform era, the government largely neglected the breakdown of the old welfare state, which resulted in a decline of social protection of the population and a rise in public discontent. Since the late 1990s, the Chinese government has paid more attention to rebuilding a social safety net, one that would serve the new economic system in the country. It has made ongoing efforts to expand and deepen the welfare system through increased funding and addressing issues emerging from various experiments.

This chapter has focused on welfare reform in three areas: pension, healthcare, and social assistance. It shows that in the twenty-first century the Party state has significantly increased investment and centralized the administration of the welfare programs in each area. The coverage of these programs has become more inclusive. However, the benefits for most participants remain far from adequate, and the levels of protection continue to be highly uneven among different segments and regions. While the emerging welfare system has achieved a degree of universalism, it has a long way to go toward an integrated and adequate safety net.

The future of social welfare in China depends as much on the country's political development as it does on its economic capacity. Thus far, the government's effort to enhance the welfare state has been primarily motivated by CCP's obsession with social stability and economic development. The instrumental nature of its policy does not bode well for a truly robust and equitable welfare state. Indeed, comparative studies find that the relative power of labor and leftist parties is a key factor shaping the welfare state (e.g. Esping-Andersen 1990). As far as China remains under the authoritarian rule of an elitist and paternalistic party, it is unlikely to create a welfare state based on social citizenship.

Questions for Discussion

1. How has China's changing economic system reshaped its welfare system?

2. Why did the CCP neglect welfare early in the reform era, yet gave it greater attention from the late 1990s onwards?

3. Is the Chinese welfare system based on social citizenship?

8

Money in the Chinese Economy

Having looked at how the "real economy," namely the production and consumption of goods and services, works in China, we turn now to the financial dimensions of the economy, examining the development of the country's fiscal and financial systems. The fiscal system – or public finance – involves the generation and the expenditure of public money. A healthy fiscal system is important not only for a country's economic growth, but also for its macroeconomic stability, strategic sector development, wealth distribution and redistribution, social welfare provision, and indirectly, for its political order. The financial system channels money among different sectors and actors in a society. It mobilizes savings for investment, facilitates information sharing, rationalizes resource allocation, diversifies risks, and cushions economic shocks. A well-developed financial system is essential for the smooth and efficient operation of the economy. In the pages that follow, we will also discuss how the Chinese state has used fiscal and financial instruments to carry out industrial policies to encourage economic development and strategic competitiveness.

The Fiscal System

Between the 1950s and the mid-1970s the Chinese fiscal system closely resembled that of the Soviet Union. As part of the planned economy, public finance was highly centralized. All revenue belonged to the national government and all expenditure was decided by the central authorities. State-owned enterprises (SOEs) made up the bulk of the urban economy. They were highly profitable despite their inefficiency thanks to the protection by the government and the absence of competition from other types of enterprises. They in turn remitted their profits to the government to fill the public coffer. Other government revenue included taxes from agricultural activities and commerce. The central government spent fiscal resources on national priorities such as defense, national infrastructure, large economic projects, higher education, and foreign aid. Local governments were given the responsibility for social services, such as public safety, healthcare, social security, housing, and primary and secondary education. Their funding came entirely from the central government (Bird and Wong 2005, Naughton 2018).

154

From Decentralization to Recentralization

The post-Mao economic liberalization involved enterprise reform and fiscal decentralization, both of which eroded the foundation of the old Soviet style fiscal system. A key to the enterprise reform of the 1980s was that the government no longer required the SOEs to turn over all their revenue. Instead, they were expected to pay taxes to the state. Soon, the tax system gave way to a contract system. Enterprises signed multi-year contracts that specified their profit remittances to the government. The goal was to motivate the SOEs to improve their productivity. After all, with their remittances fixed, the more profits they made, the more residuals they could retain. This reform weakened the traditional revenue base of the national government. Moreover, the rise of private and foreign-invested companies meant that the share of the state sector in the Chinese economy shrank sharply. Whatever revenue SOEs continued to remit to the government constituted a diminished portion of the GDP.

Fiscal decentralization was another major component of the economic reform in the 1980s. Keen to encourage local governments to develop their regional economies, in 1988 Beijing introduced a fiscal responsibility system. It specified a fixed amount of revenue local governments must turn to the center and an agreed-upon annual rate of change over a period of time. Any revenue local governments generated above and beyond the contracts would remain in their hands. Local authorities were free to use this revenue as they saw fit, including covering local government expenditure and paying bonuses to local officials. This new system boosted the enthusiasm of local officials to promote economic growth (Park et al. 1996; Jin et al. 2005). The system was a major motivation behind local government support of the rapid growth of township and village enterprises (TVEs) (Oi 1999).

While enterprise reform and fiscal decentralization provided important stimuli for China's rapid economic growth, they reduced the extractive capacity of the Chinese government, especially that of the central government. Total Chinese government revenue fell from over thirty percent of GDP in 1978 to about eleven percent in 1995–1996. Central government's share of the total revenue dropped from 40 percent in the mid-1980s to just above twenty percent in 1993. To make things worse, the decline in government revenue was accompanied by a growing need for the government to subsidize SOEs, which struggled to compete with newly established non-state enterprises in the marketplace.

Squeezed at both ends – by reduced revenue and increased expenditure – the national government fell into a fiscal crisis that challenged its power vis-à-vis the provinces and its governing capacity (Wong 2000; Wang and Hu 2001). Beijing's weakness was manifested in its poor funding for the most basic public goods for the nation, including national defense (see Box 8.1).

Then Vice Premier Zhu Rongji sounded the alarm: "the central government's finances are in very poor shape, to the point of being unsustainable . . . If we don't suitably centralize revenue . . . we won't be able to get by" (quoted in Liu et al. 2022, p. 45).

Box 8.1 "Soldiers of Fortune"

When the central government experienced a steady decline of fiscal revenue in the 1980s, it felt compelled to cut the spending on national defense. China's paramount leader, Deng Xiaoping, told the military forces that economic development was now the top national priority, and that they must serve that priority and be prepared for a shrinking defense budget. He asked the People's Liberation Army (PLA) to be diligent and frugal and continue to carry out its duty despite reduced resources allocated by the government. With the permission and even the encouragement of the government, the PLA turned to business activities to make up for the budgetary shortfall. In some ways, this was a throwback to the revolutionary era before 1949, when the communist Red Army, under economic blockades by the KMT and the Japanese, resorted to agricultural production to ensure food and clothing supplies. That tradition continued after the Chinese Communist Party (CCP) took power in 1949, with military-run farms operating in various parts of China. But, during the reform era, the PLA got involved in commercial activities far beyond agricultural sidelines. It created large real-estate firms and pharmaceutical companies. It engaged in massive arms trade and car smuggling. The armed forces became "soldiers of fortune" (Mulvenon 2001). Not only did they pursue self-sufficiency, but they also built highly profitable business concerns. From 1987 to 1993, their commercial revenue amounted to ten percent of the official defense spending. (Duan 2017).

Fiscal Reform

Beijing reacted to its dire fiscal situation by taking forceful measures to increase two ratios – the ratio between government revenue and GDP and the ratio between central government revenue and total government revenue. In 1994 it introduced a reform package, which brought major changes in three areas – tax sharing, tax modernization, and tax administration (Bahl 1999). First, the reform ended the multi-tiered system of turnover taxes – taxes based on revenue – borrowed from the Soviet model. Instead, it created a value-added tax (VAT) – a tax on transactions that would apply to all manufacturing activities at a single rate of seventeen percent. Turnover taxes were subject to manipulation by local governments, which could set the sales prices of goods and adopt drastically different taxation rates across sectors. VAT was simple and universal, much more difficult for local governments to use to maximize their own share of taxes. The reform reduced the latitude for local officials and business actors and ensured the flow of revenue to the central government. The new system also simplified and rationalized the taxation system considerably.

Second, the reform established a new tax sharing system (TSS). Unlike the old system of negotiated contracts, the new TSS institutionalized the separation among central government taxes, local government taxes, and shared taxes. It assigned exclusively to the central government excise taxes (consumption taxes on certain products such as alcohol, tobacco, and luxury cars), energy and transportation fund contribution, and income tax collected from banks and other financial institutions. Urban land-use tax, property tax, and resources tax were exclusively assigned to the local governments. VAT, salt tax, and personal income taxes were to be shared by the central and the local governments. Importantly, the expanded VAT made up nearly half of all tax revenue and was expected to go up with GDP growth regardless of profitability. By assigning 75 percent of the VAT to the central government, the new system allocated the bulk of tax revenue to Beijing (Bird and Wong 2005).

Third, in terms of tax administration, the reform created distinct tax collectors – a national tax administration responsible for collecting central and shared taxes and a local tax administration responsible for collecting local taxes. In contrast to the old setup, where the local tax bureau was in charge of collecting all the taxes, this new arrangement removed central taxes and the VAT from local administration and thus greatly reduced the opportunities for local authorities to divert central government revenue.

The fiscal reform simplified the taxation system and significantly enhanced the government's revenue generating capacity. Following its accession to the World Trade Organization (WTO) in 2001, China's exports expanded, and its economy grew exponentially. Data of the World Bank show that Chinese GDP rose from less than $1.2 trillion in 2000 to over $8.5 trillion in 2012. Accordingly, government revenue soared, growing by an annual rate of 22 percent in that period (Wong 2018, p. 274). As a result of the 1994 tax reform, the overall government revenue increased from twelve percent of GDP in 1993 to 22 percent in 2016 (Wingender 2018). With its fiscal resources rising, the government gained new capabilities to fund its favored programs.

A top priority for the national government was to improve its funding for the military and enhance its professionalism. Beginning in the mid-1990s, Beijing gradually limited the PLA's commercial activities. In 1998 the Jiang Zeming-Zhu Rongji administration banned such activities altogether. In exchange, the government committed to steady increases in the military budget. It also promised to provide additional subsidies to compensate for the loss of the military's business profits. Before the **fiscal recentralization** in 1994, the military budget fell behind inflation, amounting to a reduction of about two percent in 1993. After 1994 the trend was immediately reversed. In that year, the Chinese government increased military spending by 5.2 percent. The upward trend continued in the following years (Duan 2017). World Bank data indicate that China's military spending shot up from about $12.4 billion in 1995 to $292 billion in 2022, second only to the United States at $877 billion.

As noted in the previous chapter, after the Hu Jintao-Wen Jiabao administration came into office in the early 2000s, the CCP dramatically improved social welfare for rural as well as urban Chinese. In rural China, the government abolished agricultural taxes and subsidized new welfare programs for the peasants, including the new rural cooperative medical scheme and a basic pension scheme. In urban areas, the government extended pension and health insurance programs from the employed to all residents and enhanced social assistance for the urban poor. These programs, covering hundreds of millions of people, were enormously costly. They were made possible only by the recently gained fiscal prowess of the Chinese state (Wong 2018)

Post-Recentralization Problems

The fiscal reform in 1994 enhanced the government's taxation capability and increased its revenue significantly, but it benefited the central government far more than the local governments. Indeed, the TSS shifted large portions of the total revenue toward the central government and seriously undermined the fiscal condition of the local governments. Moreover, whereas local governments lost important sources of revenue, their responsibilities did not diminish. Post-1994, more than fifty percent of the total budget revenue went to Beijing, while the local governments were left with seventy to eighty percent of the expenditure, such as the costs of local infrastructure development, public safety, education, social services, transportation, and healthcare. The result was a major misalignment of resources and responsibilities.

With reduced tax revenue, local governments became heavily dependent on central government fiscal transfers. Prior to the reform, the national government made transfers to provinces lagging in economic development. But under the new regime, all provincial units, including those with high levels of economic development, became recipients of central transfers. In aggregate, central transfers accounted for nearly fifty percent of the provincial expenditure (Wong 2018). This changed the power balance between the center and the regions. Compared with the earlier years of the reform era, Beijing had gained more leverage over the local governments.

Even with unprecedented central government transfers, sub-national governments were poorly equipped financially to fulfill their administrative responsibilities and deliver the public services for which they were responsible. In many regions, local governments owed wages to teachers, medical staff, and civil servants. Arrears in payments into pensions and social assistance programs were common. Some local governments even owed debt to suppliers, such as utilities companies (Bird and Wong 2005). Short of fiscal revenue, local governments shifted financial responsibilities for social programs to enterprises and public service organizations (*shiye danwei*). SOEs were forced to borrow from banks, an issue we will return to in the next section. Public service organizations, including healthcare providers and schools, resorted to charging high fees. In Chapter 7, we discussed some of the detrimental consequences for the population when hospitals engaged in profit-driven activities. Similarly, despite the compulsory education guaranteed by the constitution for all children, schools were under pressure to make money on their own to compensate for the inadequate government funding. Their dependence on student fees resulted in considerable education inequality between regions and social groups of different levels of wealth (Yang et al. 2014).

As local governments struggled to fill their ever-growing fiscal gaps, they dramatically expanded "**extra-budgetary finance**" (EBF) – financial resources secured and spent outside the budget process. This involved collecting nontax payments for various services and causes. These arbitrary fees and levies imposed unfair financial and administrative burdens on businesses, households, and individuals (Zhan 2011). In this context, the sale of land leases became an important source of funding for many local governments. Land-based local government financing in turn fueled real estate development and urbanization. As noted in Chapter 3, this phenomenon harmed the interest of the peasants, many of whom lost their land in the process without fair compensation. It also sowed the seeds of real estate and financial bubbles in China (Wong 2009; Chen 2020). Since 2020, the downturn of the housing market has arguably led to an end to the real estate bubble. The full financial consequences have yet to unfold.

Another EBF strategy used by local governments was to borrow (often illegally) from banks, pension funds, unemployment insurance funds, etc. Although local governments were prohibited by law from getting into debt, they circumvented the law by creating an array of affiliated platforms, known as local government financing vehicles (LGFVs). Set up as SOEs, the LGFVs borrowed money on behalf of the local governments and the loans they took out were implicitly guaranteed by the local governments. In this way, local governments accumulated enormous amounts of hidden debt, but as long as the economy grew at a reasonable rate, the debt remained manageable. This kind of backdoor financing was part of a "grand bargain" struck by Beijing with the localities during the 1994 fiscal reform. By granting local governments the authority to establish LGFVs and to operate local state banks, the central government gave new fund-raising tools to the latter to compensate for their loss of official fiscal power, and won their support for the reform. More importantly, these new tools gave localities inducements to continue to pursue economic growth. After all, China's economic success to date had relied heavily on local governments motivated by the financial benefits they stood to gain from the GDP growth (Liu et al. 2022).

For the next fifteen years or so, this strategy worked well. Despite the fiscal shortfalls after the 1994 reform, local economies kept expanding. But, after the global financial crisis broke out in 2008, the recession in Western countries had a negative impact on Chinese exports and economic growth. With the slower growth rate, localities found it more difficult than before to get out from under the debt they had accumulated. As of 2013 the outstanding local government debt surpassed one hundred percent of the provincial revenue in all provinces and reached as high as five hundred percent in some of the poor provinces (Liu et al. 2022, p. 41).

EBF and related practices by local governments often lacked transparency. Neither the national government nor the public could easily track the generation and expenditure of EBF revenue. In this way, EBF provided fertile ground for abuse and corruption. Local government agencies and officials often used it to extract resources from enterprises and households to enrich themselves (Zhan 2011). Furthermore, EBF subverted the government's budgeting process. It also weakened Beijing's ability to use fiscal policy to achieve other policy goals. As then Minister of Finance, Lou Jiwei, put it in 2014, "The division of responsibilities between the central and local governments is unclear and unreasonable ... These problems ... affect not only the stability and sustainability of the fiscal system itself, they also [adversely] affect the national development strategy and the effectiveness of macroeconomic policy" (quoted in Wong 2018).

Chinese policymakers grew increasingly concerned about these problems. The central government began to monitor and limit local debt and demand more transparency in local government finance. In 2011, the National Audit Bureau did its first national audit of local government debt, and in 2013 it took the same step vis-à-vis the provincial governments (Liu et al. 2022). Two decades after the watershed in 1994, Beijing launched another round of fiscal reform. In August 2014, the National People's Congress (NPC) passed a revised Budget Law. It called for more comprehensive reporting of revenue and expenditure, going beyond the traditional budget to include other components of local fiscal activities, notably EBF. Indeed, following the adoption of the new law, local governments made their public finance reporting more transparent (Wong 2018). This is not to suggest that local government manipulation of data has come to a stop. Typically, local authorities rush to comply with central directives when the top leadership shows determination to address an issue. But, as soon as the leaders' focus shifts to other pressing concerns, local fudging and shirking prevail again.

The new Budget Law also authorized provincial governments to borrow funds through issuing provincial government bonds, although it stipulated that this must be carried out under the supervision of central and the provincial people's congresses. The goal was to end the off-budget activities, including the use of LGFVs, and to bring down the high, and often hidden, local government debt. Starting in 2015, a three-year "debt-swap" program gave provincial governments the right to issue government-backed bonds, converting the debts local governments incurred by LGFVs into municipal bonds. At the same time, the central government has directed local governments to cut their ties with the LGFVs. Research shows limited success of these measures. While the debt swap has changed the form of local government debt, the debt has not gone away (Liu et al. 2022). LGFVs have continued to operate and have even grown in recent years. This is in part the result of the central government's conflicting policy goals. While central government policymakers have been eager to bring local government debt under control, they are hesitant to interfere too much with local initiatives of economic growth (Wong 2018). The economic downturn during and after the Covid-19 pandemic has further undermined Beijing's resolve to reign in the fiscal activities of the localities, making it more willing to tolerate local debt for the sake of GDP growth (Liu et al. 2022).

It is too early to know the long-term effects of the closing of the backdoor financing through LGFVs and the opening of the front door of local borrowing through bond issuance. The fundamental issue is the government's failure to realign the revenue and the expenditure of different levels of governments. So long as local governments continue to shoulder vast responsibilities with limited taxation power, it will be hard for the central government to discipline their fiscal activities effectively (Wingender 2018). The central government has made some adjustments in this regard, including leaving more tax revenue in the localities and agreeing to give localities a share of the consumption tax, which used to be a tax exclusively collected by the center. There are also proposals to introduce a city-based property tax as part of local taxes. How to balance the fiscal discipline of local governments and the fiscal autonomy for the latter to promote economic growth will remain a challenge for the policymakers in China for the foreseeable future (Liu et al. 2022).

The Financial System

In many developing countries, the lack of a sophisticated financial system constitutes a bottleneck for economic growth, equality, and stability. Organizations such as the International Monetary Fund (IMF) have actively promoted financial development in middle and low-income countries. Its financial development index examines financial institutions and financial markets (their depth, access, and efficiency) (IMF 2015). Using these criteria, it ranks most advanced economies higher than emerging economies. On a scale of 0 to 1, China ranks 0.67 in 2020, below the US at 0.91, Japan at 0.93, and most other industrialized countries, but above most developing countries (IMF n.d.).

Banks and capital markets are major players in a modern financial system. Banks take in deposits from the savers and make loans to the borrowers, providing indirect financing. Capital markets – stock and bond markets – allow the savers to invest funds in the businesses they choose, providing direct financing. A well-run financial system facilitates trade, investment, production, and consumption. It also plays a vital role in the efficient allocation of financial resources in the economy. In some countries, such as Japan and Germany, banks dominate the financial system and act as the main intermediators between investors and businesses. In other countries, most prominently the United States, stock and bond markets provide the main channels through which savings flow directly into entrepreneurial activities. China has a bank-dominated financial system. Although capital markets began to develop in China in the 1990s, banks still play a much greater role in the aggregation and dispersal of financial resources in the country. In this section, we first look at the reform of the banking sector and then discuss the evolution of the capital markets.

Reforming the Banking Sector

Soon after it came to power in 1949, the CCP nationalized all the financial institutions in the county. Under the command economy, investment, production, and consumption were all subject to government planning. The banks in China then had very different structures and functions than banks in a market economy. Structurally speaking, China had a monobank system; all the banks in the country were branches of the People's Bank of China (PBC). Functionally, they did not have a role to play in financial mediation because household savings were minuscule, and investment mainly came from the government's fiscal spending. PBC branches mainly provided trade credit and payment services to facilitate the exchange of goods. They acted as the government's cashiers.

With China's turn toward a more market-oriented economy in the late 1970s, it became imperative to reform the banking system. In the early 1980s, the Chinese government made the PBC the country's central bank. At the same time, it created specialized banks to carry out commercial banking. The Agricultural Bank of China (ABC) was established in 1979 to conduct deposit-taking and lending activities in rural China, where economic reform had proceeded ahead of the urban areas. In the same year, the State Council elevated the Bank of China (BOC) from a subordinate of PBC to a separate bank. BOC mainly dealt with foreign exchange, international payments, and overseas bond issuance. Its mission was to support China's economic opening to the outside world. The China Construction Bank (CCB) had previously been a subsidiary of the Ministry of Finance and a conduit for dispersing investment funds for construction and infrastructure-related projects. It was removed from the Ministry and made into an independent bank specializing in project financing. Later, the government established the Industrial and Commercial Bank of China (ICBC), which took over all the deposit-taking and lending functions of the PBC. These state-owned commercial banks (SOCBs) came to be known as the "Big Four."

In the following years, the division of labor among the four specialized banks gradually diminished. They began to compete with one another for the same businesses. The government encouraged such competition to increase consumer choices and bank efficiency. In addition, new commercial banks emerged outside the Big Four, including the Bank of Communications, the Shenzhen Development Bank, Everbright Bank, Huaxia Bank, and Minsheng Bank. Some of them were joint stock banks, while others were affiliated with local governments or large industrial and trade groups. Non-bank financial institutions also joined the competition, such as urban credit unions, trust and investment companies, finance companies, and securities companies. With the number of financial institutions growing, there was a dramatic increase in lending. From 1978 to 1997, the total lending grew from fifty percent of the GDP to one hundred percent (Lardy 1998, p. 76).

The expansion of banks and other financial institutions notwithstanding, the Big Four continued to dominate the banking sector. From 1986 to 1995, their share of the total financial assets decreased modestly from 71.2 percent to 61 percent (Lardy 1998, p. 80). Moreover, the behavior of these banks changed little. They took in deposits from households and made most of their loans to SOEs. Following government policy, they kept the interest rates low for both deposits and loans. It was not until 2013 and 2015 respectively that the government removed its control of lending and deposit rates. The low interest rates were a hidden tax on the savers and a significant subsidy for the SOEs.

For the first fifteen years or so of the reform era, fiscal decentralization led to declining fiscal resources for the government and weakened its capacity to use public finance to support SOEs. Increasingly, the government turned to borrowing from the banks to keep the SOEs going. Over time, the SOCBs became weighed down with bad loans as many of the borrowing SOEs were poor performers in the marketplace and could not pay back the loans. In the mid-1990s, the government established three policy banks to reduce the policy responsibilities of the Big Four and enable them to act more like profit-seeking commercial banks. The new policy banks – the China Development Bank (CDB), the Export–Import Bank of China, and the Agricultural Development Bank of China – respectively specialized in lending to key industries and development in poor areas, supporting Chinese exports, and financing rural economic projects. However, their creation did not stop the large SOEs from continuing to borrow from the SOCBs for working capital. By 1995, non-performing loans accounted for an estimated 22 percent of the total loans made by China's largest banks (Lardy 1998, p. 195).

In 1997, a major financial crisis hit Asia. Investors lost their enthusiasm and optimism about the economic potential of the region and began to pull capital out. In the summer, currency speculators attacked the Thai baht and depleted the country's official foreign-exchange reserves. As the Thai currency lost much of its value, corporations and banks in Thailand found themselves unable to keep up the payment for their foreign-currency denominated debt. This led to a serious banking crisis, a downturn in investment, and then economic and political crises. The same pattern unfolded in other parts of Asia, including the Philippines, Indonesia, and Korea, with spillover effects felt as far away as Russia and Brazil.

During the **Asian financial crisis**, China seemed to be an island of stability in the region. Most observers did not know then the Chinese financial system was in no better shape than its Asian neighbors. Indeed, the share of non-performing loans in Chinese banks' lending portfolios was even higher. China avoided a crisis for two reasons. First, it had capital controls, which prevented capital from leaving the country freely, even if investors lost confidence in the local economy. Second, China was in a relatively strong balance of payments position with a robust current account surplus (greater exports than imports); its foreign-exchange reserve was $140 billion, second only to Japan's. But the crisis in the region served as a wake-up call to Chinese policymakers about the importance and fragility of financial stability. They began to speak of financial security as part of national security and were determined to make serious changes to protect it (Wang 1999).

In the short term, the government focused on rescuing the Big Four. In 1998 the Ministry of Finance injected RMB 270 billion ($32.6 billion) to recapitalize the banks. In 1999, the Chinese government created four asset-management companies to purchase the non-performing loans of each of them. Meanwhile, policymakers took steps to reform the banks to prevent the same problem from happening in the future. In 2003 they created a quasi-state-owned private equity fund, Central Huijin, to provide further help with recapitalizing the SOCBs and, more importantly, to restructure the banks as well as non-bank financial institutions. Funded by China's large foreign-exchange reserves, Central Huijin became a significant shareholder across the entire financial system. Exercising the Party state's ownership control of the SOCBs, it has played a central role in hardening the budget constraints of the banks, making their managers personally responsible for the quality of their loans, laying off redundant staff, closing unnecessary branches, and upgrading the banks' information technology. These measures were also aimed at making Chinese banks more competitive against foreign banks after China's anticipated accession to the WTO (Liu 2023).

In time, Central Huijin turned SOCBs into joint stock corporations. They sold strategic stakes to international investors and then went public on domestic and international stock markets. The listing of the big banks not only sought to generate significant amounts of new capital, but it also aimed to improve their corporate governance by subjecting them to international banking standards, disclosure requirements, and governance mandates. Going public also injected non-state equity investment in the SOCBs, partially privatizing these banks. Nevertheless, the Chinese government retained majority equity ownership in all of them. Researchers argue that this model has worked out well. The combination of the majority ownership retained by the state and a diverse investor base through public listing has struck a good balance between effective monitoring of the banks and improving their competitiveness in the marketplace. Large Chinese banks as a group outperformed their counterparts from other emerging and developed markets before and during the global financial crisis in terms of returns on assets and returns on equity (Allen et al. 2014).

At one level, the banking sector reform has been remarkably successful. The Big Four have become much more business-savvy than they once were. They have grown in assets and profitability. As of the end of 2022, ICBC, CCB, ABC, and BOC were the world's largest banks by assets (S&P Global 2023). New financial institutions, such as city banks and non-bank financial institutions, have also grown considerably in China, making the entire financial system more diverse and sophisticated. However, the reform of the Chinese banking sector has only brought limited liberalization. One indicator is how closed it remains to international competitors. At the end of 2021, foreign banks had a combined market share of 1.4 percent in China, falling below the peak of 2.3 percent in 2007 (Fitch 2022). Moreover, most Chinese banks continue to be tied to the government and subject to governmental influence. While the policy banks explicitly carry out the state's priorities, the commercial banks – under different degrees of government control – also tend to serve borrowers and projects favored by government authorities. As discussed in Chapter 5, this means China's most efficient private enterprises have chronically been subject to discrimination in accessing banking services. In that way, the financial system still hinders the overall development of the economy.

Capital Market Development

As early as the 1920s, Shanghai developed an active capital market, which ranked as a leader in East Asia. However, its operations were seriously interrupted by wars and political instability in the 1930s and 1940s. After the CCP took power in China in the late 1940s, the market disappeared altogether and only came back more than four decades later. As part of the economic reform process, Chinese government approved the creation of two stock exchanges

– the Shanghai Stock Exchange (SSE) launched in 1990 and the Shenzhen Stock Exchange (SZSE), in 1991. The SSE, located in the financial center of Pudong New District of Shanghai, is the largest stock market in mainland China by market capitalization and trading volume. The SZSE, located in the southern city of Shenzhen, a former special economic zone adjacent to Hong Kong, is known for supporting small and medium enterprises and high-tech companies. SSE began with eight listings and SZSE with six (Hu et al. 2018, p. 7). Both exchanges have grown steadily since then. By 2023 SSE had 2,263 listings whereas SZSE had 2,844 (Xinhua 2024). Because SZSE is home to many smaller companies, its capitalization is below that of SSE, even though it has more listings. In late 2021, a third exchange was established in Beijing. The Beijing Stock Exchange primarily serves small and medium-sized enterprises in China. It opened with 81 companies listed and expanded to 239 in 2023 (Xinhua 2024).

A major goal of these stock exchanges is to mobilize capital from domestic and foreign investors. Chinese companies issue A-shares quoted in RMB largely for domestic investors to acquire equities, and B shares quoted in foreign currencies mainly for foreign investors (or domestic investors using US and Hong Kong dollars to settle). In 2014 and 2016, the government created Shanghai-Hong Kong Stock Connect and Shenzhen-Hong Kong Stock Connect to facilitate the flow of capital from Hong Kong to mainland China as well as to allow qualified Chinese investors to access eligible Hong Kong shares. In terms of total market capitalization, the A-share market became the second largest in the world in 2020, only smaller than the US equity markets (Allen et al. 2024).

Companies must meet complicated and stringent requirements for listing shares to raise capital, such as their length of operations, value of assets, revenue, cash flows, and profits. But meeting these requirements is not sufficient for going public. From the 1990s through the 2010s, all the initial public offerings (IPOs) on Chinese stock exchanges had to be approved by the China Securities Regulatory Commission (CSRC), the main government regulator of the securities industry. Created in 1992, CSRC – subordinate to the State Council – has the authority to implement a centralized and unified regulatory system to ensure the lawful operations of the securities market. It has the duty and the power to investigate suspicious activities and impose penalties on illegal activities related to stock and futures markets. In 2023 CSRC announced that a new registration-based system for IPOs would replace the former approval-based system in the country's major stock exchanges. This reform promises to decentralize the control of access to individual stock exchanges, streamline the IPO process, and make the listing procedure more transparent. However, implementing the change could take a long time. In any case, this reform is unlikely to weaken the government's influence on what types of companies can enter the capital market.

Research shows that companies with the right political connections have had better chances of being approved for IPOs and they are significantly more likely to receive preferential treatment, such as higher offering price-to-earnings ratio. In addition, well-connected companies are much less likely to be selected for pre-IPO on-site auditing (Li and Zhou 2015). These patterns are likely to continue, despite the change in the formal rules for IPOs. Due to the obstacles in the domestic market, among other reasons, a large number of Chinese firms have gone outside mainland China. Many have been listed in the Hong Kong exchange (HKEX), which follows regulations similar to those in the US and is open to global investors. The second most popular external IPO destination for Chinese firms is the United States (Allen et al. 2024). However, in 2020, following accusations of accounting fraud by the US-listed Chinese company, Luckin Coffee, many major Chinese companies were delisted from the US capital market. The trend has been somewhat reversed. As of early 2024 there are 265 Chinese companies listed on American stock exchanges with a total market capitalization of $848 billion (United States–China Economic and Security Review Commission 2024).

Thus far, China's stock exchanges have primarily served SOEs and mixed ownership companies controlled by the state. A study in 2018 shows that state-controlled companies accounted for 31 percent of the A-shares companies, but they made up 61 percent of the market capitalization and 71 percent of the total revenue (Rosen et al. 2018). They have taken up much of the capital raised in the stock exchanges even though they are less productive than private enterprises. Not surprisingly, the business performance of the listed companies has been abysmal. One study shows that from 1993 to 2016 the growth rate of large company stock portfolio barely beat inflation (Hu et al. 2018). Another study finds that from 2000–2018 A-share firms performed less well than a large set of listed firms from both developed and developing countries by fifteen percent annually. In fact, the cumulative returns of the A-share market were lower than five-year bank deposits or three- and five-year government bonds in China. In real terms, investors in the domestic stock market earned essentially zero net return (Allen et al. 2024).

Overall, China's stock market is relatively insignificant as a source of capital for companies, which rely heavily on bank loans and retained earnings. As of the end of 2018, loans accounted for 54.2 percent of the financial liabilities in the nonfinancial corporate sector, higher than the euro area (27.4 percent) and Japan (24.6 percent), and much higher than the US (4.9 percent). The other side of the coin is that the share of equities and other assets for Chinese companies were much lower than other major economies, with corporate equities at nineteen percent, compared with 55.5 percent in the euro zone, 54.9 percent in Japan, and 68.8 percent in the US (Kwan 2022).

Besides generating investment, another potentially important role of the capita market is to diversify ownership of the SOEs and help improve their corporate governance. Corporate governance refers to the rules and mechanisms by which corporations are directed and controlled. It aims to address the principal-agent problem between the owners of a company and its management to ensure those who run the company serve the interests of the owners – maximizing profits and increasing share values. In theory, the stock market brings outside investors who can act as watchdogs of corporate performance and exert pressure on the companies to discipline or replace incompetent management.

Indeed, Chinese policymakers sought to use the stock market as an instrument to facilitate SOE reform in the 1990s and early 2000s (Howie and Walter 2011). Similar to the partial privatization of SOCBs discussed above, many large SOEs have become joint-stock companies and sold shares on the stock market. But in contrast to the success of SOCBs listed on overseas stock markets, most of the companies listed on China's own stock exchanges have not shown significant improvement in corporate governance. One reason is that the state typically retains controlling stakes in the listed companies and the Chinese stock exchanges lack transparency. Ordinary investors, as minority shareholders, have limited access to information and almost no influence on their operations (Howie and Walter 2011). More importantly, many of the companies listed on the stock exchanges are subsidiaries of large SOE groups, where leaders at the group level are the ultimate decision-makers for the entire group. The public knows little about the priorities and operations of the unlisted parts of the enterprise groups and have no leverage over their group level decision-making (Rosen et al. 2018).

Furthermore, in the last decade the CCP has enhanced its influence on all types of enterprises and institutionalized its dominant role in corporate governance in state-controlled companies. The personnel of company boards and Party organizations overlap significantly. Party groups and Party committees in the companies are more deeply involved in business decision-making than earlier in the reform period (Beck and Brødsgaard 2022). According to a study in 2018, thirty percent of the companies publicly traded in Shanghai and Shenzhen amended their corporate charters between 2015 and 2018 to formalize the long-standing practice of Party committees discussing "major decisions" before they go to boards of directors (Lin and Milhaupt 2020). In addition, stock market listing has not prevented state-controlled companies from subordinating the pursuit of profits and shareholder value to the Party state's priorities of industrial policy to social stability.

The poor corporate governance of listed companies has been a major disincentive for foreign participation in Chinese stock exchanges. Since 2018, Chinese A-shares have been incorporated in the MSCI Emerging Market Index, a benchmark for the equity market performance of emerging economies used by many financial institutions in the world to provide risk diversification to institutional portfolios. By 2020, China constituted approximately forty percent of the index, but its share in the emerging market equity portfolios was less than thirty percent (Cortina et al. 2023). A major concern of international investors is how the Chinese Party state affects the way Chinese companies are governed. A report in 2018 finds that of the Chinese companies included in the MSCI emerging markets index, 65 percent were ultimately controlled by the state (Rosen et al. 2018). In 2024, MSCI removed nearly 200 Chinese stocks, forcing index-tracking funds to sell off investments in Chinese companies and shifting funds to other emerging economies (Lingat 2024).

A notable characteristic of the Chinese stock market is its high volatility. In China's political environment, investors understand that companies' fortunes are closely related to government policies. Their sentiment swings between optimism and pessimism, based on their expectations of policy change, which results in sharp fluctuations on the stock market. A telling sign of the key role played by government policies is the highly correlated movement of individual stocks with one another, regardless of their specific circumstances.

Another feature of the stock exchanges in China has been the high turnover rate of stocks. Unlike mature capital markets, the Chinese stock market does not have many "patient" investors, i.e. institutional investors which hold stocks over the long term. The majority of the participants in the stock exchanges are small and medium-sized investors, including individuals, non-financial firms, security firms, and insurance companies. They behave more like hedge funds than mutual funds (Hu et al. 2018; Naughton 2018).

Perhaps the most salient difference between the Chinese stock market and their counterparts in market economies lies in the readiness of the government to intervene in the market when doing so suits its political needs. In the last decade, the Party state went beyond its routine control of the stock market on several occasions when the performance of the stocks fell dramatically over a short period of time. On each occasion, it took dramatic measures to stem the bleeding in the market to prevent a financial crisis that could threaten the overall economy (see Box 8.2). In the short run, state intervention has had the desired stabilizing effect but, in the long run, such political expediency has undermined the credibility of the regulatory regime of the Chinese capital markets, as well as investors' confidence in the direction of China's financial reform (Li et al. 2022).

Besides stock markets, bond markets are another component of a modern capital market. In fact, in developed economies, bond markets tend to be larger than stock markets. Government and corporate bonds often exceed the country's GDP. In China, the CCP government issued sovereign bonds in 1954, but from the late 1950s to the early 1980s the bond market was totally suspended. In 1983 the bond market returned with the issuance of the first enterprise bond by an SOE. Since then, the bond market has grown dramatically in size. The total debt securities outstanding shot up from $3.1 trillion in 2010 to $20.9 trillion in 2023. China's bond market ranks the second largest

Box 8.2 The Stock Market and the "National Team"

Around 2012, after a prolonged bear market, the Chinese government was eager to rally the country's financial resources to support "mass innovation" and "mass entrepreneurship." It encouraged new actors to enter the capital markets and expanded ways for investors to raise funds, including shadow borrowing from various unconventional sources. From 2012 to 2015 the SSE and SZSE experienced a continuous boom. In time, CSRC began to worry about the risks of a financial bubble. It tightened regulations over margin lending (borrowing money to invest using existing shares, managed funds and/or cash as security). This triggered a market crash as SSE and SZSE dropped more than forty percent in a few days in June 2015.

In response to this crisis, CSRC stopped all IPOs and secondary market fundraising. It prohibited key shareholders, board directors, and senior management of all listed companies from selling their shares for six months. The government mobilized a total of 21 major securities firms to invest fifteen percent of their net assets (about RMB 120 billion) in buying stocks and to commit not to reduce their trading positions until the stock market index returned to a given level. In addition, CSRC used its subsidiary, China Securities Finance Corporation (CSF), to directly coordinate liquidity injection into the market. With the support from the Chinese government, CSF raised RMB 2 trillion from various financing channels, including capital injection, issuance of short-term notes, funds committed by the 21 major securities firms mentioned above, and credit from the Chinese central bank as well as SOCBs. Toward the end of the year, the market began to stabilize. In November, CSRC allowed IPOs again, but tightened the regulation of margin-financing (Li et al. 2022).

The state-affiliated financial institutions that worked together around CSRC and CSF came to be known as the "National Team." After playing a major role in calming the stock market in 2015, the National Team stepped in again when stocks fell sharply in 2018 due to the trade war between China and the United States. The same pattern repeated itself in 2020, when the Covid-19 pandemic pushed down the stock market. (Rothko Investment Strategy 2020)

in the world, surpassed only by the US bond market of $51.3 trillion (World Economic Forum 2023). The variety of debt issuance has also expanded, offering a range of products including government and quasi-government bonds, credit bonds, financial bonds issued by financial institutions, Treasury futures, green bonds, and asset-backed securities (Schipke et al. 2019).

The public sector dominates the bond market in China. An IMF report in 2019 indicates that until then more than sixty percent of the bonds were sovereign, policy bank, and local government bonds, or bonds issued by government-affiliated organizations (Schipke et al. 2019). More recent data collected by the Asian Bond Monitor of the Asian Development Bank show that from 2021 to 2024, government bonds accounted for 64 to 66 percent of the total bond market in China. For instance, at the end of 2023 the total amount of local currency bonds outstanding in China was RMB 140.363 trillion, of which RMB 92.981 trillion were government bonds and RMB 47.367 trillion were corporate bonds. The latter include bonds issued by SOEs, private companies, and financial institutions (AsianBondOnline n.d.). As noted earlier in this chapter, local governments faced with growing fiscal problems have turned to borrowing to fill the fiscal gap. In 2023, local government bond issuances amounted to RMB 9.3 trillion, not far behind Treasury bond issuances of RMB 11 trillion (Xinhua 2024).

The Chinese bond market is made up of two components – the interbank market, which resembles the interbank market in developed economies, and the exchange market, which is part of the SSE and SZSE. The interbank market is by far the more important of the two, accounting for about ninety percent of bond financing (Schipke et al. 2019). The government sells bonds mainly to commercial banks through the interbank market; the banks are required to buy these bonds and typically hold them to maturity. On the other hand, corporate bonds and some enterprise bonds are traded on the SSE and SZSE, where the investors are relatively small and the turnover is relatively high.

Many government agencies participate in the regulation of China's capital market, with the CSRC playing a central role in regulating the stock exchanges. How effective is it in enforcing regulations and protecting investors' interests? The evidence is mixed. One study finds that firms targeted by the CSRC's enforcement actions suffer wealth losses of around one or two percent in the five days surrounding the event. In addition, the firms in question have a greater rate of auditor change, a much higher incidence of qualified audit opinions, increased CEO turnover, and wider bid–ask spreads. These negative consequences for the firms suggest that the actions of the CSRC have teeth (Chen et al. 2005). In contrast, according to another study, the CSRC has not investigated many insider trading cases and there are few convictions for insider trading offences in China. It argues that the CSRC has not been able to enforce the regulations strictly because most insider trading cases involve high-ranking government and Party officials and the CSRC does not have the power to impose discipline and penalties on these powerful actors (Cheng 2008).

To summarize: China's financial development during the reform era has created a large number of financial institutions and led to enormous growth of financial assets. China is home to the world's largest banks, and it now has the world's second largest capital market in terms of total market capitalization. However, the operation of the financial system remains under heavy state control. The big banks and the stock markets channel large volumes of savings cheaply to the inefficient SOEs. In this process, they deprive hundreds of millions of individual depositors and investors of a fair chance to grow their wealth. In addition, dynamic private enterprises have limited access to capital, either through banking or the issuance of stocks and bonds. Such a system has been a major contributor to the persistent misallocation of financial resources in Chinese economy. Moreover, neither the banks nor the non-state shareholders have provided effective oversight of enterprises and corporations and have largely failed to fulfill their function in improving corporate governance.

Financial Instruments of the Developmental State

The Chinese Party state dominates the country's economy in two major ways. On the one hand, it does so through its ownership of large SOEs in the so-called "lifeline industries" (*mingmai chanye*). On the other hand, the Chinese government uses similar policy instruments as Japan and the newly industrialized economies of Taiwan and Korea to guide national economic development. In Chapter 4 we examined the important role of the state sector in the Chinese economy. In this section, we turn our attention to the government's use of developmental policies, also known as industrial policies. Such policies often involve market-defying practices to promote selected industries and companies, including trade protection, special licenses, government funded research consortia, and favorable tax policies. But the most important are financial subsidies.

A developmental state typically directs financial institutions to channel financial resources to sectors and enterprises which are too risky for private capital and thus unlikely to develop on their own, but which have significant positive spillover effects for the national economy. For instance, in the aftermath of the Korean War (1950–1953), South Korea was devastated and impoverished. It had no comparative advantage in the development of capital-intensive industries. However, when military strongman Park Chung-hee took over the country in 1961, he and his advisors adopted policies to encourage the development of capital-intensive industries which they believed were essential for national security and for long-term national economic development. Financial policy played a major role in their strategy. Under state guidance, 57.9 percent of Korea's total bank loans between 1962 and 1985 were policy loans in support of heavy and chemical industries (Chang, 1993, p. 141). The Korean government was also keen to cultivate large business groups, known as chaebols, making them national champions that could compete on the world stage. By the end of 1981, among a total of 298 types of state-controlled bank loans, 221 were policy loans extended to the chaebols (Woo, 1991, p. 12).

A similar story unfolded in Taiwan around the same period. After its defeat by the CCP on the Chinese mainland in the late 1940s, the Kuomintang (KMT) retreated to the island of Taiwan. During the 1950s, the KMT government took control of all the banks through the Bank of Taiwan. It mobilized the banks' resources to support its import substitution industrialization strategy, which sought to replace foreign imports with domestic production and thus build up local industrial capacity. When giving generous financial support to large firms and SOEs, policymakers focused their attention on augmenting investment and directing its composition, much more than on increasing the efficiency of resource use (Wade 1990). This strategy was a key factor in Taiwan's economic miracle.

As noted above, the financial system of contemporary China is dominated by the banking sector and the state has majority ownership of the largest banks. These banks have benefited from China's extraordinarily high domestic savings, which, according to the World Bank, have ranged from 36 to 51 percent of the GDP since 1990, much higher than the world average of 23 to 28 percent of GDP in this time period. They take in large amounts of savings from society at low costs and channel them to industries and enterprises favored by the government. Through its influence over the banks, the government has been able to sustain large SOEs in industries crucial to national security (e.g. energy), economic upgrading (e.g. high-tech industries), and state revenue (e.g. telecom). Aside from the banks, the Chinese state has full control of the stock and bond markets. The government has routinely used these capital markets to provide its favored industries and companies with financial resources (Baek 2005).

Through its control of the financial system, the Chinese state has been able to implement industrial policies designed to promote selected industries considered to be strategically important and, more broadly, national economic growth. In defying the market logic, it has accelerated the growth of sectors ranging from shipbuilding to aircraft manufacturing, from conventional automobiles to electrical vehicles, and from semi-conductors to solar panels. Take shipbuilding as an example, In the early 2000s, China's shipbuilding industry contributed to less than ten percent of global production. The Chinese government designated it as a pillar industry in the eleventh and the twelfth five-year plans (2006–2010 and 2011–2015). Policy lending to this industry amounted to RMB 550 billion from 2006 to 2013, including RMB 330 billion devoted to entry subsidies, RMB 159 billion to production subsidies, and RMB 51 billion to investment subsidies. In a few years, China overtook Japan and Korea and became the world's leading shipbuilder, measured in output (Barwick et al. 2019).

Another example comes from the energy sector. In 2005 the NPC passed the Renewable Energy Law, giving clear legislative support for the development of renewable energy. Since the eleventh five-year plan, the government has made the development of renewable energy a priority, out of concern about energy security and the environment. Because developing renewable energy is costly and risky, especially in the early stages, the Chinese government has used massive subsidies to jump-start the industry (Chen and Lees 2016). As of 2015, the policy bank CDB had over RMB 1.5 trillion in outstanding loans to green energy projects. In 2015 alone, it provided RMB 137.1 billion in green project financing. Meanwhile, commercial banks had extended more than RMB 8 trillion in total outstanding loans to green energy firms. In addition, green energy companies have raised large amounts of funding from Chinese capital markets in recent years (Ji and Zhang 2019). Today, China stands at the forefront of the production of several forms of renewable energy – hydro, wind, solar, and biomass.

China has been a manufacturing powerhouse since the 1990s. However, Chinese leaders have been increasingly unsatisfied with the low level of sophistication of Chinese manufactured products. They are concerned that China is stuck in the so-called "middle-income trap" like many developing countries which achieved middle income decades ago but have not been able to join the ranks of rich countries. Their progress has been hampered by wage increase and reduced competitiveness in standardized, labor-intensive manu-facturing. The lack of technological innovation has limited their ability to transition to higher value-added activities. In 2015, the Chinese State Council launched a program dubbed **"Made in China 2025"** (MIC 2025), which sought to upgrade China's manufacturing capabilities by encouraging local innova-tion, especially in high-tech sectors (see Box 8.3).

The Chinese developmental state has much in common with other East Asian development states, but it also has its own characteristics. One example is the innovative method it uses for raising development funds. CDB, a policy bank that has become the world's largest development bank, provides an illustration. Although CDB has mostly invested in long-term and large-scale public projects, it has not been funded by fiscal revenue or state-subsidized funds. Instead, it raises most of its funds from China's capital markets through bond issuance. What makes it possible for CDB to do so cheaply and thus to lend cheaply is the state's credit guarantee for CDB bonds, which gives CDB bonds a credit level equal to government bonds (Chen 2020).

In another example, the Chinese state has created hundreds of sharehold-ing firms owned by different levels of the government. They invest broadly in the economy, including the private sector, to facilitate the development and upgrading of certain types of industries. For instance, part of MIC 2025 has been the establishment of "government industrial guidance funds" in strate-gic sectors, including semiconductors, artificial intelligence, electric vehicles, and others. These funds are provided by the state but matched by private investment and managed by private capital management companies. This has provided the state with a new way to deploy its control of capital to guide the direction of economic development. While it serves the state's purposes, it

Box 8.3 Made in China 2025

MIC 2025 is an industrial policy aiming to make China a global leader in high-tech manufacturing. The government uses state guidance and funding to promote advances in sectors such as information technology, automated machine tools and robotics, aircraft and aeronautical equipment, maritime vessels and marine engineering equipment, advanced rail equipment, new energy vehicles, electrical generation and transmission equipment, agricultural machinery and equipment, new materials, and pharmaceuticals and medical devices. Since its launch, the program has been a lightning rod. Critics in the West, especially in the United States, argue that MIC 2025 is a statist project that violates market principles and discriminates against foreign investment. They accuse China of questionable means to acquire advanced technology, including forced technology transfers, theft of intellectual property, and cyber espionage. American policymakers also worry that Chinese development of high-tech manufacturing, much of which could be used for military as well as civilian purposes, would pose a serious threat to the national security of the United States and its allies. In the last few years, the Chinese government has toned down the rhetoric of MIC 2025, but it has continued to pursue the goals embodied in the program. Meanwhile, the US government under both the Trump and the Biden administrations has imposed trade sanctions, investment restrictions, and technology export control to address American concerns.

has, however, the typical problems of public funding, including moral hazard, corruption and resource misallocation. In addition, the involvement of the Party state has caused alarm and suspicions among other governments about the intention of Chinese companies (Chen and Rithmire 2020). This is likely to hinder their participation in foreign investment and international technology transfer.

A striking feature of the Chinese developmental state is the deep involvement of local governments. Instead of having one national government implementing its industrial policy, China has thousands of local governments each seeking to promote their own goals and priorities. After the tax reform in 1994 led to serious fiscal shortfalls, local officials have turned to the development of real estate and the use of LGFVs to generate revenue. They build industrial parks, invest in infrastructure, and offer tax breaks to attract developers and manufacturing companies. Many local governments have been able to expand their coffers and compensate for the revenue losses due to the fiscal recentralization. However, just as many of them have not fared well. They have borrowed trillions of dollars from the banks to develop the local economy. But miscalculations, corruption, and other problems have hindered their ability to pay back the loans. As a result, they have accumulated large volumes of debt, leaving a time bomb that could explode at any time (Su and Tao 2017; Liu et al. 2022). The investment bank, Goldman Sachs, estimated that as of the end of 2022, official local government debt reached RMB 94 trillion. According to the *Financial Times*, the debt of two-thirds of local Chinese governments exceeds the global benchmark (Cheng and Lin 2023).

Conclusion

The focus of this chapter has been the evolution of China's fiscal and financial systems. The fiscal system has seen centralization, decentralization, and recentralization through the decades, as the Chinese state seeks to balance fiscal discipline and incentives for local economic agents. In the early years of the reform era, the decentralization of fiscal authority and revenue gave rise to tremendous economic development momentum in many regions, but seriously weakened the power of the national government. Later, fiscal recentralization strengthened Beijing's control of public finance and capacity to implement its policy priorities, including increasing national defense spending and improving the welfare system. However, the new fiscal system created serious mismatches of resources and mandates, leaving the local governments struggling with debt and worsening the problem of EBF.

China's financial system has come a long way since the monobank system of the Maoist era. Chinese banks and capital markets rank among the largest in the world, but there are major inefficiencies in the distribution of financial resources. Most notably, the power of the state and its interest in supporting the state sector have undermined the private sector's access to formal financing. By depriving private entrepreneurs of much-needed financial resources, the Chinese financial system dampens their dynamism and productivity, which in turn hinders national economic development. In addition, state control of the financial institutions has rendered them ineffective as mechanisms for improving corporate governance.

The financial system has been a vital part of China's industrial policy. The Party state has been quite skillful in using both fiscal and financial instruments to achieve its development goals. China's success in developing strategic industries such as shipbuilding and green energy owes much to state-guided investments. However, the developmental state is not always effective. While it may have a critical role to play in the catching up phase of economic development, state intervention may become counterproductive later on. The CCP's heavy-handed intervention in the banks and the capital markets has prolonged misallocation of financial resources. It has also made it difficult for Chinese companies to participate in the global economy in an era of intensified geopolitical competition, as their ties to the Chinese government often lead to suspicions that they are not genuine commercial actors but servants of the Party state.

Questions for Discussion

1. How has the Chinese fiscal system shaped local government behavior in the reform era?

2. Are China's state-owned banks commercial actors or instruments of the government?

3. How do Chinese stock markets differ from their counterparts in Western countries?

9

Macroeconomic Policy

In market economies, governments use macroeconomic policy to avoid rapid and excessive changes in prices, economic output, and employment. Macroeconomic stability is essential for producers, investors, and consumers to formulate expectations and carry out their economic activities rationally and efficiently. In the long run, this is conducive to fostering strong and sustainable economic growth.

The main tools of macroeconomic policy are fiscal policy and monetary policy, although to a lesser extent exchange rate policy can also serve macroeconomic management. During periods of economic expansion, the demand for capital, goods, and services tends to outstrip their supply, leading to rapid price increases. The government can counter the risk of runaway inflation by tightening fiscal policy (e.g. increasing taxes) and monetary policy (e.g. increasing interest rates), thus discouraging investment and spending. It can also let the value of the country's currency appreciate to reduce the price for imports. In times of economic slowdown or recession, the government can adopt the opposite macroeconomic policies. It can increase government spending (fiscal policy), lower interest rates (monetary policy), and devalue the home currency (exchange policy) to stimulate investment, consumption, and exports.

While all three types of policies are useful, monetary policy has been by far the most important instrument of macroeconomic management since the 1980s. In this context, the central bank has been a key actor. When the economy overheats, the central bank typically raises interest rates and reserve requirements (the amount of cash that banks must keep in their vaults or deposit at the central bank as a portion of the deposits they have from their customers), thus reducing the money supply and containing inflation. When the economy is sluggish, the central bank usually lowers interest rates and reserve requirements, increasing the supply of money and encouraging investment and consumption.

In the first section of this chapter, we examine China's macroeconomic management during the reform era. By and large, the government has maintained a remarkable level of stability. In this process, the People's Bank of China (PBC), the Chinese central bank, has played a crucial role. The next section traces the evolution of the PBC and analyzes how it has become the effective manager of monetary policy. The final section discusses the economic imbalance in China, which the government has acknowledged since the early 2000s, and the challenges for economic rebalancing.

Macroeconomic Management

The Chinese government is relatively new to macroeconomic management. During the Maoist era, the government determined production targets for goods and services and regulated their prices; there was no risk of inflation or deflation. It also guaranteed full employment for all (despite hidden unemployment or underemployment). There was no need for a macroeconomic policy to balance price stability and employment. With the onset of economic liberalization in the late 1970s, market mechanisms began to play an increasingly important role in the allocation of resources. The demand and supply for goods and services rose and fell, and prices fluctuated accordingly. Periods of high investment and consumption often saw growing inflation, whereas periods of economic slowdown were characterized by shrinking production and increasing unemployment. Chinese policymakers had to learn to manage the ups and downs of business cycles that they previously attributed exclusively to capitalist societies.

China's economic reform was incremental. In the early years, even as various components of the economy became gradually liberalized, the legacy of a command economy remained strong. In macroeconomic management, Chinese government used a combination of direct administrative control and indirect market-based levers. In the twenty-first century, the use of indirect levers has become more mature and institutionalized, especially in the realm of monetary policies. However, administrative intervention has not disappeared. In fact, it often comes back strongly during times of crises, as we will discuss later in the chapter.

Since the 1980s, China has undergone about a dozen macroeconomic cycles (Figure 9.1). In the beginning, price fluctuation was quite dramatic, forming a **boom-and-bust** pattern. During the boom period, investment rose quickly, supported by expansionary fiscal and monetary policies. Rapid economic growth was followed by a sharp rise in inflation. The government then tightened its macroeconomic policies, curbing investment and restricting back lending. Often inflation persisted, so more tightening ensued. Finally, inflation subsided while the economy slowed down. In response to the bust, the government turned to expansionary macroeconomic policies, enabling another round of economic growth led by increases in investment. A brief examination of some of the cycles illustrates the evolving mechanisms and effectiveness of China's macroeconomic management.

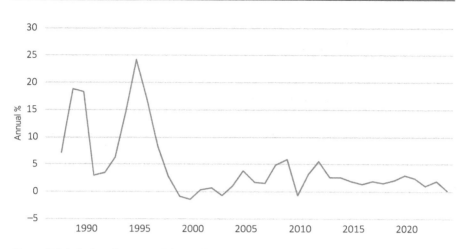

Figure 9.1 Inflation, Consumer Prices 1987–2023
Source: World Bank Group.

Early Boom-and-Bust Cycles

From the late 1970s to the late 1990s, Chinese economy underwent four rounds of expansion and contraction (Khor and Fetherston 1991; Yusuf 1994). In round one, economic liberalization in 1978 quickly led to a period of economic expansion accompanied by inflation. The government reacted by restricting credit quantity, raising interest rates, forcing sales of treasury bonds, and vetting investment projects more stringently. The result was shrinking investment, declining inflation and an economic slowdown by 1981. Round two started with the launch of urban enterprise reform in 1984. With rising wages and bonuses came increased aggregate demand and inflation. Beijing stiffened its control of foreign exchange and credit supply, and it raised both the interest rates and the reserve requirements on banks. These measures brought inflation down by 1986. In the third round, further enterprises reform and price liberalization led to a sharp rise in inflation in 1987 and 1988. In the face of public anger and political instability, including the Tiananmen movement in mid-1989, Chinese policymakers halted the reform initiatives and adopted a program of "rectification" in late 1989 (see Box 9.1). They drastically cut back state investment and tightened monetary policy. These measures successfully reined in price increases, but also dampened economic growth. According to the World Bank, China's GDP growth dropped to a mere 3.9 percent in 1990, the lowest since 1978.

The fourth round of the boom-and-bust cycles began in 1992, when Deng Xiaoping's famous southern tour reignited economic reform and pulled the country out of the post-Tiananmen doldrums. Investment – especially in real estate – grew rapidly, by 93.5 percent in 1992 and 124.9 percent in 1993. The frantic economic expansion pushed inflation up to 14.7 percent in 1993. Vice

> ### Box 9.1 Inflation and Political Instability
>
> In contemporary China, perhaps more than in most countries, inflation is not only an economic problem but also a highly sensitive political issue. A historical perspective helps shed light on this phenomenon. In the 1930s and the 1940s, Japan's invasion of China and the poor management of the economy by the Kuomintang (KMT) government led to chronic inflation and – at times – hyperinflation. The economic hardship it inflicted upon ordinary people led to growing social discontent. In the late 1940s, runaway inflation turned out to be a major contributor to the collapse of the KMT regime and the triumph of the Chinese Communist Party (CCP). In the 1950s, the new communist government quickly succeeded in stabilizing prices and, in doing so, solidified popular support for the new regime. Ever since then, in the minds of Chinese policymakers, inflation has been associated with political trouble. Indeed, double-digit inflation was an important factor underlying the political turmoil in 1989. With the official consumer price index (CPI) increasing by thirty percent in Beijing between 1987 and 1988, ordinary people were concerned that they could no longer afford staple goods (Vogel 2011, 600–601). When the students took to the street to demand greater freedom and democracy, many workers and other citizens joined them primarily driven by their grievances about inflation, corruption, and an erosion of their economic welfare. (Walder and Gong 1993)

Premier Zhu Rongji, who was also Governor of PBC, China's recently established central bank, led a series of measures to restrict credit and investment. They included withdrawing unauthorized loans, raising interest rates, and imposing administrative guidelines against excessive real estate development. Zhu threatened to fire local officials if they failed to follow the order of reducing local bank lending. Inflation came down quickly (Yu 2015).

As Figure 9.1 shows, the early macroeconomic cycles were more volatile compared with the later cycles. This was largely due to the government's lack of refined and effective policy tools during this period of economic transition. Despite incremental steps toward marketization, the government continued to rely mainly on the traditional method of quantitative credit control. The State Council, in coordination with the State Planning Commission, made credit plans as part of the overall economic planning process. This meant PBC did not have the ability to adjust its credit policy according to the changing economic circumstances. In a market economy, producers and consumers respond to changes in the cost of borrowing. The adjustment of interest rates is an important monetary policy instrument. But, for many economic actors in China's partially reformed economy, this was not a consideration. State-owned enterprises (SOEs) had access to cheap credit. Moreover, with only "soft budget constraints," they could count on the guaranteed financial support from the government. The cost of borrowing did not feature in their decisions about investment and production (Yusuf 1994; Brandt and Zhu 2001). The rigidity of the credit plans and the irrelevance of interest rates greatly limited the government's ability to finetune its macroeconomic management.

The Maturation of Macroeconomic Management

In the late 1990s, China's economic reform entered a new stage. Two changes were especially consequential for macroeconomic management. On the one hand, the state sector was transformed. The policy of "grasping the big and letting go the small" freed the government from years of expensive subsidies of the money-losing SOEs. On the other hand, the significant expansion of the non-state sector meant a larger portion of economic actors were now responsive to indirect macroeconomic levers, such as interest rates and exchange rates. When PBC changed its benchmark lending and deposit rates, it could influence the financial costs of enterprises and, to a certain degree, household saving behavior. The adjustment of exchange rates could affect the fortunes of enterprises engaged in international trade and investment. In addition, as discussed in Chapter 8, a modern financial system had taken shape in China around that time. The reform of the banks and the creation of capital markets provided new indirect levers for the government to use to influence the macroeconomic situation.

When the Asian financial crisis (AFC) struck in 1997, China managed to avoid the economic collapse of many of its neighbors. But the turmoil in the region had a serious negative impact on China's exports and foreign investment inflow. In response, policymakers in Beijing introduced countercyclical monetary and fiscal policies. PBC cut the reserve requirement ratio and reduced its benchmark interest rates multiple times. After some hesitation, the government also intervened with a proactive fiscal policy in the second half of 1998. Chinese Ministry of Finance sold RMB 100 billion of bonds to commercial banks to fund investment in infrastructures. In addition, the government instructed the commercial banks to extend RMB 100 billion in loans to supplement the government's infrastructure investment. With these expansive macroeconomic policies, investment rebounded strongly. In real estate, investment decreased in 1997 but grew by 13.7 percent in 1998. It rose further by 21.5 percent in 2000. China's GDP growth picked up pace again in 2000 (Yu 2015).

Once recovered from the impact of the AFC, Chinese economy expanded rapidly. As in the past, the growth was led by investment. Even as overproduction and overcapacity became prevalent, the growth rate of investment accelerated. Concerned about economic overheating, PBC increased banks' reserve requirements and raised benchmark interest rates more than once. It even imposed new limits on bank lending. However, the economy did not cool down, and inflation continued to rise. In 2007 China's GDP growth exceeded fourteen percent, a level comparable with the historical height registered in 1992. In early 2008, the annualized growth rate of CPI reached 8.7 percent, the highest in eleven years (Yu 2015).

The global financial crisis (GFC) in 2008 and the ensuing economic recession in many industrialized countries had serious ripple effects on the developing countries, including China. Faced with shrinking export markets and downward pressure on economic growth, the Chinese government quickly shifted from contractional to expansionist macroeconomic policies. In September 2008, PBC loosened monetary policy (lowering reserve requirements and interest rates). In November of that year, the State Council announced a RMB 4 trillion ($586 billion) economic **stimulus package** to be spent over 27 months. In relative terms, this was equal to three times the size of the US stimulus program following the GFC.

The expansionist macroeconomic policies worked well in the short term. Chinese economy rebounded quickly. However, as critics point out, the stimulus package created considerable negative consequences in the longer run; many of the projects receiving stimulus funding were rushed without careful feasibility studies. Indeed, some of them had previously been rejected by the government because they went against the country's industrial policies. Massive investment in questionable projects resulted in waste and overcapacity, especially in capital-intensive, energy-intensive and even polluting industries (Cai 2015). Moreover, the implementation of the stimulus package worsened local government debt. Of the RMB 4 trillion in total, the central government only contributed less than RMB 1.2 trillion; local governments were expected to come up with the rest of the funds. To fill the funding gap, Beijing encouraged local governments to create "local financing platforms" to borrow from banks, using future government revenue or land as collateral. By the end of 2014, the total local government debt had reached RMB 24 trillion. The central government had to rescue many local governments from bankruptcy (Perkins 2018).

For years after the GFC, a major focus of China's economic policy involved dealing with housing stock surplus, industrial overcapacity, particularly in coal and steel, as well as the debt hangover that resulted from the stimulus program. In late 2015, the government launched the so-called "structural reforms on the supply side" to tackle these issues. The title of the reform initiative suggested that the supply side of the economy far exceeded the demand side and required reduction. However, the government's macroeconomic policy was haphazard and inconsistent with this goal. Within the Party state, there were two influential groups of policymakers, who disagreed over the relative urgency of economic structural reform versus near-term economic growth. Those concerned about the long-term sustainability of the economy sought to push through structural reform, even though that involved a contractionary macroeconomic policy and slower economic growth. Those keen to maintain a high annual economic growth rate tried to extend a loose macroeconomic environment and postpone the difficult economic restructuring (Naughton 2016).

In any event, the Covid-19 pandemic sidelined all attempts at structural reform and ended any tightening of macroeconomic policy. Similar to its reaction to the GFC, the Chinese government unleashed a RMB 3.6 trillion ($500 billion)-stimulus program in May 2020 to fend off the downward pressure on economic growth. The central bank reduced the reserve requirements on banks, encouraging banks to expand their lending to enterprises. Other government agencies deferred tax payments by companies, and increased subsidies for businesses. Just like the last round, the stimulus policies have been investment-focused and business-oriented, offering relatively little support for households to boost their consumption.

All things considered, the Chinese government has had a successful record in macroeconomic management. Calculations based on World Bank data show that from 1978 to 2022, Chinese economy grew by an average of over nine percent, with an annual average inflation rate of 4.4 percent. This is not only far superior to the record of the other transitional economies of Eastern Europe and the Soviet Union/Russia, but it also compares favorably with the newly industrialized economies of East and Southeast Asia. Moreover, since the beginning of the reform era, the government's use of macroeconomic policy instruments has become more diverse and sophisticated, as manifested by the increasingly smooth macroeconomic cycles. However, it is worth noting that administrative intervention remains alive and well as part of the government's toolbox for macroeconomic management. In the next section, we focus on a key player in China's macroeconomic management – the Chinese central bank.

The Central Bank

The central bank is a relatively young institution in China, and yet it has become a key player in macroeconomic management. As mentioned at the beginning of the chapter, governments can use fiscal and monetary policies to smooth out business cycles. However, the former is not as versatile as the latter. Beijing has not often used fiscal policy to spend its way out of economic downturns. It has only used fiscal stimulus on a large scale twice – in response to the AFC in the late 1990s and the GFC a decade later (Yu 2015). Fiscal tools are even less useful in fighting inflation and curbing economic overheating (e.g. by imposing new taxes). Far more often, governments resort to monetary policy conducted by the central bank.

Conventional wisdom stipulates that a central bank must be independent to be effective in conducting monetary policy. To keep inflation in check, central bankers must tighten monetary policy. This shrinks the supply of money in the economy and typically results in reduced investment and employment and rising costs of living. It is not a situation politicians would like to have on their hands. Political leaders concerned about public support are almost always tempted to direct the central bank to keep monetary policy loose and economic growth strong. The central bank needs sufficient autonomy to counter such political influence and focus on containing inflation even when it is unpopular. Only a central bank that is insulated from the rest of the government can succeed in its mission of maintaining price stability and ensure the long-term well-being of the economy (Cukierman 1992; Alesina and Summers 1993).

Seen from this perspective, China stands out as a puzzle. Comparative evaluations of **central bank independence** (CBI) rank China quite low relative to many other countries (Dincer and Eichengreen 2014). The PBC, by law, works under the guidance of the State Council. Furthermore, according to the Chinese constitution, all government agencies operate under the leadership of the CCP. Since the late 1990s, the Party has used its Central Financial Work Commission and other mechanisms to ensure its priorities are implemented by monetary as well as financial policies. Meanwhile, PBC's sub-national branches are subject to the political influence of the regional Party and government officials. How do we reconcile the low level of CBI with PBC's success in macroeconomic management?

Evolution of the PBC

During the era of planned economy, PBC was merely a subsidiary of the Ministry of Finance (MOF), allocating funds according to government instructions. In 1983, the State Council designated PBC as the country's central bank. It began to assume a role in controlling credit in the financial system and liquidity in the financial institutions. However, operating in an economy that was still heavily controlled by the state and being subject to the direction of the State Council, PBC had limited means to curb the excessive supply of credit and serious inflation in the late 1980s.

In 1995 the National People's Congress (NPC), China's legislature, passed the Law of the People's Republic of China on the People's Bank of China, which officially confirmed PBC's central bank status. The new law stipulated three main functions of the bank: (1) to formulate and implement monetary policy and to maintain the stability of the RMB, thus promoting economic growth, (2) to implement financial supervision and regulation, and (3) to provide financial services, such as maintaining payment and settlement, management of the national treasury, and management of foreign-exchange reserves. The law explicitly stipulated that PBC was to operate under the leadership of the State Council.

In the late 1990s, Chinese policymakers gained a heightened awareness of the importance of financial stability. The AFC's assault on the surrounding countries showed how financial troubles could lead to political and economic chaos. The Chinese government held the first National Financial Work Conference in November 1997. It made an important decision to restructure the PBC system. Previously, PBC branches had been subordinate to provincial and local governments. Driven by their desire for fast economic development, these sub-national governments often pressured PBC branches to adopt a generous credit policy. With their career on the line, PBC officials routinely complied with local authorities, allowing investment and other spending to expand out of hand. The restructuring of the PBC system created nine supra-provincial regional branches, which was designed to free them from the political influence of provincial and local governments (Wang 1999).

In the following years, Chinese policymakers paid close attention to the worldwide movement toward greater CBI and inflation targeting. Such a trend had begun with industrialized economies in the late 1970s and was catching on beyond the Western world (Arnone et al. 2007). In 2002, the government held the Second National Financial Work Conference, at which it decided to establish the China Banking Regulatory Commission (CBRC). The CBRC was put in charge of supervising the banking sector, which had been overshadowed by heavy debt, low capitalization, and a lack of transparency. This would free the PBC from financial supervision, thus allowing it to better focus its attention on price stability and to act more autonomously to control inflation. Research shows that before this conference PBC was inflation-accommodating, but afterwards it adopted an anti-inflation policy (Girardin et al. 2017).

A decade after the AFC, the GFC wreaked havoc on the global economy and once again drove home the danger of financial instability. After taking immediate measures to counter the economic consequences of the crisis, the Chinese government went on to enhance the coordination between monetary policy and financial regulatory policy. In 2013, the State Council established a Financial Regulatory Coordination Joint Ministerial Committee (JMC). In 2017 another National Financial Work Conference created a Financial Stability and Development Committee (FSDC). The FSDC replaced the JMC as the State Council's coordinating mechanism for financial stability and development. The PBC was given a prominent coordinating role in both of these inter-agency arrangements, serving as their secretariat. Meanwhile, the central bank itself went through significant restructuring, taking on the dual task of financial regulation and monetary policy (Zheng and Wang 2021).

Operations of the Central Bank

Nominally, PBC works under the leadership of the State Council rather than independently. Furthermore, the central bank ranks near the bottom within the State Council's formal hierarchy, not only below the Ministry of Foreign Affairs and Ministry of Defense, but also below the National Development and Reform Commission (NDRC) and MOF. However, operationally, since its creation PBC has gradually gained considerable *de facto* authority and autonomy. This has been an important factor in China's successful macroeconomic management.

A key source of PBC's *de facto* autonomy and authority lies in the professionalism and expertise of the bank staff (see Box 9.2). Monetary policy is an abstract concept. Its effect works through the intermediation of financial

---

Box 9.2 Zhou Xiaochuan, the Technocratic Central Banker

The success of the Chinese central bank as a macroeconomic manager owes a great deal to one individual – Zhou Xiaochuan. Born in 1948, Zhou came from a revolutionary family. His father was a senior government official and a political patron of Jiang Zemin, CCP leader for much of the 1990s. He studied science and technology and received a PhD in automation and systems engineering at the elitist Tsinghua University in 1985. He first worked in various economic bureaucracies in the government and then took up leadership positions in several financial institutions, including the Bank of China, the State Administration of Foreign Exchange (SAFE), the China Construction Bank, and the China Securities Regulatory Commission. In between, he spent 1987–1988 as a visiting scholar at the University of California, Santa Cruz. Having amassed a great deal of knowledge and practical experience in economic and financial matters, he became the Governor of PBC in 2002, a post he held for an unprecedented fifteen years.

During his tenure, Zhou recruited many talented economists and bankers with international education and work experience. Together they created an increasingly sophisticated monetary policy framework using modern policy instruments. Zhou's rare combination of technical expertise, political acumen, and personal charisma played a vital role in the effectiveness of PBC's policy operations. His reformist orientation contributed strongly to China's financial liberalization, including interest rate and exchange rate reform, and the internationalization of the RMB. In 2019, Zhou won the United Kingdom's Central Banking lifetime achievements award in recognition of his high levels of integrity, intellectual rigor and bold reforms. (Central Banking Staff 2019)

institutions. As the financial market develops and new financial instruments come into being, the effect of monetary policy and the uncertainties involved become increasingly difficult for most politicians to master. This gives the central bank, where financial technocrats congregate, a significant advantage in making and implementing monetary policy.

In the process of making monetary policy, typically it is PBC that develops the initial proposal stemming from its technical expertise. The proposal is then submitted to the State Council and forms the basis of the latter's policy choice. Indeed, as a well-informed insider observed in the mid-1990s, "the policy option provided by the central bank is often the only option, or there is little room for alternatives . . . In the end the policy outcome often suits the central bank's intention. This can be seen as a kind of technical autonomy, which to some extent compensates for the lack of decision-making autonomy" (Xie 1995). Although the Party has the final say on all policy issues, China's monetary policy is often the result of negotiation between PBC and CCP leadership (Bell and Feng 2013). With the development of China's financial market and the marketization of various factors, monetary policy has become even more complex and technical, further strengthening the hands of the professionals. In 2010, PBC's monetary policy committee tripled the number of external experts, while the number of officials on the committee remained the same (Zheng and Wang 2021).

Another source of PBC's autonomy and authority is the decline of traditional macroeconomic control instruments. Central banks try to keep price stability by adjusting the supply of money in the economy. Money can be classified according to its liquidity. M1 refers to currency in circulation plus overnight deposits. It is highly liquid. M2 includes M1 plus less liquid money, such as savings and time deposits, certificates of deposits, and money market funds. In the early years of the reform era, the Chinese government had a quantitatively based monetary policy. The State Council issued targets of RMB lending and M2 growth. With China's financial development came new forces affecting monetary supply, including large-scale shadow banking – underground financial activities that create credit outside the traditional banking system. Under these circumstances, government planned RMB lending and M2 growth could no longer capture the total amount of financing in the Chinese economy. In fact, the State Council stopped publicly announcing RMB lending target in 2011 and M2 growth target in 2018 (Zheng and Wang 2021). The end of government pronouncement of these intermediate targets has given the central bank greater flexibility in managing money supply according to its own judgments.

PBC's autonomy and authority have also grown thanks to the increasing marketization of the Chinese economy. Staffed with well-educated and liberal-minded economists, the central bank has persistently pushed for more market-based interest rates over the years. In 1996, when China established a national interbank market, PBC quickly removed its control of China Interbank Offered Rate (CHIBOR), allowing the participating banks to decide lending and borrowing rates on their own. In 2007 PBC launched the Shanghai Interbank Offered Rate (SHIBOR), which is widely seen by the financial community as the most market-driven interest rate benchmark in China. In 2019, PBC updated its Loan Prime Rate mechanism to form a market-based benchmark loan rate. These reform measures have given the central bank a potent new monetary policy instrument – open market operations (OMO). OMO is a major monetary policy instrument used by central banks in market economies. The central bank buys or sells short-term government bonds and other securities in the open market to influence the money supply in the economy. As PBC conducts OMO on market interest rates, it has considerable *de facto* authority and exercises a high degree of operational autonomy from the State Council.

Finally, technology has enhanced PBC's *de facto* autonomy and authority. PBC has been a pioneer among the central banks of major economies in the world in exploring the potential and implications of financial technology (fintech). In 2019, it released the Fintech Development Plan for 2019–2021, providing guidance for establishing "pillars and beams" for the fintech sector. In 2022, it issued a second plan for 2022–2025 to further develop China's fintech sector, with an emphasis on digitalization, financial innovation, data capacity and security, smart risk control, standard setting, green financing, and inclusive financing. PBC's development of central bank digital currency (CBDC) has been especially noteworthy. It began research and development in this area in 2014 and accelerated its pace in 2019. Since then, PBC has expanded field experiments, allowing residents in many cities to open e-wallets (Xu 2022). The development of fintech has in turn given the PBC enhanced capability for financial monitoring and policy implementation.

China's impressive macroeconomic management record during the reform era owes a great deal to PBC's deft conduct of monetary policy. As the above discussion shows, while lacking institutionalized independence from the Party state, the Chinese central bank has developed considerable *de facto* autonomy and authority. Relying on professional expertise, the Chinese central bank has maintained price stability and financial stability for the country's economic development. However, all is not well with central banking and macroeconomic management in China. Compared to more mature market economies, monetary policy in China has been much more reliant on quantitative instruments, such as the credit plan, reserve requirements, and lending quota. This is especially true in times of crisis. While these instruments have been effective in the short term, they are clumsy and distort the allocation of resources (Geiger 2008; Naughton 2018). In the long run, macroeconomic management will need to be based more on market-determined interest rates.

Economic Imbalance

One of the prominent macroeconomic features of China in recent decades has been the extraordinarily high levels of national savings. According to World Bank data, from 2000 to 2022 China's gross domestic savings averaged 45.7 percent of its GDP. This put China's savings rate well above most countries in the world, including other high-savings East Asian economies. For instance, Japan's savings rate peaked at around forty percent in the early 1990s, while Korea's highest rate was just above forty percent in the late 1980s.

Economists express the national income identity as Y=C+I+G+X–M, where Y stands for national income, C, I, G denote consumption by households, investment by businesses and spending by government, and X and M represent exports and imports. We can rewrite the equation as Y–C–G=I+(X–M), and then S=I+(X–M), where S stands for savings, which equals national income minus household consumption and government spending. This shows that a high savings rate means high investments and/or net exports. Since 1994, China has consistently had a current account surplus mainly due to its positive net exports. World Bank data show that China's current account surplus reached ten percent of its GDP in 2007. In 2022, the figure stood at 2.2 percent. This represents a persistent imbalance between high exports and low domestic demand, which is more salient than the records of post-World War II Japan and Germany, two of the most competitive exporters in the world. At the same time, the Chinese economy is also marked by an imbalance between high investment and low consumption. The World Bank reports that from 1990 to 2022, the global average of final consumption by households and non-profit institutions serving households ranged from 55 to 61 percent of GDP. In the same period, that figure for China was significantly lower, ranging from 34 to 46 percent.

The dual imbalance of China's economy – between exports and imports and between investment and consumption – is highly problematic. The heavy dependence on exports poses a serious challenge for China's foreign economic relations, especially for its relations with the United States. China's large current account surplus has been a chronic source of tension in their bilateral relations. From 2001 to 2023, US imports of goods and services from China rose from $103 billion to $448 billion while its exports to China grew from $25 billion to $195 billion, creating a chronic and significant trade deficit (Siripurapu and Berman 2024). For years, American politicians and media have criticized China for having stolen American jobs and devastated American manufacturing industries. In the last few years, US policymakers have expressed growing concern that Chinese exports of higher-end products, such as electric vehicles, threaten American leadership in strategic industries. In May 2024, President Joe Biden signed an executive order that quadrupled tariffs on Chinese electric cars to one hundred percent (Tankersley 2024). Meanwhile, US officials have tried to rally support from European allies, which have also suffered from the massive inflow of cheap Chinese products, to resist China's exports of its "excess industrial capacity" (Rappeport and Alderman 2024).

Thanks to its current account surplus, China has accumulated enormous foreign reserves, which reached a high of nearly $4 trillion in 2014. Data of the IMF shows that as of March 2024, China's foreign reserves stood at $3.25 trillion, still the largest in the world, well above the second ranking Japan at $1.29 trillion. China invests large portions of its foreign reserves in US government securities, which are highly liquid and relatively safe. This has generated unhappy reactions in the US from time to time. Pundits question the wisdom of America's dependence on Chinese financing of its debt. Some US policymakers and analysts even blamed China for having created the "saving glut" that encouraged excessive and substandard lending in the United States in the early 2000s, which ultimately led to the financial crisis in 2008 (see, for example, Bernanke 2005; Bergsten 2008).

China's investment-led economic growth pattern has already shown its limitations. Connected with this, one study shows that the contribution of capital accumulation to GDP growth peaked at five percentage points for 2008–2013 and declined to three percentage points for 2014 to 2018. As the capital intensity of production rises, an ever-higher investment rate is needed to keep the growth contribution from capital accumulation at its current level. It will likely require an investment rate of roughly 55 percent of GDP to prevent this contribution from continuing to decline (Higgins 2020). Moreover, the capital-intensive development model did not provide many employment opportunities for the population and thus pathways for ordinary people to improve their living standards. As these distortions accumulated, the sustainability of China's economic growth became questionable. In 2007, in his report to the NPC, Chinese Premier, Wen Jiabao, already pointed out that China's growth strategy was "unstable, unbalanced, uncoordinated and ultimately unsustainable" (cited in Yu 2012).

The key to rebalancing the Chinese economy lies in increasing domestic consumption. This was something CCP leaders recognized two decades ago. In December 2004, a Central Economic Work Conference made an announcement to fundamentally change the country's economic growth strategy, turning from one led by investment and export to one based on expanding domestic consumption. In the following years, Chinese leaders repeatedly emphasized the importance of strengthening domestic consumption as an engine of economic growth.

To make the transition to a consumption-based development model requires increasing the income for households, especially low-income groups, who are more likely than high-income groups to spend any extra income they make on consumption. The administration of Hu Jintao and Wen Jiabao drafted a plan for income redistribution reform aimed at helping low-income groups.

In 2006, the government eliminated agricultural taxes for farmers. Beijing also raised the income-tax threshold for individuals, from 800 yuan a month to 1,600 yuan in 2005, to 2,000 yuan in 2007 and, again to 3,000 yuan in 2011. In late 2012, the 18th CCP Congress promised to double urban and rural household income between 2010 and 2020 (Wang 2014).

As discussed in Chapter 7, in the twenty-first century, the government has gradually improved the welfare system. The pension, healthcare, and social assistance programs have all expanded their scope and depth, covering larger portions of the population with greater benefits. The development of a better social safety net has somewhat diminished the pressure on households to set funds aside for the financial risks of old age, sickness, and loss of employment. This has led to reduced precautionary household savings. The level of household savings declined from 42 percent of the disposable income in 2010 to less than 35 percent in 2019, although it went back up to 38 percent in 2020 during the Covid pandemic (Huang and Lardy 2023).

However, household savings are only part of the national savings, which also include corporate savings and government savings. Corporate savings (profits minus dividends) surged in the 2000s following China's entry into the World Trade Organization (WTO), a function of large profits and low dividend payout. Government savings (the government's disposable income minus its final consumption expenditure) also rose sharply in the twenty-first century, benefiting from revenue from the export boom after the WTO accession. China's government savings constitute a larger share of the GDP than other major economies, mainly because of China's tendency to use fiscal revenue for public investment and its low expenditure on public service, such as social welfare and education (Zhang et al. 2018). As a result of these factors, China's national savings rate has been unusually high and its consumption unusually low compared with other countries in the world.

The lack of progress in economic rebalancing is especially salient in the persistently high level of investment in the Chinese economy. Since the early 2000s, investment has been over forty percent of the country's GDP, well above the world average of about 25 percent (Pettis 2023). A major obstacle for shifting the engine of growth from investment to consumption lies in the lack of public participation in public finance policymaking. If history is any guide, the creation of a domestic consumption-led growth regime requires a democratic political system. There need to be independent trade unions to ensure workers' interests and voices receive serious consideration in the policymaking process. As discussed in Chapter 6, this has not been possible under the one-party political system in contemporary China.

In theory, the national legislature is the highest organ of state power and the government's budget is subject to NPC approval. In reality, however, NPC is little more than a rubber stamp that automatically approves budgetary decisions made by the bureaucracy. The NDRC and the MOF are the chief bureaucratic agencies making the budget, and they follow the priorities and preferences of the CCP leadership. Without meaningful involvement of the public in the decision-making process, it is little wonder that public finance routinely ignores social services and welfare and, instead, focuses on investment projects favored by the CCP. In a telling example, when the GFC hit in 2008, many Western governments adopted counter-cyclical fiscal measures with significant upfront consumption elements. In contrast, Beijing went right back to the familiar playbook of investment-led economic growth. The Chinese stimulus package was predominantly investment-focused. Of a total of RMB 4 trillion, infrastructure projects constituted 72 percent of the funds (Naughton 2009).

Another pillar sustaining the investment-driven development model is the state-controlled financial system. As discussed in Chapter 8, the Party state controls all the big banks and exercises considerable influence on the financial markets. These financial institutions allocate financial resources to industries and enterprises selected by the government. For decades, the large SOEs favored by the government have had easy access to credit. The low interest rate for borrowing has contributed to the SOEs' high investments and high profits. With China's capital control policy, households have been forced to put their savings in domestic banks (and real estate market). The prolonged low interest rates for deposits have deprived them of a fair return on their assets and limited their consumption.

Since 2021 the Chinese government has emphasized its commitment to "common prosperity," calling for high-income individuals and businesses to give back more to society. On the surface, this could mean a redistribution policy that will encourage household consumption. However, the target of wealth reduction has been private entrepreneurs rather than large SOEs or the government. In fact, the CCP's touting of common prosperity seems to be primarily an instrument to control China's private enterprises from challenging the Party's authority.

The same political factors hindering the shift away from investment to consumption – the Party state's focus on development, the vested interests of powerful bureaucracies, and the weakness of popular voice for better living conditions – have also hampered the transition away from export dependence. A recent analysis of data from 1994 to 2018 indicates heightened importance of exports in China's GDP growth after the GFC. It concludes that the transition from an export-led growth strategy proceeded far more slowly than the government's rhetoric would suggest (Liu et al. 2019).

Local political economy constitutes an additional barrier for the transition. For instance, the Pearl River Delta in southern China pioneered foreign trade development early in the reform era. Over time, its success in the international market created various stakeholders in the export-based economic development. The Hong Kong firms funding the exporting enterprises benefited from the cheap labor and land in Guangdong. The township and village enterprises gained from doing the contract work. Local governments profited from the revenue generated from these business operations. When the central government called for economic restructuring, relocation, and reorientation from export to domestic sales, only limited cooperation was forthcoming from below. The actors and institutions supporting the export industries have evolved into obstacles for new patterns of economic development (Yang 2012).

Nevertheless, compared with the still serious imbalance between investment and consumption, there has been more improvement in rebalancing exports and domestic demand. According to the World Bank, the ratio between Chinese export and GDP declined from a high of 36 percent in 2006 to a low of 21 percent in 2022. China's dependence on export is now lower than the world average of 31 percent, even though it is still much higher than the twelve percent of the United States in 2022, a comparably large economy.

This progress has been in large part the result of changes in the international environment. Although trade frictions have existed for years in China's relations with the United States and other countries with which it has persistent trade surpluses, the tension has increased dramatically since Donald Trump's election in 2016. During that Trump presidency, the US government launched a trade war against China, imposing punishing tariffs on Chinese goods. Since then, President Joe Biden has kept those tariffs and introduced more restrictions on technology and investment flows between China and the United States, describing the two countries as locked in "extreme competition". Moreover, Biden has actively rounded up traditional and new allies to confront China economically as well as strategically. Talks about "de-coupling" and "de-risking" permeate Western policy discussions of economic relations with China. Between 2017 and 2022, while China's total exports to the United States increased, the share of US imports from China fell from 22 percent to sixteen percent (Borges and Palazzi 2023),

Chinese policymakers may well have miscalculated Washington's accumulated frustration with China's trade advantage over recent decades and underestimated its determination to take more decisive actions against China. They may have been too optimistic that economic interdependence and US corporate interest would sustain American policy of engagement with China. But, with Trump's confrontational policy and Biden's continuation of the same policy, albeit with a more multilateral format, Chinese leaders have abandoned their illusion. They have also taken notice of the broader backlashes against globalization in the United States and other Western industrialized countries, which have been major export markets for Chinese products, and come to the conclusion that China has to turn away from the old export-led development model toward a greater emphasis on increasing domestic demand. In 2020 the Standing Committee of the CCP's Politburo proposed a "new development program of mutual benefit through domestic-international dual circulation." In 2022, the 20th CCP National Congress added the "dual circulation" strategy to the Party's constitution. The Party state has made it a priority to try to reduce China's reliance on trade with the United States and other potentially hostile powers. This is an economic necessity in an increasingly fragmented global economy. It is also a geopolitical imperative for China as it seeks to limit its vulnerability to political pressures from the West.

Conclusion

In this chapter we have explored the macroeconomic management in China during the reform era. The success of the Chinese government in this policy area has been essential to the smooth economic development of the country so far. In this process, the Chinese central bank has played a crucial role. Although the PBC is a relatively new institution and lacks formal independence, it has developed considerable *de facto* autonomy and authority in its operations. With its impressive professionalism and expertise and with the development of China's financial market, the Chinese central bank has become increasingly mature and deft in the conduct of monetary policy.

On the other hand, China's economic development has been seriously out of balance. For decades, it has been heavily dependent on exports for growth, and it continues to rely too much on investment, neglecting domestic household consumption. This model has proven to be unsustainable as China faces an increasingly hostile international environment and diminishing return to investment. Lately, the international environment has forced China to reduce its reliance on exports in driving economic growth. But there has been little improvement in the imbalance between high investment and low consumption. The difficulty of changing this pattern lies in continued state control of the political and financial institutions and the lack of genuine public participation in policymaking.

Questions for Discussion

1. What policy tools does the Chinese government use to maintain macroeconomic stability?

2. How has the People's Bank of China contributed to China's economic success?

3. Why has it been so difficult to rebalance the Chinese economy from its heavy reliance on investment and – until recently – exports?

10

In Search of Clear Waters and Green Mountains

In 2005, Xi Jinping was the Communist Party Secretary of Zhejiang Province in eastern China. During a visit to Yucun, a village making the transition from mining to rural tourism, he commented that "clear waters and green mountains are (as valuable as) mountains of gold and silver (*lüshui qingshan jiushi jinshan yinshan*)." He was praising the village for having cleaned up the pollution of its former mining industry and returned the area to its natural beauty, while also benefiting from new and much cleaner lines of business. Since Xi became leader of the Chinese Communist Party (CCP) in 2012, this slogan has been widely promoted as the government's new development philosophy. In Xi's words, "The ecological environment itself is the economy. Protecting the environment is developing productivity" (Xinhua 2021a).

Meanwhile, a new phrase – "**ecological civilization** (*shengtai wenming*)" – has become popular in China's official discourse. First included in the CCP documents at its 18th National Congress in 2012, it refers to sustainable economic development based on harmony between human society and the natural environment. Since then, this concept has gained increased currency. In 2015 it appeared in the country's five-year economic plan for the first time. In 2018 it was incorporated in China's amended constitution. It is a frequent topic in the public speeches by Chinese leaders. In his keynote speech at COP15 on biodiversity held in China in 2021, Xi stated that "We shall take the development of an ecological civilization as our guide to coordinate the relationship between man and nature" (Xinhua 2021b).

The rhetoric of "clear waters and green mountains" and "ecological civilization" has been accompanied by new policy initiatives, ranging from the creation of ecological zones around the nation to the greening of the Belt and Road Initiative (BRI). They reflect a growing awareness on the part of the CCP leadership of the seriousness of China's environmental problems and the dire consequences they pose for the country. This chapter examines environmental degradation in three areas – air, water, and land. We will discuss the economic and human costs of the deteriorating quality of China's environment. We will also analyze how Chinese political economy has shaped the environmental policies and their implementation. This chapter ends by touching on the role of environmental issues in Chinese foreign relations.

Environmental Degradation

Until the twentieth century, China was largely an agrarian society. Over two millennia of intensive agricultural production involved large-scale deforestation and massive water management systems. These practices no doubt left footprints on the natural world (Elvin 2004; Burke and Pomeranz 2009). However, the damage to the natural environment by farming and irrigation engineering was minimal compared with what was to come with industrialization.

When the CCP came to rule China in 1949, it was eager to transform the poor agrarian nation into a strong industrial power. The government wasted no time in mobilizing natural and human resources to build up modern industries, especially the heavy industries related to national defense. With revolutionary zeal, Chinese leader Mao Zedong declared war on nature. His famous mantra was to struggle against heaven and earth (*yu tian dou, yu di dou*). With total confidence, he predicted the inevitable triumph of man over nature (*ren ding sheng tian*). Nationwide campaigns, such as the Great Leap Forward in the 1950s and the Third Front Movement in the 1960s, were carried out without careful consideration of the negative effects on the environment. Claiming agricultural land from lakes and killing sparrows to protect crops, the Maoist policies certainly damaged the natural environment. However, much worse problems came later, after the CCP introduced market-oriented economic reforms in the late 1970s.

The meteoric rise of the Chinese economy in the last few decades, especially since the 1990s, has been accompanied by a steady deterioration of the natural environment in China. From the "airpocalypses" in major Chinese cities to the **cancer villages** in the rural areas, from the rapidly falling water tables in the north to the shrinking lakes in the south, and from contaminated agricultural produce to mysterious dead pigs floating down the river, environmental problems are increasingly affecting people's lives as well as the country's economy. In this section, we examine three areas of environmental degradation – air, water, and land.

Air Pollution and Climate Change

In the summer of 2008, Beijing hosted the 29th International Olympic Games. This was an extremely important international event for the Chinese, a dream finally coming true after years of lobbying the Olympic Committee and the international community, and a "coming out party" for a rising China. The government spared no efforts and resources to clean up the city, shutting down factories and restricting traffic flows for months ahead of time. The weather was good during the Games. Nevertheless, the air quality in Beijing was still much worse than at the previous several Olympics. The levels of particulate matter in the air were double the levels in Athens, tripling those in Atlanta, and 3.5 times higher than those in Sydney during the recent Games they hosted. The levels of coarse particulate matter were too high by the standards of the World Health Organization (WHO) 81 percent of the time, while the most dangerous particulate matter (smaller than 2.5 microns, or PM 2.5) reached unacceptable levels one hundred percent of the time (Wang et al. 2009). In the mid-2010s, Chinese cities were plagued by serious air pollution, frequently experiencing smog that turned midday into dusk. From time to time, people had to stay indoors to avoid breathing in hazardous particles. In 2014 only eight out of the 74 biggest Chinese cities passed the government's own basic air quality standards (BBC 2015).

The air quality in China has improved significantly in the last decade. According to the Air Quality Life Index report published by the University of Chicago in 2023, air pollution in China declined 42.3 percent from 2013 to 2021. However, China's air pollution is still six times the level set by the WHO's guideline, which causes a reduction of 2.5 years in life expectancy (Greenstone and Hasenkopt 2023). According to IQAir, as of mid-2024, sixteen of the twenty cities in the world with the worst air quality are in China (IQAir n.d.).

A major source of air pollution lies in the heavy use of coal to power and heat the country. Coal is not only dirtier than clean energy sources such as solar and wind, but it is also more polluting than other fossil fuels such as oil and gas. The mining of coal emits methane while the burning of coal produces considerable airborne toxins and pollutants, including sulfur dioxide, nitrogen oxides, mercury, lead, and other heavy metals. Coal-related air pollution has severe health consequences. It is associated with asthma, cancer, heart and lung ailments, and neurological problems. It also causes acid rain and global warming.

China has limited supplies of oil and gas but is richly endowed with coal. Coal has played a major role in fueling the country's extraordinary economic growth. Between 2001 and 2013, China's economy roughly tripled and so did its coal consumption. In 2013, China consumed 4.24 billion tons of coal. For a few years thereafter, coal consumption dropped, but as of 2018, coal still made up 59 percent of the country's total energy consumption and over fifty percent of coal consumption worldwide (Columbia University n.d.). In 2022, China's use of coal rose again, to just short of five billion tons and 53 percent of the global consumption (Energy Information Administration 2023).

The growing number of automobiles in China constitutes another important source of air pollution. Since the 1990s, the Chinese government has made the automobile industry a pillar industry. By late 2022, the number of vehicles in the country had reached 415 million (Xinhua 2022). Recent research shows that transportation accounts for ten percent of the country's total carbon emissions (International Energy Agency 2021). Automobile exhaust has particularly worsened the air quality in Chinese cities. According to China's Ministry of Ecology and Environment (MEE), in 2018 vehicle emissions accounted for about 45 percent of the air pollution in Beijing and nearly thirty percent of it in Shanghai (CSIS n.d.).

The negative impact of air pollution on the population is devastating. Research finds that each year air pollution leads to between one to two million premature deaths in China. In 2019, 1.42 million deaths were attributable to the high level of PM 2.5, whereas another 363,000 deaths resulted from household air pollution from burning solid fuels (Health Effects Institute 2020). Air pollution is also responsible for various chronic diseases, including stroke, ischemic heart disease, chronic obstructive pulmonary disease, and lung cancer (Yin et al. 2020).

The same economic activities polluting the air have also added to the emission of greenhouse gas (GHG). In 2006, China became the largest emitter of GHG, overtaking the United States (see Figure 10.1). Although, on a per capita basis, China's emission is still well below the US level, as of 2023 it is responsible for 35 percent of the global CO2 emissions, fifteen percent higher than those of all the advanced economies combined (International Energy Agency 2023). Besides the intense coal production and consumption and the fast-growing automobile use, another major contributor to GHG emission is the frenzy of urbanization. According to World Bank data, from 1980 to 2022, the proportion of Chinese population living in urban areas has grown from nineteen percent to 64 percent. Building new cities and towns involves enormous amounts of high-energy products, such as cement and steel.

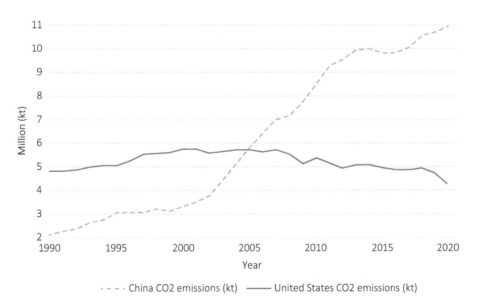

Figure 10.1 CO2 Emissions in China and the United States 1990–2020
Source: World Bank Group.

Compared with the effects of air pollution, the consequences of climate change are less visible and immediate, but they are no less real. If the current trend of global warming continues, coastal cities in China, including Shanghai, could be submerged in the coming decades. If the global average temperature rises by 2°C by the end of the century, land currently inhabited by about 43 million people in China could be underwater (CFR n.d.). In recent years, China has already seen unprecedented floods, snowstorms, sandstorms, and other extreme weather phenomena. For instance, in July 2021, Zhengzhou, the capital city of Henan Province in central China, had the equivalent of a year's average rainfall in just three days. The record downpour trapped passengers of the subway, killing twelve people. The flooding forced the evacuation of over 200,000 people (BBC 2021). Climate change will only become more salient in the absence of drastic counter measures.

Water Shortage and Pollution

China is home to over 1.4 billion people, roughly twenty percent of the global population, but its freshwater resources rank sixth in the world, only six percent of the global total. This combination makes China one of the most water-scarce countries, with its per capita water resources a mere 28 percent of the world average. A common way to measure the seriousness of water shortage is the percentage of the annual withdrawal of a country's freshwater resources. When that figure exceeds 25 percent, it means that the area is "water stressed." Figure 10.2 shows China's dire and growing water stress since 1980. Moreover, its water distribution is highly uneven both across time and across space. Precipitation varies dramatically from year to year and through each year, with typically hot and wet summers and cold and dry winters. Drought and flooding are frequent occurrences. Geographically, North China (north of the Yangtze River Basin) takes up 63.5 percent of the nation's territory, but only nineteen percent of the national water resources (Ministry of Water Resources n.d.).

In recent decades, the rapid economic growth in China has exacerbated water shortage. With only fourteen percent of the water used for the basic needs of hydration, sanitation, hygiene, and cooking, 62 percent goes to agriculture and 22 percent to industry and power generation (University of Southern California 2021). Moreover, economic development has aggravated deforestation and climate change, which, in turn, have added to the reduction of the country's freshwater supply. Thousands of rivers and lakes have disappeared. Even the Yellow River, the cradle of the Chinese civilization, has often been unable to reach the sea. Groundwater depletion is also significant. According to research by scholars in the Chinese Academy of Sciences, the water table in the North China Plain has declined by six to eight billion tons each year since 2002 (Chen 2018). As a result of the falling water table, parts of

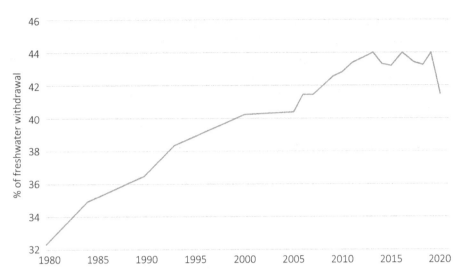

Figure 10.2 Level of Water Stress in China 1980–2020 (freshwater withdrawal as a proportion of available freshwater resources)
Source: Food and Agriculture Organization.

the city of Beijing are falling into the earth by more than fourteen centimeters a year (Reddy 2021).

The water scarcity in northern China has been so severe that the Chinese government has resorted to a gargantuan engineering project to divert water from the Yangtze River in the south to the arid land in the north. Through three routes of man-made water ways stretching hundreds of miles – east, central, and west – this project aims to transfer approximately 45 billion cubic meters of water each year. Since the construction began in 2003, the eastern and the central routes have been completed, while the western route remains a blueprint. While this ambitious engineering project has offered a partial solution to the uneven water distribution between the north and the south, it has also had serious environmental consequences. In addition to the involuntary relocation of hundreds of thousands of people, the project has caused considerable loss of water and estuary salination in the water-providing areas. The water transferred is often polluted and not suitable to use for many purposes. The quantity of the transferred water is insufficient to replenish the ground water in the water receiving areas and may indeed bring about secondary salination (Wilson et al. 2017).

Besides water shortage, China's breakneck economic growth in the reform era has significantly worsened water pollution. Increasing volumes of untreated wastewater from households, agricultural runoff, aquaculture discharge, other forms of land exploitation, and chemicals and toxins released by industries have all worsened the quality of the limited supply of water in the country. In 2018, MEE reported that 6.9 percent of surface water in China's river basins was too polluted for any use, and another 18.9 percent was only suitable for agricultural or industrial use, but not for human consumption. Meanwhile, it noted 15.5 percent of the groundwater in China was unsuitable for any use and another 70.7 percent was clean enough only for agricultural and industrial purposes, but could not be used for drinking without proper treatment (CSIS 2020).

The excessive heavy metals, toxic compounds, bacteria, and parasites in polluted water pose a danger for the health of fish and humans alike. For example, in 2013, dead fish covered a river in Hubei province in central China, looking like snowflakes. Authorities uncovered 220,000 pounds of dead fish, which they said had been poisoned by ammonia from a chemical plant (*Guardian* 2013). With hundreds of millions of people drinking water from hazardous sources, waterborne diseases are prevalent, especially in rural China. For example, in the early 2000s, the Huai River in eastern China was so polluted that people in the countryside near it suffered from abnormally high cases of spontaneous abortions, birth defects, and cancer. Young men in the area were not fit enough for military service (Economy 2004). Epidemiologists point out that drinking water contamination is a major risk factor for digestive system (stomach, liver, esophageal, and colorectal) cancers. They estimate about eleven percent of digestive cancer cases in China are attributable to chemical contaminants in drinking water (Zhang et al. 2010). In some areas, large portions of the population are inflicted (see Box 10.1).

Box 10.1 China's "Cancer Villages"

Yanglingang is a small village in Jiangsu Province, not far from Shanghai. In 2013, it was home to only a few hundred people. In the previous decade, at least eleven villagers had died from cancer and more cases were emerging. Surrounded by chemical, pharmaceutical, and power plants, the small fishing village had no choice but to live with the pollution, including drinking the water contaminated by the waste from these plants. Residents had long suspected of a connection between the arrival of the plants in a newly established industrial zone nearby and the soaring number of cancer cases among them. A four-hour drive to the north of Yanglingang sits the village of Dongxing. A chemical factory began to operate on the edge of the village in 2000. It reportedly produced 2,000 tons of the carcinogenic chemical chlorophenol each year. Ducks, chickens, and geese began to die *en masse*. More than one hundred residents developed cancer between 2000 and 2005. In February 2013, the Chinese government first acknowledged the existence of "cancer villages," which Chinese media, academics and NGOs estimated to number well over 400, spreading across every province, except Qinghai and Tibet in the far west. (Kaiman 2013)

Water pollution in turn makes water shortage even worse. Polluted water is unsafe for drinking, so pollution exacerbates the scarcity of drinking water. Moreover, it takes a lot of relatively clean water to dilute the dirty water, so that the quality of the water could meet the standard for specific usage. In areas where surface water quality is bad, people resort to exploiting groundwater, which, in turn, reduces the water underground. While northern China is short of water around the year, even southern China is plagued by quality-induced water shortage (Ma T. et al. 2020).

Desertification and Soil Pollution

In addition to air and water, the land in China has seen accelerated degradation in recent decades. There are many forms of land degradation, including deforestation, soil erosion (the loss of soil through the action of wind and water), desertification, and soil pollution. They tend to be related and reinforce each other. According to the United Nations Convention to Combat Desertification (UNCCD), land degradation is "the result of human-induced actions which exploit land, causing its utility, biodiversity, soil fertility, and overall health to decline." The current agricultural practices in many countries in the world are causing soils to be eroded up to one hundred times faster than natural processes replenish them (UNCCD n.d.). In this section, we focus on desertification and soil pollution.

Desertification is a process in which fertile land becomes desert. Between a quarter and a third of Chinese territory is covered in desert. The biggest deserts include the Taklimakan in the far west, the Ordos, west of Beijing, and the Gobi, which straddles the Inner Mongolia Autonomous Region of China and the Republic of Mongolia. The vast Gobi Desert, which occupies roughly 400,000 square miles in China, sends sand and dust across many areas in the north and northwest of the country every year.

Desertification can be caused by climate change and/or human activities. Changing climate can affect soil quality, vegetation cover, species composition, and the hydrologic cycles in drylands. Human economic activities include land reclamation for agriculture, increased animal grazing, excessive logging, and the exploitation of underground water. Researchers find that in China social economic factors account for 79.3 percent of the desertification whereas climate change is responsible for 20.6 percent (Feng et al. 2015).

For decades, China has combated desertification with various programs. Since 1978, the government has carried on the Great Green Wall of China project, which involves planting a 3,000-mile strip of protective vegetation and eventually billions of trees to prevent the expansion of the northern deserts. This project, the biggest tree-planting program in human history, is expected to continue until 2050. In 1949, the forest coverage of China was ten percent. Four decades into this project, nearly a quarter of China's territories were covered (Stanway 2021). In the early 2000s, the government launched a Grain-for-Green program, encouraging farmers to convert grain fields to forests or grassland by rewarding them with grain and cash subsidies. The program has contributed significantly to the increased vegetation of hilly regions, including in the central Loess Plateau (Liu et al. 2020).

Thanks to these government-sponsored programs, the frequency of severe dust and sandstorms has decreased in the twenty-first century. However, the problem is far from being solved. For example, in May 2017, Beijing was covered by thick orange clouds formed by sand and dust from the Gobi Desert. The air quality index scores for PM10 – particulate matter with a diameter of ten microns or less – for Beijing and surrounding cities ranged between 900 and 999, the monitor's maximum reading, many times over the WHO's recommended score of no higher than fifty (Feng 2017). Elsewhere, the encroaching deserts continue to destroy farmland and force villagers to abandon their homes.

The rapid economic development of China has led to soil pollution on an ever-larger scale. Agricultural production's prolonged use of fertilizers and pesticides has lowered soil quality. Mining, smelting, and the combustion of coal and petrol add heavy metals to the ground. According to a report issued by the Chinese government in 2014, contaminants such as cadmium, mercury, arsenic, copper, lead, nickel, DDT, and PAHs are the major pollutants of soil in China (Li et al. 2019). A recent study of soil quality across three decades (1989–2018) in the Pearl River Delta in southern China shows that most of the sampling sites were contaminated by one or more heavy metals and there was an increasing trend in heavy metal contamination over time (Li et al. 2020). Another study finds that heavy metals exceed the standard levels in central, southwest, and south China. Furthermore, it reveals that mineral exploitation and industrial production are prominent in the most severely polluted provinces, while sewage, irrigation and the abuse of fertilizer are major culprits in agricultural areas. In addition, urban development in densely populated provinces has also contributed to the problem (Wu et al. 2022).

Soil contamination directly affects food safety among other things. High concentrations of heavy metals are not only toxic to most plants and other organisms, but also threaten human and animal health through the food chain. High levels of copper exposure lead to brain and kidney damage, liver cirrhosis, and intestinal irritation. Cadmium is a cause of kidney failure, osteoporosis, and cancers. Lead exposure results in losses of neurological function. Research finds high levels of heavy metal toxicity in the grains and vegetables grown in many parts of China, so much so that many farmers – except the poorest and most desperate – avoid eating the crops they have grown (Qin et al. 2021).

The Political Economy of Environmental Policies

The growing environmental problems in China have been closely connected to the rapid growth of Chinese agriculture and industry, as well as the large-scale infrastructure construction and urbanization. Some scholars hypothesize that environmental degradation is inevitable during the early stages of economic modernization but, as economic development reaches a certain level, the situation will improve because of greater demands from the public for environmental goods, improved industrial structure, and technological advance. The so-called Environmental Kuznets Curve (EKC) depicts an inverted-U shaped relationship between economic development and the environment.

The evidence of EKC is mixed. In China, some forms of environmental degradation seem to have turned the corner; for instance, the total SO2 emissions peaked in 2006, as did water pollution. However, other problems have continued to worsen, such as biodiversity loss and GHG emissions. While scholars disagree on the validity of EKC, most recognize that economic development does not automatically lead to improved environmental performance (Carson 2010). Government policies and regulations make a big difference. In this section, we explore how the Chinese government has dealt with the environmental challenges, and we explain the underlying political economy logic.

Chinese policymakers first became aware of the necessity to pay attention to environmental degradation in 1972, when a Chinese delegation went to the United Nations Conference on Human Environment in Stockholm. Until then, they had thought of environmental pollution as a problem only in capitalist societies. In 1974 the State Council established a Leading Group of Environmental Protection, which evolved into the National Environmental Protection Agency in 1988, a vice-ministerial organization. A decade later, the Agency became the State Environmental Protection Administration (SEPA) and was upgraded to the ministerial level. In 2008 SEPA was made the Ministry of Environmental Protection, a cabinet ministry. Most recently, in 2018, the Ministry expanded to become the MEE.

Beginning in the early 1970s, the Chinese government took incremental steps in developing an environmental agenda. In 1973 the First National Conference on Environmental Protection formulated the first national strategy on environmental protection. In 1983, the Second National Conference declared environmental protection a basic national principle. In 1994 China issued a White Paper on China's Population, Environment, and Development in the Twenty-first Century, which laid out a broad strategy to achieve sustainable development. In 1996 it developed the first five-year plan on environmental protection.

Despite its growing environmental awareness, the Chinese government still prioritized economic development far above any environmental concerns. A turning point in the official attitude came early in the Hu Jintao and Wen

Jiabao administration (2002–2012). Unlike their predecessors, who overwhelmingly stressed GDP growth, Hu and Wen conceived a new "**scientific outlook on development**," which sought to redefine development in light of the worsening environment as well as the growing inequality in China. Calling for a people-centered approach to development, the Hu-Wen government placed a strong emphasis on environmental protection alongside wealth redistribution. In 2004 the CCP endorsed the idea of **Green GDP**, which would include the resource and environmental costs in GDP accounting (Rauch and Chi 2010).

After Xi succeeded Hu as the CCP General Secretary in 2012, the Chinese government intensified its efforts on environmental protection. As noted earlier in this chapter, the concept of ecological civilization has become an important theme of official discourse. In addition to expanding the authority of MEE, the government has made many new environmental laws and regulations, set concrete targets for pollution reduction and renewable energy expansion, added environmental performance to the evaluation of cadres, and given permission for social groups to sue local polluters. The forcefulness of the Party state in imposing environmental standards and punishing failures of enforcement constitutes a form of "authoritarian environmentalism," which has even earned admiration from some international environmentalists (Li and Shapiro 2020).

In addition, China has also participated in international environmental agreements in numerous areas, such as sustainable development, atmospheric environmental protection, freshwater resources utilization and protection, marine pollution control, biological resources protection, land resources protection, hazardous substances and activities management, waste management, environmental protection in polar regions, and environmental protection in outer space (Jiang 2015). Notably, China signed the Paris Climate Agreement in 2016 and promised to begin to reduce its carbon emissions after 2030. In 2020, President Xi surprised the world by announcing to the United Nations General Assembly that China would peak its emissions "well before" 2030. He further made a significant new target for carbon neutrality by 2060 (Hilton 2024).

The formal commitments made by the Chinese government are impressive. However, the reality on the ground is more complicated. Enormous resources have gone into addressing a variety of environmental problems, and government subsidies and other incentives have facilitated the rapid growth of renewable energy. China has been the world's largest producer of wind and solar power for some years, and it has increased its lead in renewable energy over time. In 2022, China installed about as much solar capacity as the rest of the world combined. In 2023, it doubled that amount and commissioned as much solar capacity as the entire world did in 2022. In the same period, its wind power capacity grew by 66 percent year-on-year (Hilton 2024). Related to the development of renewable energy, the environmental cost per unit of

GDP has been decreasing, even as the environment is still worsening. A study shows that from 2004 to 2017, the growth rate of environmental cost annually slowed from ten percent to two percent. The share of the environmental cost in the GDP decreased from 3.05 percent to 2.23 percent in that period (Ma G. et al. 2020).

On the other hand, China's environmental management remains poor compared with that of other countries and, although solar, wind, and other renewables now account for half of China's installed capacity, this has not prevented a surge in permits for new coal-fired power plants. In fact, as of 2023, China still generates about seventy percent of its electricity from fossil fuels, which means that the actual use of renewable energy falls far behind installed capacity (Hilton 2024). The Yale Center for Environmental Law and Policy's Environmental Performance Index ranks 180 countries on climate change performance, environmental health, and ecosystem vitality. In 2022, China still ranked 160th on the index, approaching the bottom of the list. Three factors have hindered the implementation of environmental protection policies in China – the government's competing priorities, the fragmentation of the governance system, and the weakness of civil society.

Competing Priorities

When the post-Mao reformers came into power in the late 1970s, they faced a country on the brink of economic bankruptcy and a people tired of prolonged low living standards. It was not surprising that their top priority was to grow the economy. In Deng Xiaoping's words, "development is the indisputable truth *(fazhan shi ying daoli)*." Environmental protection was peripheral to the thinking of Chinese policymakers.

In the early twenty-first century, the deterioration of the environment became a salient policy challenge for the Chinese government. Chinese leaders were particularly alarmed by the economic costs of environmental degradation and by the political threat embedded in rising public anger about various environmental problems. To a lesser extent, criticisms of China's environmental performance by the international community also contributed to the intensified attention to this matter by the Chinese government.

For decades, the Chinese government has been obsessed with the GDP growth rate. However, GDP figures completely ignore the resource and environmental costs of development. As early as the 1970s, a new green national accounting system emerged that subtracted such costs from GDP figures. In 1993 the United Nations Statistics Division developed the System of Environmental–Economic Accounting (SEEA) as a basic framework for green GDP. Calculations based on SEEA guidelines suggest that the environmental cost was between three and ten percent of China's GDP in the 1980s and 1990s. In 2007, the report of the CCP's 17th National Congress admitted that the most serious problem for China's social and economic development was that "the resource and environmental costs of economic growth are too large." A technical team of Chinese environmental scientists finds that the cost of environmental degradation in China increased from RMB 511.82 billion in 2004 to RMB 1,892.42 billion in 2017 (Ma G. et al. 2020).

In addition to economic costs, environmental degradation generated increasing public dissatisfaction in China. According to a 2015 Pew opinion poll, 76 percent of those surveyed agreed that air pollution was a very big (35 percent), or moderately big (41 percent) problem; 75 percent regarded water pollution as a very big (34 percent), or moderately big (41 percent) problem (Wike and Parker 2015). Protests proliferated as people became more and more aware of the health risks brought by pollution and other kinds of environmental hazards. Moreover, after the 1990s, environmentally driven social unrest spread from the rural areas to the cities, increasingly involving China's prosperous middle class. As these social unrests drew larger and more heterogeneous groups, they became a growing concern for the government (Steinhardt and Wu 2016).

For the CCP, it has become an imperative to balance economic growth and environmental protection because poor performance in either area could undermine its legitimacy. In the twenty-first century, the Party state has apparently tried to downplay GDPism and to pay more attention to sustainable development. However, its impulse for economic growth remains strong. When push comes to shove, the government has proven to be willing to sacrifice the environment: a study of pollution enforcement among state-owned enterprises (SOEs) controlled by the central government reveals that the latter has implicitly tolerated the SOEs' shirking of pollution regulations in the pursuit of better economic performance (Eaton and Kostka 2017).

China's economic growth slowed down steadily in the 2010s, from over ten percent in 2010 to six percent in 2019. The onset of the Covid pandemic in 2019 further worsened the headwind. As the CCP is still keen to keep a GDP growth rate of around five to six percent annually, it has relaxed environmental regulations. In connection with this, the government has reversed the reduction of coal-powered production of steel and cement and heavy manufacturing. In fact, there has been an accelerated increase of new coal power capacity in the current five-year plan period (2021–2025) compared to either of the previous two five-year plan periods (Centre for Research on Energy and Clean Air 2021). In 2023, China started construction of 70.2 GW of new coal power capacity, nineteen times more than the rest of the world combined, at 3.7 GW (Global Energy Monitor 2024).

Fragmented Authoritarianism

Another obstacle hindering the implementation of China's ambitious environmental policies lies in the fragmentation of the political system. In a country as vast as China, Beijing needs the cooperation of provincial and local governments to implement its policies. Indeed, the Environmental Law of China stipulates that local governments are primarily responsible for enforcing environmental regulations. However, the authoritarian nature of the CCP regime notwithstanding, the governance of the country is often incoherent. As many studies have shown, local officials are often ineffective in enforcing environmental rules and regulations.

Motivation and capacity go a long way in explaining the lack of effectiveness (Qi and Zhang 2014). First, the cadre evaluation system in China shapes the incentives of local officials. During the reform era, local GDP growth has been the most important and quantifiable criterion for assessing the performance of Party and government functionaries. Leaders of areas with high economic growth are the most likely to be promoted to higher ranks. This gives local cadres strong inducements to promote economic development even if that comes at the expense of the environment.

Second, fiscal necessities have a significant impact on local government behavior. Since the fiscal reform in 1994, subnational governments have had to deal with much higher expenditure than their tax revenue. As a strategy to cope with this dire situation, many local governments have gone out of their way to attract industries to boost their fiscal resources. This often means applying environmental standards leniently, if at all, to investment projects. Officials look the other way when enterprises, including many township and village enterprises, pollute the environment.

Third, local governments are constrained by their capacity. They have inadequate funding for various administrative tasks, including the implementation of environmental policy. Ironically, many local environmental agencies are subsidized by the pollution discharge fees paid by the very enterprises they are supposed to regulate. Furthermore, they lack reliable data on environmental quality and pollutant emissions. These data are typically provided in a bottom-up fashion and are often subject to distortion and manipulation by self-serving enterprises and lower-level officials. Research shows that caught between their limited capacity and public expectations for environmental protection, local governments often engage in "performance governance" – appearing responsive to public opinion, demonstrating benevolent intentions, and making efforts visible to the public. But their theatrical deployment of language, symbols, and gestures do not substantially address the environmental problems (Ding 2020).

The experiment with the Green GDP offers a telling example of the lack of local cooperation. After the central government endorsed the idea in 2004, ten regions carried out a pilot project in 2005 and a nationwide study was scheduled for 2006. The report of the result was delayed indicating trouble with the experiment. To begin with, it is inherently difficult to quantify resource and environmental damage (e.g. calculating the cost of the extinction of a species, the soil erosion due to the loss of trees, and the health problems from pollution). But more importantly, local governments have close and strong ties with local enterprises, making them reluctant to enforce environmental measures that would increase the cost of doing business. Moreover, local officials could distort data to paint a "greener" picture, thus rendering these data unreliable. In 2009 the Green GDP experiment was cancelled (Rauch and Chi 2010).

Local governments are all laggers in enforcing environmental rules, however. Studies show variation in their approaches to environmental protection. In richer regions, local authorities are more likely to enforce those rules because the citizens in their jurisdictions are more demanding of clean air and water. Moreover, service industries tend to make up a large part of the local economy. Unlike low-end manufacturing industries, the service sector is not usually undermined by high environmental policies. In addition, local governments in the richer regions have more resources available for implementing environmental protection measures. In contrast, in poorer regions, the importance of polluting industries to local economic development continues to sabotage the enforcement of environmental rules (Kostka and Nahm 2017; van Rooij et al. 2017).

The negative effect of local shirking does not imply that centralizing power in the hands of the national government will necessarily ensure effective enforcement of environmental rules. In the last decade, there has been a clear tightening of control by the central government, diminishing the power and autonomy of sub-national governments. Beijing has subjected local officials to close monitoring and has shown little tolerance of non-compliance with central directives. While the centralizing trends have helped make environmental policy enforcement stricter and more frequent, that has not led to better environmental performance. Scholars point to several plausible reasons for this phenomenon. One of them is the lack of strength of most administrative sanctions. Although violating environmental rules brings fines, the level of those fines is quite low, and not sufficient to change the behavior of the polluters. Another factor is that the center and the local governments make similar calculations about the trade-off between economic development and environmental protection. When it comes to the poorer regions, which depend heavily on polluting enterprises for economic growth, both levels of governments are willing to make compromises on environmental enforcement (Kostka and Nahm 2017; van Rooij et al. 2017).

Weak Civil Society

Civil society, sometimes labelled "the third sector," refers to the sector of a society that is neither part of the government nor the corporate world. It consists of voluntary organizations that work on behalf of community and public causes, such as labor unions, chambers of commerce, charitable organizations, religious groups, professional associations, and hobby clubs. In Western countries, there is a general assumption that civil society organizations are autonomous from the government. Indeed, they are often called non-government organizations (NGOs).

During the Maoist era, China had no civil society to speak of. The entire country was organized and controlled by the government. During the reform era, a nascent civil society has emerged in China, but it is weak and vulnerable, operating in a narrow and shifting political space granted by the Party. Some of the social organizations (*minjian zuzhi*, the preferred label in official lingo) have limited autonomy from the government, while others are directly tied to the government – aptly nick-named government-organized NGOs (GONGOs). In between there are groups with different levels of closeness with the government, labelled semi-GONGOs (Schwartz 2004).

Environmental NGOs are among the oldest and most prominent civil society actors in contemporary China. The first environmental groups emerged in the mid-1990s, including pioneers such as Friends of Nature (FON) and Global Village Beijing. Most environmental NGOs tend to focus on education and conservation. Their activities are often non-controversial, ranging from organizing birdwatching and tree-planting to promoting sorting garbage and recycling plastic. Some NGOs have taken up advocacy, exposing environmental problems hidden from the public and mobilizing opposition to environmentally damaging projects and practices (see Box 10.2).

Some environmental NGOs have used the legal system to help victims of environmental pollution. A well-known example is the Center for Legal Assistance for Pollution Victims (CLAPV). Founded in 1998 by two law professors, it is based at the Chinese University of Politics and Law in Beijing. It provides legal information for individuals, businesses, and communities so that the latter could use this information to defend their rights in courts. However, CLAPV only selects a tiny fraction of the numerous requests it receives each year. In some of the cases, CLAPV has been successful in stopping the pollution and/or obtaining compensation for the victims, but it has been very careful in choosing which cases to take on because of the political risks involved in confronting powerful actors (van Rooij 2010). CLAPV's approach has won international respect as well as government recognition. Its long-time director, Professor Wang Canfa, has frequently been invited to be a law consultant for MEE. In 2024, he was given an honorary doctorate by the Vermont Law and Graduate School in the United States.

Box 10.2 The Nu River Dam Project

Nu River, also known as Salween River in Southeast Asia, originates on the Tibetan Plateau and flows through southwestern China, Myanmar, and Thailand. With dramatic turns and drops, the Nu River forms breathtakingly beautiful landscapes and contains great potential for hydropower. In 2003 the Chinese government approved a large hydropower project on the river. Consisting of a series of thirteen dams on the lower reaches of the river, it aimed to create 21 million kilowatts of electric power and to accelerate the economic development of the river valley regions. Local communities and environmental activists from other parts of the country leapt into action to protect one of the last free-flowing rivers in China, home to many ethnic minorities as well as 6,000 plant species, and over 25 percent of the world's diverse animal species (International Rivers n.d.). They worried that the damming project would seriously damage the renowned natural beauty of the region and its extraordinary biodiversity and threaten the cultural heritage of the many ethnic groups there. The project would also force masses of hillside villagers to relocate and take away the livelihood of many more. Environmental NGOs organized public events, engaged the media, and collected petition signatures. Their campaign caught the attention of the national government. Premier Wen Jiabao took note of the "high level of social concern." Soon, the government ordered the project to be suspended, until a careful study of its environmental impact could be completed (Yang and Calhoun 2007). In 2016, the dams proposed for the Nu mainstream were removed from China's thirteenth five-year plan. (International Rivers n.d.)

Another way for environmental NGOs to push for better environmental protection through the legal system is environmental public interest litigation (EPIL). EPIL is a framework that allows parties without any direct involvement in a situation to bring lawsuits to defend public environmental interests. It has long been a practice in Western countries, especially the United States. EPIL was first introduced to China in the 1980s, but it was not until 2012 that it became confirmed by Chinese Civil Procedure Law. In the last decade, EPIL suits have increased dramatically, and environmental NGOs have actively participated in them by helping identify violations and contributing information and expertise to the legal proceedings. According to a recent study, by the end of 2020, the courts had accepted 587 EPIL lawsuits filed by environmental NGOs, and 28 of those were designated as model cases by the Supreme People's Court, meaning they were likely to play a significant role in guiding judicial practice in the future (Chu 2023).

Despite such progress, the work of Chinese environmental groups has had a very limited effect on environmental protection in China. For instance, the campaign against the Nu River dam project in 2003 led to its suspension by the Chinese government. But, around 2018, a somewhat scaled-down version of the hydropower project in the area appeared in government planning documents. This time, there was not the kind of media attention and public debate of fifteen years earlier because of the much more oppressive political atmosphere under Xi's rule (Standaert 2020). As of mid-2024, processes of assessment and approval were moving ahead with this project (China Power 2024). Meanwhile, although NGOs like CLAPV have helped some victims of pollution, the small number of court cases they are able to aid are a drop in the bucket. When it comes to EPIL, unlike in many other countries, the main players are not NGOs but the government's procuratorates, which are responsible for seventy to eighty percent of the thousands of such cases each year. In some years, their share is more than ninety percent (Xia and Wang, 2023). Chinese NGOs are limited by their financial resources, ability to gather evidence, and concern about potential political risks (Li and Song 2024).

To understand the limited role of NGOs in China's environmental governance, one needs to remember the nature of the CCP regime. As a Leninist party, the CCP has always seen alternative organizations as a grave threat to its monopoly of power. Although the Chinese government has allowed social organizations to emerge and develop in the reform era, it has made it clear that this does not mean that citizens are free to organize themselves to pursue their beliefs and interests. The Party state manipulates the political space for NGOs through its control of social organization registration, regulation of their structure and activities, Party-building in those organizations, and outright cracking down when it views these organizations as having crossed a red line. Chinese NGOs have had to be strategic in navigating a highly restrictive system, which often means aligning their operations with the Party's priorities and avoiding controversial issues (Saich 2000; Nie and Wu 2022). In this context, the personal quality and political capital of the organizational entrepreneurs (often the founders) play a big role in the NGOs' fate (see Box 10.3).

Finally, funding is a major challenge for Chinese environmental groups. In contrast to the environmental GONGOs, which receive generous financial support from the government, other environmental groups are almost all poorly funded. The larger and better-known among them obtain grants from outside the country. Take FON as an example. As of 2021, among its main funders are German EED Foundation, Department of Culture and Science and Technology of the French Embassy, US-based Rockefeller Brothers Fund, American Bar Association, US-based Natural Resources Defense Council, Germany-based MISEREOR Foundation, US-based Delta Environmental & Educational Foundation, US-based PAMC Health Foundation, and the Cultural

> ## Box 10.3 Liang Congjie and Friends of Nature
>
> Friends of Nature (FON) is the oldest and arguably best-known environmental NGO in China. Its main founder, Liang Congjie, was a historian and came from a legendary Chinese family. His father, Liang Sicheng, and mother, Lin Huiyin, were renowned historians of Chinese architecture trained in the United States. His grandfather, Liang Qichao, was an influential reformist thinker in the late nineteenth and early twentieth centuries. In March 1994, the younger Liang and three colleagues registered FON as China's first legally recognized NGO. In contrast to the confrontational techniques of international environmental groups, such as Greenpeace, FON took pains to work with the Chinese government rather than against it. Its collaboration with government authorities helped the enforcement of environmental laws and the protection of endangered species. Liang became a symbol of environmentalism in China and enjoyed the respect of government officials and the public alike. He was also widely admired by the international community. In 1998, he met with US President Bill Clinton and UK Prime Minister Tony Blair when they visited China for a discussion of environmental policies. He won numerous honors and awards at home and abroad. Much of the early success of FON was attributable to Liang's personal stature and political capital. After he stepped down from the leadership position in 2004, FON went through a difficult time in developing its institutional capacity without Liang. It took several years to formulate a shared organizational mission, vision, and set of values. (Zhuang et al. 2022)

and Education Section of the British Embassy (China Development Brief n.d.). But in getting support from overseas, these social groups often incur suspicion and hostility from the government, endangering their operations and even existence (Schwartz 2004; Yang 2005).

In democratic countries, NGOs are a major force in keeping the government accountable on environmental issues and in helping to enforce environmental regulation. The absence of a vibrant civil society in China continues to limit the role of social groups in environmental governance. This trend is unlikely to change because of the CCP's deep-seated fear of public mobilization outside its organizational structure. As long as the Party state views NGOs as potentially threatening to its monopoly of power, environmental groups, along with other types of NGOs, will be marginal to the policy process and will indeed remain precarious in their very existence. China's authoritarian environmentalism may well expand regulations and meet some quantifiable targets in the short run. But the progress it produces is uneven, often costly for the citizens, and likely to be unsustainable in the long run (Li and Shapiro 2020).

Environmental Issues in Chinese Foreign Relations

The sheer size of China and its important role in international trade and investment mean its environmental problems have broad consequences for the rest of the world. China has been a top contributor to global warming. The dusts and acid rain from China reach its neighboring countries and beyond. Chinese demand for energy and raw materials has intensified pollution, erosion, and deforestation in faraway land. The environmental challenges for China are thus also challenges for the world. Chinese cooperation is essential for global efforts to slow down and potentially reverse environmental degradation. This section discusses China's controversial role in global environmental governance by examining China's behavior in climate change negotiations, its involvement in international trade of solar panels, and its initiative for greening the BRI.

Climate Change Negotiations

China's involvement in international climate governance goes back a long way, and its position has evolved significantly over time (Pearson 2019; Kopra 2019). China was a founding participant in the United Nations Framework Convention on Climate Change (UNFCCC) in 1992. The Rio Convention signed that year called for countries to take on "common but differentiated responsibility" in combating climate change. Later, the Kyoto Protocol of 1997 separated developed and developing countries, setting emission reduction targets for the former but not the latter. The Chinese government, along with the Group of 77 developing countries, insisted on a "firewall" between the wealthy and the poor countries in shouldering the costs of fighting climate change. Chinese leaders emphasized that addressing climate change should not come at the expense of economic progress and that developing countries like China must protect their "right to development."

By the mid-2000s, Chinese economy had become one of the largest in the world (overtaking Japan as number two in 2010), and China, a top GHG emitter (overtaking the United States as number one in 2006). Under these new circumstances, it was increasingly difficult for China to continue to define itself as just another developing country. In fact, many of China's erstwhile allies in the global South began to urge China to take on more responsibilities in fighting climate change. In 2009 the Chinese government made concrete pledges to the international community that it would reduce domestic carbon intensity from 2005 levels and increase non-fossil fuels in primary energy consumption. It also accepted limited international verification. In 2011, China played a constructive role in the UN Climate Change Conference in Durban. It agreed to enter another round of negotiations with other parties to develop a climate agreement among all major emitters by 2015, dismantling the distinction between developed and developing countries.

In 2014, China and the United States reached a groundbreaking bilateral agreement, which formed the foundation of the landmark Paris Agreement of 2015. Under the Paris Agreement signed by 196 parties, countries agree to make their nationally determined contribution to the collective goal of limiting global warming to 1.5 to 2 degrees Celsius. Every five years they would come together to assess the collective progress and update their national actions in a transparent way. China was among the first nations to ratify the agreement. In the following years, it more than lived up to its commitment under the agreement, "overdelivering" in its performance (Pearson 2019).

China's changing behavior in international negotiations reflects the evolution of the leadership's thinking. As discussed earlier in this chapter, the rapid deterioration of air, water, and soil quality and other kinds of environmental degradation at home have convinced the government to recalculate the balance between economic development and the environment. Meanwhile, Chinese policymakers have come to recognize that international cooperation is necessary to deal with many transnational environmental challenges, including global warming.

An additional important factor shaping the thinking of Chinese leaders lies in China's evolving identity and international political ambition. With the ascendance of the Chinese economy, the idea of China as a "responsible great power" has gradually taken hold in the imagination of the Chinese elite. As early as the Asian financial crisis in 1997–1998, this new self-identity played a key role in the decision by the Chinese government to adopt a no-devaluation policy. Although that policy incurred economic costs for the country, it improved China's international image, especially among its Asian neighbors (Wang 2002). When it comes to international cooperation in combating climate change, China sees another opportunity to project itself as a responsible great power. The withdrawal of the United States from the Paris Agreement during the Trump administration widened the opportunity for China to act as a leader on the world stage. Beijing has declared repeatedly that China would not dilute its commitment. In President Xi's words, "Taking a driving seat in international cooperation to respond to climate change, China has become an important participant, contributor, and torchbearer in the global endeavor for ecological civilization" (Kopra 2019). Although the Biden Administration has revived US participation in the Paris Agreement, the Chinese government continues to highlight its willingness to lead. As noted earlier in the chapter, Xi announced in 2020 that China would reach peak emissions well before 2030, ahead of the timeline it pledged under the Paris Agreement.

However, China's emerging leadership in international climate change negotiations is more limited than these declarations imply. Xi's strong statement was not followed up with any specific steps as to how the country would strengthen its climate commitments. For instance, at the Bonn Conference on climate change in 2017, China got together with other emerging economies, including Brazil, India, and South Africa, and resumed the pursuit of the division between the developed and the developing countries that the Paris Agreement had abandoned. They demanded that the future conferences should formally discuss the failure of developed countries in implementing their climate commitments and the limited flow of climate finance from the rich to the poor countries (Kopra 2019). Moreover, China's lofty rhetoric on the international stage has not always translated into action on the ground. As mentioned earlier, in the last few years China has continued to increase its coal power capacity at an alarming rate. As of 2023, fossil fuel still accounted for seventy percent of China's electricity (Hilton 2024).

Trade Disputes over Solar Panel Exports

China was a late comer to the technologies of renewable energy, such as wind and solar power. The pioneers were research centers and companies in Europe, North America, and Japan. But, once the Chinese government decided to make it a strategic priority to develop renewable energy, progress has been fast and furious. The solar-electric panel industry offers a vivid example.

In the late 1990s, the German government pushed hard for rooftop solar panels. Its incentive program led to soaring demand for solar panels in the country. Unable to meet the demand, German manufacturers provided the capital, technology, and experts to help manufacturers in China make solar panels to fill the gap. This created an excellent opportunity for China to grow its rudimentary solar power industry. With governmental encouragement and subsidies (mainly tax credits), Chinese companies hired more foreign experts and shopped for machinery and polysilicon supplies around the world. China's cheap and disciplined labor force and its existing semiautomatic manufacturing facilities quickly made these emerging companies competitive.

Between 2008 and 2013, Chinese companies drove down the prices for solar panels in the world by eighty percent. While this greatly accelerated the transition to solar power both inside and outside China, it seriously undermined the solar panel producers in other countries, many of whom lost market shares and even went bankrupt. By 2012, Chinese manufacturers had captured sixty percent of the global photovoltaic (PV) module market (Hughes and Meckling 2017).

In 2011 and 2013, in response to industry petition, the US government investigated possible Chinese dumping of solar cells and modules in the American market. It found that the Chinese imports had injured US producers and thus imposed antidumping and countervailing duties on Chinese products. These tariffs were a triumph of the protectionist coalition of domestic manufacturers in the United States and congressional interests (Hughes and Meckling 2017). In 2012, the European Commission announced it was launching an antidumping investigation into solar PV cells, wafers, and modules imported from

China. Industrial actors were not all in support of the investigation. Increasing the prices of imports from China would obviously benefit the local PV manufacturers. But it would also hurt the interest of upstream producers such as polysilicon and equipment exporters to China, and downstream retailers and installers of PV projects. There was also significant division between defenders of fair trade and promoters of green energy, and between the European Commission and individual European Union (EU) member countries with different stakes in maintaining good relations with China. In 2013, through a compromise solution, Chinese exporters agreed to abide by minimum import conditions when selling their products to the EU (Goron 2018). In 2018, the EU removed the anti-dumping tariffs after re-evaluating the effects of the tariffs on producers and on users of solar panels (McWilliams et al. 2024).

These trade barriers notwithstanding, China's competitiveness in solar panel production remains formidable. In 2022, over 95 percent of Europe's solar panels came from China (IEA, 2023). Moreover, China's share in all the main manufacturing stages of solar panels has exceeded eighty percent by 2022. For key elements including polysilicon and wafers, China's share is expected to rise to more than 95 percent in the coming years (IEA 2022). China's strong capacity in the solar panel industry poses a dilemma for Western countries. Both the EU and the United States have ambitious plans to transition from fossil fuel to renewable energy. In the EU, if existing patterns hold, the goal of expanding solar power from 263 GW in 2024 to almost 600 GW by 2030 will almost exclusively depend on solar panels imported from China. This dependence has raised concerns about the EU's economic security and geopolitical vulnerabilities (McWilliams et al. 2024).

Likewise, the US goal is to expand its current 100 GW of solar energy capacity by more than 500 GW by the end of 2030 (Solar Energy Industries Association 2021). To achieve its goal, the US has relied heavily on imported solar panels. In 2022, the US Commerce Department began to investigate if solar panels imported from four Southeast Asian countries – Vietnam, Malaysia, Thailand, and Cambodia – circumvented American trade rules by using Chinese-sourced materials without paying applicable duties. The investigation contributed to a major drop in solar installation forecasts, as the four countries under investigation account for more than eighty percent of the solar panel imports for the United States. Installers were concerned that the government could impose retroactive taxes and that the cost of future purchases would go up dramatically (National Public Radio 2022).

"Green BRI"

China's President Xi announced the ambitious BRI in 2013, a multi-trillion-dollar project connecting China with the rest of the world. The land route – the "Silk Road Economic Belt" – consists of roads and railways through Central

Asia to Europe. The sea route – the "21st Century Maritime Silk Road" – runs through Southeast Asia, South Asia, the Middle East, and Africa. With its focus on infrastructure development, BRI potentially has lasting consequences for the environment of over one hundred and fifty countries which have signed up for the project. Analysts have identified a myriad of environmental risks of the BRI, ranging from increased GHG emission by the power plants to changed patterns of transportation (e.g. Gallagher and Qi 2018, Losos 2019). Public opinion surveys indicate widespread concerns in the host countries of Chinese investment about the adverse environmental impacts of BRI projects (Nedopil 2022).

Partly in response to international criticisms and concerns, the Chinese government began to emphasize greening the BRI around 2017. A series of official guidelines came out of various government agencies, including the State Council, the People's Bank of China, the Ministry of Finance, the National Reform and Development Commission, the Ministry of Commerce, the State-owned Assets Supervision and Administration Commission, the MEE, the Chinese Banking and Insurance Regulatory Commission, and the Ministry of Foreign Affairs. These guidelines typically encourage BRI projects to follow host-country environmental regulations and try to incorporate international environmental standards. At the first Belt and Road Forum for International Cooperation in 2017 and the second such forum in 2019, Chinese leaders emphasized the BRI would promote green and clean development. In October 2020, under the leadership of MEE, five ministries issued the "Guidance on promoting investment and financing to address climate change," which promotes "the active integration of climate investment and financing into the 'Belt and Road' construction" (Nedopil 2022)

However, the discourse on greening the BRI has been vague and is inconsistently implemented. On the one hand, China has made green finance – investments in financial assets that address climate change and other environmental concerns – a flagship of its financial policies. In particular, it has issued offshore green bonds to finance low-carbon infrastructure in the wealthier regions along the Belt and Road, offering business opportunities for emerging Chinese firms in renewable energy. On the other hand, in developing countries, China has invested heavily in brown projects associated with carbon emissions and other environmental damages, such as coal-fired power plants, oil pipelines, mines, and massive transportation infrastructure. From 2013 to mid-2020, China invested nearly $300 billion in energy-related projects under the BRI, with fossil-fuel related investments making up 72 percent of the total. NGOs and thinktanks have published reports on the environmental abuses by Chinese companies operating abroad (Nedopil 2022).

The **Asian Infrastructure Investment Bank** (AIIB) is a new China-led multilateral development bank. Launching its first investment projects in 2016, it has worked in many BRI countries helping with infrastructure development. Despite its mantra of being "lean, clean and green," it has a lower share of climate finance in its portfolio than other major multilateral development banks. By August 2021, AIIB had invested $4.7 billion in energy-related projects, of which $1.5 billion (31 percent) went into fossil fuels, $1.1 billion (24 percent) funded renewable energies, and the remainder supported energy transmission and distribution (Nedopil 2022).

Skeptics describe the Chinese conception of "green development" as akin to greenwashing. China defines hydropower as "green," even though hydropower plants are often detrimental to the environment. In addition, the Chinese government believes that poverty reduction and modernization are important means of reducing damages to the environment and of improving access to clean water. It often equates economic development with environmental improvement, which is quite different from international norms (Harlan 2021). A recent study concludes that the Chinese government has used green finance as a tool for building up China's soft power along the Belt and the Road, but the rhetorical signals of greening the BRI are undermined by the lack of green finance action (Nedopil 2022).

Conclusion

China's rising economy has been accompanied by its deteriorating environment. Just as its economic miracle has been a focus of worldwide attention, its environmental challenge is becoming increasingly a global concern. In this chapter, we have briefly reviewed environmental degradation in three realms – air, water, and land. While there has been improvement in some areas, the general trend is still one of environmental decline. China's per capita consumption and pollution is still smaller than many other countries but, given its population size, its environmental footprint is considerable, and will likely grow in the years to come.

Domestic economic and political pressure has contributed to the government's shift from its single-minded pursuit of GDP growth to a greater emphasis on environmental protection than in the recent past. But there are still significant obstacles for achieving sustainable development in China. We have highlighted some of these obstacles – the competition between the economic and the environmental priorities for the Party state, the fragmented nature of the Chinese political system, and the absence of a strong and effective civil society in China.

In the international arena, China has been an influential and controversial environmental actor. On the one hand, the Chinese government has made important contributions to international negotiations on environmental issues, including the all-important fight against climate change. Chinese companies have helped accelerate the transition to renewable energy worldwide.

On the other hand, China continues to oscillate between advocating green standards and investing in brown practice and projects. There is a clear gap between China's strong signals of environmental commitment and the insufficient green actions on the ground.

Questions for Discussion

1. How has China's environment deteriorated in the reform era?

2. Why has the Chinese government become more attentive to the environment in recent years?

3. Has China been a lagger or a leader in combating climate change?

11

Laying Eggs with Borrowed Hens

At the end of the Cultural Revolution (1966–1976), China was not only poor, but also quite isolated from the world economy. World Bank data show that in the late 1970s China's exports accounted for only five percent of its GDP, much below the global figure of over sixteen percent. With the onset of post-Mao reform, the Chinese government not only initiated economic liberalization at home, but also quickly expanded economic interactions with the rest of the world. In fact, the official rhetoric always paired the reform policy with this opening-up policy (*gaige kaifang*). Over a period of around ten years, the Chinese economy became more foreign-trade oriented than most other major economies. World Bank figures show exports in 1990 accounted for about nine percent of Chinese GDP, roughly the same as the US. By 2006 however, China's exports had climbed to 36 percent of GDP, three times that of the United States (ten percent).

As well as trade, foreign capital inflow is another major indicator of a country's integration with the global economy. Prior to the reform era, the Chinese government totally banned the inflow of foreign capital. But this changed dramatically under the reform-and-open policy framework. By far the most important form of foreign capital inflow has been foreign direct investment (FDI), i.e. investment by foreign companies that involves at least ten percent of the equity and thus gives the investor considerable influence on the business. Since the early 1990s China has been the top or the second most popular destination of FDI worldwide. Portfolio foreign investment – short-term passive investment by foreigner investors – has also entered China through the newly created Chinese capital market and through Chinese companies' overseas listing.

China's shift from near economic autarchy to a hub of international trade and capital flow is the subject of this chapter. We will examine how this extraordinary transformation has taken place and explore its impact on China's economic growth. Focusing on foreign trade and FDI, we will see how China has implemented a policy of "laying eggs with borrowed hens (*jieji xiadan*)" – using foreign markets and capital to develop its economy.

Foreign Trade

International trade involves the exchange of goods and services across state borders. According to the classical economic theory of David Ricardo, countries have different comparative advantages, i.e. they can produce some things more efficiently than other things. International trade is welfare-improving because it enables countries to specialize in making what they are more efficient at making and exchange them for the products that they cannot produce very efficiently. Trade makes all parties better off than if they produce everything they need on their own (see Box 11.1).

Box 11.1 Ricardo's Model

The key concept in Ricardian theory is comparative advantage. To illustrate how it works, consider Ricardo's ideal example of a world made up of two countries – England and Portugal – which produce two products – cotton and wine. It takes England 100 hours of labor to produce one unit of cloth or 5/6 unit of wine. Meanwhile, in Portugal 100 hours of labor can turn out 10/9 unit of cloth and 10/8 unit of wine. If each country is on its own, it requires 220 hours to make one unit of cloth and one unit of wine in England and 170 hours to produce the same in Portugal. But if the two countries trade with each other, then England can specialize in the production of cloth, in which it has a comparative advantage (over its production of wine) and Portugal can focus on the production of wine, where its comparative advantage lies. In that scenario, England can spend 220 hours producing 2.2 units of cloth and Portugal can spend 170 hours making 2.215 units of wine. Their combined output is greater than if both countries engage in making both products (2.2 > 2 units of cloth and 2.215 > 2 units of wine). And if the two countries trade with each other, each of them can enjoy more of both products than if they remain autarkic. (Ricardo 1817/2004)

In reality, the economic consequences of international trade have not always been beneficial to all participants. Many developing countries deeply involved in international trade remain poor and vulnerable. Structural economics, which emerged in the late 1940s and is critical of Ricardian economic thought, attributes this phenomenon to the unfavorable terms of trade faced by the developing countries, i.e. they export low-value primary goods to developed countries while importing high-value manufactured goods from the latter (Prebisch 1950; Singer 1950). This kind of unequal exchange has not only failed to improve the welfare of the developing countries but has in fact often locked them in an inferior and dependent position in the world economic hierarchy.

Theorists of different persuasion have marshalled empirical evidence to support their respective claims and the debate goes on. However, what is clear is that the effects of international trade in a capitalist system vary. While some developing countries have benefited a great deal from international trade and gained upward mobility, most of the global South economies have been trapped on the lower rungs of the development ladder (e.g. Mahutga 2006). China stands out as one of a minority of developing countries that have benefited enormously from participating in international trade. In this section, we trace the evolution of Chinese foreign trade, discuss its impact on the country's economic development, and explore the political economy underlying the China's trade policy.

Evolution of Chinese Foreign Trade

When the Chinese Communist Party (CCP) came into power in 1949, the newly established People's Republic of China (PRC) quickly formed a strategic alliance with the Soviet Union. "Leaning toward one-side" in the Cold War meant terminating existing economic relations with the Western bloc. In the following years China conducted foreign trade primarily with the Soviet Union and other communist countries in the Eastern bloc. It imported fuel, steel, and machinery, and exported textiles and processed food. But within a decade, the Sino-Soviet alliance frayed. From the late 1950s to the early 1960s, the two communist giants argued bitterly over their political and ideological differences. The CCP were critical of the de-Stalinization policy of new Soviet leader, Nikita Khrushchev, and his policy of peaceful coexistence with the United States. Mao accused the Soviet Union of revisionism – a betrayal of Marxism and Leninism. The economic relationship between China and the Soviet Union deteriorated as well. By the end of the 1960s, the military of the two countries confronted each other in border clashes. China found itself estranged from both the East and the West in a bipolar world.

Data of the World Bank show that in 1970 and 1971, Chinese imports and exports combined made up only five percent of the country's GDP. The economic setback during the Great Leap Forward in the late 1950s and the Cultural Revolution from the mid-1960s to the mid-1970s led to serious shortages of everything; there was little surplus to export. This in turn resulted in a scarcity of foreign exchanges. The government took every measure to conserve its limited reserve of hard currencies to cover the cost of grain imports and the purchase of critical industrial input from overseas. In the mid-1970s, the Chinese economy began to recover from the rock bottom, with an increase in the production of textiles and petroleum among other things. For a brief period, the Chinese government planned to use the earnings from exporting petroleum to pay for imports of modern equipment and advanced technologies. But it soon became clear that China's oil reserves were far below expectations. New ways had to be found to generate much-needed foreign exchanges.

In the late 1970s, China opened new trade channels in the Pearl River Delta (PRD) adjacent to the British colony of Hong Kong. With Beijing's permission, local enterprises in this area, including many township-and-village enterprise (TVEs) began to engage in export-processing (EP) operations funded by Hong Kong investors. In the previous three decades, Hong Kong had become a manufacturing powerhouse, but the rising costs of labor and land eroded Hong Kong's competitiveness over time. When China opened its door, Hong Kong manufacturers were eager to move their production to the mainland. They shipped materials to Guangdong province next door, had them assembled there, and then returned the products to Hong Kong, all the while keeping the materials and the products under their ownership. This was a win–win arrangement; the Hong Kong firms were able to reduce their cost of manufacturing, while their Chinese contractors earned processing fees paid in foreign exchanges. Seeing the benefit of the EP model, the Chinese government established four special economic zones (SEZs) – three in Guangdong neighboring Hong Kong and one in Fujian, a province located near Taiwan. The growing numbers of EP enterprises in the SEZs expanded Chinese exports without having to restructure China's formal foreign-trade regime.

The Chinese foreign-trade system in the reform era should be understood as consisting of two trade regimes – EP trade and "ordinary trade" (Naughton 2018). After the initial success of EP trade in the SEZs, the Chinese government launched a "Coastal Development Strategy," expanding the EP model to the entire coastal region. The Yangtze River Delta in eastern China, around Shanghai, Jiangsu, and Zhejiang, quickly caught up with the PRD in trade openness. At the beginning, most of the EP took place in low-end manufacturing of textiles, garments, footwear, and toys. Later it included more sophisticated industries such as electronics, auto parts, steel, and machinery.

In contrast to EP trade, China's ordinary trade changed little in the early years of the reform era. Still under the traditional command economy, exports and imports were exclusively controlled by a handful of state-owned **foreign-trade companies** (FTCs). The government set the value of the Renminbi (RMB) unrealistically high without considering the international supply and demand for currencies. Both the state monopoly of foreign trade and the arbitrary exchange rates were designed to restrict foreign trade and to insulate the domestic economy from the world economy. It was not until the mid-1990s that the regime governing ordinary trade began to change. The FTCs lost their monopoly as the government granted permission to more and more enterprises to engage in foreign trade. The central bank abolished the old foreign exchange regime, increasingly linking the exchange rates to market conditions. Under the new foreign-trade system, normal tariffs and non-tariff barriers became the main instruments for protecting the domestic market. When China intensified its efforts to join the World Trade Organization (WTO)

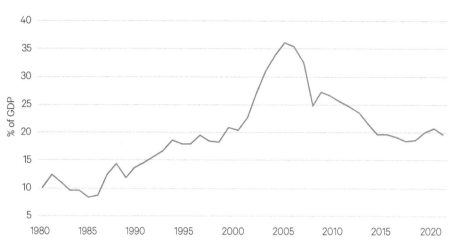

Figure 11.1 China's Exports of Goods and Services 1980–2020
Source: World Bank Group.

in the late 1990s, the government accelerated trade liberalization by dramatically lowering tariffs and reducing non-tariff barriers.

Following China's accession to the WTO in 2001, its exports climbed sharply (see Figure 11.1). World Bank data indicate that China's trade surplus (exports minus imports) reached an extraordinarily high level of seven percent of its GDP in 2006–2008. While cheap products from China brought substantial benefits to consumers everywhere, the competition they posed destroyed many manufacturing businesses in other countries. Foreign government and business communities blamed China for unfair trade practice, including the low value of the RMB, which kept Chinese exports ultra-competitive in the international market. In response, the Chinese government further liberalized the exchange rate, allowing the Chinese currency to appreciate against other currencies. Moreover, in the wake of the global financial crisis (GFC) of 2008, the Chinese government introduced a large-scale economic stimulus package, which increased its purchase of foreign goods and services. As a result, Chinese foreign trade became more balanced between exports and imports. According to the World Bank, in 2010 and 2011, China's trade surplus dropped to about two percent of the GDP.

The combined growth of EP trade and ordinary trade has propelled China to the status of a global trade leader. In 2013 it became the world's largest trading power in goods, a position it has maintained since. In retrospect, the evolution of Chinese foreign trade has been a remarkable story. China's exports of goods made up one percent of the global total in 1980 and rose to four percent in 2000. In 2020, China's share reached nearly fifteen percent, well ahead of the United States and Germany, each around eight percent (Nicita and Razo 2021).

Trade and Economic Development

As noted above, international trade has not always served economic development well. Historically, only in a small number of developing countries did trade enhance the productivity of the enterprises and improve the living standards of the people. Until China came along, the most prominent cases of success were post-World War II Japan and the newly industrialized economies (NIEs) of Korea, Taiwan, Singapore, and Hong Kong. In a widely cited report published in the early 1990s, the World Bank attributed the so-called East Asian economic miracle to an export-led development strategy (World Bank 1993). In a recent study that includes China, the United National Industrial Development Organization similarly attributes the success of East and Southeast Asian economies to the "outward-oriented industrialization" strategy, defined as "a strategy that aims to extensively re-organize an economy for the purpose of manufacturing by exporting goods for which the nation has a comparative advantage" (Seric and Tong 2019).

China has largely followed the export-led development strategy of Japan and the Asian NIEs. Systematic studies across time and regions show that export has been one of the two external engines of economic growth in China, the other being FDI (Lardy 1995; Yao 2006). The positive effect of trade on Chinese economic development is two-fold. First, it has enabled China to profit from its comparative advantage, as described by the Ricardian trade theory. For much of the reform era, China has enjoyed a strong comparative advantage in labor-intensive productions thanks to its cheap, disciplined, and relatively well-educated work force. Through international trade, China has become the workshop of the world. In this process, the Chinese have created jobs and wealth on a scale unprecedented in human history. Second, international trade has exposed Chinese companies to intense competition from around the world. Enterprises engaged in exports have been forced to continuously improve their productivity through technological and managerial upgrading (Lardy 1995).

The prevailing view among many observers is that China's economic development depends heavily on foreign trade, especially on selling Chinese goods to Western countries, and that international demand has raised wages for Chinese workers and increased their consumption. But some researchers disagree. They contend that China's reliance on export is significantly lower than implied by the headline exports-to-GDP ratio. Moreover, they propose that exports have contributed to China's economic growth not through their multiplier effect on the demand side but, instead, through their impact on the supply side. By exporting to the world market, Chinese firms find themselves at the frontier of international competition, compelled to improve their efficiency and total factor productivity (He and Zhang 2010). This is an area where further research is warranted.

To the extent that exports have been an engine behind China's economic success, it is important to recognize that their positive impact is not only because of the quantity of trade but also because of its quality. Starting with labor-intensive goods, China has gradually expanded its export basket to include a wide range of highly sophisticated products. In the early twenty-first century, China's export bundle was that of a country whose income-per-capita level was three times higher. For instance, the video recorders and TV and video monitors exported by China then had higher unit values than Korean exports in these product lines (Rodrik 2006). Comparative studies show a robust positive relationship between the productivity level of a country's export and the subsequent rate of economic growth experienced by that country. China's rapid economic growth owes as much to the content of its exports as to the volume.

However, the export-led development model has its problems. China's extraordinary performance in exports, especially following its entry into the WTO, caused a so-called "China shock" in developed countries. The influx of goods made in China eroded the manufacturing base in many of those countries, where import-competing businesses shrank, and workers suffered stagnant wages and rising unemployment. The United States, the European Union and other countries have harshly and frequently criticized the policies and practices behind China's strong exports, including persistent state subsidies of industries ranging from steel and aluminum to solar panels and electric vehicles. From time to time, China has been subject to WTO sanctions and retaliatory trade measures by other governments.

In addition to international backlashes, policymakers in China have also come to realize the inherent unsustainability of an export-dependent development model. China has accumulated large amounts of dollar earnings as a result of its trade surplus. The Chinese government has invested heavily in dollar assets, including US government debt. The wealth of China is thus vulnerable to changes in American financial health and monetary policy. Indeed, during the GFC the Chinese Premier, Wen Jiabao, openly expressed worries about the "safety" of China's $1 trillion investment in US Treasury bonds and other American debt. Speaking at an international forum, he asked the Obama administration to offer assurances that these securities would maintain their value (Wines et al. 2009).

Political Economy of Foreign-Trade Reform

Like other aspects of the Chinese economy, the development of foreign trade has been shaped by many political factors. In this discussion of the political economy undergirding China's foreign-trade reform, we briefly examine the politics of the CCP's management of trade liberalization and the policy controversy surrounding China's accession to the WTO.

As part and parcel of the gradualist economic reform strategy of the CCP, the restructuring of China's foreign-trade system has proceeded incrementally. The government has carefully managed the pace and scope of trade liberalization according to political as much as economic calculations. In the early years of the open policy, China allowed EP trade in relatively remote areas in the southern provinces of Guangdong and Fujian. Only after witnessing the model's success in generating employment and foreign currency earnings did the government extend it from the SEZs to the entire coastal region, all the time avoiding changing the traditional foreign-trade system. This can be seen as a parallel to the macroeconomic and industrial reforms, both of which followed a strategy of **"growing out of the plan"** (Naughton 1995). It introduced new market dynamics without abolishing the old system, thus avoiding causing immediate losses to the powerful stakeholders in the status quo, such as the FTCs and the millions of inefficient domestic enterprises that could not compete against imported goods. When the government turned to dismantling the monopoly of state-owned FTCs, it took more than a decade to phase in the change. In the 1992–1993 period China had 8.61 million industrial enterprises, and only 839 had been granted the right to trade directly in the international market (Lardy 1995).

Another dimension of liberalizing the foreign-trade system was to develop a more market-driven exchange rate regime. According to World Bank data, in 1980 the official exchange rate set one RMB yuan at $1.5. At this rate, exporting goods had no chance of making any profits because the foreign exchange earnings could hardly cover the production costs denominated in RMB. Meanwhile, the demand for cheap foreign exchange far exceeded the supply, which the government controlled tightly and made available only for a small number of high-priority imports.

China's reformers recognized the need to abandon the unrealistic exchange rate in order to encourage exports and to expand importers' access to hard currencies. However, they were concerned that devaluing the RMB would lead to serious inflation and macroeconomic chaos. They believed that macroeconomic instability was a major problem with the "big bang" reforms that had brought down communist regimes in the former Soviet Union and Eastern European countries. Cautiously, they introduced an internal settlement exchange rate, which was linked to market supply and demand, while still keeping the official exchange rate, which was commanded by the government. Such a dual-track system was in place for over a decade, allowing the government to slowly devalue the Chinese currency and to loosen its control of foreign exchanges. It was not until the mid-1990s that a unified exchange rate emerged, providing a sound foundation for China's soaring foreign trade.

The piecemeal approach to foreign-trade reform reached its limits in the late 1990s, when China entered a new stage in its pursuit of WTO membership. To understand that turning point, we need to briefly trace the history of China's relationship with the international trade regime.

At the end of World War II, the Republic of China (ROC) under the Kuomintang (KMT) participated in the Bretton Woods Conference in 1944, where it became a founding member of the International Monetary Fund (IMF) and the World Bank. Delegates to the Bretton Woods Conference also recommended the establishment of an International Trade Organization (ITO). However, the ITO was never created because of opposition in the US Senate. In its place, a General Agreement on Tariffs and Trade (GATT) signed by 23 nations in 1947 became a multilateral framework for governing international trade. The ROC government was a founding party to the GATT. When the PRC broke out of its diplomatic isolation in the 1970s, it took over the seat held by the ROC in various international organizations. In 1980, it joined the IMF and the World Bank. In 1986, it applied to resume China's status as a contracting party to the GATT. The negotiation was complicated by the socialist characteristics of the Chinese economy. After the CCP cracked down on the Tiananmen movement in 1989, China became an international pariah, which further delayed the negotiations. By the mid-1990s, the Chinese economy had come to depend so much on foreign trade that the government was determined to join the GATT's successor organization, the WTO, to stabilize and enhance China's access to the international market.

To be accepted by the WTO, China had to meet a long list of conditions set forth by the trade body. In the shadow of WTO membership negotiations, China implemented numerous difficult reform measures in the late 1990s. This was not an easy process because of the hardship those measures would impose on certain sectors and groups in China. Various government bureaucracies, many SOEs, as well as nationalist pundits argued that if China were to accept the WTO's conditions of market openness, Chinese businesses would face crippling competition from foreign companies. For instance, they worried that Chinese farmers would be hurt by cheaper and better agricultural products from other countries. They were also concerned that China was to become entangled in the global capitalist network that would erode the country's sovereignty, possibly reducing China to an "appendage" of the West (Fewsmith 2001). On the other hand, establishment economists working for the government drew optimistic conclusions from their research and modeling about China's ability to absorb the disruptions of WTO membership (Naughton 2002).

The reformers in the government led by the no-nonsense Premier, Zhu Rongji, pushed hard for China to meet the requirements for WTO accession. From their point of view, globalization was an unstoppable tide. China should join the world trade body even if it was costly, or it would be marginalized in a globalized trading system. Perhaps more importantly, they saw an opportunity in the tough negotiations about China's WTO membership. The concessions

China was asked to make, such as improving policy transparency, reducing protection of the SOEs, and greater exposure to international competition, would bring about politically difficult but economically sensible restructuring the country needed (Fewsmith 2001). In other words, they were keen to use this international pressure to overcome domestic opposition to economic liberalization beyond trade.

Foreign Direct Investment

Throughout history foreign capital has played an important role in the economic development in many parts of the world. At one time, in the nineteenth century, the United States and other European settlement areas relied on foreign capital to build their infrastructure, especially the railways (Eichengreen 1995). In the post-World War II era, developing countries in Latin America, Asia, and Africa drew foreign investment to assist their industrialization (Stallings 1990). International capital flow is potentially beneficial for both the capital exporters and the host countries of foreign capital. It allows capital owners to find higher profit margins in areas where capital is relatively scarce. It also enables countries with limited domestic savings to use foreign investment to help jump-start their economic development.

However, just as international trade has not always promoted economic development, foreign capital has also had mixed results for capital-importing countries. Scholars have debated the costs and benefits of foreign investment for developing countries (Stallings 1990). Standard business literature stresses the benefits FDI brings to the host countries, including capital, technology, employment, and international market access (Dunning 1993). In contrast, dependency theorists are critical of foreign capital, blaming it for the underdevelopment of the poor countries in the global South. They contend that foreign investors extract more profits from the host countries than the capital they bring in, that multinational corporations (MNCs) often adopt technologies that are old and/or do not help the employment, environmental, or industrial upgrading of the host countries, and that they marginalize the low-income regions and groups, thus worsening the inequality in the host countries (Higginbottom 2013). More nuanced research suggests that the impact of foreign capital is varied, depending on circumstances. For instance, countries with strong state capacity (e.g. East Asian NIEs) can better control foreign capital and make it serve their national economic development than those without such capacity (e.g. countries in Latin America) (Haggard 1990). Moreover, it matters how concentrated foreign investment is. The more foreign investment, especially FDI, is owned by a single investing country, the less autonomy the host state has in making use of foreign capital for its long-term economic growth (Kentor and Boswell 2003).

When it comes to China, there is widely shared consensus among scholars that foreign capital has played a vital and positive role in the country's economic development. This is especially true of FDI, which far exceeds foreign bank loans and foreign portfolio investment made through capital markets. In this section, we examine the evolution of FDI in China, its impact on the Chinese economy, and the political economy of China's FDI policy.

Evolution of FDI in China

Following the establishment of the PRC in 1949, China not only stopped trading with the West, but also prohibited any investment from the capitalist countries. Only a limited amount of economic aid came into the country from the Soviet Union, which in any case was halted by the early 1960s following the Sino-Soviet split. For the rest of the Maoist era, Chinese economic development was entirely funded by domestic savings. In the late 1970s, the economic reform re-opened China to foreign investment alongside foreign trade.

In 1979, the National People's Congress passed the Law on Joint Ventures Using Chinese and Foreign Investment. The government sought to utilize foreign capital to help launch China's economic modernization. Initially, only the four SEZs in Guangdong and Fujian were open to foreign investment. They enticed foreign enterprises by setting low tax rates, streamlining bureaucratic procedures, and allowing duty-free import of components for EP trade. In the early 1990s, the establishment of Pudong SEZ in Shanghai, China's historical industrial center, constituted a symbolic and significant step up in China's economic openness to foreign capital. In the years that followed, more and more coastal regions obtained permission to host foreign companies and the FDI flow took off (see Figure 11.2). Local governments competed fiercely with

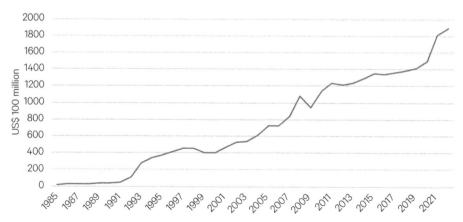

Figure 11.2 FDI Inflow 1985–2021
Source: Based on data from Chinese Ministry of Commerce, "Statistical Bulletin of FDI in China, 2023."

each other to attract foreign investment. A favorite strategy was to build "development zones" that built infrastructure for industrial and commercial use and provided favorable regulatory and tax policies. Some of these zones were successful, but some never received any FDI. Indeed, the uneven distribution of FDI worsened the inequality among regions, leaving inland provinces further behind coastal China in economic development.

In the twenty-first century, FDI inflow has continued to grow, although the feverish competition among local governments has diminished somewhat for two reasons. First, as domestic Chinese enterprises catch up with and even exceed foreign companies in their technological and production capacity, national and local governments have rolled back the red carpet for foreign capital. For China, FDI is no longer a main source of capital or advanced technologies. Second, to comply with the conditions of WTO accession, the Chinese government has had to grant "national treatment" to foreign enterprises. It has gradually stopped both discriminatory and extra-favorable policies toward foreign investors; the latter was a major reason underlying local enthusiasm toward FDI. For example, in 2008 Chinese legislations unified the income-tax rates for all enterprises, which removed an important privilege of foreign investors who used to enjoy lower tax rates than Chinese businesses.

A remarkable feature of FDI development in China is its unusual sources. In the early years of the reform era, FDI in China came primarily from Hong Kong and Taiwan. A study published in 2005 found that the European Union, the US, and Japan (the so-called Triad) supplied ninety percent of the world's FDI, but they only accounted for 25 percent of FDI in China from the early 1980s to the end of the 1990s. In comparison, Hong Kong and Taiwan made up 58 percent of the FDI flowing into mainland China (Zhang 2005). The dominance of Hong Kong and Taiwan investors then can be attributed to socio-cultural ties between them and mainland China, the human networks they had access to through family ties, as well as the economic complementarity Hong Kong and Taiwan had with mainland China.

When China first began to reform the socialist economy and to open its door to international capital, it lacked the institutions of a modern capitalist system. The absence of an effective legal system was not conducive to the security of private property and contractual rights. Many MNCs aspired to sell their products to the Chinese market but stayed away from China because of the perceived risks of investing there. Hong Kong and Taiwan businesses were less deterred than their counterparts from the Triad. Thanks to their understanding of Chinese language and culture and their access to personal networks in Chinese society, many of them were able to navigate the convoluted bureaucracies and manage the uncertainties of operating under a weak legal system (Wang 2001).

Economically, there was ready synergy among mainland China, Hong Kong and Taiwan. From the 1950s to the 1970s, Hong Kong and Taiwan had grown their economies by exporting manufactured goods. They had developed worldwide market networks. However, by the 1980s, their manufacturing industry was squeezed by rising wages and land prices in their territories. Luckily, mainland China began to open its door at this critical juncture. The abundant cheap labor and land and the welcoming policy of the Chinese government made the SEZs ideal sites for Hong Kong and Taiwan manufacturers to relocate their manufacturing operations. From Beijing's perspective, the export orientation of the Hong Kong and Taiwan companies suited China well. Together the three economies formed a so-called "**China Circle**" (Naughton 2018).

While Hong Kong and Taiwan firms were eager to participate in the EP trade in the SEZs, MNCs from the Triad of the EU, US, and Japan were more interested in making goods for China's domestic market. China's reluctance to open its market in the early years of economic reform limited the inflow of FDI from the Triad companies (Zhang 2005). As the Chinese government became more willing to grant market access to foreign companies, and as the legal system governing FDI matured, MNCs from the Triad increased their investment in China. In the period leading up to China's accession to the WTO, such FDI grew steadily. From 1997 to 2002, American companies' share of FDI in China rose from 7.16 percent to 10.28 percent, whereas Hong Kong's share fell from 45.59 percent to 33.86 percent (Zhang 2022).

However, this trend did not last long. The GFC slowed down FDI from the Triad countries as their domestic economic situation deteriorated. In 2008 Hong Kong's FDI in mainland China bounced back to 44.41 percent, whereas the US share dropped to 3.19 percent. In the following years, Hong Kong accounted for an ever-larger portion of FDI inflow to China, reaching 72.6 percent in 2022, when European and American companies only took up 6.3 percent and 1.2 percent respectively (Ministry of Commerce 2023).

The more recent explosion of investment flow from Hong Kong to mainland China cannot be explained by the same social-cultural and economic factors underlying the earlier episode of Hong Kong/Taiwan dominance of FDI in China. It is instead the result of new development in China and in Hong Kong. The maturing of Chinese industry in recent years has reached such a degree that many companies are keen to greatly expand their businesses. However, the financial system in China remains underdeveloped and has been especially inapt in supporting the private sector. On the other hand, after moving its manufacturing industry to mainland China during the 1980s, Hong Kong reinvented itself as an international financial hub with a modern financial market. Large Chinese corporations have increasingly used Hong Kong to raise capital for their expansion. They have also established subsidiaries in Hong Kong to take advantage of the regulatory advantages there. A large portion of FDI from Hong Kong is "roundtripping" investment made by subsidiaries mainland investors have established in Hong Kong.

Besides the role of Hong Kong and Taiwan, another large source of FDI in China can be found in tax havens such as the British Virgin Islands (BVI), the Cayman Islands, and Samoa. These territories with low or no taxes for non-domiciled investors are often used by companies and wealthy individuals for tax evasion. In fact, BVI was the second largest foreign investor in China from 1985 to 2006. Scholars estimate that much of the FDI from these areas originates from other places, such as Taiwan, the US, and UK (Naughton 2018). Many MNCs use foreign subsidiaries in tax havens to obscure the true locations of their operations and to minimize their tax obligations. Researchers tracing the ultimate parent companies of these subsidiaries find that developed countries' investment in large emerging markets is dramatically larger than previously thought. One instance of this is shown in a study of the national accounts of the US in 2017, which estimates that they understated the American position in Chinese firms by nearly $600 billion (Coppola et al. 2021). When we combine this distortion with the composition of Hong Kong's FDI in the mainland, it is clear that the reality of FDI in China is far more complex than official statistics represent.

FDI and Economic Development

The impact of FDI on China has been largely positive, which is consistent with the expectations of standard economic theory. One study shows that from 1986 to 2005 China's real GDP grew by an average of 11.77 percent annually, of which 1.4 percent can be attributed to FDI-generated capital formation and knowledge spillovers; that is quite significant given the scale of the Chinese economy (Chen 2011). FDI has been especially critical for China's export-oriented development strategy. In 1985 foreign invested enterprises (FIEs) only accounted for one percent of China's exports. By 2005 their contribution had reached 58 percent, it remained at that high level through 2010 (Naughton 2018).

How does FDI facilitate exports specifically and economic development more generally? First, MNCs typically possess superior technology, which improves the efficiency of production and the quality of products. This factor, combined with their management know-how and access to international markets, enhances the export performance of the companies they invest in. Second, the presence of MNCs stimulates the local economy by bringing competitive pressure, improved infrastructure, and technology diffusion through backward and forward linkages. As a result, large numbers of domestic companies become more competitive, and many become exporters in the international market.

Furthermore, in a globalized economy, production of goods and services has become highly fragmented. Global value chains (GVCs) integrate various activities taking place in different countries, such as research and development, design, production, marketing, distribution, and after-sale support. GVCs consist of different subsidiaries of the same company or different companies situated in different jurisdictions. FDI offers a major link by which developing countries join the GVCs. The enormous amount of FDI in China has brought Chinese manufacturing companies deep into many GVCs. This has not only facilitated Chinese exports, but has also promoted indigenous innovation in China, thus upgrading the entire Chinese economy. This upgrading effect is especially prominent among Chinese companies that have reached relatively high positions in the GVCs (Yang et al. 2020).

While FDI has had a positive impact on Chinese economic development overall, its specific effects vary across regions, depending on local economic and technological conditions. For example, its benefits for economic growth through knowledge spillovers have been more prominent in the advanced coastal provinces than in the less-developed inland provinces (Wu and Chen 2016). Moreover, investors from different parts of the world differ in their impact. Research shows that due to their superiority in technology and innovation, firms from OECD countries have generally played a much greater role in inter-industry spillovers than firms from Hong Kong and Taiwan (Wei and Liu 2006).

Political Economy of FDI Inflow

Interestingly, while China has followed the export-oriented development strategy of Japan and the Asian NIEs, it has adopted a very different approach to FDI. These neighboring economies welcomed foreign aid and foreign bank loans in launching their economic miracles, but they were extremely reluctant to let in FDI. Post-World War II Japan was notorious for its restrictive policy toward FDI and for how little FDI inflow it allowed. Even after Japan became the world's second largest economy in the 1980s and after it gradually liberalized its market, its FDI intake ranked well below other industrialized countries and even below some large developing countries. This was not only part of the government's nationalist industrial policy, but also the result of maneuvers by Japanese businesses eager to safeguard their own interests from foreign competition. Indeed, informal barriers put in place by private companies in Japan stayed on long after official restrictions were lifted and continued to hinder foreign businesses seeking to establish themselves in Japan (Mason 1992). Similarly, Korea and Taiwan also exerted significant controls over FDI in the early years of their post-World War II economic takeoff. Like Japan, from the 1950s to the 1980s, they limited FDI inflow to no more than one percent of the GDP. After the late 1990s, with their policies becoming more open to foreign capital, FDI inflow still remained below two percent of their GDP. In contrast, FDI in China grew quickly after the 1980s, reaching a peak of six percent of the GDP in 1994. Thereafter, FDI as a percentage of

Chinese GDP diminished as the size of the Chinese economy expanded, but it stayed above two percent until 2007 (Naughton 2018).

Why has China been so welcoming of FDI? To explain it, we need to examine the government's political and economic calculations. When the CCP decided to implement economic reform in the late 1970s, it was determined not to let it erode the one-party political system. This meant maintaining a strong state-owned economic sector supporting the CCP's economic and political power and preventing the formation of a robust independent bourgeoisie. The Chinese government rejected whole-sale privatization. Although it has allowed some private businesses to function, it has maintained a strict political pecking order of businesses in terms of their access to financial support. Large SOEs have been the most privileged in such a hierarchy. Although they are often inefficient, they have consistently enjoyed favorable treatment by the government and by the financial institutions under state control. In contrast, private enterprises, which consistently outperform SOEs, face serious discrimination under China's "socialist market economy." It is difficult for them to borrow from the banks and to raise capital in the stock and bond markets. They also operate under risky conditions due to the insecurity of their property rights. In this context, FDI inflow fills a vital gap in the Chinese economy by providing privately owned and efficient enterprises without a domestic privatization program. FDI also brings capital mobility across different regions and different economic sectors, thus helping to overcome the fragmentation of the Chinese economy rooted in its socialist bureaucratic nature (Huang 2003).

Economic liberalization in China has broken the old social contract between the CCP and the working class. FDI has given the Chinese government a way to avoid having to confront the workers' discontent about the downside of marketization. As described in chapter 6, foreign companies entered China well before domestic economic restructuring and provided labs for capitalist labor market practices, including short-term labor contracts, managerial autonomy in setting wages, and sharp curtailment to enterprise-funded welfare. Their efficient performance exerted competitive pressure on Chinese enterprises to adopt similar rules and mechanisms of labor management. Politically, the presence of FIEs allowed the CCP to reformulate the debate over SOE reform. When the Fifteenth Party Congress in 1997 declared a policy of "grasping the big and letting go the small," it presented the downsizing of the state sector as part of a battle between Chinese national industry and foreign industry. It portrayed the end the so-called "iron rice bowl" (guaranteed employment) for many SOE workers as necessary to ensure Chinese industrial survival in the face of fierce foreign competition. The replacement of a socialist narrative by a nationalist narrative enabled the CCP to maintain its legitimacy despite its abandonment of certain socialist principles (Gallagher 2011).

Whether by design or by experimentation and learning, China's generous FDI policy has served the CCP's political and economic interests well. The massive inflow of foreign capital has allowed the Party to achieve fast economic development without creating a strong domestic capitalist class. At the same time, FDI has given the CCP a tool to divert working class discontent about their suffering under marketization and thus helped prevent the workers from becoming a powerful force for political change. In this sense, FDI has enabled the Chinese government to delay political liberalization (Huang 2003, Gallagher 2011).

In many other developing countries, openness to FDI has resulted in foreign businesses overpowering domestic industries and government losing control over the economy. Indeed, it is precisely the concern about such negative effects that has led Japan and the Asian NIEs to take a highly cautious approach toward FDI. The Chinese government was well aware of such risks. From the beginning of its open policy, it was careful to establish its own terms for foreign capital's entry and adopted various policies to ensure that FDI serve the Party state's economic and political interests.

In the early years of the reform era, Chinese regulators stipulated that foreign investors must partner with Chinese enterprises in order to operate in China. Foreign companies typically formed equity joint ventures or contractual joint ventures with local partners (Pearson 1992). Under these arrangements, foreign companies investing in China were often pressured to transfer their technologies, share their management knowhow, incorporate local content in their products, and otherwise serve China's needs (see Box 11.2). Foreign investors felt compelled to abide by the policies of the Chinese government because the size of the Chinese economy, its large labor pool and tremendous market potential meant China was in a strong bargaining position in the negotiations.

After China's accession to the WTO, it abandoned the joint venture requirements and allowed more foreign companies to establish wholly foreign-owned enterprises. Researchers find that the shift has reduced technology spillovers; compared with joint ventures, FIEs wholly owned by foreign investors are less likely to transfer technologies. But the government has continued to use other means to influence foreign capital. Since 2002 the Chinese government has regularly issued guidelines for FDI, classifying industries where foreign capital is "encouraged," "permitted," "restricted," or "prohibited." The guidelines are revised every few years according to the government's priorities. The 2017 guidelines introduced a negative list, which specified the industries where FDI was restricted or prohibited. The assumption was that FDI would be free to enter all the industries not on the list. In the last few years, the negative list has been shortened, apparently seeking to further liberalize the FDI regime. In reality, however, other barriers remain significant, rendering the apparent opening up of the negative list practically meaningless.

Box 11.2 Foreign Capital and China Unicom

During the Maoist era, China had an extremely primitive telecommunication infrastructure. By the mid-1990s it had become clear that this was a bottleneck for economic development. In 1994, the government decided to break the monopoly of telecom services by the Ministry of Post and Telecommunications and allowed the creation of a new company – China Unicom. At the beginning, Unicom was poorly funded. The combined investment by all of its sixteen shareholders (government ministries, SOEs, and local governments) was roughly $156 million, hardly sufficient to build a mobile network in one city. It also did not have the necessary expertise or technology. Thus, Unicom turned to foreign investors for help.

Chinese law at that time did not allow foreign participation in telecom operations because of the political importance and national security sensitivity of the sector. Working closely with government bureaucracies, Unicom developed a China-China-Foreign (CCF) scheme to attract foreign investment while minimizing foreign influence. Under the CCF framework, a foreign company would partner with a Chinese business entity owned by a shareholder of Unicom but unrelated to telecom to form a joint venture. This joint venture would not be allowed by Chinese law to directly operate or manage a telecom network. It would form a second joint venture with Unicom's subsidiaries, which were allowed to operate in the telecom sector. Through this legally dubious arrangement, the foreign company would indirectly invest capital, provide equipment and technology, and teach Unicom how to operate a modern telecom network. In return, the foreign company would get "installation and consultation fees."

From 1995 to 1997, Unicom partnered with 32 international telecom companies from eleven countries and implemented 46 CCF projects across the country. With billions of dollars brought in, Unicom built the most technologically advanced system of the time with a total capacity of about 2 million lines. Once Unicom obtained strong financial and technological positions, the CCF framework was dismantled around 2000, leaving the foreign companies unhappy and disgruntled. For all their capital investments and technology transfers, they failed to get a foothold in the lucrative telecom sector of China. (Zhao 2022)

Conclusion

After decades of near autarky, the PRC began to join the global economy in the late 1970s. China's participation in international trade and its absorption of foreign capital have both contributed significantly to its economic development. Scholarly studies show that foreign trade and FDI have been the twin engines for Chinese rapid economic growth. Furthermore, trade, FDI and economic growth have been mutually reinforcing.

China's success in utilizing foreign trade and foreign capital for its own development purposes is rare among developing countries. To some extent this can be attributed to the size of the country, especially its large labor pool and huge market potential, which provides it with significant bargaining chips when it comes to negotiations with trading partners and foreign investors. But just as important has been the government's shrewd management of China's engagement with the global economy. The CCP took an incremental approach to China's economic opening, first experimenting in the SEZs and then liberalizing other parts of the country to foreign trade and investment. The trade reform started with modest EP in the SEZs, followed by restructuring the ordinary trade regime years later. Similarly, China's FDI policy first insisted on joint ventures between foreign capital and domestic enterprises, and only subsequently granted permission for wholly foreign owned enterprises.

The reformist leaders have shown a highly pragmatic approach to foreign trade and foreign investment. When they view foreign competition as a useful instrument to bring about domestic economic restructuring, they have welcomed foreign presence and input. This was a driving force behind the Chinese government's dogged efforts to join the WTO, and its generous policies toward MNCs investing in China. But when they see foreign economic entities as threatening, they do not hesitate to block their entry or kick them out. The above example of the treatment of foreign investors in China Unicom's projects highlights this point well.

Questions for Discussion

1. What role did the special economic zones play in the initial stages of China's economic reform?

2. How has foreign direct investment contributed to China's economic development in the reform era?

3. What were the costs and benefits of China's accession to the World Trade Organization for different groups in China and for other countries?

12

China's "Going Out" Policy

Until the turn of the century, the world felt China's economic rise largely through its exports of goods, particularly manufactured products. Since then, China's international economic presence has greatly expanded and become much more multidimensional than before. In the late 1990s, then Chinese leader, Jiang Zemin, suggested that China's open policy must be two-dimensional. On the one hand, China needed to attract foreign companies to come into the country. On the other hand, Chinese companies should start to operate overseas. In the early twenty-first century, the Chinese government officially adopted a "going out (*zou chu qu*)" strategy. The tenth five-year plan made in 2000 called for competitive Chinese companies to invest abroad and to operate multinationally.

In 2013 President Xi Jinping launched a grandiose "Belt and Road Initiative" (BRI), consisting of the "Silk Road Economic Belt" and the "21st Century Maritime Silk Road". Under the BRI framework, which combines investment and development aid, many Chinese companies have expanded their operations overseas. A recent report by the Green Finance and Development Center indicates that as of 2023, China has cumulatively invested over $1 trillion in BRI projects, including $634 billion in construction contracts and $419 billion in non-financial investments (C. Wang 2024).

In this chapter, we first examine China's outward foreign direct investment (OFDI) – what has motivated it, how it has evolved, what impact it has had on China and the rest of the world. We will also explore its underlying political economy. The second part of the chapter studies the rising development aid by China. The focus will be on the distinctive Chinese characteristics of the aid and its impact on the recipient countries. These issues have attracted much international attention and controversy.

Outward Foreign Direct Investment

China has utilized foreign capital extensively in its economic development in the reform era. With the initiation of China's going out strategy two decades ago, the movement of capital has become increasingly a two-way street. Similar to the inflow of capital to China, the outflow of capital from China has

241

mainly taken the form of direct investment. In contrast, portfolio investment through institutional or individual purchase of foreign stocks and bonds has been quite limited under the country's persistent capital control regime.

Motivations

Traditional literature on FDI is based on studies of multinational corporations (MNCs) based in Western industrialized countries. It shows that these companies invest abroad out of a variety of motivations – exploiting natural resources and cheap labor located in other countries, accessing overseas markets behind trade barriers, and acquiring technology not available domestically. Research shows several of these motivations to be at work in Chinese OFDI as well. Early studies find Chinese investment to be concentrated in developing economies with rich natural resources and in developed economies with advanced technology and large markets (Huang and Wang 2011; Kolstad and Wiig 2012). They indicate that resources, technology, and market access have been important motivations for Chinese OFDI. They also make it clear that Chinese investment pursues different goals in different countries. Chinese companies go to developing countries primarily in search of natural resources whereas they invest in developed countries mainly to obtain technology and markets.

An unusual driver of Chinese OFDI is the desire to better manage the country's large foreign-exchange reserves. Thanks to China's growing current account surplus (mostly trade surplus, i.e. export–imports), from 2004 to 2014, China's foreign-exchange reserves rose steeply from $500 billion to almost $4 trillion, which more than tripled the amount for Japan, the world's second largest holder of forex reserves (Xinhua 2014). The Chinese government invested most of the foreign reserves in US government debt, mainly Treasury bills (short-term maturity), notes (medium-term maturity), and bonds (long-term maturity). While these assets are highly liquid and relatively safe, they offer low rates of return. Some commentators in China complained about the government's wasteful handling of the nation's wealth in this way. In addition, Chinese policymakers as well as the public were uneasy about the resulting financial dependence on the United States. OFDI emerged as a useful way of diversifying the investment of the country's large foreign reserves and of generating better returns. Meanwhile, the government created several sovereign wealth funds (SWFs), including the China Investment Corporation and the SAFE Investment Company (under the State Administration of Foreign Exchange or SAFE). They acquired foreign assets outside US government debt, which were often less liquid but more profitable (Liu 2023).

In the last decade, an increasingly salient motivation for OFDI has been China's desire to export its industrial overcapacity and environmental hazards. Chinese economic growth has been driven more by investment than by consumption. Years of investment-led growth, featuring rapid industrialization, real estate development, and infrastructure construction, have accumulated excessive production capacity and resulted in serious environmental pollution. In 2014 the State Council's Guiding Opinions on the Promotion of International Capacity Cooperation and Equipment Manufacturing identified twelve target sectors that had overcapacity to export – steel, non-ferrous metals, construction materials, railways, electricity, chemicals, textiles, automotive, information and communications technology, engineering machinery, and aerospace and marine engineering. The government leveraged against its foreign-exchange reserves and funneled funds to provincial governments and state-owned enterprises (SOEs) to support the offshoring of projects in these sectors (Kenderdine and Ling 2018). Since China launched the BRI in 2013, growing numbers of OFDI projects along the Belt and the Road have been in sectors characterized by overcapacity and environmental pollution. The recipient countries are often in dire need of FDI to develop their infrastructure and industries. Those with relatively poor institutions – government effectiveness, regulatory quality, rule of law, control of corruption – have been especially receptive of overcapacity and pollution-related Chinese OFDI (Nugent and Lu 2021).

Evolution

Although Chinese OFDI has only a short history, it has already gone through significant changes. First, there has been a shift in sectoral focus. At the beginning, Chinese investment abroad centered around the natural resources sector. With the downturn in global energy and commodities prices in 2014, many of China's OFDI projects in those areas suffered substantial losses. The poor financial return of such investments was one reason why Chinese investors became more interested in other sectors. In 2022, in terms of deal value (the value of investment deals), 55 percent of total Chinese OFDI was concentrated in the technology, media, and telecom (TMT) sector, health care and life sciences, and real estate, hospitality, and construction industries. By deal volume (the number of investment deals), half of the investments occurred in TMT, advanced manufacturing and mobility, and health care and life sciences sectors (Wu 2024).

The sectoral shift has also been driven by policymakers' concern about the "middle income trap." To avoid being trapped like many other middle-income countries in the global South and ultimately join the ranks of the rich countries, China needs to move up the technological and value chain. The Chinese government has eagerly encouraged Chinese companies to go out to acquire the most advanced technologies in the world. A recent study shows that Chinese OFDI from 2003 to 2018 was positively associated with host-country technology development. Countries with more patent applications by residents and higher percentages of R&D in GDP attracted more Chinese OFDI (Martins et al. 2023).

Second, the actors in China's OFDI have changed. In the early days of going out, SOEs were the main players, while other types of enterprises were largely excluded from participation. With the diversification of investment from mega projects in natural resources to other areas, opportunities arose for non-state-owned enterprises to jump on the bandwagon. In 2011 the government passed the twelfth five-year plan, which encouraged capable private enterprises to also go out. It allowed banks and other financial institutions to support non-SOEs in their overseas investment. A survey conducted by the China Council for the Promotion of International Trade in 2011 found that private enterprises particularly appreciated the government's foreign-exchange policy support, insurance for expatriates, simplification of approvals such as customs clearance, and the provision of information on investment opportunities (Suavant and Chen 2014). Official speeches indicate that as of 2017, private enterprises contributed about seventy percent of new OFDI, and in that year non-state-owned enterprise investment surpassed OFDI by SOEs for the first time (Molnar et al. 2021).

Researchers emphasize that private enterprises behave differently from those controlled by the state. Many SOEs invest in countries with abundant natural resources, undeterred by their often-risky political environments. Private firms tend to follow a straightforward business logic, going where there are market opportunities. They have also been quite active in the manufacturing sector in some parts of the developing world where they find low-waged labor force (Gu 2009; Shen 2015). Moreover, scholars also find that private enterprises vary among themselves in their OFDI orientation. For example, an important subgroup of private enterprises are family-owned businesses. Family firms owned by a lone founder, who is typically highly entrepreneurial, are more likely to engage in OFDI than those owned by multiple family members, who see themselves as family guardians (Wei et al. 2020).

Third, the geographic distribution of Chinese OFDI has shifted. Initially, Chinese investment in developed countries fell far behind that in the developing countries. After the 2008 global financial crisis, Western industrialized countries eagerly welcomed Chinese investment to prop up their recession-stricken economies. Chinese investors became actively involved in mergers and acquisitions, acquiring equities in cash-strapped companies in North America and Europe (Hanemann and Rosen 2011; Munier 2014). In the last five years or so, stricter investment screening by North American and European countries in the name of national security has led to a decline in Chinese FDI in those areas. At the end of 2022, thirteen percent of the outbound mergers and acquisitions by Chinese companies were in North America, and 10.2 percent, in Europe (Wu 2024).

Impact

When American MNCs led the initial post-World War II wave of FDI in the 1960s and 1970s, policy analysts became concerned about how that was going to affect the domestic economy of the United States. To the extent companies use FDI to circumvent the trade barriers by producing their products in the countries where they want to sell their products, it could decrease the home country's exports. In addition, the outflow of capital could reduce domestic investment and employment opportunities. Moreover, the creation of subsidiaries in foreign countries or joint ventures with foreign enterprises typically involves technology transfer, which can undermine the technological lead of the investing companies and their home country (Gilpin 1975). So far studies of Chinese OFDI have not uncovered these negative effects. In fact, China seems to have been largely successful in using OFDI to strengthen its domestic economy.

With regard to trade, while OFDI can substitute for exports of finished goods, it can also increase the demand for intermediate products, equipment, and technology from China. Statistical analysis indicates that Chinese investment abroad is correlated with higher exports and imports; China trades more with countries hosting Chinese FDI. In other words, OFDI seems to have fostered trade rather than supplanted the latter (Abeliansky and Martínez-Zarzoso 2019).

Second, theoretically speaking, OFDI could drain capital from the domestic economy. However, this "crowding out" effect may be minimal if domestic savings are high, especially if they are higher than domestic investment needs. OFDI can also reduce the cost of natural resources and labor and thus increase the returns of domestic production. In that case, it can actually stimulate domestic investment. Empirical research shows that Chinese OFDI has generally increased domestic investment rather than crowded it out. This is especially true in industries dominated by SOEs. A plausible explanation is that SOEs have privileged access to financial resources in China's state-controlled financial system, including the country's massive foreign reserves. The abundant supply of capital means their investment abroad does not involve a tradeoff with investment at home (You and Solomon 2015).

Third, contrary to conventional wisdom, OFDI has not diminished China's technological lead. Instead, it has played a positive and significant role in stimulating innovation and technological upgrading in China. Chinese companies benefit from their presence in countries with higher levels of technological development in several ways. Through establishing research and development centers in those countries, they take advantage of local infrastructure and local human resources. By setting up strategic alliances with technologically advanced companies, they acquire knowledge about specific products and processes. Cross-border mergers and acquisitions have been particularly helpful to Chinese firms' domestic innovation. They are associated with higher research and development spending and greater number of patent applications. However, these benefits are concentrated in OFDI in advanced industrialized countries, involving vertical integration (i.e. integration among different but related businesses), and in competitive and knowledge-intensive markets (Howell et al. 2020).

While China's OFDI has had a largely positive impact on the domestic economy, its effects on the host countries and the global economy are more mixed. Chinese officials and officials of many developing countries hosting Chinese OFDI claim that Chinese investment has helped the host countries. But various civil society organizations and Western governments are more critical. Many of them contend that Chinese investment has done more harm than good. Scholarly research so far has not produced definitive answers to this complex question.

Some studies show that Chinese OFDI has indeed produced positive economic outcomes for the host countries. It has, for example, improved host country infrastructure (Waqar et al. 2021). It has also brought in much-needed capital, created jobs and led to technology spillover among host-country companies with high absorptive capacity (Mebratu et al. 2015). In some countries, it has promoted social welfare as measured by the human development index, which includes education and health indicators as well as GDP per capita (Allou et al. 2020).

On the other hand, Chinese investment may well have worsened the institutional environment in the host countries. Chinese companies do not hesitate to operate in countries with relatively low governance capacity, government accountability, poor regulations, rampant corruption, and underdeveloped legal systems (Kolstad and Wiig 2012; Mohan and Tan-Mullins 2019). The BRI seems to have intensified this trend. Some researchers conclude that even as the BRI promotes economic growth through infrastructure development and enhances certain aspects of human development, it has not improved the civil political rights in those societies (Sutherland et al. 2020). Moreover, Chinese OFDI provides host countries with an alternative to Western MNCs. The latter have been under extensive civil society scrutiny for decades and have established certain corporate social responsibility standards. Although these standards have not prevented them from engaging in investment activities that damage the local environment, indigenous communities, and the rights of some groups, they have been more sensitive to public pressure and more willing to push for better environmental and governance practice through their investment in developing countries. The growth of Chinese investment in those countries may have weakened their will and leverage with regard to enforcing their traditional standards (Frost and Ho 2005).

Political Economy

China's OFDI is not an automatic extension of the country's economic development. Instead, it has been profoundly shaped by government policies. Before 2000, the Chinese government actively wooed FDI to China to bring in much-needed capital, technology, management knowhow, and access to the international market. At the same time, it allowed a small number of SOEs to invest abroad, mainly to facilitate exports and imports and to earn foreign exchanges. These included state-owned trading companies, engineering and construction companies, labor services companies, and SOEs' subsidiaries in Hong Kong. From 1982 to 1991, China's annual average OFDI flow was a paltry $537 million. In the 1990s, especially after Deng Xiaoping's famed Southern tour in 1992, Chinese OFDI rose to a higher level, averaging $2.686 billion annually from 1992 to 1999 (Wang and Gao 2019). But the government was still cautious.

At the turn of the century, the Chinese government began to relax its regulations of OFDI. This was the final stage of China's push to join the World Trade Organization (WTO), when the authorities accelerated the broad economic liberalization required by the WTO. It was also then that the government launched the going out policy. In 2004, the State Council promulgated the Decision on Reforming the Investment Systems. Following this decision, the National Development and Reform Commission, the Ministry of Commerce, SAFE, and other government agencies simplified and speeded up the procedures for approving investment projects overseas.

However, the volume of Chinese OFDI has not been on a linear trajectory (see Figure 12.1). It grew steadily for over a decade after 2004, reaching a peak in 2016. But in 2017 the trend was reversed. After a dramatic drop in that year, OFDI from China has remained stagnant at a lower level. The change was triggered by a change in government policy. From 2016 to 2017, China experienced a significant exodus of capital and its foreign-exchange reserves decreased by $1 trillion (Bradsher 2017). Alarmed, policymakers tightened the monitoring and control of capital outflow, especially investment by private enterprises and companies suspected of profit-hiding and money laundering (Molnar et al. 2021).

In more recent years, other unfavorable factors – many political in nature – have diminished the momentum of Chinese OFDI. In many developed countries there has been rising anxiety about Chinese investment. Policymakers and the public alike have expressed concern about the influence of the CCP on Chinese companies, which makes them potentially threatening to host country national security and national interest. They have also criticized China's state subsidies for those companies, which gives them unfair advantages in business competition. The authorities of Australia, the European Union, and the United States have all enhanced their scrutiny and restrictions of Chinese FDI. Last, but not least, the Covid pandemic dragged down Chinese OFDI after 2020.

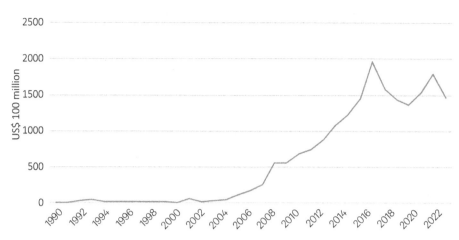

Figure 12.1 China's Outward Foreign Direct Investment 1990–2022
Source: UNCTAD.

Traditional theories of FDI argue that companies investing abroad tend to have firm-specific advantages, which typically include ownership of financial resources, technology, marketing capabilities, brands, and management competencies. Contrary to conventional wisdom, Chinese companies investing abroad often have no competitive advantage internationally or even domestically (Huang and Wang 2011). In fact, this is a common characteristic of many global South-based MNCs. Instead of firm-specific advantages, they seem to benefit from "government-created advantages," such as privileged access to cheap capital in their home countries and the political backing of their home governments (Matthew 2006; Adarkwah and Malonæs 2022).

Researchers distinguish different types of policies used by the Chinese government to guide OFDI. Regulatory policies focus on regulation and supervision. They aim to control who can make OFDI and how. They also consist of mechanisms to monitor Chinese enterprises operating overseas. Supportive policies involve services and promotion. They seek to compensate for the disadvantages Chinese investors encounter overseas by gathering and sharing information with the latter. Above all, they include the provision of specific advantages for Chinese companies operating abroad, especially in accessing finance (Yin et al. 2021).

In China, the state-dominated banking system has played a major role in supporting OFDI. The policy banks, especially China Development Bank and the Export–Import Bank of China, and the large commercial banks, such as the Bank of China, the Industrial and Commercial Bank of China, and the China Construction Bank, have mobilized and channeled massive amounts of funds to companies engaged in the going out campaign. A comparative study shows that China leads Japan and Korea, two developmental states known for state involvement in economic development, in bank lending to companies investing abroad. From 2003 to 2011, bank loans amounted to 58 percent of Chinese OFDI, much higher than Japan's 15.6 percent and Korea's 20.3 percent. The Chinese government has been willing and able to use bank loans to finance OFDI to such a degree because many of the borrowers are SOEs and because Chinese savings and foreign-exchange reserves are even more abundant than Japan's and Korea's (Gallagher and Irwin 2014).

The Chinese government does not encourage every kind of investment abroad; it takes a selective approach in its support of OFDI. A key factor in determining the government's attitude lies in the type of capital involved. A recent study distinguishes among three kinds of capital – tactical, competitive, and crony. *Tactical capital* follows a political logic, either aiming to serve the strategic interests of the Chinese state or seeking to enhance the political prestige and power of the investing firms and their managers. *Competitive capital* pursues conventional business goals, such as market shares and profits. *Crony capital*, often accumulated through ill-acquired access to land, credit, and assets undergoing privatization in China, seeks safety from state expatriation. The Chinese government treats these types of capital differently. It typically deploys and disciplines tactical capital, enables competitive capital, and constrains crony capital (Rithmire 2022). For example, the tightening of OFDI control around 2017 was largely directed at the "irrational growth" of investment overseas in real estate, hotels, cinemas, entertainment, and sports clubs, which was typically found in the projects of crony capital.

It may be tempting to infer the type of capital from the ownership of the investing companies. But one cannot assume that SOEs are always engaged in tactical capital, and private business is necessarily the source of competitive capital. Enterprises under various ownership have produced all three kinds of capital (Rithmire 2022). Research on such SOEs as State Grid and China's national oil companies demonstrates that their OFDI has sought commercial as well as national strategic goals (Xu 2017; Norris 2016). Other studies echo the theme that SOEs tend to carry the twin missions of supporting the state and expanding markets (Li and Cheong 2019). Large SOEs enjoy considerable autonomy in making business decisions, and they often prioritize their own commercial interests. The Chinese government has condoned this tendency because it sees the commercial success of SOEs as consistent with China's national interests (Jiang 2014).

While crony capital constitutes a major component of OFDI seeking refuge from the Chinese state, many legitimate private enterprises also resort to OFDI as a way to escape from the reach of the government. They are routinely discriminated in China's state-dominated economy. In addition, similar to their counterparts in other emerging economies, they are vulnerable to the grabbing hands of government officials, such as corruption, regulatory uncertainty, poor intellectual property rights protection, and arbitrary political interference. For these enterprises, OFDI constitutes a form of institutional escapism (Shi et al. 2017).

In recent years, Western countries – notably the United States – have become increasingly suspicious of Chinese OFDI on their territories. Given the Party state's prominent role in Chinese economy in general and in OFDI in particular, they are deeply worried that Chinese firms may be instruments of government policy regardless of their ownership. Many of them have put in place expanded mechanisms to review and discourage Chinese investment projects in high-tech industry and other industries seen as related to national security (Pearson et al. 2022). Many scholars believe this perception overestimates the strategic nature of Chinese OFDI. They argue that Chinese companies investing abroad are mostly driven by economic motives rather than policy goals. Moreover, Chinese companies compete against each other for business opportunities (ten Brink 2015). Indeed, Chinese media and policy analysts have been critical of the bad behavior of some large SOEs operating overseas, blaming them for incurring economic and political costs for the country, including financial losses and reputation damages (see Box 12.1).

Box 12.1 The Poland Fiasco

In 2009 a group of Chinese SOEs led by China Overseas Engineering Group Company (COVEC) won a bid to build two sections of the A2 Highway in Poland, stretching 49 kilometers between the capital city of Warsaw and the German border. This was the first infrastructure project by a Chinese group in a member country of the European Union (EU) and was thus potentially a major step in establishing China's presence in EU's construction sector. The low bid of the Chinese group (under fifty percent of the Polish budget) generated complaints and disbelief from the competitors, but the Polish government accepted the bid. Soon after the project got underway, it became clear that the Chinese companies had underestimated the costs. In May 2011 the Chinese group failed to pay its Polish subcontractors on time, and the project came to a stop. Polish contractors and workers staged angry protests. In June, the Chinese group abandoned the project. The Polish side demanded compensation exceeding $270 million and a ban on the Chinese group from bidding for projects in Poland for three years. According to analyses in the Chinese media, the Chinese companies involved had been too eager to enter the European market and had not done their homework. They had exaggerated China's advantage in cheap labor and then tried to change the contract midway to absorb the higher costs, not appreciating this would be impossible in Poland's transparent public finance system and institutionalized contract system. Chinese pundits argued that this fiasco caused serious financial losses and damaged China's reputation. (Wang 2011)

Development Aid

Besides OFDI, China's going out campaign also includes an increasing outflow of development aid. Unlike investment overseas, foreign aid is a well-established component of China's foreign economic relations. Only a few years after the founding of the People's Republic, the newly established communist regime began to provide economic and technological assistance to other developing countries. Throughout the Maoist era, in accordance with its policy of solidarity with the Third World, the Chinese government continued to send aid to newly independent countries in Asia and Africa, even as China itself remained one of the poorest nations in the world.

After the death of Mao Zedong, his successors shifted their focus to domestic economic reform and modernization. The Chinese government drastically reduced foreign aid in the 1980s and 1990s. But in the last two decades, having successfully developed its own economy, China has revived and expanded its foreign aid programs. From 2004 to 2009, Chinese annual commitment of foreign aid shot up from $10 billion to $124 billion. After peaking in 2016 at $142 billion, China's annual commitment declined, with only $44 billion committed in 2021 (Aiddata.org n.d.).

Chinese foreign aid includes not only bilateral aid provided to individual foreign countries, but also contribution to the World Bank and other multilateral development institutions. The latter has also increased over time. In 1990 China held 2.87 percent of the shares of International Bank of Reconstruction and Development, the largest member institution of the World Bank Group. In 2020, its shares rose to 6.01 percent. Furthermore, China has led the creation of two new multilateral development banks – the Beijing-based Asian Infrastructure Investment Bank (AIIB) and the Shanghai-based **New Development Bank** (NDB). As of 2024, China accounts for about 31 percent of the AIIB's shares and about 19 percent of the NDB's shares.

Like other donor countries, China uses development aid to promote its own interests. For instance, in the Maoist era, the Chinese government provided assistance to African countries to help with their urgent needs in infrastructure development, medical service, and agriculture. This won China friendship, good will and, most importantly, political support on the international stage. African governments actively backed the government of the People's Republic's effort to claim China's seat at the United Nations, which was occupied by the *Kuomintang* government that escaped to Taiwan in the late 1940s. It was not until 1971 that representatives from Beijing were finally seated at the UN General Assembly. Mao gratefully acknowledged that "It is our African brothers who have carried us into the United Nations." During the reform era, China has used foreign aid to enhance economic ties with developing countries, which has helped it obtain access to natural resources and opened business opportunities for Chinese companies overseas (Xue 2014).

The recent surge of Chinese foreign aid has alarmed many observers, not only because of its rapid expansion but also because of its lack of transparency and its unconventional characteristics. How is Chinese aid different from the aid given by traditional donors? What has been the impact of the growing Chinese aid? Is China undermining the existing development aid regime?

Development Aid with Chinese Characteristics

International aid for development was an idea that emerged in the early twentieth century, with important input from thinkers in developing countries, including Sun Yat-sen, the founding father of modern China (Helleiner 2019). After World War II, Western industrialized countries became major providers of international development aid through both bilateral and multilateral channels. In the early 1960s, these donor countries created national development agencies and institutionalized their development assistance programs. Around the same time, the Organization of Economic Cooperation and Development (OECD) established the **Development Assistance Committee** (DAC) as a venue for consultation and coordination among its member countries.

In the late 1960s, DAC adopted official development assistance (ODA) as the "gold standard" of foreign aid. ODA promotes poverty reduction in developing countries. It is concessional in character and includes a grant element of at least 25 percent. DAC donors often attach political conditions to their loans, requiring recipients to implement governance reform. They provide program funding (e.g. budget support, balance of payment support, and trust funds) as well as project funding. Their projects typically follow internationally agreed-upon standards of social and environmental safeguards.

China is not a member of the OECD and its DAC and is therefore not required to report its aid using the DAC categories and measures. The Chinese government has also opted out of other major standards initiatives, including the International Aid Transparency Initiative. Researchers find it difficult to gauge Chinese foreign aid. Studies of Chinese development financing often overestimate or underestimate its magnitude, depending on what definitions they use (Bräutigam 2011; Sears 2019). In addition, Chinese development aid differs from the DAC framework in several ways, including the types of financing, the focus of assistance, and the conditions of lending.

In terms of types of financing, Chinese bilateral programs include some ODA – grants and concessional loans aimed at poverty reduction in the recipient countries. But the bulk of its development financing falls into what DAC defines as other official flows (OOF), which refers to "grants to developing countries for representational or essentially commercial purposes; official bilateral transactions intended to promote development, but having a grant element of less than 25%; and, official bilateral transactions, whatever their grant element, that are primarily export-facilitating in purpose" (OECD 2024).

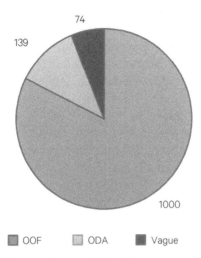

Figure 12.2 Chinese Development Finance 2000–2021
Source: Based on data from Dreher, A., Fuchs, A., Parks, B.C., Strange, A., and Tierney, M.J. (2022) *Banking on Beijing: The Aims and Impacts of China's Overseas Development Program.* Cambridge University Press.

Chinese OOF consists primarily of export credits and non-concessional loans with substantial economic benefits accruing to Chinese lenders and contractors (Bräutigam 2011; Dreher et al. 2018; Chin and Gallagher 2019). Although Chinese ODA has increased in the twenty-first century, it is only a minor component of Chinese official development finance (see Figure 12.2). It pales by comparison with the non-concessional lending by Chinese banks, especially the two giant policy banks – China Development Bank and the Export Import Bank of China (Chen 2020).

With regard to the sectoral focus, most of China's bilateral development finance has gone into extraction and infrastructure rather than poverty alleviation. From 2008 to 2021, China's total official commitment of development financing amounted to $498 billion. The top three sectors were extraction and pipelines ($128 billion), transport ($115 billion), and power (87 billion) (Ray 2023). Together these sectors accounted for a whopping 66 percent of the total, a sharp contrast with the traditional donors, whose aid typically focuses on health, education, and core administration. This is because China's development finance is often intertwined with the promotion of Chinese economic and business interests.

Unlike traditional donors, who often tie their aid to political demands, such as governance reform by the recipient, the Chinese government extends development assistance without political conditions, with the notable exception that the recipient country recognizes that Taiwan is part of China. China often proudly touts its development financing as pragmatic and genuinely aimed at meeting the needs of the developing countries. It likes to point out the distinction between China's principle of non-interference in the domestic affairs of other countries and the political agenda underlying Western aid (Xue 2014).

These differences between Chinese aid and DAC norms are rooted in a fundamental disagreement in the understanding of development financing. DAC members – mostly traditional donors in the global North – view their aid programs through a hierarchical lens. They see themselves as more advanced than the developing countries in the global South. As such, they deem it as an obligation to provide guidance and assistance for the backward countries and to help the latter reduce poverty, develop their economy, and improve the well-being of their people. On the contrary, Chinese policymakers emphasize equality among countries and the virtue of economic cooperation. For them, aid is not charity but aims to provide "mutual benefit" and common development for the provider and the recipient. The Chinese government is unapologetic for its use of development aid to promote Chinese trade with developing countries and to secure natural resources (Bräutigam 2011).

Another source of the distinctive features of Chinese aid is its relatively limited capacity. As a developing country itself, China has enormous financial needs at home, which poses constraints on its direct fiscal allocation and subsidies for aid projects. Instead, the Chinese state has resorted to various other means to assist fellow developing countries. Government-backed guarantees and resource-backed collaterals are two notable methods to increase the creditworthiness of projects that are otherwise un-bankable (Chen 2020). Many of the development projects financed by China in Africa and Latin America have been made possible by the use of oil revenue of the recipient countries as collaterals (see Box 12.2).

The unconventional characteristics of China's foreign aid have generated both positive and negative reactions. The apparent absence of an ideological dogma renders Chinese aid flexible. With no political strings attached (except when it comes to accepting Chinese sovereignty over Taiwan), Chinese aid is highly attractive to many governments of developing countries. Having suffered in the hands of Western colonialism and the post-colonial arrogance of traditional donors, many countries in the global South have warmly welcomed Chinese development aid for this reason.

On the other hand, Chinese aid often displays a strong tendency to promote China's economic interests. In this regard, it is reminiscent of Japan's foreign-aid programs at an earlier time, when they were typically tied to exporting Japanese equipment and products and to Japan's access to natural resources in the aid-receiving countries (Stallings and Kim 2017). The international development community criticized Japan for years. Under pressure from other OECD members, Japan has in recent decades moved closer toward the DAC

Box 12.2 Oil for Infrastructure and Housing

China has emerged as a major funder for development projects in Africa and South America in recent decades. To circumvent the borrowers' low credit rating, China has made loans to the resource-rich countries by having the latter guarantee repayment using the proceeds from selling those resources. The oil-rich country of Angola offers a good illustration. When Angola emerged from 27 years of civil war in 2002, it faced severe shortages of infrastructure and housing. China happened to be launching its going out strategy and was eager to explore economic opportunities in Africa for commercial and political purposes. Chinese policy banks began to provide Angola credit facilities worth billions of dollars for infrastructure construction. China also got involved in financing the construction of new urban centers around big cities to ease the massive housing shortfall in that country. Many of the loans provided by China were secured by Angolan oil, either under China–Angola bilateral co-operation agreements or through private contracts. Chinese banks used their loans to pay Chinese construction firms working on the projects in Angola, and the repayment for the loans was guaranteed by oil sales by Angola to Unipec, a subsidiary of the Chinese oil giant Sinopec. (Benazeraf and Alves 2014)

framework of development aid. A study of Chinese and Japanese aid programs in Africa shows that Japan has been more attentive to the recipient countries' needs and their quality of governance and institutions than China is (Furuoka 2017). China has become the new target of this type of criticism by the international development community.

Effects

The OOF in Chinese foreign aid, including non-concessional lending and export credit, has brought direct economic gains to China, such as exports and labor contracts. In addition, development aid brings indirect economic benefits by facilitating OFDI. Investment overseas typically faces a variety of country risks – political instability, corruption, financial market turmoil, and host government intervention. Past research shows that foreign aid can ameliorate some of these risks. Grants and loans, technical support, funding for education programs, and support of public health programs, for instance, can improve the business environment, economic infrastructure, human capital, and the governance and legal systems in the recipient countries. In so doing, development aid makes the recipient countries safer and more conducive for FDI inflows (Selaya and Sunesen 2012).

Running parallel to – and at times overlapping with – the country's growing OFDI, Chinese development aid has indeed had a positive impact on the latter. A recent study examines a sample of 124 countries assisted by China from 2000 to 2019. It finds that foreign aid significantly reduces the investment risks in the recipient countries, especially political risks (e.g. government instability) and financial risks (e.g. exchange rate instability). Furthermore, Chinese aid improves the image of Chinese enterprises and enlists assistance from the host-country government and its ruling party for Chinese businesses. An intriguing finding of this study is that the beneficial effect of foreign aid on OFDI is exclusive. While Chinese foreign aid encourages OFDI from China, aid from other countries such as Japan, the United States, and European countries, has a negative impact on Chinese OFDI to the recipient countries (Wang et al. 2022).

Other research presents a more nuanced view, arguing that Chinese foreign aid has been helpful to OFDI only under certain conditions. The type of aid matters. Complementary foreign aid, i.e. aid that fills gaps in local economic and social infrastructure and human capital, promotes FDI. In contrast, aid in the form for material capital that flows directly into the production sector competes with other types of capital in the sector and crowds out FDI (Liao et al. 2020).

In addition to its economic impact, foreign aid has important political effects. As an essential component of economic statecraft, it can help donor countries turn their economic leverage into political influence over the recipient countries. By promising and providing aid, donors can encourage and reward friendly policies of the recipients. On the other hand, the withholding or withdrawal of aid can deter or punish unfriendly behavior. Either way, aid has the potential to serve important political and strategic purposes (Baldwin 2020).

Research on the political effects of Chinese aid shows a mixed picture. On the one hand, coming with no (political) strings attached and providing much-needed assistance to recipient countries in an efficient way, Chinese aid has been welcomed in many developing countries. Even in countries where the public exhibits ambivalence toward China's economic presence, research shows that local communities by and large have a positive perception of aid as well as investment from China; the negative perceptions are primarily associated with trade-related issues (Morgan 2019). In addition, studies show that Chinese aid projects have been especially effective in generating a pro-China attitude among supporters of the incumbent political party. This is because in the context of neopatrimonialism and patronage politics in many African and Asian developing countries, the ruling elite tend to benefit disproportionately from China's largess (Chen and Han 2021; Mohan and Tan-Mullins 2019).

The political payoff for China can be seen in the voting patterns in international organizations. An examination of aid data and voting alignment at the

UN General Assembly from 2000 to 2014 finds that non-concessional aid flows from China have led to foreign-policy alignment between China and democratic recipient countries (Raess et al. 2022). Another study shows that Chinese foreign aid has decreased the ability of the United States to use American aid to buy support and manipulate voting at the UN General Assembly (Xun and Shuai 2018). In other words, Chinese aid has indirectly increased China's political influence relative to its main rival on the international stage.

On the other hand, Chinese aid has generated a political backlash from Western countries and some corners of the global South. An influential perspective portrays Chinese aid as a form of predatory economic policy. A prime example cited in this vein is Sri Lanka's Hambantota Port project. From 2010 onwards, China provided over a billion dollars to finance the construction of the port, the second largest in Sri Lanka. However, the port turned out not to be commercially viable, operating under capacity and losing money. When the Sri Lankan government found itself under financial stress, it negotiated an agreement to lease the port to China for 99 years. This has given rise to a new discourse that describes Chinese development finance as "**debt trap**" diplomacy.

Proponents of the debt trap narrative claim that the Chinese government uses development financing as a deliberate and coordinated effort to lure poor countries to take on unsustainable loans from China. When these borrowers are unable to keep up with the payment for the loans, China seizes control of assets in those countries to advance its economic and strategic interests. Others are more lenient, allowing for the possibility that China may have accidentally fallen into its own debt trap through profligate and uncoordinated lending, but they also blame Chinese financing for having exacerbated the debt crisis in many developing countries. While attacks of this kind mostly come from Western countries, this view is also shared by some critics in developing countries. Indeed, the phrase itself originally came from an Indian think tank, which produced a critical report of China's involvement in Sri Lanka's Hambantota Port. It was quickly picked up by the mass media and policy circles in the West and around the world (Bräutigam 2020).

The Chinese government has tried hard to rebuke the accusation. Meanwhile, scholarly research shows no support for the narrative. For instance, the Hambantota Port project was not proposed by China, but by the Sri Lankan government. Sri Lanka's debt distress was primarily the result of excessive borrowing on Western-dominated capital markets rather than Chinese loans. The $1.1 billion generated by the lease of the port to a Chinese SOE was used by the Sri Lankan government to pay down other debts and boost foreign reserves (Jones and Hameiri 2020). But so far these counter-arguments have largely fallen on deaf ears, and references to debt trap diplomacy continue to feature prominently in debates about Chinese foreign aid.

Conclusion

OFDI and development aid have been two major components of China's going out strategy in the last two decades. Having benefited from incoming FDI since the early years of its economic reform, China has become an exporter of FDI since the early twenty-first century. Some of the motivations behind China's OFDI are consistent with findings of studies of Western capital-exporting countries – access to resources and market, acquisition of technology, and export of overcapacity and environmental hazards. Others are particular to China's circumstances, such as better management of its foreign-exchange reserves. Over the last two decades, Chinese OFDI has widened its focus beyond accessing resources, especially to technology acquisition. Private enterprises have joined SOEs in investing abroad. And the geographic presence of Chinese companies has expanded from the global South to the global North. Thus far, OFDI has served China's economic development well, particularly through the technology spillover effect. Its impact on the host countries has been more mixed, including some dubious effects on the local institutions.

Following a brief hiatus in the 1980s and 1990s, China has revived and greatly expanded its foreign aid programs in the last two decades. Operating outside DAC, Chinese development financing shows different characteristics from the aid programs of the traditional donors. While the Chinese government provides some ODA, its aid has been dominated by OOF. The Chinese government emphasizes that its aid does not come with political conditions, and China does not interfere with the domestic affairs of the recipient countries. On the other hand, China is explicit in using aid to enhance economic cooperation that benefits China as well as the recipients. Besides the direct economic gains of non-concessional lending, Chinese aid has served China's economic interests by reducing the risks for its OFDI in the developing countries. Politically, it has improved China's relations with many developing countries' governments and increased their support of China on the international stage. At the same time, Chinese aid has also made China a target of strong criticisms by Western countries and some critics in the developing countries.

Questions for Discussion

1. Why are some recipient countries ambivalent toward foreign direct investment from China?

2. How does Chinese development aid differ from Western foreign aid?

3. What is your assessment of the effects of China's Belt and Road Initiative for China and the world?

Conclusion

After a long history of being at the center of *Tianxia* (all under heaven) and the interlude that was the century of national humiliation from the mid-nineteenth to the mid-twentieth century, China came under the rule of a communist regime in 1949. The Chinese Communist Party (CCP) proclaimed its determination to make the country rich and strong again. However, the economic experiment with Maoist socialism failed miserably; China remained poor and underdeveloped, when several of its neighbors – Japan and the newly industrialized economies (NIEs) of Korea, Singapore, Taiwan, and Hong Kong – modernized quickly in the post-World War II era. In the late 1970s, the CCP launched an economic reform program to change the country for the better and to re-establish its own legitimacy in the eyes of the disillusioned population. Today, China is the world's second largest economy. Its wealth and might have elevated it from the periphery to the center of the international system. The CCP prides itself for having restored the country to its rightful place in the world and realized the China Dream of national rejuvenation.

The economic rise of contemporary China has attracted intense interests globally. Scholars and pundits have debated vigorously how China has achieved its economic miracle. Is there a China model (CM) for development? If so, what are its main elements? What are its strengths and weaknesses? In this final chapter, we briefly visit the CM debate and reflect on these questions in light of China's economic performance detailed in the previous chapters.

A Chinese Development Model?

Two decades ago, a think tank in London published an article entitled "The Beijing Consensus: Notes on the New Physics of Chinese Power" (Ramo 2004). It argues that China has achieved its economic success by adopting a distinctive development approach characterized by three elements. First, it values innovation and seeks innovation-led productivity growth. Second, it aims not only to increase the size of the economy, but also to achieve equitable distribution of wealth. Third, it emphasizes national self-determination, rejecting Western attempts to impose their will or development policies.

The article uses the term **"Beijing Consensus"** to describe China's approach to contrast it with the so-called **"Washington Consensus,"** a set of ten market-oriented policy recommendations first proposed in 1989 by John Williamson, a Washinton DC-based economist, for Latin American countries. These recommendations later came to symbolize the neoliberal tenets advocated by the US government and the international financial institutions based in Washington DC – the International Monetary Fund and the World Bank. The term of Beijing Consensus suggests the potential for China to offer other countries an alternative to Western economic orthodoxy that preaches marketization, deregulation, liberalization, and privatization. This article gained immediate and widespread attention. Academics and commentators inside and outside China reacted with various rejoinders. Some were sympathetic to the thesis, while many were critical of it, pointing out that despite the government's rhetoric, China had not been a leader in innovation and had a poor record in equitable and sustainable development (Kennedy 2010). The official response from the Chinese government, however, was rather muted.

A few years later, another round of debate about China's development experience took place, as China successfully hosted the 2008 Olympics and as many countries around the world fell into a global financial crisis (GFC) that originated in the United States. The Beijing Olympics shone a spotlight on the tremendous economic growth China had achieved in recent decades, while the GFC exposed serious problems of Western economies in general, and the US economy in particular. The following year saw the celebration of the sixtieth anniversary of the founding of the People's Republic of China (PRC) and the commemoration of the thirtieth year of the beginning of the CCP's economic reform program.

This proved to be an opportune moment to distill China's development experience. Chinese opinion leaders spoke confidently of "the China model (*zhongguo moshi*)," "the China path (*zhongguo daolu*)," "the China speed (*zhongguo sudu*)," and "the China miracle (*zhongguo qiji*)." Meanwhile, Western commentators showed greater recognition of the Chinese model of state-led economic development, and some even expressed growing doubts about the Anglo-Saxon model of market capitalism (e.g. Fukuyama 2011). Again, the Chinese government stayed aloof from the debate. Speaking at a press conference during the 4th Ministerial Meeting of the Forum of China–Africa Cooperation in 2009, Premier Wen Jiabao pointed out that neither the Washington Consensus nor the Beijing Consensus offered guidance for Africa's development; Africans should make policies according to their own circumstances and follow an African model of development (Wen 2009).

With Xi Jinping's ascendance to China's political apex in 2012–2013 (first as General Secretary of the CCP and then as President of the PRC), the discourse on the CM entered a new stage. Unlike the previous rounds of debate, the Chinese government emerged from the shadow and stepped into the limelight, with Xi himself acting as the chief spokesperson. Xi has repeatedly called on the Chinese people to have confidence in China's own theory, path, institutions, and culture (*lilun zixin, daolu zixin, zhidu zixin, wenhua zixin*). He attributes the economic success of China not only to the reform policies in the post-Mao era, but also to the CCP's leadership through the generations and, indeed, to China's long and rich history since ancient times. Echoing Xi's rhetoric, nationalist pundits argue that China's unique qualities have enabled the country's remarkable social and economic achievements. The official CM discourse consists of multiple layers. It emphasizes the imperative for China to follow its own path of development, finding Chinese solutions for Chinese problems. It claims that China's economic and political superiority over the Western systems is clearly demonstrated by the rise of China and the decline of the West. It even offers the Chinese experience to other developing countries as an alternative to Western models of modernization (Zhao 2017).

The self-congratulatory tone of the Chinese discourse on the CM reached a climax during the first two years of the Covid-19 pandemic. Although the earliest cases of Covid infection appeared in China, the government quickly contained the spread of the virus by imposing draconian control over the population. At the height of the pandemic, Chinese officials and citizens expressed disbelief and contempt regarding the helplessness of Western governments in protecting their citizens. The talk of China's institutional superiority was prevalent in the mass media (including social media) and government leaders' speeches.

Different Versions of the China Model

Despite the wide use of the term, the CM remains an amorphous notion, without a clear or commonly accepted definition. A popular version describes it as a combination of a market economy and an authoritarian political system (e.g. Halper 2010; Kurlantzick 2013). Historically, market economy has, over the long run, gone hand-in-hand with liberal democracy. China has implemented market-oriented reform for decades since the late 1970s. However, economic liberalization aside, the CCP has maintained its monopoly of power and changed little in its authoritarian rule, leading to a system of "capitalism without democracy" (Tsai 2007). Sympathizers of such a system credit it for China's rapid economic development. Some argue that the insulation of the Chinese state from interest group pressure and regional demands makes it a "neutral government," which has been single-minded in its pursuit of national economic growth (Yao 2010). Others contend that the Party state has been critical in maintaining political stability in a country as vast and diverse as China. Moreover, state control of land and raw materials, state ownership of large enterprises, state management of the financial system, and a united group of selfless and capable cadres, combined with a free labor market and markets for commodities and assets, have led to a successful model of development (e.g. Pan 2009).

Another version of the CM focuses on the incremental process of Chinese reform. Unlike the former Soviet Union/Russia and the former communist countries in Eastern Europe, China avoided the so-called "shock therapy" of rapid restructuring of the old socialist economy. Instead, Chinese economic reform has proceeded step by step and, in many areas, liberalization has only gone part of the way. For instance, industrial reform did not initially involve abolishing economic planning and privatizing the state-owned enterprises (SOEs). In fact, for years the government was committed to allocating the same resources to the SOEs as before the reform and keeping their workers employed and paid as they had been under the planned economy. At the same time, the government allowed a non-state sector to develop, which was more efficient and gradually took up bigger shares of the economy. This dual-track strategy allowed economy to "grow out of the plan" accomplished something remarkable – reform without losers, at least for a while (Naughton 1995; Lau et al. 2000). Supporters of this model argue that it prevented the serious discontent and dislocation that plagued the "big bang" reform in the Soviet Union/Russia and Eastern Europe. It gave the CCP plenty of opportunities to learn from small mistakes and adapt to unexpected circumstances.

A third interpretation of the CM sees it as a variation of the **East Asian model** of economic development. Pioneered by Japan and practiced by the region's NIEs, the East Asian model features high savings, an educated population, export-led growth and, above all, a development-oriented state. Staffed by dedicated and capable bureaucrats, the state makes economic development plans and uses industrial policies – subsidies, tax incentives, research funding, infrastructure development, and trade protection – to facilitate the advancement of selected sectors and companies. Like its East Asian counterparts, the Chinese government is strongly oriented toward economic development, makes long-term plans, supports strategic industrial sectors with financial resources and other preferential policies, and encourages domestic companies to compete in the international market. It is true that China differs from its neighboring economies in important ways, including the legacy of a command economy and its international environment – economic globalization rather than the Cold War – during its takeoff. But by and large, the CM shares the main features of the East Asian model (Peerenboom 2007; Boltho and Weber 2009).

A fourth perspective on the CM stresses that the Chinese state has played a much more dominant role in the economy than the developmental states of East Asia. They use a different label for the Chinese system – state capitalism – to highlight the combination of a significantly marketized economy and a large and influential state sector (e.g. Naughton and Tsai 2015). Despite the market-oriented reform in urban China since the 1980s, SOEs continue to be the pillars in China's strategic industries. Indeed, since the mid-2000s, the CCP has demonstrated an ever-stronger desire to maintain a robust state sector in the long run. Being the owner of SOEs, the Chinese state has channeled enormous amounts of financial and other resources to them, regardless of their varied competitiveness and efficiency. Meanwhile, it has restricted the growth of private enterprises by depriving them of a level playing field and much-needed financial support. Furthermore, even with the introduction of considerable market-based policy instruments, Beijing's management of the economy retains strong elements of central command. These characteristics set China apart from other East Asian economies (e.g. Boltho and Weber 2009). A more recent formulation of the CM along these lines emphasizes the expanded role of the CCP in governing the economy, elevating state capitalism to Party state capitalism (Pearson et al. 2023).

Finally, some analysts believe China's economic success comes from its adoption of market principles. A report issued by the World Bank in 1993 argues that the East Asia economic miracle has been made possible by sound macroeconomic management, high level of domestic savings and investments, flexible labor markets, promotion of exports, a friendly business environment, and other pro-market policies (World Bank 1993). Echoing these themes, some scholars point out that despite its claim to socialism, China has adopted most of the elements of the Washington Consensus on its way to economic success, especially in the 1980s (e.g. Kennedy 2010; Williamson 2014; Huang 2010). They do not see anything particularly Chinese about China's development strategy in the reform era. In some ways, the concept of a CM is neither justifiable nor useful.

Three Features of the Chinese Development Experience

It is not the purpose of this book to adjudicate among these contending perspectives on the CM. In fact, our analysis of the various aspects of Chinese political economy in the previous chapters highlights the complexity of China's development experience. Three features of the Chinese experience are especially noteworthy. First, China's approach to economic development has *changed over time* during the reform era. Second, the governance of different economic sectors *varies considerably*. Third, the institutions and policies in the reform era have developed not from a blueprint, but through *pragmatic experimentation*.

The post-Mao reform era began over four decades ago. In this period, China's approach to economic development has evolved significantly. Scholars differ in their characterization of the evolution. Some distinguish between the rural-centered entrepreneurial model of the 1980s and the urban-centered statist model since the 1990s (Huang 2010). Others highlight the shift in China's development approach around the turn of the century with the transition from the Jiang Zemin and Zhu Rongji era to the Hu Jintao and Wen Jiabao era.

Unlike their predecessors, who single-mindedly pursued GDP growth, Hu and Wen called for a new people-centered notion of development (Dickson 2011). Still others see the GFC in 2008 as a watershed, after which state intervention in the economy increased significantly (Yao 2010).

The account of China's political economy in this book supports this dynamic view of the CM. In the initial stage of reform, the most momentous change in both the rural and the urban areas was the introduction of material incentives and market opportunities. In rural China, household farming replaced collective production and dramatically increased agricultural output. The newly established township and village enterprises (TVEs) competed fiercely in the market place and thrived by meeting market demands. In urban China, SOE workers were rewarded for higher productivity and managers were given certain authority to make production decisions. At the same time, the government gave permission for other types of enterprises to operate, including collectively owned enterprises, private enterprises, foreign invested enterprises. While the SOEs improved their efficiency, the non-state sector grew even more rapidly. The rising industrial output was a major component of the country's GDP growth, which according to World Bank data averaged 9.5 percent from 1980 to 1990. The early success of the post-Mao reform in China was clearly the result of economic liberalization.

Starting in the 1990s, market-oriented reform lost momentum. Under the somewhat oxymoronic banner of "a socialist market economy," further economic liberalization was hindered and diverted in various ways. In the late 1990s, after years of subsidizing and protecting the SOEs, the government decided to streamline the state sector, making it leaner and stronger. The Party state redoubled its support of the large SOEs in strategic sectors, turning many of them into gigantic enterprise groups. With generous government subsidies and preferential policies, they became "national champions," monopolizing key industries such as energy, resource, infrastructure, defense, and telecom. Meanwhile, private entrepreneurs found their business environment to be increasingly risky and their access to formal financing more and more restricted. In the twenty-first century, the state has continued to splurge its resources on the SOEs. In connection with this, much of the government's 4-trillion-yuan stimulus package following the GFC went to the state sector, with few benefits for the private sector, resulting in tremendous waste recognized by the government's own experts. This is a far cry from the liberalizing model of the 1980s; it contains prominent features of state developmentalism and state capitalism.

Besides its evolution over time, China's approach to economic development has been marked by variation across sectors, which involves seemingly contradictory elements. For instance, in the early years of economic reform, the government implemented a dual pricing system. Industrial input and output within the planned economy were priced by administrative means, while the same input and output outside the plan had their prices determined by the supply and demand in the marketplace. This was but one manifestation of the mixture of command and market principles in the Chinese economy. Similarly, until the mid-1990s, China's foreign-trade system consisted of two mutually contradictory regimes. Ordinary trade remained under the monopoly of the state-owned foreign trade companies and operated with an exchange rate set artificially high by the government. Meanwhile, **export-processing trade** followed the market logic and was fully integrated into the global capitalist system.

The varied nature of the CM can also be found in the multiple types of TVEs that emerged at the height of rural economic liberalization. Those in southern Jiangsu adhered to the practice of collective ownership and communal welfare. Their counterparts in Wenzhou, Zhejiang, featured strong individual entrepreneurship. Meanwhile, TVEs in the Pearl River Delta in Guangdong were enmeshed with Hong Kong businesses. Elements of socialism, market capitalism, and globalization were all components of this important dimension of China's rural industrialization. Likewise, the SOEs experienced the economic reform in different ways, culminating in the bifurcation of the state sector in the late 1990s. At that time, the government adopted a policy of "grasping the big and letting go the small." The state stopped taking care of the smaller SOEs, letting them fend for themselves in the marketplace. Many of those enterprises went bankrupt or were acquired by other companies. The large SOEs in strategic industries, on the other hand, continued to operate under state control and state protection.

Some scholars argue that the apparent contradictions within the Chinese economic system are a defining feature of the CM. About a decade ago, McNally (2012) observed that Sino capitalism is a combination of neoliberalism and neo-statism. It consists of both top-down state led development and bottom-up entrepreneurial accumulation. These two institutional arrangements occupy different realms of the Chinese economy. While the state-controlled entities dominate finance and strategic industries, private and foreign invested enterprises compete in retail and manufacturing. These two types of capitalism are complementary and compensate each other. Since then, the line between neoliberalism and neo-statism has become even more blurred. On the one hand, the government has encouraged private capital to join state capital to operate in previously restricted industries. The goal is to use "mixed ownership" to increase the competitiveness of the former SOEs. On the other hand, through the so-called reverse mixed ownership reform, various funds owned and guided by the state have gone into non-state-owned enterprises, including private high-tech companies. At the same time, the Party has deepened its penetration of all types of enterprises.

A prominent feature of the CM is its pragmatic experimentalism (Heilmann 2008; Ang 2018). Deng Xiaoping's famous mantra – "it does not matter if a cat is white or black; if it can catch mice, it is a good cat" – captures the pragmatism of China's reformers. Although Deng was given the title of the "chief architect" (*zong shejishi*) of China's reform and modernization by foreign media and then the CCP itself, he did not have a blueprint to follow in guiding China's development. Indeed, the first generation of reform leaders around Deng described their efforts to change the country as a great experiment. Not knowing exactly where the path forward was, they were ready to improvise and explore. Their strategy was to "cross the river by groping the stones (*mozhe shitou guohe*)."

In the previous chapters, we have seen many cases where major policy change came via trial and error, rather than carefully thought-out design. One example of this is the household responsibility system, which was introduced at the beginning of the rural reform, and which emerged from the spontaneous and clandestine experiments of desperately poor villagers. Only after the practice produced favorable results and received the endorsement of enlightened local government officials did it gain the attention of the national leaders and finally become a nationwide policy. Similarly, China first tested economic opening to the world in a very confined area in southern China, far away from the country's economic and political centers. The government created four so-called special economic zones in Guangdong and Fujian, giving them permission to engage in export processing and to host foreign invested enterprises. As those experiments proved to be highly successful in growing China's international trade and attracting foreign capital, policymakers in Beijing extended similar policies, first to the coastal regions and then to the rest of the country.

The remarkable record of China's four-decade-long economic growth has led to heated discussions inside and outside the country about its development model. There is no consensus on the precise meaning of the CM. Contending perspectives emphasize different factors that have contributed to Chinas economic success. What this book demonstrates is that the CM has evolved over time. It also shows that the CM consists of multiple components that can seem mutually contradictory but have coexisted and even complemented each other. One can conclude that to the extent that there has been a consistent theme in the economic development strategy in contemporary China, it is one of pragmatic experimentation and adaptation.

A Successful Model?

The widespread interest in China's development model comes from its apparently spectacular success. The world wants to know how that country has achieved the fastest and most sustained economic growth in human history, lifting hundreds of millions of people out of poverty and turning a socialist backwater into a global economic superpower in such a short time. Compared with the former Soviet Union and other post-socialist countries in Eastern Europe, China has managed its transition much more smoothly and with far better economic outcomes. Furthermore, during the GFC and the early stages of the Covid-19 pandemic, the Chinese economy showed greater resilience than the United States and many other developed countries, raising doubts about the superiority of Western economic and political systems.

Limitations and Problems of the China Model

However, the CM – in its various manifestations – has serious limitations and problems. As we have seen earlier in this book, while the reform era has seen rapid economic growth, it has not been kind to all groups of Chinese citizens. The CCP, large SOEs, the educated elite, skilled professionals, and multinational corporations have gained a great deal of power, wealth, and/or opportunities, but many peasants, workers, and private entrepreneurs have experienced relative (and sometimes even absolute) deprivation and found themselves in precarious positions.

Rural economic reform from the late 1970s through the 1980s gave peasants unprecedented incentives and opportunities to increase their productivity and better their lives. Since the 1990s, however, rural China has been squeezed by the state-led urbanization project. Local governments, which have faced continued fiscal pressure since the tax reform in 1994, have turned to land grabbing for industrial and commercial development. Many villagers have been coerced into selling their land cheaply and relocating to newly created peri-urban areas. In this process, they have lost their ancestral homes, traditional ways of life, and the safety net provided by a plot of land. Meanwhile, in their new homes on the edges of the cities, they face an unfamiliar and unforgiving environment, where they lack the skills and resources to compete for jobs and business opportunities. Aggrieved peasants have tried to resist this form of "gangster capitalism" by petition, protests, and riots, but their demands have largely fallen on deaf ears, and their battles have mostly been lost.

China's rapid economic development has been made possible by its cheap and disciplined labor. The transfer of large numbers of laborers from agriculture to industry and from the rural to the urban areas played a key role in the country's transformation. Migrant workers have manufactured China's exports, built its skyscrapers, constructed the roads, railways, ports, and powerlines across the country, and provided a myriad of services in Chinese cities. However, they have remained at the bottom of the socio-economic hierarchy. Doing the hardest, dirtiest and most dangerous jobs, they are paid low wages and have little protection against injuries, illness, unemployment, and old age. Living in the margins of the cities, they and their children face discrimination in every aspect of life. They have formed a precariat proletariat – labelled by some as "precariat" – in contemporary China.

Another group of the new precariat consists of former SOE workers, who have lost their jobs during the restructuring of the state sector. Deprived of the "iron rice bowl" they had held for years, and lacking the skills and mentality to compete in the new capitalist labor market, many have been unable to find re-employment or start their own businesses. From the late 1990s to the early 2000s, thousands of labor protests and riots involving millions of workers showed the depth of their frustration and despair. The government tried to appease them by addressing their concerns piecemeal but offered no systematic and institutionalized policies to improve their livelihood.

The Party state has long been aware of the unfair treatment of rural migrants and the desperate situation of the castaway former SOE workers. However, it has been unwilling to reform the neoliberal labor market that has been the source of their misery. After all, that market has given China a huge comparative advantage in global economic competition, turning it into a manufacturing superpower. Moreover, under CCP's authoritarian rule, labor has been forbidden to organize. Without independent trade unions and meaningful political representation, Chinese workers have not been able to have their say in the making of laws and policies.

Neoliberalism has dominated Chinese welfare policy as much as its labor policy. When collective agriculture ended and the planned economy declined in the 1980s, the economic foundation of the old socialist welfare state began to crumble. In the following years, the CCP obsessed with GDP growth, ignored the need to build a social safety net suitable for an increasingly marketized economy. Beginning in the late 1990s, under the pressure of rising social tension, the Chinese government made more efforts to develop a new welfare system. Thus far, the Party state has chosen a welfare model that combines conservative/corporatist and liberal elements. It differentiates benefits by the recipients' status. Separate pension and healthcare systems privilege government employees and SOE workers over informal sector employees, and they offer greater protection for urban *hukou* holders than the rural population. These programs reinforce rather than ameliorate the existing social economic stratification. Meanwhile, the welfare system provides meager and means-tested social assistance programs, which stigmatize those in need and leave them struggling on, barely above subsistence. Compared with mature capitalist societies, the post-socialist welfare system in China remains quite rudimentary, suffering from major institutional and implementation gaps. As a result, the inequality of the neoliberal marketplace is exacerbated by the welfare system.

A main reason for the lamentable state of social welfare for the Chinese population lies in the instrumental approach of the government to welfare provision. For the Party state, the overwhelming top priority is to maintain social stability, sustain economic growth, and ensure its legitimacy. It has been willing to invest in a social safety net to the extent it serves these purposes. But its commitment to the well-being of the population, especially the less powerful groups, is limited. Unless, and until, the government is genuinely concerned about the intrinsic rights of ordinary people – their social citizenship – it will not ensure a robust welfare state. Unfortunately, such a government is unlikely to emerge under the current political regime.

The rapid growth of the Chinese economy has been made possible in no small part due to the dynamism in the private sector. Private enterprises have consistently shown greater efficiency than the SOEs. The Chinese government recognizes the value of private entrepreneurs and has allowed them to operate and grow their businesses. However, the Party state has always privileged SOEs over the private companies. For a long time, the latter were kept away from the strategic industries, such as energy, telecom, and defense. Although the government has encouraged private capital to join the state capital in some of the formerly restricted sectors in recent years, the role of the private enterprises is limited and subordinate to the state. The state-controlled financial system systematically discriminates against private entrepreneurs, depriving them of the capital needed to increase their production and to weather economic downturns. Moreover, government agencies and officials routinely extract resources from private enterprises for fiscal and personal gains. The absence of a level playing field and a reliable system of rule of law render private enterprises vulnerable to considerable risks and uncertainties.

Over the decades, CCP has formed a symbiotic relationship with private businesses. It does not provide the latter with institutionalized protection but has often tolerated their institution-bending strategies, such as "wearing a red hat" (posing as collective enterprises and paying for local government protection), financing their businesses through informal channels (e.g. using financial intermediaries and services outside the state-controlled banks and capital markets), and engaging in corruption (e.g. using bribery and other questionable means to obtain favors from government officials). However, this expedient arrangement does not change the precarious existence of private businesses. Their *ad hoc* deals with local governments and individual officials are volatile and risky. Raising funds outside the formal channels has sometimes led to severe punishment, including the death sentence, for the daring entrepreneurs. The discrimination against the private sector is not only unfair, but it also restricts the potential of China's economic growth in the long run.

In the last decade, the Chinese economy has clearly passed the miracle stage. According to World Bank data, from 1978 to 2015 Chinese GDP grew at an average of 9.7 percent a year, and from 2016 to 2023, the average annual rate of growth was down to 5.7 percent. At the beginning of the thirteenth five-year plan (2016–2020), Chinese leaders admitted that a more slowly growing economy would be the "new normal." The World Bank estimates that

Chinese GDP will grow by only 4.5 percent in 2024. A simple and obvious reason for the slower growth is the much bigger size of the Chinese economy compared with the past. In 1978 China's economy was merely RMB 368.87 billion. In 2016, it reached RMB 74.64 trillion, more than 200 times larger. By 2023, this figure had grown to RMB 126 trillion. Against a much larger base, new growth constitutes a smaller portion of the existing economy.

There are other factors underlying the new normal. First, when China was a backward economy, it was relatively easy to emulate more advanced economies. Taking advantage of technology transfer and other forms of learning, China was able to leapfrog stages of development. Once the "catching up" phase is over, China must rely more on its own research and development to keep its productivity growing. In fact, the government has been calling for indigenous innovation for two decades. But for various reasons, the progress in this regard has been slow and limited.

Second, China's demographics have changed. Due to longer life expectancy and declining fertility rates, its population has been aging faster than most other countries in modern times. According to the World Health Organization (WHO), in 2019, 254 million Chinese were over the age of sixty. By 2040, that number will rise to 402 million, or 28 percent of the population (WHO n.d.). Along with aging, the population is shrinking. As has been mentioned, in 2022 China recorded the first drop in population in sixty years and this trend will likely continue. A report by the United Nations indicates that China's population could decline to 1.3 billion in 2050 and then plummet to only 770 million in 2100 (Rieffel and Wang 2024). An aging and shrinking population means a declining labor force and rising welfare costs, both of which drag down the country's economic growth.

Third, Chinese economic growth in recent decades has been based on heavy investment, particularly investment in infrastructure and real estate. At the same time, household consumption level has stayed very low, too weak to be the main driver for economic growth. Capital accumulation has constituted three-quarters of growth in the last decade. As the development of infrastructure and real estate slows down, profitable investment opportunities in these areas have narrowed. Moreover, investment in business, which concentrates in the state sector, has also shown diminishing returns. This has weakened a major engine of growth.

Last, but not least, China's international environment has deteriorated significantly in recent years. At the start of the reform era, China enjoyed ever improving relations with the United States and other industrialized countries. For political as well as economic reasons, the West was eager to see the former communist country move toward a market economy and integrate into the capitalist global system. Expanded international trade, foreign capital inflow, and technology transfer all contributed significantly to China's rapid economic development. Even though the suppression of the Tiananmen movement of

1989 showed the world the CCP was not about to give up its monopoly of power, Western governments resumed their engagement with China after a brief hiatus. They hoped and assumed that economic liberalization and the emergence of a middle class would ultimately move China toward political democratization.

But, in the last decade, a new consensus has formed in the United States and, to a lesser extent, other industrialized countries, that the policy of engagement with China has failed; rather than nudging China toward political liberalization, cooperation with China in the economic realm seems to have only further strengthened its authoritarian regime and its state-dominated approach to development. They have expressed growing concerns about Chinese behavior, ranging from intellectual property theft to commercial espionage, and from arbitrary restriction of rare earth exports to the choking of critical supply chains. Fearing China's existential threat to the so-called "liberal international order," they have fought trade wars against China, set new restrictions on foreign investment from and into China, tightened control of technology sharing with Chinese companies and research institutions, and imposed sanctions on Chinese entities suspected to be related to the Chinese military. This has greatly worsened the conditions for China's pursuit of economic growth and upgrading.

Some of these problems faced by China are structural, such as the size of its economy, the end of the catching-up phase, and demographic change. But other problems are rooted in institutional arrangements and policies. These include, for instance, the limited progress made in indigenous innovation, the diminishing returns on investment, the persistently low level of consumption, and the rising tension in China's relations with the United States and other industrialized countries.

There is room for the Chinese government to modify the CM to confront these challenges. Innovation requires freedom of thinking and encouragement of diverse ideas. A more open and tolerant political and ideological space can improve the conditions for innovation. Continued economic growth calls for a more efficient allocation of capital. The financial system can help by funneling more funding resources to private entrepreneurs than the SOEs. Domestic consumption has enormous untapped potential in stimulating China's economic development. Increasing wages for the working class and reducing inequality can greatly increase the spending power of households and sustain economic growth for years to come. Finally, reversing the trend of greater state dominance of the economy will not only unleash people's innovation capacity, entrepreneurship, and consumption power, but it will also ease the tension between China and Western countries, creating a more conducive environment for much-needed international economic cooperation to continue.

Finally, the successful economic growth achieved by the CM has been accompanied by serious environmental problems. For decades, the government of

China focused on keeping up the GDP growth rate, neglecting the damage of its policies to the ecological system. The result has been alarming pollution of the air, water, and soil, as well as losses of water and arable land, among other things. Environmental degradation has incurred heavy economic costs and led to rising public discontent. In the twenty-first century, the government has become increasingly attentive to environmental protection.

When green development and economic growth go hand-in-hand, as in the expansion of renewable energy, China has made remarkable progress thanks in part to government guidance and financial subsidies. But, when environmental and economic priorities compete against each other, the Party state has largely stuck with its obsession with the latter, sacrificing the environment for the sake of growth. Unlike in democratic countries, China lacks a vibrant civil society to hold the government accountable. This situation will likely continue if two aspects of the CM – the dominant role of the state and its authoritarian nature – remain unchanged.

Thus, despite its achievement of rapid economic growth, the CM has obvious problems and limitations. It has benefited some groups in Chinese society much more than others, leading to extraordinary inequality in a nominally socialist society governed by a self-proclaimed communist government. Moreover, the Chinese miracle has lost some of its luster, with slower GDP growth since the mid-2010s and with alarming environmental degradation. Dealing with these challenges requires adjustments of key dimensions of the CM, particularly the role of the state in the economy and the nature of the political system.

Why Debate the CM?

The debate about the CM is not only of academic interest, but also has political and policy implications (Ferchen 2013). At the international level, it has been part of the larger political and strategic contestation between China and Western industrialized countries. The economic rise of China and the expansion of its global economic influence through trade, investment, aid, and other means are a source of growing anxiety for the US and its allies. If developing countries in the world view the CM – however it is interpreted – as an attractive alternative to the neoliberal ideology of market fundamentalism, it would strengthen China's ideational leadership (an important element of soft power), which in turn could threaten the hegemonic status of the United States and the West-led "liberal international order."

The Chinese government has not shied away from its criticisms of the Washington Consensus even though it has not explicitly advocated a Beijing Consensus. Under Xi Jinping, it has become bolder in promoting China's development model. In a speech at the 2015 UN Sustainable Development Summit, Xi proposed a Center for International Knowledge on Development. In spring

2017, the Center was officially established in Beijing with the mandate to enhance research on development theories and promote knowledge-sharing on international development issues with other countries. The contest of development models has added a new layer to the power competition between China and the United States.

Inside China, discussions of the CM have provided an outlet for different groups to express their political views and promote their policy preferences. The government and establishment intellectuals praise the CCP for its leadership and credit its leadership for China's economic miracle. The **New Left** – a group of public intellectuals intensely critical of neoliberalism and its negative effects on socio-economic inequality – supports state-led development but advocates an even more central role of the state in combating the problems of a market economy. Among other things, the New Left emphasizes the need to increase the central government's fiscal prowess and redistributive capacity. For them the strength of the CM lies in the government's ability to harness market forces to serve national interests. In contrast to the discourse of the government and the New Left is the faint voice of China's liberal intellectuals. This group of individuals was always a minority and has been largely silenced in recent years under Xi's tightening of the ideological straitjacket. Their view of the CM is highly critical. They believe social justice is not served by the unchecked power of the Party state but depends on a well-functioning market and a strong civil society. In other words, the current CM is flawed; what China needs going forward is greater economic and political freedom.

Throughout this book, we have seen many twists and turns in China's economy over time, and – with them – the changing fortunes of the nation. During the reform era, China has achieved unprecedented economic growth and poverty reduction. In the process, it has gained greater international influence. But into the third decade of the twenty-first century, that momentum seems to be slipping. China now faces slower economic growth, ballooning debt burdens, rising unemployment, and an apparent loss of consumer and investor confidence. This is not only bad news for China, but it may also have serious consequences for many other countries. After all, in the post GFC era, China emerged as a major engine of the global economy. Data from the World Bank show that, from 2013 to 2021, China's contribution to global economic growth averaged 38.6 percent, greater than that of the Group of Seven countries combined (Xinhua 2022). China's future, and the future of much of the world, depends on major adjustments of the existing CM, including further economic and political liberalization. The stakes are high for the Chinese people, and for the rest of the world.

Questions for Discussion

1. How does the China model need to change to meet today's challenges?

2. Can the CCP government make the adjustments necessary to keep the Chinese economy growing?

3. What can other developing countries learn from China's economic development experience in recent decades?

Glossary

All-China Federation of Trade Unions: The official mass organization for Chinese labor. Its dual identity includes being an instrument of the Party state and serving the interest of the workers.

Asian financial crisis: A financial crisis (1997–1998) that began with a currency crisis in Thailand and spread to other areas in East and Southeast Asia. It led to widespread economic recession and political turmoil that set the region back after decades of economic growth.

Asian Infrastructure Investment Bank: A multilateral development bank established in 2016 and headquartered in Beijing. China played a leading role in the creation of the bank, which has over one hundred members and focuses on investing in infrastructure to promote economic development.

barefoot doctors: Mao-era rural paramedics with rudimentary medical training, who provided basic prevention-oriented healthcare to the peasants under the cooperative medical system.

Beijing Consensus: A label used by some to summarize the factors underlying China's economic success, including innovation, equitable distribution of wealth, and national self-determination.

Belt and Road Initiative: A grandiose initiative launched by Xi Jinping in 2013, which seeks to use infrastructure development to connect the economy of China with that of other countries on multiple continents. The "Silk Road Economic Belt" consists of roads and railways through landlocked Central Asia to Europe. The "21st-Century Maritime Silk Road" envisions ports and sea lanes through Southeast Asia and South Asia to the Middle East and Africa.

boom-and-bust: A term to describe the swings between rapid economic growth accompanied by high inflation and economic slow-down. Such volatile macroeconomic cycles were common in China during the early period of the reform era.

cancer villages: Rural areas where environmental pollution has dramatically increased the occurrence of cancer among residents, often resulting in many deaths in a single village.

central bank independence: Autonomy of the central bank from the political leaders in conducting monetary policy. Some theorists believe this is the institutional foundation for effective control of inflation.

century of humiliation: A period in Chinese history when China suffered humiliating defeats by foreign powers and lost its sovereignty, beginning with the first Opium War (1839–1841), to the end of the war of resistance against Japan in 1945.

China Circle: The economic region consisting of mainland China, Hong Kong, and Taiwan. Economic ties grew among the three economies in the 1990s and beyond, despite on-and-off political tension. Synergy and cooperation have brought remarkable growth to the region.

commune: Large organization for collective agriculture and rural administration in China from the late 1950s to the late 1970s. Consisting of thousands of households, it was subdivided into brigades and production teams.

comprador bourgeoisie: Individuals who were private business owners before the communist takeover of China in 1949, and who were deemed by the Chinese Communist Party to be collaborators with, and representatives of, foreign interests.

Confucianism: An ancient philosophy attributed to the teachings of Confucius (c. 551–479 BCE) and adopted by Chinese rulers since the Han Dynasty (206 BCE–220 CE). It emphasizes respect for traditions and prescribes appropriate behavior and relationships based on hierarchy, rituals, and ethics.

Cooperative Medical System: The healthcare system in rural China under collective agriculture. Funded by peasants' premium contributions, the village Collective Welfare Fund, and subsidies from higher levels of government, it provided basic healthcare for rural residents.

crossing the river by groping the stones: A mantra of post-Mao reform leaders, who described their efforts to change the country as a pragmatic experiment without a blueprint.

debt trap: A narrative that claims that the Chinese government uses development financing as a deliberate and coordinated effort to lure poor countries to take on unsustainable loans from China, thus allowing China to advance its economic and strategic interests in those countries.

Glossary 277

dependence ratio: The ratio of the dependent population (the very old and the very young) to the working-age population.

Development Assistance Committee: A component of the Organization of Economic Cooperation and Development (OECD), which offers a venue for consultation and coordination among its member countries on development aid. Its official development assistance has long been regarded as the "gold standard" of foreign aid.

developmental state: A state which focuses on national economic development and uses policy tools, notably financial subsidies, to promote strategic economic sectors and enterprises.

dibao: Urban Minimum Living Guarantee System, a government-provided welfare program which aims to provide a safety net for the urban poor.

East Asian model: A development model pioneered by Japan and practiced by several newly industrialized economies in East Asia. It features high savings, an educated population, export-led growth, and, above all, a developmental state.

ecological civilization: A concept promoted by the Chinese government, especially under Xi Jinping. It calls for sustainable economic development based on harmony between the human society and the natural environment.

export-processing trade: A special form of foreign trade, where manufacturers assemble materials from companies abroad and return the products to those companies, all the while keeping the materials and the products under the latter's ownership.

extra-budgetary finance: Financial resources secured and spent by the government outside the budget process. This often involves arbitrary fees and levies and (often illegal) borrowing from banks.

first Opium War: A war between Britain and China from 1839 to 1841, which resulted from Britain's use of the opium trade to balance its trade deficit with China. When the Qing government took measures to stop the inflow of opium to China, Britain sent its navy in retaliation and won a decisive victory over China.

fiscal decentralization: A process whereby the central government grants local governments greater authority in collecting and spending tax revenue. This was a major component of China's economic reform in the 1980s.

fiscal recentralization: A reduction of local authority in collecting and spending tax revenue. Such a policy, introduced in 1994, has greatly enhanced the fiscal resources for the central government at the expense of the local governments.

floating population: Migrants from rural China, who work in other locales, especially industrial centers in coastal cities. Doing the jobs shunned by urban Chinese, most of them do not have official urban status and the entitlements that brings.

foreign direct investment: Investment by foreign companies that involves at least ten percent of the equity, and thus gives the investor considerable influence over the business.

foreign-trade companies: State-owned companies with the exclusive rights to import and export products under a command economy.

fragmented authoritarianism: An authoritarian political system, characterized by internal division and competition among different bureaucracies and different levels of governments. It often undermines the coherence of policymaking and the effectiveness of policy implementation.

GDP per capita: Gross domestic product divided by the country's population. It is often used as a broad measure of average living standards.

Government Insurance Scheme: A welfare program funded by government budget for the employees of government and public service organizations. Dating back to the Maoist era it covered the healthcare expenses for the employees, retirees, and their dependents. It also extended benefits to students and disabled veterans.

grasping the big and letting go the small: A strategy for reforming the state-owned enterprises (SOEs) in the late 1990s. The government cut loose the smaller SOEs, letting them go out of business or become privatized, and focused its attention and resources on improving the financial condition and business performance of the big SOEs.

Green GDP: A national accounting system that takes account of the resource and environmental costs of economic development. It subtracts such costs from standard GDP figures.

growing out of the plan: A prominent phenomenon of China's gradualist economic reform process, where early economic growth came from the newly created non-state sector while the state-owned enterprises remained largely untouched.

household responsibility system: Also known as "household contracting," it was first implemented in rural China in the late 1970s. It allocates collectively owned land among rural households. Once the households have fulfilled the agricultural procurement quota under contract, they can keep the products or sell them in the market.

hukou: A household registration system introduced in the 1950s to monitor and control internal population movement, especially from the rural areas to the cities. Based on one's birth, the household registration status severely discriminates against people originating from rural China.

iron rice bowl: Guaranteed employment for state-owned enterprise workers under socialism.

Janus-faced business associations: Business associations that are not only vehicles for the expression of business interests but are also "transmission belts" for the Party state to communicate its will to the entrepreneurs.

joint venture: A business arrangement that brings two or more partners together to form a new enterprise. This was the main channel for foreign direct investment to enter China in the early years of the reform era.

kuaikuai: A horizontal chain of command in the Chinese government system, where government agencies follow the order from local leaders first and foremost.

Labor Insurance Scheme: A welfare program in state-owned enterprises under socialism. Funded by the enterprises, it covered the healthcare expenses for the employees, retirees, and their dependents.

Made in China 2025: An industrial policy program launched by the Chinese government in 2015. It seeks to use state guidance and subsidies to promote indigenous innovation and thus upgrade China's manufacturing capabilities, especially in high-tech sectors.

national bourgeoisie: Individuals who were private business owners before the communist takeover of China in 1949 and who were deemed by the Chinese Communist Party to be patriotic and indigenous entrepreneurs.

national champions: Large companies aided and protected by the state, which have come to dominate one or more sectors of the national economy and compete effectively on the international stage.

National People's Congress: China's legislative body, in charge of making and amending laws of the country. Nominally the highest organ of state power, it routinely rubber-stamps policies made by the Chinese Communist Party.

National Team: A group of big and state-affiliated financial institutions, which has followed government guidance and intervened in the Chinese stock market to rescue it from sharp declines.

Needham puzzle: A two-part puzzle raised by Joseph Needham about Chinese history – why China had been far in advance of other civilizations in science and technology early on and why it fell behind after the seventeenth century.

New Development Bank: A new multilateral development bank established in 2015 and headquartered in Shanghai. Founded by Brazil, Russia, India, China, and South Africa, it is also known as the BRICS bank. Its main goal is to mobilize financial resources for infrastructure projects and sustainable development.

New Left: A group of public intellectuals highly critical of neoliberalism and its negative effects on socio-economic inequality. They favor China's state-led development and advocate an even more central role of the state in combating the problems of a market economy.

Party state: A term to describe the fusion of the Chinese Communist Party with the government of China, where the Party is the decision-maker and the state organs are supervised by the Party and implement the Party's decisions.

People's Bank of China: The Chinese central bank, which plays an important role in the making of China's monetary policy and maintaining macroeconomic stability.

permanent migrants: Highly educated and skilled migrants, who are granted local *hukou* and thus enjoy all the privileges of local citizens.

Political bureau (Politburo): The decision-making body of the Central Committee of the Chinese Communist Party. Made up of two dozen or so members, it is nominally elected by the Central Committee but is typically a product of intra-Party power struggle. Its standing committee is the most powerful center in Chinese politics.

precariat: Migrant workers and laid-off SOE workers, whose employment and livelihood are precarious. Oscillating between exploitation and exclusion by capital, this group faces even harsher conditions than those of the "proletariat" in Chinese cities.

red capitalists: Private entrepreneurs in the reform era, who are members of the Chinese Communist Party. Some of them are former managers of state-owned enterprises, and were already Party members before becoming business owners. Others are private entrepreneurs who have joined the Party more recently.

rightful resistance: A popular form of rebellion in rural China that employs official rhetoric against the corrupt and oppressive behavior of local cadres.

scientific outlook on development: A concept promoted by the Chinese government during the Hu Jintao and Wen Jiabao administration. Calling for a people-centered approach to development, it sought to shift away from a single-minded focus on GDP growth to more sustainable development and more equitable wealth redistribution.

Self-Strengthening Movement: A movement led by some provincial leaders of the late Qing Dynasty advocating learning from the West to modernize China's military and industry. It turned out to be too little and too late to save China from repeated defeats by Western powers and, later, Japan.

shock therapy: A reform strategy adopted by the Soviet Union/Russia and some former socialist countries in Eastern Europe, characterized by rapid privatization of the state-owned enterprises and removal of administrative control of prices. It caused serious short-term economic dislocations.

soft budget constraint: The elastic financial constraint faced by state-owned enterprises, which can count on guaranteed government bailouts to survive.

special economic zones: Geographic areas that were granted special economic liberalization policies at the beginning of the reform era. Four of the earliest such areas in Guangdong and Fujian were pioneers in opening China to international trade and foreign direct investment.

stimulus package: Government spending program in response to economic downturn. It typically consists of expansionist fiscal and monetary policies, designed to stimulate investment and/or consumer spending.

temporary migrants: The status of most rural migrants who work in urban China. Even if they have spent many years working in the cities, they are not granted local *hukou* and the entitlements that come with it.

Three Represents: A new self-definition adopted by the Chinese Communist Party in the early twenty-first century, portraying the Party as representing advanced productive forces, advanced culture, and the fundamental interests of the majority of the Chinese people. It opened an important door to welcome private entrepreneurs into the Party.

Tiananmen movement of 1989: A protest in Beijing – centered around Tiananmen Square – and other cities in the spring of 1989. Led by students and joined by workers and ordinary citizens, it criticized the rising corruption and demanded freedom and democracy. After several weeks, it was suppressed by the Chinese military.

tiaotiao: Vertical chain of command in the Chinese government system, where government agencies prioritize the guidance from their counterparts at higher administrative levels.

tied aid: Foreign aid that requires recipients to use the aid to purchase equipment and products from the donor country. It is a strategy of export promotion frowned upon by the OECD's Development Assistance Committee.

township and village enterprises: Enterprises that arose in rural China early in the reform era. While many of them were formally under collective ownership, they largely followed market principles and conditions in their operation.

Washington Consensus: A set of policy recommendations by Washington-based international financial institutions and the US government for economic liberalization in developing countries, which emphasizes privatization, deregulation, and marketization.

wearing a red hat: The practice whereby privately owned enterprises register as collectively owned township and village enterprises. This makes the enterprises seem to be part of the socialist system and offers them political protection in the transitional economic system.

work units (*danwei*): Total institutions in urban China under planned economy, including enterprises as well as government and service organizations. They not only turned out products and provided employment and welfare, but they were also instruments of social control.

yi'nao: Incidents where doctors and nurses are harassed and even violently attacked because of patient disappointment with the outcomes of medical treatment. They are rooted in a deep distrust in the profit-making orientation of hospitals.

References

Abeliansky, A. and Martínez-Zarzoso, I. (2019) "The relationship between the Chinese 'going out' strategy and international trade," *Economics*, 13(1): 1–18.

ACFTU (n.d.) "*Quanzong zhuyao zhize* (Major Responsibilities of the ACFTU)," https://www.acftu.org/jgsz/.

Adarkwah, G. and Malonæs, T. (2022) "Firm-specific advantages: A comprehensive review with a focus on emerging markets," *Asia Pacific Journal of Management*, 39: 539–585.

Ahlers, A.L. and Schubert, G. (2013) "Strategic modelling: 'Building a new socialist countryside' in three Chinese counties," *China Quarterly*, 216: 831–849.

Ahlstrom, D. and Bruton, G.D. (2001) "Learning from successful local private firms in China: Establishing legitimacy," *Academy of Management Perspectives*, 15(4): 72–83.

Aiddata.org (n.d.) "China's global development footprint."

Aiddata.org. (n.d.) "Global Chinese development finance."

Aivazian, V.A., Ge, Y., and Qiu, J. (2005) "Can corporatization improve the performance of state-owned enterprises even without privatization?" *Journal of Corporate Finance*, 11(5): 791–808.

Alesina, A. and Summers, L. (1993) "Central bank independence and macroeconomic performance: Some comparative evidence," *Journal of Money, Credit and Banking* 25(2): 151–162.

Allen, F., Qian, J., Shan, C., and Zhu, J.L. (2024) "Dissecting the long-term performance of the Chinese stock market," *Journal of Finance*, 79(2): 993–1054.

Allen, F., Qian, J., Shan, S., and Zhao, M. (2014) "The IPO of Industrial and Commercial Bank of China and the 'Chinese Model' of privatizing large financial institutions," *European Journal of Finance*, 20(7–9): 599–624.

Allen, R. (2011) *Global Economic History: A Very Short Introduction*. Oxford University Press.

Allou, E., Adeleye, B., Cheng, J., and Abdul, R. (2020) "Is there a nexus between China outward foreign direct investment and welfare in Côte d'Ivoire? Empirical evidence from the Toda–Yamamoto procedure," *African Development Review*, 32(3): 499–510.

Anderson, K., Huang, J., and Ianchovichina, E. (2004) "Will China's WTO accession worsen farm household income?" *China Economic Review*, 15: 443–456.

Ang, Y. (2018) *How China Escaped the Poverty Trap*. Cornell University Press.

References

AP (2022) "China party says nearly 5 million members probed for graft."

Arnone, M., Laurens, B., Segalotto, J.F., and Sommer, M. (2007) "Central bank autonomy: Lessons from global trends," *IMF Staff Papers*, 56(2): 263–296.

AsianBondOnline (n.d.) "People's Republic of China: Size and composition."

Atherton, A. and Newman, A. (2016) "The emergence of the private entrepreneur in reform era China: Re-birth of an earlier tradition, or a more recent product of development and change?" *Business History*, 58(3): 319–344.

Bach, D., Newman, A., and Weber, S. (2006) "The international implications of China's fledgling regulatory state: From product maker to rule maker," *New Political Economy*, 11(4): 499–518.

Backhouse, E. and Bland, J. (1914) *Annals and Memoirs of the Court of Peking*. Boston: Houghton Mifflin.

Baek, S-W. (2005) "Does China follow 'the East Asian development model'?" *Journal of Contemporary Asia*, 35(4): 485–498.

Bahl, R. (1999) *Fiscal Policy in China. Taxation and Inter-Governmental Fiscal Relations*. South San Francisco: The 1990 Institute, University of Michigan Press.

Bai, C., Lu, J., and Tao, Z. (2006) "Property rights protection and access to bank loans: Evidence from private enterprises in China," *Economics of Transition*, 14(4): 611–628.

Bai, X. (2011) "Tongren yiyuan yisheng beikan shijian diaocha" (Investigative Report on the Incident of the Slashing of Tongren Hospital Doctor).

Baldwin, D. (2020) *Economic Statecraft: New Edition*. Princeton University Press.

Barboza, D. (2010) "After suicides, scrutiny of China's grim factories," *New York Times*, June 6.

Barboza, D. (2016) "How China built 'iPhone City' with billions in perks for Apple's partner," *New York Times*, December 29.

Barwick, P., Kalouptsidi, M., and Zahur, N. (2019) "China's industrial policy: An empirical evaluation" (No. w26075). National Bureau of Economic Research.

Batra, G., Kaufmann, D., and Stone, A. (2003) *Investment Climate around the World: Voices of Firms from the World Business Environment Survey*. Washington, DC: World Bank.

BBC (2015) "Most China cities fail to meet air quality standards."

BBC (2021) "China floods: 12 dead in Zhengzhou train and thousands evacuated in Henan."

Beck, K. (2023) "Reforming the Chinese state sector: Mixed ownership reforms and state–business relations," *Journal of Contemporary China*, 32(140): 264–279.

Beck, K. and Brødsgaard, K. (2022) "Corporate governance with Chinese characteristics: Party organization in state-owned enterprises," *China Quarterly*, 250: 486–508.

Bell, S. and Feng, H. (2013) *The Rise of the People's Bank of China*. Harvard University Press.

Benazeraf, D. and Alves A. (2014) "'Oil for housing': Chinese-built new towns in Angola."

Bergsten, C. (2008) "A partnership of equals: How Washington should respond to China's economic challenge," *Foreign Affairs*, July–August: 57–69.

Bernanke, B. (2005) "The global savings glut and the U.S. current account deficit," Remarks by Governor Ben S. Bernanke at the Virginia Association of Economics, Richmond, VA, March 10.

Bernstein, T. and Lü, X. (2003) *Taxation Without Representation in Contemporary Rural China*. Cambridge University Press.

Bian, Y. (1994) *Work and Inequality in Urban China*. State University of New York Press.

Bird, R.M. and Wong, C.P. (2005) "China's fiscal system: A work in progress," Rotman School of Management Working Paper, 07–11.

Blumenthal, D. and Hsiao, W. (2005) "Privatization and its discontents: The evolving Chinese health care system," *New England Journal of Medicine*, 353(11): 1165–1170.

Bodde, D. (1991) *Chinese Thought, Society, and Science: The Intellectual and Social Background of Science and Technology in Pre-Modern China*. University of Hawaii Press.

Boltho, A. and Weber, M. (2009) "Did China follow the East Asian development model?" *European Journal of Comparative Economics*, 6(2): 267–286.

Borges, C. and Palazzi, A. (2023) "The U.S–China relationship amid China's economic woes."

Bradsher, K. (2017) "How China lost $1 trillion," *New York Times*, February 7.

Brandt, L. and Lim, K. (2020). "Accounting for Chinese exports," University of Toronto, Department of Economics.

Brandt, L. and Zhu, X. (2001) "Soft budget constraint and inflation cycles: a positive model of the macro-dynamics in China during transition," *Journal of Development Economics*, 64(2): 437–457.

Brandt, L., Hsieh, C., and Zhu X. (2008) "Growth and structural transformation in China," in Brandt, L. and Rawski, T. eds., *China's Great Economic Transformation*. Cambridge University Press, pp. 683–728.

Brandt, L., Huang, J., Li, G., and Rozelle, S. (2002) "Land rights in rural China: Facts, fictions, and issues," *China Journal*, 47: 67–97.

Branstetter L. and Lardy, N. (2008) "China's embrace of globalization," in Brandt, L. and Rawski, T.G. eds., *China's Great Economic Transformation*. Cambridge University Press, pp. 633–682.

Bräutigam, D. (2011) "Aid 'with Chinese characteristics': Chinese foreign aid and development finance meet the OECD–DAC aid regime," *Journal of International Development*, 23(5): 752–764.

Bräutigam, D. (2020) "A critical look at Chinese 'debt-trap diplomacy': The rise of a meme," *Area Development and Policy*, 5(1): 1–14.

Breslin, S. (2012) "Government–industry relations in China: A review of the art of the state," in Walter, A. and Zhang, X. eds., *East Asian Capitalism: Diversity, Continuity, and Change*. Oxford University Press, pp. 29–45.

Broadberry, S., Guan, H., and Li, D.D. (2018) "China, Europe, and the great divergence: a study in historical national accounting, 980–1850," *Journal of Economic History*, 78(4): 955–1000.

Brødsgaard, K. and Li, X. (2013) "SOE reform in China: Past, present and future," *Copenhagen Journal of Asian Studies*, 31(2): 54–78.

Brown, K. (2018) "The anti-corruption struggle in Xi Jinping's China: An alternative political narrative," *Asian Affairs*, 49(1): 1–10.

Brown, L. (1995) *Who Will Feed China? Wake-up Call for a Small Planet.* W.W. Norton & Company.

Brown, W. and Cao, X. (2023) "Trade unions in China: The dynamics of labour relations and state-ancillary unionism in transition," *Routledge Handbook of Chinese Business and Management*, pp. 169–184.

Buckley, C., Wang, V., and Bradsher, K. (2022) "Living by the code: In China, Covid-era controls may outlast the virus." *New York Times*, January 30.

Burke III, E. and Pomeranz, K. eds. (2009) *The Environment and World History.* University of California Press.

Burns, J. (2019) *The Chinese Communist Party's Nomenklatura System.* Routledge.

Cai, F. (2015) "Haste makes waste: Policy options facing China after reaching the Lewis turning point," *China & World Economy*, 23(1): 1–20.

Cai, F., Park, A., and Zhao, Y. (2008) "The Chinese labor market in the reform era," in Brandt, L. and Rawski, T.G. eds., *China's Great Economic Transformation.* Cambridge University Press, pp. 167–214.

Cai, Y. (2002) "The resistance of Chinese laid-off workers in the reform period," *China Quarterly*, 170: 327–344.

Cai, Y. (2003) "Collective ownership or cadres' ownership? The non-agricultural use of farmland in China," *China Quarterly*, 175: 662–680.

Carothers, C. and Zhang, Z. (2023) "From corruption control to everything control: The widening use of inspections in Xi's China," *Journal of Contemporary China*, 32(140): 225–242.

Carson, R. (2010) "The environmental Kuznets curve: Seeking empirical regularity and theoretical structure," *Review of Environmental Economics and Policy*, 4(1): 3–23.

CCDI (n.d.) "Zhongyang yiji dang he guojia jiguan, guoqi he jinrong danwei ganbu zhiji shencha" (Central level Party and State agencies, SOEs, and financial units cadres: investigation under discipline implementation).

Center for Strategic and International Studies (CSIS) (n.d.) "Is air quality in China a social problem?"

Central Banking Staff (2019) "Lifetime achievement: Zhou Xiaochuan."

Centre for Research on Energy and Clean Air (CREA) 2021 "China dominates 2020 coal plant development."

Chan, A. (1993) "Revolution or corporatism? Workers and trade unions in post-Mao China," *Australian Journal of Chinese Affairs*, 29: 31–61.

Chan, A. and Unger, J. (2009) "A Chinese state enterprise under the reforms: What model of capitalism?" *China Journal*, 62: 1–26.

Chan, C. and Hui, E. (2012) "The dynamics and dilemma of workplace trade union reform in China: The case of the Honda workers' strike," *Journal of Industrial Relations*, 54(5): 653–668.

Chan, H. (2009) "Politics over markets: Integrating state-owned enterprises into Chinese socialist market," *Public Administration and Development*, 29(1): 43–54.

Chan, J., Selden, M., and Pun, N. (2020) *Dying for an iPhone: Apple, Foxconn, and the Lives of China's Workers*. Haymarket Books.

Chan, K. (2010) "Fundamentals of China's urbanization and policy," *China Review*: 63–93.

Chang, H.-J. (1993) "The political economy of industrial policy in Korea," *Cambridge Journal of Economics*, 17: 131–157.

Che, L., Du, H., and Chan, K.W., (2020) "Unequal pain: A sketch of the impact of the Covid-19 pandemic on migrants' employment in China," *Eurasian Geography and Economics*, 61(4–5): 448–463.

Chen, A. (2016) "The politics of the shareholding collective economy in China's rural villages," *Journal of Peasant Studies*, 43(4): 828–849.

Chen, C. (2011) *Foreign Direct Investment in China: Location Determinants, Investor Differences and Economic Impacts*. Edward Elgar.

Chen, C. (2018) "Impact of China's outward foreign direct investment on its regional economic growth," *China & World Economy*, 26(3): 11–21.

Chen, C. (2020) "Peasant protests over land seizures in rural China," *Journal of Peasant Studies*, 47(6): 1327–1347.

Chen, C., Chang, L., and Zhang, Y. (1995) "The role of foreign direct investment in China's post-1978 economic development," *World Development*, 23(4): 691–703.

Chen, F. (2003) "Industrial restructuring and workers' resistance in China," *Modern China*, 29(2): 237–262.

Chen, G. and Lees, C. (2016) "Growing China's renewables sector: A developmental state approach," *New Political Economy*, 21(6): 574–586.

Chen, G., Firth, M., Gao, D.N., and Rui, O.M. (2005) "Is China's securities regulatory agency a toothless tiger? Evidence from enforcement actions," *Journal of Accounting and Public Policy*, 24(6): 451–488.

Chen, H. and Rithmire, M. (2020) "The rise of the investor state: State capital in the Chinese economy," *Studies in Comparative International Development*, 55(3): 257–277.

Chen, J. (2021) "Huaxi Village: The rise and fall of the "richest village in China."

Chen, J. and Han, S.M. (2021) "Does foreign aid bifurcate donor approval? Patronage politics, winner–loser status, and public attitudes toward the donor," *Studies in Comparative International Development*, 56(4): 536–559.

Chen, L. and Naughton, B. (2016) "An institutionalized policy-making mechanism: China's return to techno-industrial policy," *Research Policy*, 45(10): 2138–2152.

Chen, M. (2020) "Beyond donation: China's policy banks and the reshaping of development finance," *Studies in Comparative International Development*, 55(4): 436–459.

Chen, M. (2020) "State actors, market games: Credit guarantees and the funding of China Development Bank," *New Political Economy*, 25(3): 453–468.

Chen, N. (2018) "Water table falling in China: Research."

Chen, W. (2007) "Does the colour of the cat matter? The red hat strategy in China's private enterprises," Management and Organization Review, 3: 58.

Chen, X. (2012) *Social Protest and Contentious Authoritarianism in China*. Cambridge University Press.

Cheng, II. (2008) "Insider trading in China: The case for the Chinese Securities Regulatory Commission," *Journal of Financial Crime*, 15(2): 165–178.

Cheng, L. and Lin, A. (2023) "The local government debt that threatens China's economy," *Financial Times*, August 23.

Cheng, T. and Selden, M. (1994) "The origins and social consequences of China's hukou system," *China Quarterly*, 139: 644–668.

Chew, D.C. (1990) "Civil service pay in China, 1955 to 1989: Overview and assessment," *International Review of Administrative Sciences*, 56(2): 345–364.

Chi, Y. and Rauch, J. (2010) "The plight of green GDP in China," *Consilience: Journal of Sustainable Development*, 3(1): 102–116.

Chin, G. and Gallagher, K. (2019) "Coordinated credit spaces: The globalization of Chinese development finance," *Development and Change*, 50(1): 245–274.

China Daily (2019) "Over 84% companies in China are private," *China Daily*, November 28, 2019.

China Development Brief (n.d.) "Friends of nature."

China Power (2024) 规划总院承担的《龙盘工程防灾减灾效应研究》大纲顺利通过评审 (The "Investigation of disaster prevention and disaster reduction effects of Longpan Project" conducted by the Planning Institute has passed evaluation and review).

Chiu P. (2002) "You fangliao dao gongchang: Qingdai qianqi mianbu zihao de jingji yu falü fenxi" (From putting-out system to factory system: An economic and legal analysis of cotton textile workshop in Early Qing), *Lishi yanjiu*, 1: 75–87.

Chou, C.C. (2018). "China's bureaucracy in the open-door legislation: The Labor Contract Law in focus," *Journal of Chinese Political Science*, 23(2): 217–234.

Chu, J. (2023) "From peripheral actors to established players: Environmental NGOs' participation through public notice-and-comment procedures and environmental public interest litigation in China," *Journal of Contemporary China*: 1–19.

Chu, S.C. and Liu, K.C. (1994) *Li Hung-Chang and China's Early Modernization*. ME Sharpe.

Chuang, J. (2014) "China's rural land politics: Bureaucratic absorption and the muting of rightful resistance," *China Quarterly*, 219: 649–669.

Chuang, J. (2015) "Urbanization through dispossession: Survival and stratification in China's new townships," *Journal of Peasant Studies*, 42(2): 275–294.

Chung, J. (2000) *Central Control and Local Discretion in China: Leadership and Implementation during Post-Mao Decollectivization*. Oxford University Press.

Clarke, D.C. (2007) "Legislating for a market economy in China," *China Quarterly*, 191: 567–585.

Columbia University (n.d.) "Guide to Chinese climate policy."

Coppola, A., Maggiori, M., Neiman, B., and Schreger, J. (2021) "Redrawing the map of global capital flows: The role of cross-border financing and tax havens," *Quarterly Journal of Economics*, 136(3): 1499–1556.

Cortina, J., Peria, M., Schmukler, S., and Xiao, J. (2023) *The Internationalization of China's Equity Markets*.

Council on Foreign Relations (n.d.) "China's fight against climate change and environmental degradation."

CSIS (2020) "How does water security affect China's development?"

CSIS (n.d.) "How is China feeding its population of 1.4 billion?"

CSIS (n.d.) "Is China the world's top trader?"

Cukierman, A. (1992) *Central Bank Strategy, Credibility, and Independence: Theory and Evidence*. MIT Press.

Da Silva, J. (2024) "EU hits Chinese electric cars with new tariffs," July 4.

Daly, J. (2014) *Historians Debate the Rise of the West*. Routledge.

De Graaff, N. (2014) "Global networks and the two faces of Chinese national oil companies," *Perspectives on Global Development and Technology*, 13(5–6): 539–563.

Démurger, S. and Xu, H. (2011) "Return migrants: The rise of new entrepreneurs in rural China," *World Development*, 39(10): 1847–1861.

Démurger, S., Gurgand, M., Li, S., and Yue, X. (2009) "Migrants as second-class workers in urban China? A decomposition analysis," *Journal of Comparative Economics*, 37(4): 610–628.

Deng, G. (2002) *The Premodern Chinese Economy: Structural Equilibrium and Capitalist Sterility*. Routledge.

Deng, X. (1991) "Opening speech at the Twelfth National Congress of the Communist Party of China," in *Selected Works of Deng Xiaoping, vol. 2: 1978–1982*. Beijing: Foreign Languages Press.

Derleth, J. and Koldyk, D.R. (2004) "The Shequ experiment: Grassroots political reform in urban China," *Journal of Contemporary China*, 13(41): 747–777.

Dickson, B. (2000) "Cooptation and corporatism in China: The logic of party adaptation," *Political Science Quarterly*, 115(4): 517–540.

Dickson, B. (2003) *Red Capitalists in China: The Party, Private Entrepreneurs, and Prospects for Political Change*. Cambridge University Press.

Dickson, B.J. (2007) "Integrating wealth and power in China: The Communist Party's embrace of the private sector," *China Quarterly*, 192: 827–854.

Dickson, B. (2011) "Updating the China model," *Washington Quarterly*, 34(4): 39–58.

Dincer, N. and Eichengreen, B. (2014) "Central bank transparency and independence: Updates and new measures," *International Journal of Central Banking*, March: 189–253.

Ding, I. (2020) "Performative governance," *World Politics*, 72(4): 525–556.

Dollar, D. (2016) "China as a global investor," in Song, L., Garnaut, R., Cai, F., and Johnston, L. eds., *China's New Sources of Economic Growth, vol. 1*. Canberra: Australian National University Press, pp. 197–214.

Dossani, R., Bouey J., and Zhu, K. (2020) "Demystifying the Belt and Road initiative: A clarification of its key features, objectives, and impacts," Rand Corporation.

Dreher, A., Fuchs, A., Parks, B., Strange, A., and Tierney, M. (2018) "Apples and dragon fruits: The determinants of aid and other forms of state financing from China to Africa," *International Studies Quarterly*, 62(1): 182–194.

Dreher, A., Fuchs, A., Parks, B.C., Strange, A., and Tierney, M.J. (2022) *Banking on Beijing: The Aims and Impacts of China's Overseas Development Program*. Cambridge University Press.

Duan, X. (2017) "Intergovernmental fiscal relations and military spending in China, 1980–2013," *China: An International Journal*, 15(3): 77–99.

Dunning, J.H. (1993) "Assessing the costs and benefits of foreign direct investment: some theoretical considerations," in Artisien, P., Rojec, M., and Svetličić, M. eds., *Foreign Investment and Privatization in Eastern Europe*. London: Palgrave Macmillan, pp. 34–81.

Eaton, S. (2016) *The Advance of the State in Contemporary China: State–Market Relations in the Reform Era*. Cambridge University Press.

Eaton, S. and Hasmath, R. (2021) "Economic legitimation in a new era: Public attitudes about state ownership and market regulation," *China Quarterly*, forthcoming.

Eaton, S. and Kostka, G. (2017) "Central protectionism in China: The 'central SOE problem' in environmental governance," *China Quarterly*, special section "Central–local relations and environmental governance in China."

Economist (2012) "iPadded: The trade gap between America and China is much exaggerated."

Economist (2023) "How to sneak billions of dollars out of China."

Economist (2024) "Why so many Chinese graduates cannot find work," April 18.

Economy, E. (2004) *The River Runs Black: The Environmental Challenge to China's Future*. Cornell University Press.

Eichengreen, B. (1995) "Financing infrastructure in developing countries: Lessons from the railway age," *World Bank Research Observer*, 10(1): 75–91.

Elvin, M. (1984) "Why China failed to create an endogenous industrial capitalism," *Theory and Society* 13(3): 379–391.

Elvin, M. (2004) *The Retreat of the Elephants: An Environmental History of China*. Yale University Press.

Energy Information Administration (2023) "China."

Esping-Andersen, G. (1990) *Three Worlds of Welfare Capitalism*. Princeton University Press.

Fairbank, J. (1986) *The Great Chinese Revolution, 1800–1985*. Harper & Row.

Fairbank, J. and Goldman, M. (2006) *China: A New History*. Harvard University Press.

Fan, C. (2002) "The elite, the natives, and the outsiders: Migration and labor market segmentation in urban China," *Annals of the Association of American Geographers*, 92(1): 103–124.

Fang, X. (2012) *Barefoot Doctors and Western Medicine in China*. Rochester: University of Rochester Press.

Feng, E. (2017) "Beijing chokes in Gobi desert sandstorm," *Financial Times*, May 4.

Feng, Q., Ma, H., Jiang, X., Wang, X., and Cao, S. (2015) "What has caused desertification in China?" *Scientific Reports*, 5(1): 1–8.

Feng W., Zuo X., and Ruan D. (2002) "Rural migrants in Shanghai: Living under the shadow of socialism," *International Migration Review*, 36: 520–545.

Ferchen, M. (2013) "Whose China model is it anyway? The contentious search for consensus," *Review of International Political Economy*, 20(2): 390–420.

Fewsmith, J. (2001) "The political and social implications of China's accession to the WTO," *China Quarterly*, 167: 573–591.

Fewsmith, J. (2016) *Dilemmas of Reform in China: Political Conflict and Economic Debate*. Routledge.

Fitch. (2022) "China banks dashboard: December 2022 – foreign banks in China."

Fortune (2024) "Global 500."

Frank, A. (1998) *ReOrient: Global Economy in the Asian Age*. University of California Press.

Frazier, M. (2002) *The Making of the Chinese Industrial Workplace: State, Revolution, and Labor Management*. Cambridge University Press.

Frazier, M. (2004) "China's pension reform and its discontents," *China Journal*, 51: 97–114.

Frazier, M. (2017) "Social policy and public opinion in an age of insecurity," in Kuruvilla, S., Lee, C.K., and Gallagher, M.E. eds., *From Iron Rice Bowl to Informalization: Markets, Workers, and the State in a Changing China*. Cornell University Press, pp. 61–80.

Freese, B. (2003) *Coal: A Human History*. Penguin Books.

Friedman, E. (2022) *The Urbanization of People: The Politics of Development, Labor Markets, and Schooling in the Chinese City*. Columbia University Press.

Frost, S. and Ho, M. (2005) "'Going out': The growth of Chinese foreign direct investment in Southeast Asia and its implications for corporate social responsibility," *Corporate Social Responsibility and Environmental Management*, 12(3): 157–167.

Fu, D. (2018) *Mobilizing Without the Masses: Control and Contention in China*. Cambridge University Press.

Fukuyama. F. (2011) "US democracy has little to teach China," *Financial Times*, January 17.

Furuoka, F. (2017) "Determinants of China's and Japan's foreign aid allocations in Africa," *African Development Review*, 29(3): 376–388.

Gallagher, K. and Irwin, A. (2014) "Exporting national champions: China's outward foreign direct investment finance in comparative perspective," *China & World Economy*, 22(6): 1–21.

Gallagher, K. and Qi, Q. (2018) "Policies governing China's overseas development finance: Implications for climate change." Boston, MA.

Gallagher, M. (2002) "'Reform and openness': Why China's economic reforms have delayed democracy," *World Politics*, 54(3): 338–372.

Gallagher, M. (2007) *Contagious Capitalism: Globalization and the Politics of Labor in China*. Princeton University Press.

Gallagher, M. (2011) *Contagious capitalism: Globalization and the Politics of labor in China*. Princeton University Press.

Gallagher, M. (2014) "China's workers movement and the end of the rapid-growth era," *Daedalus*, 143(2): 81–95.

Gallagher, M. and Dong, B. (2017) "Legislating harmony: Labor law reform in contemporary China," in Kuruvilla, S., Lee, C.K., and Gallagher, M.E. eds., *From Iron Rice Bowl to Informalization: Markets, Workers, and the State in a Changing China*. Cornell University Press, pp. 36–60.

Gao, Q. (2010) "Redistributive nature of the Chinese social benefit system: Progressive or regressive?" *China Quarterly*, 201: 1–19.

Gao, Q. (2013) "Public assistance and poverty reduction: The case of Shanghai," *Global Social Policy*, 13(2): 193–215.

Gao, Q. (2017) *Welfare, Work, and Poverty: Social Assistance in China*. Oxford University Press.

Gao, Q., Yang, S., and Li, S. (2012) "Labor contracts and social insurance participation among migrant workers in China," *China Economic Review*, 23(4): 1195–1205.

Gao, Q., Zhang, Y., and Zhai, F. (2019) "Social assistance in China: Impact evaluation and policy implications," *China: An International Journal*, 17(1): 3–9.

Garrett, G. (1998) *Partisan Politics in the Global Economy*. Cambridge University Press.

Ge Y., Song L., Clancy R., and Qin Y. (2019) "Studies on left-behind children in China: Reviewing paradigm shifts," *Child and Adolescent Development in China: New Directions for Child and Adolescent Development*, 163: 115–135.

Geiger, M. (2008) "Instruments of monetary policy in China and their effectiveness: 1994–2006," United Nations Conference on Trade and Development.

Giles, J., Park, A., and Cai, F. (2006) "How has economic restructuring affected China's urban workers?" *China Quarterly*, 185: 61–95.

Gilpin, R. (1975) *US Power and the Multinational Corporation*. Basic Books.

Girardin, E., Lunven, S., and Ma, G. (2017) "China's evolving monetary policy rule: from inflation-accommodating to anti-inflation policy," Bank for International Settlements, BIS Working Papers, No. 641.

Glanz, J., Hvistendahl, M., and Chang, A. (2023) "How deadly was China's covid wave?" *New York Times*, February 15.

Global Energy Monitor (2024) "Boom and bust coal 2024."

Golan, J., Sicular, T., and Umapathi, N. (2014) "Any guarantees? China's rural minimum living standard guarantee program." Washington, DC: World Bank, Social Protection and Labor, Discussion Paper 1423.

Gold, T. (1984) "Just in time: China battles spiritual pollution on the eve of 1984," *Asian Survey*, 24(9): 947–974.

Goron, C. (2018) "Fighting against climate change and for fair trade: Finding the EU's interest in the solar panels dispute with China," *China–EU Law Journal*, 6(1): 103–125.

Greenstone, M. and Hasenkopf, C. (2023) *AIR QUALITY LIFE INDEX® | 2023 Annual Update*. University of Chicago.

Gu, J. (2009) "China's private enterprises in Africa and the implications for African development," *European Journal of Development Research*, 21(4): 570–587.

Guardian (2013) "China finds 100,000 kg of poisoned dead fish in river."

Guo, F., Huang, Y., Wang, J., and Wang, X. (2022) "The informal economy at times of COVID-19 pandemic," *China Economic Review*, 71: 101722.

Guo, Y., He, A. and Wang, F. (2022) "Local policy discretion in social welfare: explaining subnational variations in China's de facto urban poverty line," *China Quarterly*, 249: 114–138.

Haggard, S. (1990) *Pathways from the Periphery: The Politics of Growth in the Newly Industrializing Countries*. Cornell University Press.

Haggard, S. and Huang, Y. (2008) "The political economy of private-sector development in China," in Brandt, L. and Rawski, T.G., eds., *China's Great Economic Transformation*. Cambridge University Press. pp. 337–374.

Hale, T. and Leahy, J. (2024) "China has finally unveiled its property rescue plan. Will it be enough?"

Halper, S. (2010) *The Beijing Consensus: How China's Authoritarian Model Will Dominate the Twenty-First Century* (vol. 16). Basic Books.

Hamilton, G. (2006) *Commerce and Capitalism in Chinese Societies*. London: Routledge.

Hanemann, T. and Rosen, D.H. (2011) "Chinese FDI in the United States is taking off: How to maximize its benefits?" *Columbia FDI Perspectives*, no. 49.

Hao, Y. and Johnston, M. (1995). "Reform at the crossroads: An analysis of Chinese corruption," *Asian Perspective*, 19(1): 117–149.

Harlan, T. (2021) "Green development or greenwashing? A political ecology perspective on China's green Belt and Road," *Eurasian Geography and Economics*, 62(2): 202–226.

He, C. and Ye, J. (2014) "Lonely sunsets: impacts of rural–urban migration on the left-behind elderly in rural China," *Population, Space and Place*, 20(4): 352–369.

He, D. and Zhang, W. (2010) "How dependent is the Chinese economy on exports and in what sense has its growth been export-led?" *Journal of Asian Economics*, 21(1): 87–104.

He, X. (2021) "Pressures on Chinese judges under Xi," *China Journal*, 85(1): 49–74.

Health Effects Institute (2021) *State of Global Air 2020*.

Heffernan, M. (2013) "What happened after the Foxconn suicides," August 7, 2013, MoneyWatch, CBS News.

Heilmann, S. (2008) "Policy experimentation in China's economic rise," *Studies in Comparative International Development*, 43(1): 1–26.

Heilmann, S. and Melton, O. (2013) "The reinvention of development planning in China," *Modern China*, 39(6): 580–628.

Helleiner, E. (2019) "Multilateral development finance in non-Western thought: from before Bretton Woods to beyond," *Development and Change* 50(1): 144–163.

Higginbottom, A. (2013) "The political economy of foreign investment in Latin America: Dependency revisited," *Latin American Perspectives*, 40(3): 184–206.

Higgins, M. (2020) "China's growth outlook: Is high-income status in reach?" *Economic Policy Review*, 26(4): 69–98.

Hillenbrand, M. (2023) *On the Edge: Feeling Precarious in China*. Columbia University Press.

Hilton, I. (2024) "How China became the world's leader on renewable energy."

Honig, E. and Zhao, X. (2019) *Across the Great Divide: The Sent-Down Youth Movement in Mao's China, 1968–1980*. Cambridge University Press.

Hou, Y. (2019) *The Private Sector in Public Office: Selective Property Rights in China*. Cambridge University Press.

Howell, A., Lin, J., and Worack, S. (2020) "Going out to innovate more at home: Impacts of outward direct investments on Chinese firms' domestic innovation performance," *China Economic Review*, 60: 101404.

Howie, F. and Walter, C. (2006). *Privatizing China: Inside China's Stock Markets*. Wiley.

Hsing, Y. (2010) *The Great Urban Transformation: Politics of Land and Property in China*. Oxford University Press.

Hsueh, R. (2011) *China's Regulatory State: A New Strategy for Globalization*. Cornell University Press.

Hu, A. (2012) "The global spread of neoliberalism and China's pension reform since 1978," *Journal of World History*, 23(3): 609–638.

Hu, A. and Jefferson, G. (2008) "Science and Technology in China," in Brandt, L. and Rawski, T.G. eds., *China's Great Economic Transformation*. Cambridge University Press, pp. 286–336.

Hu, G. X., Pan, J., and Wang, J. (2018) *Chinese Capital Market: An Empirical Overview*. Cambridge: National Bureau of Economic Research, Working Paper 24346.

Huang, P. C. (2002) "Development or involution in eighteenth-century Britain and China? A review of Kenneth Pomeranz's *The Great Divergence: China, Europe, and the Making of the Modern World Economy*," *Journal of Asian Studies*, 61(2): 501–538.

Huang, T. (2023) "Why China's housing policies have failed," Washington DC: Peterson Institute for International Economics, *Working Papers*, 23(5).

Huang, T. and Lardy, N. (2023) "Can China revive growth through private consumption?" Peterson Institute for International Economics.

Huang, T. and Lovely, M. (2023) "Half a year into China's reopening after COVID, private economic activity remains weak," Peterson Institute for International Economics.

Huang, T. and Veron, N. (2024) "China's state vs. private company tracker: Which sector dominates?"

Huang, Y. (1996) "Central–local relations in China during the reform era: The economic and institutional dimensions," *World Development*, 24(4): 655–672.

Huang, Y. (2003) *Selling China: Foreign Direct Investment During the Reform Era*. Cambridge University Press.

Huang, Y. (2008) *Capitalism with Chinese Characteristics: Entrepreneurship and the State.* Cambridge University Press.

Huang, Y. (2010) "Debating China's economic growth: The Beijing consensus or the Washington consensus," *Academy of Management Perspectives*, 24(2): 31–47.

Huang, Y. and Tao, K, (2010) "Causes and remedies of China's external imbalances," China Center for Economic Research Working Paper Series, Peking University, No. E2010002, 25 February.

Huang, Y. and Wang, B (2011) "Chinese outward direct investment: Is there a China model?" *China & World Economy* 19(4): 1–21.

Hughes, L. and Meckling, J. (2017) "The politics of renewable energy trade: The US–China solar dispute," *Energy Policy*, 105: 256–262.

Hung, H. (2008) "Agricultural revolution and elite reproduction in Qing China: The transition to capitalism debate revisited," *American Sociological Review*, 73(4): 569–588.

Huntington, S. (1993) *The Third Wave: Democratization in the Late Twentieth Century.* University of Oklahoma Press.

Huo, X. and Lin, M. (2019) "Understanding welfare stigma in China: An empirical study of the implementation of urban dibao," *China: An International Journal*, 17(1): 29–47.

Hurst, W. (2004) "Understanding contentious collective action by Chinese laid-off workers: the importance of regional political economy," *Studies in Comparative International Development*, 39(2): 94–120.

Hurst, W. (2009) *The Chinese Worker after Socialism.* Cambridge University Press.

IMF (2015) "Rethinking financial deepening: Stability and growth in emerging markets."

IMF (n.d.) "Financial Development Index Data Base."

International Energy Agency (IEA) (2022) *Solar PV Global Supply Chains: An IEA Special Report.*

International Energy Agency (2021) "Global energy review: CO2 emissions in 2021."

International Energy Agency (2023) "The changing landscapes of global emissions."

International Rivers (n.d.) "Nu River campaign."

IQAir (n.d.) "Air quality in Beijing."

Jefferson, G. and Rawski, T. (1994) "Enterprise reform in Chinese industry," *Journal of Economic Perspectives*, 8(2): 47–70.

Jefferson, G.H. and Rawski, T. (1999) "Ownership change in Chinese industry," in *Enterprise Reform in China: Ownership, Transition, and Performance*, ed. G.H. Jefferson and I. Singh. Oxford University Press, pp. 23–42.

Ji, Q. and Zhang, D. (2019) "How much does financial development contribute to renewable energy growth and upgrading of energy structure in China?" *Energy Policy*, 128: 114–124.

Jiang, J., Qian, J., and Wen, Z. (2018) "Social protection for the informal sector in urban China: Institutional constraints and self-selection behaviour," *Journal of Social Policy*, 47(2): 335–357.

Jiang, X. (2015) "China's participation in major international environmental agreements," in *Research Handbook on Chinese Environmental Law*, ch. 18, pp. 395–426. Edward Elgar Publishing.

Jiang, Y. (2014) "Red trojan horses? A new look at Chinese SOEs' outward investment," *Journal of China and International Relations*, 2(1): 1–25.

Jin, H., Qian, Y., and Weingast, B. (2005) "Regional decentralization and fiscal incentives: Federalism, Chinese style," *Journal of Public Economics*, 89(9–10): 1719–1742.

Jing, J. (2003) "Environmental protests in rural China," in Perry, E. and Selden, M. eds., *Chinese Society: Change, Conflict and Resistance*, pp. 205–222. London: Routledge.

Johnson, G. (1992) *The Political Economy of Chinese Urbanization: Guangdong and the Pearl River Delta Region* (vol. 185). Westport: Greenwood Press.

Jones, L. and Hameiri, S. (2020) "Debunking the myth of 'debt-trap diplomacy'," Chatham House, p. 19.

Jones, L. and Zou, Y. (2017) "Rethinking the role of state-owned enterprises in China's rise," *New Political Economy*, 22(6): 743–760.

Kaiman, J. (2013) "Inside China's 'cancer villages'," *Guardian*.

Kan, K., (2019) "A weapon of the weak? Shareholding, property rights and villager empowerment in China," *China Quarterly*, 237: 131–152.

Kanamori, T. and Z. Zhao (2004) *Private Sector Development in the People's Republic of China*. Manila: Asian Development Bank Institute.

Kasa, K. (1998) "Could Russia have learned from China?" Research Department, Federal Reserve Bank of San Francisco.

Kaske, E. (2011) "Fund-raising wars: Office selling and interprovincial finance in nineteenth-century China," *Harvard Journal of Asiatic Studies*: 69–141.

Keister, L.A. (2000) *Chinese Business Groups: The Structure and Impact of Interfirm Relations during Economic Development*. Oxford University Press.

Kelliher, D. (1992) *Peasant Power in China: The Era of Rural Reform, 1979–1989*. Yale University Press.

Kenderdine, T. and Ling, H. (2018) "International capacity cooperation – financing China's export of industrial overcapacity," *Global Policy*, 9(1): 41–52.

Kennedy, S. (2008) *The Business of Lobbying in China*. Harvard University Press.

Kennedy, S. (2010) "The myth of the Beijing Consensus," *Journal of Contemporary China* 19(65): 461–477.

Kentor, J. and Boswell, T. (2003) "Foreign capital dependence and development: A new direction," *American Sociological Review*, 68(2): 301–313.

Khor, H. and Fetherston, M. (1991) "China: Macroeconomic cycles in the 1980s," International Monetary Fund.

Knight, J. and Song L. (1999) "Employment constraints and sub-optimality in Chinese enterprises," *Oxford Economic Papers*, 51(2): 284–299.

Knight, J. (2014) "China as a developmental state," *The World Economy*, 37(10): 1335–1347.

Ko, K. and Weng, C. (2012) "Structural changes in Chinese corruption," *China Quarterly*, 211: 718–740.

Kolstad, I. and Wiig, A. (2012) "What determines Chinese outward FDI?" *Journal of World Business*, 47(1): 26–34.

Kopra, S. (2019) *China and Great Power Responsibility for Climate Change*. Taylor & Francis.

Kostka, G. and Nahm, J. (2017) J. "Central–local relations: Recentralization and environmental governance in China," *China Quarterly*, 231: 567–582.

Kroeber, A. (2015) "Making sense of China's stock market mess," Brookings Institution.

Kurlantzick, J. (2013) "Why the 'China model' isn't going away," *Atlantic*, March 21.

Kuruvilla, S., Lee, C.K., and Gallagher, M.E. eds. (2017) *From Iron Rice Bowl to Informalization: Markets, Workers, and the State in a Changing China*. Cornell University Press.

Kwan, C.H. (2022) "China's shift from indirect to direct financing – Improving the quality of listed companies as the key to success," Research Institute of Economy, Trade and Industry.

Lancet (2014) "Violence against doctors: Why China? Why now? What next?"

Landes, D.S. (2006) "Why Europe and the West? Why not China?" *Journal of Economic Perspectives*, 20(2): 3–22.

Lardy, N. (1995) "The role of foreign trade and investment in China's economic transformation," *China Quarterly*, 144: 1065–1082.

Lardy, N. (1998) *China's Unfinished Economic Revolution*. Washington DC: Brookings Institution Press.

Lardy, N. (2014) *Markets over Mao: The Rise of Private Business in China*. Columbia University Press.

Lardy, N. (2019) *The State Strikes Back: The End of Economic Reform in China?* Washington DC: Peterson Institute for International Economics.

Lau, L., Qian, Y., and Roland, G. (2000) "Reform without losers: An interpretation of China's dual-track approach to transition," *Journal of Political Economy*, 108(1): 120–143.

Lee, C. (2016) "Precarization or empowerment? Reflections on recent labor unrest in China," *Journal of Asian Studies*, 75(2): 317–333.

Leonard, J. (1984) *Wei Yuan and China's Rediscovery of the Maritime World*. Harvard University Asia Center.

Leung, J.C. (2006) "The emergence of social assistance in China," *International Journal of Social Welfare*, 15(3): 188–198.

Leutert, W. (2018) "The political mobility of China's central state-owned enterprise leaders," *China Quarterly*, 233: 1–21.

Leutert, W. and Eaton, S. (2021) "Deepening not departure: Xi Jinping's governance of China's state-owned economy," *China Quarterly*, 248(1): 200–221.

Leutert, W. and Vortherms, S.A. (2021) "Personnel power: Governing state-owned enterprises," *Business and Politics*, 23(3): 419–437.

Li, C. (2016) "Holding 'China Inc.' together: The CCP and the rise of China's Yangqi," *China Quarterly*, 228: 927–949.

Li, R. and Cheong, K. (2019) *China's State Enterprises: Changing Role in a Rapidly Transforming Economy.* Singapore: Palgrave Macmillan.

Li, C., Sanchez, G., Wu, Z., Cheng, J., Zhang, S., Wang, Q., Li, F., Sun, G., and Meentemeyer, R.K. (2020) "Spatiotemporal patterns and drivers of soil contamination with heavy metals during an intensive urbanization period (1989–2018) in southern China," *Environmental Pollution*, 260: 114075.

Li, C., Zheng, H., and Liu, Y. (2022) "The hybrid regulatory regime in turbulent times: The role of the state in China's stock market crisis in 2015–2016," *Regulation & Governance*, 16(2): 392–408.

Li, G. and Zhou, H. (2015) "Political connections and access to IPO markets in China," *China Economic Review*, 33: 76–93.

Li, H. and Zhou, L. (2005) "Political turnover and economic performance: The incentive role of personnel control in China," *Journal of Public Economics*, 89(9–10): 1743–1762.

Li, J. and Zhan, J.V. (2023). "Environmental clientelism: How Chinese private enterprises lobby under environmental crackdowns," *China Quarterly*, 255: 679–696.

Li, L. (2016) "The rise of the discipline and inspection commission, 1927–2012: Anticorruption investigation and decision-making in the Chinese Communist Party," *Modern China*, 42(5): 447–482.

Li, L. (2019) "Politics of anticorruption in China: Paradigm change of the Party's disciplinary regime 2012–2017," *Journal of Contemporary China*, 28(115): 47–63.

Li, L. and Fu, H. (2017) "China's health care system reform: progress and prospects," *International Journal of Health Planning and Management*, 32(3): 240–253.

Li, M. and Walker, R. (2021) "Need, justice and central–local relations: The case of social assistance in China," *Public Administration*, 99(1): 87–102.

Li, Q., Zhang, L., and Jian, W. (2023) "The impact of integrated urban and rural resident basic medical insurance on health service equity: Evidence from China," *Frontiers in Public Health*, 11: 1106166.

Li, S. (2023) "Sunflower seed seller extraordinaire," *Beijing Review*, December 14.

Li, T., Liu, Y., Lin, S., Liu, Y., and Xie, Y. (2019) "Soil pollution management in China: A brief introduction," *Sustainability*, 11(3): 556.

Li, X. and Song, Z. (2024) "A critical examination of environmental public interest litigation in China – reflection on China's environmental authoritarianism," *Humanities and Social Sciences Communications*, 11(1): 1–12.

Li, Y. and Shapiro, J. (2020) *China Goes Green: Coercive Environmentalism for a Troubled Planet.* Polity.

Liang, Z., Li, Z., and Ma, Z. (2014) "Changing patterns of the floating population in China, 2000–2010," *Population and Development Review*, 40(4): 695–716.

Liao, H., Chi, Y., and Zhang, J. (2020) "Impact of international development aid on FDI along the Belt and Road," *China Economic Review*, 61: 101448.

Lichtenberg, E. and Ding, C. (2009) "Local officials as land developers: Urban spatial expansion in China," *Journal of Urban Economics*, 66(1): 57–64.

Lieberman, V. (2009) *Strange Parallels: Southeast Asia in Global Context, c. 800–1830, Volume 2: Mainland Mirrors: Europe, Japan, China, South Asia, and the Islands.* Cambridge University Press.

Lieberthal K. and Oksenberg, M. (1988) *Policy Making in China: Leaders, Structures, and Processes.* Princeton University Press.

Lin, C., Ye, L., and Zhang, W. (2023) "Transforming informal work and livelihoods in China" in Gary S. Fields et al. eds., *The Job Ladder: Transforming Informal Work and Livelihoods in Developing Countries.* Oxford, 2023, online edn, Oxford Academic, April 20, 2023.

Lin, J. (1990) "Collectivization and China's agricultural crisis in 1959–1961," *Journal of Political Economy*, 98(6): 1228–1252.

Lin, J. (1995) "The Needham puzzle: Why the industrial revolution did not originate in China," *Economic Development and Cultural Change*, 43(2): 269–292.

Lin, J. (2011) *Demystifying the Chinese Economy.* Cambridge University Press.

Lin, K.C. (2017) "Enterprise reform and wage movements in Chinese oil fields and refineries," in Kuruvilla, S., Lee, C.K., and Gallagher, M.E. eds., *From Iron Rice Bowl to Informalization: Markets, Workers, and the State in a Changing China*, Cornell University Press, pp. 83–106.

Lin, L. (2017) "Reforming China's state-owned enterprises: From structure to people," *China Quarterly*, 229: 107–129.

Lin, L. and Milhaupt, C. (2013) "We are the (national) champions: understanding the mechanisms of state capitalism in China," *Stanford Law Review*, 65(4): 734–760.

Lin, L. and Milhaupt, C. (2020) "Party building or noisy signaling? The contours of political conformity in Chinese corporate governance," *European Corporate Governance Institute*, Law Working Paper No. 493.

Lin, Q., Tan, S., Zhang, L., Wang, S., Wei, C., and Li, Y. (2018). "Conflicts of land expropriation in China during 2006–2016: An overview and its spatio-temporal characteristics." *Land Use Policy*, 76, pp. 246–251.

Lingat, J.R. (2024). "MSCI axes dozens more Chinese stocks from global indices." *Financial Times*, August 22.

Lipset, S. (1960) *Political Man: The Social Bases of Politics.* Garden City, NY: Double Day and Company.

Liu, A., Oi, J., and Zhang, Y. (2022) "China's local government debt: The grand bargain," *China Journal*, 87(1): 40–71.

Liu, M., Margaritis, D., and Zhang, Y. (2019) "The global financial crisis and the export-led economic growth in China," *The Chinese Economy*, 52(3): 232–248.

Liu, R., Li, T., and Greene, R. (2020) "Migration and inequality in rental housing: Affordability stress in the Chinese cities," *Applied Geography*, 115: 102138.

Liu, T. and Sun, L. (2016) "Pension reform in China," *Journal of Aging and Social Policy*, 28(1): 15–28.

Liu, Y. (2002) "Reforming China's urban health insurance system," *Health Policy*, 60(2): 133–150.

Liu, Y. and Zhou, Y. (2021) "Reflections on China's food security and land use policy under rapid urbanization," *Land Use Policy*, 109: 105699.

Liu, Z. (2023) *Sovereign Funds: How the Communist Party of China Finances its Global Ambitions*. Harvard University Press.

Liu, Z., Wang, J., Wang, X., and Wang, Y. (2020) "Understanding the impacts of 'Grain for Green' land management practice on land greening dynamics over the Loess Plateau of China," *Land Use Policy*, 99: 105084.

Long, C. and Yang, J., (2016) "What explains Chinese private entrepreneurs' charitable behaviors? – A story of dynamic reciprocal relationship between firms and the government," *China Economic Review*, 40: 1–16.

Looney, K. (2015) "China's campaign to build a new socialist countryside: Village modernization, peasant councils, and the Ganzhou model of rural development," *China Quarterly*, 224: 909–932.

Losos, E. A., Pfaff, L., Olander, S., Mason, and S. Morgan (2019) "Reducing environmental risks from Belt and Road Initiative investments in transportation infrastructure," Policy Research Working Paper, No. 8718. World Bank, Washington, DC.

Lu, Y. and Sun, T. (2013) "Local government financing platforms in China: A fortune or misfortune," IMF Working Paper WP/13/243.

Lubman, S. (1999) *Bird in a Cage: Legal Reform in China after Mao*. Stanford University Press.

Ma, D. (2008) "Economic growth in the Lower Yangzi region of China in 1911–1937: a quantitative and historical analysis," *Journal of Economic History*, 68(2): 355–392.

Ma, G., Peng, F., Yang, W., Yan, G., Gao, S., Zhou, X., Qi, J. et al. (2020) "The valuation of China's environmental degradation from 2004 to 2017," *Environmental Science and Ecotechnology*, 1: 100016.

Ma, J., Lu, M., and Quan, H. (2008) "From a national, centrally planned health system to a system based on the market: lessons from China," *Health Affairs*, 27(4): 937–948.

Ma, L. and Christensen, T. (2020) "Mapping the evolution of the central government apparatus in China," *International Review of Administrative Sciences*, 86(1): 80–97.

Ma, L. and Fan, M. (1994) "Urbanisation from below: The growth of towns in Jiangsu, China," *Urban Studies*, 31: 1625–1645.

Ma, T., Sun, S., Fu, G. et al. (2020) "Pollution exacerbates China's water scarcity and its regional inequality," *Nature Communications*, 11(1): 1–9.

Ma, Z. (2002) "Social–capital mobilization and income returns to entrepreneurship: The case of return migration in rural China," *Environment and Planning A*, 34(10): 1763–1784.

Maddison, A. (2007) *Chinese Economic Performance in the Long Run*, 2nd edn. Paris: Organization of Economic Cooperation and Development.

Mahutga, M.C. (2006) "The persistence of structural inequality? A network analysis of international trade, 1965–2000," *Social Forces*, 84(4): 1863–1889.

Mark, J. (2024) "China's local government debts are coming due."

Marquis, C. and Qiao, K. (2022) *Mao and Markets: The Communist Roots of Chinese Enterprise*. Yale University Press.

Martins, J., Gul, A., Mata, M., Haider, S., and Ahmad, S. (2023) "Do economic freedom, innovation, and technology enhance Chinese FDI? A cross-country panel data analysis," *Heliyon*, 9(6).

Maskin, E., Qian, Y., and Xu, C. (2000) "Incentives, information, and organizational form," *Review of Economic Studies*, 67(2): 359–378.

Mason, M. (1992) *American Multinationals and Japan: The Political Economy of Japanese Capital Controls, 1899–1980*. Harvard University Asia Center.

Mathews, J. (2006) "Dragon multinationals: New players in 21st century globalization," *Asia Pacific Journal of Management*, 23(1): 5–27.

McGregor, R. (2010) *The Party: The Secret World of China's Communist Rulers*. Penguin UK.

McMorrow R. and Yu, S. (2021) "The vanishing billionaire: How Jack Ma fell foul of Xi Jinping," *Financial Times*, April 15.

McNally, C. (2002) "Strange bedfellows: Communist party institutions and new governance mechanisms in Chinese state holding corporations," *Business and Politics*, 4(1): 91–115.

McNally, C. (2012) "Sino-capitalism: China's reemergence and the international political economy," *World Politics*, 64(4): 741–776.

McWilliams, B., Tagliapietra, S., and Trasi, C. (2024) "Smarter European Union industrial policy for solar panels."

Mebratu, S., Wu, R., Yang, L. (2015) "Technology spillovers from Chinese outward direct investment: The case of Ethiopia," *China Economic Review*, 33: 35–49.

Meisner, M. (1999) *Mao's China and After: A History of the People's Republic*. Simon and Schuster.

Meng, Q., Fang, H., Liu, X., Yuan, B., and Xu, J. (2015) "Consolidating the social health insurance schemes in China: Towards an equitable and efficient health system," *Lancet*, 386 (10002): 1484–1492.

Meng, Q., Mills, A., Wang, L., and Han, Q. (2019) "What can we learn from China's health system reform?" *British Medical Journal*, 365.

Meng, X. (2012) "Labor market outcomes and reforms in China," *Journal of Economic Perspectives*, 26(4): 75–102.

Meng, X. and Zhang, J. (2001) "The two-tier labor market in urban China: Occupational segregation and wage differentials between urban residents and rural migrants in Shanghai," *Journal of Comparative Economics*, 29(3): 485–504.

Mertha, A. (2005) "China's 'soft' centralization: Shifting tiao/kuai authority relations," *China Quarterly*, 184: 791–810.

Meunier, S. (2014) "'Beggars can't be choosers': The European crisis and Chinese direct investment in the European Union," *Journal of European Integration*, 36(3): 283–302.

Miao, M. (forthcoming) "Coded social control: China's normalization of biometric surveillance in the post-Covid-19 era (July 13, 2023)", *Washington Journal of Law, Technology & Arts.*

Minard, P. (2015) "Government discretion: How high a barrier to entry for Chinese private enterprises?" *Journal of Asian Public Policy,* 8(2): 134–148.

Ministry of Commerce (2023) "Statistical Bulletin of FDI in China, 2023."

Ministry of Finance (2024) "Minying qiye tiaoqi private enterprises shoulder the "large beams" of foreign trade development," January 25.

Ministry of Water Resources (n.d.) *Water Resources in China.*

Minzner, C. (2018) *End of an Era: How China's Authoritarian Revival is Undermining Its Rise.* Oxford University Press.

Mohan, G. and Tan-Mullins, M. (2019) "The geopolitics of South–South infrastructure development: Chinese-financed energy projects in the global South," *Urban Studies,* 56(7): 1368–1385.

Molnar, M., Yan, T., and Li, Y. (2021) "China's outward direct investment and its impact on the domestic economy," OECD Economics Department Working papers, no. 1685.

Moore, B. (1993) *Social Origins of Dictatorship and Democracy: Lord and Peasant in the Making of the Modern World.* Boston: Beacon Press.

Morgan, P. (2019) "Can China's economic statecraft win soft power in Africa? Unpacking trade, investment, and aid," *Journal of Chinese Political Science,* 24: 387–409.

Morris, C. (2022) "Spatial governance in Beijing: Informality, illegality, and the displacement of the 'low-end population'," *China Quarterly,* 251: 822–842.

Moulder, F. (1976) *Japan, China, and the Modern World Economy: Toward a Reinterpretation of East Asian Development ca. 1600 to ca. 1918.* Cambridge University Press Archive.

Mulvenon, J. (2001) *Soldiers of Fortune: The Rise and Fall of the Chinese Military–Business Complex, 1978–1998.* ME Sharpe.

Nahm, J. (2017) "Exploiting the implementation gap: Policy divergence and industrial upgrading in China's wind and solar sectors," *China Quarterly,* special section "Central–local relations and environmental governance in China."

Nathan, A. (2003) "Authoritarian resilience," *Journal of Democracy,* 14(1).

Nathan, A. (2019) "The New Tiananmen Papers," *Foreign Affairs,* 98(4): 80–91.

National Public Radio (2022) "Solar projects are on hold as U.S. investigates whether China is skirting trade rules."

National Public Radio (2022) "Why China's 'zero COVID' policy is finally faltering," November 30.

Nature Conservancy (2016) *China's Urban Water Blueprint.*

Naughton, B. (1988) "The Third Front: Defence industrialization in the Chinese interior," *China Quarterly,* 115: 351–386.

Naughton, B. (1995) *Growing Out of the Plan: Chinese Economic Reform, 1978–1993.* Cambridge University Press.

Naughton, B. (2002) "China's economic think tanks: Their changing role in the 1990s," *China Quarterly,* 171: 625–635.

Naughton, B. (2006) *The Chinese Economy: Transitions and Growth*. MIT Press.

Naughton, B. (2009) "Understanding the Chinese stimulus package," *China Leadership Monitor*, 28(2): 1–12.

Naughton, B. (2010) "The impact of the Tiananmen crisis on China's economic transition," in *The Impact of China's 1989 Tiananmen Massacre*, pp. 166–190. Routledge.

Naughton, B. (2016a) "Supply-side structural reform: Policy-makers look for a way out," *China Leadership Monitor*, 49(1).

Naughton, B. (2016b) "Two trains running: Supply-side reform, SOE reform and the authoritative personage," *China Leadership Monitor*, 50(19): 1–10.

Naughton, B. (2018) *The Chinese Economy: Adaptation and Growth*, 2nd edn. MIT Press.

Naughton, B. and Tsai, K.S. eds. (2015) *State Capitalism, Institutional Adaptation, and the Chinese Miracle*. Cambridge University Press.

Nedopil, C. (2022) "Green finance for soft power: An analysis of China's green policy signals and investments in the Belt and Road Initiative," *Environmental Policy and Governance*, 32(2): 85–97.

Nee, V. and Opper, S. (2012) *Capitalism from Below: Markets and Institutional Change in China*. Harvard University Press.

Needham, J. (1981) *Science in Traditional China: A Comparative Perspective*. Hong Kong: Chinese University Press.

Ng, K. and He, X. (2017) *Embedded Courts: Judicial Decision-Making in China*. Cambridge University Press.

Ngai, P. (2005) *Made in China: Women Factory Workers in a Global Marketplace*. Duke University Press.

Ngai, P. and Chan, J. (2012) "Global capital, the state, and Chinese workers: The Foxconn experience," *Modern China*, 38(4): 383–410.

Ngok, K. and Huang, G. (2014) "Policy paradigm shift and the changing role of the state: The development of social policy in China since 2003," *Social Policy and Society*, 13(2): 251–261.

Ngok, K. and Zhu, G. (2007) "Marketization, globalization and administrative reform in China: A zigzag road to a promising future," *International Review of Administrative Sciences*, 73(2): 217–233.

Nicita A. and Razo, C. (2021) "China: The rise of a trade titan," UNCTAD.

Nie, L. and Wu, J., (2022) "Strategic responses of NGOs to the new party-building campaign in China," *China Information*, 36(1): 46–67.

Nolan, P. and Wang, X. (1999) "Beyond privatization: Institutional innovation and growth in China's large state-owned enterprises," *World Development*, 27(1): 169–200.

Norris, W. (2016) *Chinese Economic Statecraft: Commercial Actors, Grand Strategy, and State Control*. Cornell University Press.

North, D. (1990) *Institutions, Institutional Change and Economic Performance*. Cambridge University Press.

North, D. and Thomas, R. (1973) *The Rise of the Western World: A New Economic History*. Cambridge University Press.

Nugent, J. and Lu, J. (2021) "China's outward foreign direct investment in the Belt and Road Initiative: What are the motives for Chinese firms to invest?" *China Economic Review*, 68: 101628.

O'Brien, K. (2008) *Reform without Liberalization: China's National People's Congress and the Politics of Institutional Change*. Cambridge University Press.

O'Brien, K. and Han, R. (2009) "Path to democracy? Assessing village elections in China," *Journal of Contemporary China*, 18(60): 359–378.

O'Brien, K. and Li, L. (2004) "Suing the local state: Administrative litigation in rural China," *China Journal*, 51: 75–96.

O'Brien, K. and Li, L. (2006) *Rightful Resistance in Rural China*. Cambridge University Press.

OECD (n.d.) "Agriculture Support."

OECD (2024) "Other official flows (OOF)."

Oi, J. (1999) *Rural China Takes Off: Institutional Foundations of Economic Reform*. University of California Press.

Pampel, F. and Williamson, J. (1989) *Age, Class, Politics and the Welfare State*. Cambridge University Press.

Pan, F., Zhang, F., and Wu, F. (2021) "State-led financialization in China: The case of the government-guided investment fund," *China Quarterly*, 247: 749–772.

Pan, W. (2009) "Dangdi zhonghua tizhi (Contemporary Chinese System)," in *Zhongguo Moshi: Jiedu Renmin Gongheguo 60 nian (The China Model: Interpreting 60 Years of the People's Republic)*. Beijing: Zhongyang bianyi chubanshe, pp. 1, 3–88.

Park, A., Rozelle, S., Wong, C., and Ren, C. (1996) "Distributional consequences of reforming local public finance in China," *China Quarterly*, 147: 751–778.

Parris, K. (1993) "Local initiative and national reform: The Wenzhou model of development," *China Quarterly*: 242–263.

Pastor, R. and Tan, Q. (2000) "The meaning of China's village elections," *China Quarterly*, 162: 490–512.

Pearson, M. (1992) *Joint Ventures in the People's Republic of China*. Princeton University Press.

Pearson, M. (1994) "The Janus face of business associations in China: Socialist corporatism in foreign enterprises," *Australian Journal of Chinese Affairs*, 31: 25–46.

Pearson, M. (1997) *China's New Business Elite*. University of California Press.

Pearson, M. (2005) "The business of governing business in China: Institutions and norms of the emerging regulatory state," *World Politics*, 57(2): 296–322.

Pearson, M. (2019) "China and global climate change governance," in *Handbook on the International Political Economy of China*, pp. 411–423. Edward Elgar Publishing.

Pearson, M., Rithmire, M., and Tsai, K. (2022) "China's party-state capitalism and international backlash: From interdependence to insecurity," *International Security*, 47(2): 135–176.

Pearson, M., Rithmire, M., and Tsai, K. (2023) *The State and Capitalism in China*. Cambridge University Press.

Peerenboom, R. (2006) "What have we learned about law and development?

Describing, predicting, and assessing legal reforms in China," *Michigan Journal of International Law*, 27(3): 823–871.

Peerenboom, R. (2007) *China Modernizes: Threat to the West or Model for the Rest?* Oxford University Press.

Pei, M. (1997) "Citizens v. mandarins: Administrative litigation in China," *China Quarterly*, 152: 832–862.

Pei, M. (2006) *China's Trapped Transition: The Limits of Developmental Autocracy*. Harvard University Press.

People's Bank of China. (2019) "For a green belt and road with green finance."

Perkins, D.H. (2018) "The complex task of evaluating China's economic reforms," in Garnaut, R., Song, L., and Cai, F. eds., *China's 40 Years of Reform and Development 1978–2018*. Canberra, ANU Press, pp. 135–154.

Perkins, D.H. and Yusuf, S. (1984) *Rural Development in China*. Washington DC: The World Bank.

Perotti, E., Sun, L., and Zou, L. (1999) "State-owned versus township and village enterprises in China," *Comparative Economic Studies*, 41: 151–179.

Pettis, M. (2023) "What will it take for China's GDP to grow at 4–5 percent over the next decade?"

Polo, M. (1903) *The Book of Ser Marco Polo: The Venetian Concerning Kingdoms and Marvels of the East*, vols. 1 and 2, trans. and ed. Colonel Sir Henry Yule. Charles Scribner's Sons, 1903, ed. Sue Gronewald.

Pomeranz, K. (2000) *The Great Divergence: China, Europe, and the Making of the Modern World Economy*. Princeton University Press.

Pong, D. (2003) *Shen Pao-chen and China's Modernization in the Nineteenth Century*. Cambridge University Press.

Potter, P. (2004) "Legal reform in China: Institutions, culture, and selective adaptation." *Law & Social Inquiry*, 29(2): 465–495.

Potter, S. (1983) "The position of peasants in modern China's social order," *Modern China*, 9(4): 465–499.

Prebisch, R. (1950) *The Economic Development of Latin America and Its Principal Problems*. New York: United Nations.

Pringle, T. (2011) *Trade Unions in China: The Challenge of Labour Unrest*. London: Routledge.

Prosterman, R., Hanstad, T., and Ping, L. (1996) "Can China feed itself?" *Scientific American*, 275(5): 90–96.

Przeworski, A. and Limongi, F. (1997) "Modernization: Theories and facts," *World Politics*, 49(2): 155–183.

Qi, Y. and Zhang, L. (2014) "Local environmental enforcement constrained by central–local relations in China," *Environmental Policy and Governance*, 24(3): 216–232.

Qian, W. (1985) *The Great Inertia: Scientific Stagnation in Traditional China*. London: Taylor & Francis.

Qian, Y. and Weingast, B. (1996) "China's transition to markets: Market-preserving federalism, Chinese style," *Journal of Policy Reform*, 1(2): 149–185.

Qin, G., Niu, Z., Yu, J., Li, Z., Ma, J., and Xiang, P. (2021) "Soil heavy metal pollution and food safety in China: Effects, sources and removing technology," *Chemosphere*, 267: 129205.

Raess, D., Ren, W., and Wagner, P. (2022) "Hidden strings attached? Chinese (commercially oriented) foreign aid and international political alignment," *Foreign Policy Analysis*, 18(3).

Ramo, J. (2004) *The Beijing Consensus*. London: Foreign Policy Centre.

Rappeport, A. and Alderman, L. (2024) "U.S. seeks to join forces with Europe to combat excess Chinese goods," *New York Times*, May 21.

Rauch, J. and Chi, Y. (2010) "The plight of green GDP in China," *Consilience*, 3: 102–116.

Ravina, M. (2017) *To Stand with the Nations of the World: Japan's Meiji Restoration in World History*. Oxford University Press.

Ray, R. (2023) "'Small is beautiful' A new era in China's overseas development finance?" Global Development Policy Center, Boston University.

Reddy, G. (2021) "American supply chains face a dire threat from China's water shortages," *The Hill.*

Remington, T. (2018) "Bureaucratic politics and labour policy in China," *China: An International Journal*, 16(3): 97–119.

Ricardo, D. (1817/2004) *Principles of Political Economy and Taxation*. Dover Publications.

Rieffel, L. and Wang, X. (2024) "China's population could shrink to half by 2100."

Rithmire, M. (2022) "Going out or opting out? Capital, political vulnerability, and the state in China's outward investment," *Comparative Politics*, 54(3): 477–499.

Rithmire, M. and Chen, H. (2021) "The emergence of mafia-like business systems in China," *China Quarterly*, 248(1): 1037–1058.

Rodrik, D. (2006) "What's so special about China's exports?" *China & World Economy*, 14(5): 1–19.

Rosen, D., Leutert W., and Guo S. (2018) "Missing link: Corporate governance in China's state sector," Asia Society.

Rossabi, M. (1983) *China Among Equals: The Middle Kingdom and Its Neighbors, 10th–14th Centuries*. University of California Press.

Rothko Investment Strategies (2020) "The national team and co.: China's ¥53 trillion experiment."

Rozelle, S. (1996) "Stagnation without equity: Patterns of growth and inequality in China's rural economy," *China Journal*, 35: 63–92.

S&P Global (2023) "The world's 100 largest banks, 2023."

Sagers, J. (2006) *Origins of Japanese Wealth and Power: Reconciling Confucianism and Capitalism, 1830–1885*. Palgrave Macmillan.

Saich, T. (2017) "The politics of welfare policy: Towards social citizenship?" in Carrillo, B., Hood, J., and Kadetz, P. I. eds., *Handbook of Welfare in China*. Edward Elgar Publishing, pp. 81–97.

Saich, T. (2000) "Negotiating the state: The development of social organizations in China," *China Quarterly*, 161: 124–141.

Sargeson, S. (2013) "Violence as development: Land expropriation and China's urbanization," *Journal of Peasant Studies*, 40(6).

SASAC (n.d.) "What we do."

Satia, P. (2018) *Empire of Guns. The Violent Making of the Industrial Revolution*. Stanford University Press.

Sauvant, K. and Chen, V. (2014) "China's regulatory framework for outward foreign direct investment," *China Economic Journal*, 7(1): 141–163.

Schell, O. (1995) *Mandate of Heaven: The Legacy of Tiananmen Square and the Next Generation of China's Leaders*. Simon and Schuster.

Schipke, A., Rodlauer, M., and Longmei, Z. (2019) *China's Bond Market: Characteristics, Prospects, and Reforms. The Future of China's Bond Market*. Washington DC: International Monetary Fund.

Schran, P. (1974) "Institutional Continuity and Motivational Change: The Chinese Industrial Wages System, 1950–1973," *Asian Survey*, 14(11): 1014–1032.

Schwartz, B. (1960) "Totalitarian consolidation and the Chinese model," *China Quarterly*, 1: 18–21.

Schwartz, J. (2004) "Environmental NGOs in China: Roles and limits," *Pacific Affairs*, 77(1): 28–49.

Schwartz, J. and Evans, R. (2007) "Causes of effective policy implementation: China's public health response to SARS," *Journal of Contemporary China*, 16(51): 195–213.

Sears, C. (2019) "What counts as foreign aid: Dilemmas and ways forward in measuring China's overseas development flows," *The Professional Geographer*, 71(1): 135–144.

Selaya, P. and Sunesen, E. (2012) "Does foreign aid increase foreign direct investment?" *World Development*, 40(11): 2155–76.

Seric, A. and Tong Y. (2019) "'East Asian Miracle' through industrial production and trade lenses."

Shambaugh, D. (2008) *China's Communist Party: Atrophy and Adaptation*. University of California Press.

Shen, X. (2015) "Private Chinese investment in Africa: Myths and realities," *Development Policy Review* 33(1): 83–106.

Shi, W., Sun, S., Yan, D. and Zhu, Z. (2017) "Institutional fragility and outward foreign direct investment from China," *Journal of International Business Studies*, 48(4): 452–476.

Shih, V., Adolph, C. and Liu, M. (2012) "Getting ahead in the Communist Party: explaining the advancement of central committee members in China," *American Political Science Review*, 106(1): 166–187.

Shin, J. (2021) "What is the "Great Green Wall" of China?"

Shirk, S. (1993) *The Political Logic of Economic Reform in China*. University of California Press.

Simpson, K. (2019) "Just how green is the Belt and Road?" *The Interpreter*. Lowy Institute. January 23.

Singer, H. (1950) "Distribution of gains between investing and borrowing countries," *American Economic Review (Papers and Proceedings of the Sixty-Second Annual Meeting of the American Economic Association)*, 40(2): 473–485.

Singh, I., D. Ratha, and G. Xiao, 1993. "Non-state enterprises as an engine of growth: An analysis of provincial industrial growth in post-reform China," Working paper, Transition and Macro Adjustment Division, Washington DC: The World Bank.

Siripurapu, A. and Berman, N. (2024) "The contentious US–China trade relationship," Council on Foreign Relations.

Sivin, N. (1985) "Why the scientific revolution did not take place in China – or did it?" *Environmentalist*, 5(1): 39–50.

Solar Energy Industries Association. (2024) "American renewable energy manufacturing: 100 GW by 2030."

Solinger, D. (1993) "China's transients and the state: A form of civil society?" *Politics & Society*, 21(1): 91–122.

Solinger, D. (1999) *Contesting Citizenship in Urban China: Peasant Migrants, the State and the Logic of the Market*. University of California Press.

Solinger, D. (2002) "Labour market reform and the plight of the laid-off proletariat," *China Quarterly*, 170: 304–326.

Solinger, D. (2014) "The state, the poor, and the Dibao: Three models of the wellsprings of welfare and lessons for China," in Guo S. ed. *State–Society Relations and Governance in China*. Lanham, MD: Lexington Books, pp. 3–13.

Stallings, B. (1990) "The role of foreign capital in economic development," in Gereffi, G. and Wyman, D. eds., *Manufacturing Miracles: Paths of Industrialization in Latin America and East Asia*. Princeton University Press, pp. 55–89.

Stallings, B. and Kim, E. (2017) *Promoting Development: The Political Economy of East Asian Foreign Aid*. Springer.

Standaert, M. (2020) "With activists silenced, China moves ahead on big dam project," *Yale Environment 360*.

Standaert, M. (2021) "Despite pledges to cut emissions, China goes on a coal spree."

Stanway, D. (2021) "The Great Green Wall: China's farmers push back the desert one tree at a time," *Reuters*, July 19.

Steinhardt, H. and Wu, F. (2016) "In the name of the public: Environmental protest and the changing landscape of popular contention in China," *China Journal*, 75(1): 61–82.

Stevenson, A. (2021) "China moves against private tutoring companies, causing shares to plunge," *New York Times*, July 26.

Su, F. and Tao, R. (2017) "The China model withering? Institutional roots of China's local developmentalism." *Urban Studies*, 54(1): 230–250.

Su, J. and He, J. (2010) "Does giving lead to getting? Evidence from Chinese private enterprises," *Journal of Business Ethics*, 93(1): 73–90.

Sullivan, L. (1988) "Assault on the reforms: Conservative criticism of political and economic liberalization in China, 1985–86," *China Quarterly*, 114: 198–222.

Sutherland, D., Anderson, J., Bailey N., and Alon, I. (2020) "Policy, institutional fragility, and Chinese outward foreign direct investment: An empirical examination of the Belt and Road Initiative," *Journal of International Business Policy*, 3: 249–272.

Swanson, (2022) "Biden administration clamps down on China's access to chip technology."

Tankersley, J. (2024) "Biden doesn't want you buying an E.V. from China. Here's why," *New York Times*, May 27.

Tanner, M. (1999) *The Politics of Lawmaking in Post-Mao China: Institutions, Processes, and Democratic Prospects*. Oxford University Press.

Tanner, M. (2019) "Organizations and politics in China's post-Mao law-making system," in *Domestic Law Reforms in Post-Mao China*, pp. 56–93. Routledge.

Taylor, B. and Li, Q. (2007) "Is ACFTU a union and does it matter?" *Journal of Industrial Relations*, 49: 701–715.

ten Brink, T. (2015) "Chinese firms 'going global': Recent OFDI trends, policy support and international implications," *International Politics*, 52(6): 666–683.

TheGlobalEconomy.com. (n.d.) "Household consumption, percent of GDP – Country rankings."

Thompson, N. (2023) "China's restless workers," *The Diplomat*.

Tsai, K. (2005) "Capitalists without a class: Political diversity among private entrepreneurs in China," *Comparative Political Studies*, 38(9): 1130–1158.

Tsai, K. (2007) *Capitalism Without Democracy: The Private Sector in Contemporary China*. Cornell University Press.

Tsai, K. (2009) "Beyond banks: The local logic of informal finance and private sector development in China," in Li, J. and Hsu, S. eds., *Informal Finance in China: American and Chinese Perspectives*. Oxford University Press, pp. 80–103.

UNCCD (n.d.) "Land Degradation Neutrality."

United States–China Economic and Security Review Commission (2024) "Chinese companies listed on major U.S. stock exchanges."

University of Southern California (2021) "Running out of water."

Van Rooij, B. (2010) "The people vs. pollution: Understanding citizen action against pollution in China," *Journal of Contemporary China*, 19(63): 55–77.

Van Rooij, B., Zhu, Q., Li, N., and Wang, Q. (2017) "Centralizing trends and pollution law enforcement in China," *China Quarterly*, special section "Central–local relations and environmental governance in China."

Vogel, E. (2011) *Deng Xiaoping and the transformation of China*. Belknap Press of Harvard University Press.

Wade, R. (1990) *Governing the Market: Economic Theory and the Role of Government in East Asian Industrialization*. Princeton University Press.

Wakeman, F. (1993) "Voyages," *American Historical Review* 98(1): 1–17.

Walder, A. (1986) *Communist Neo-Traditionalism: Work and Authority in Chinese Industry*. University of California Press.

Walder, A. and Gong, X. (1993) "Workers in the Tiananmen protests: The politics of the Beijing Workers' Autonomous Federation," *Australian Journal of Chinese Affairs*, 29: 1–29.

Walker, K. (2006) "'Gangster capitalism' and peasant protest in China: The last twenty years," *Journal of Peasant Studies*, 33(1): 1–33.

Wang, B. and Gao, K. (2019) "Forty years development of China's outward foreign direct investment: Retrospect and the challenges ahead," *China & World Economy*, 27(3): 1–24.

Wang, B., Yu, M., and Huang, Y. (2013) "Financial constraints on Chinese outward direct investment by the Private sector," in Garnaut, R., Cai, F.. and Song, L. eds., *China: A New Model for Growth and Development*. Canberra: ANU Press, pp. 321–340.

Wang, C. (2024) "China Belt and Road Initiative (BRI) Investment Report 2023," Green Finance and Development Center.

Wang, F. (2005) *Organizing Through Division and Exclusion: China's Hukou System*. Stanford University Press.

Wang, H. (1999) "The Asian financial crisis and financial reforms in China," *Pacific Review* 12(4): 537–556.

Wang, H. (2001) *Weak State, Strong Networks: The Institutional Dynamics of Foreign Direct Investment in China*. Oxford University Press.

Wang, H. (2002) "China's exchange rate policy in the aftermath of the Asian financial crisis," in J. Kirshner, ed., *Monetary Order: Ambiguous Economics, Ubiquitous Politics*. Cornell University Press pp. 153–171.

Wang, H. (2014) "The limits of the exchange rate weapon in addressing China's role in global imbalance," in Helleiner, E. and Kirshner, J. eds., *The Great Wall of Money: Politics and Power in China's International Monetary Relations*. Cornell University Press, pp. 99–126.

Wang, H. and Huang, J. (2023) "How can China's recent pension reform reduce pension inequality?" *Journal of Aging and Social Policy*, 35(1): 37–51.

Wang, H., Yang, H., Li, F., and Zhang, M. (2022) "Does foreign aid reduce the country's risk of OFDI? The Chinese experience," *International Studies of Economics*,

Wang, J. (2023) "Minying jingji wenbu maixiang gao zhiliang (Private economy takes solid steps toward high quality)," *People's Daily*, May 31.

Wang, S. and Hu, A. (2001) *The Chinese Economy in Crisis: State Capacity and Tax Reform*. Armonk: East Gate.

Wang, V. (2024) "China appears to backpedal from video game crackdown," *New York Times*, January 23.

Wang, W., Primbs, T., Tao, S., and Simonich, S. (2009) "Atmospheric particulate matter pollution during the 2008 Beijing Olympics," *Environmental Science & Technology*, 43(14): 5314–5320.

Wang, X. (2011) "中海外波兰遭遇索赔 终止只为避免更糟结局 (COVEC, subject to compensation demand, stops project to avoid worse outcomes)," *Economic Information*.

Wang, X., Hui, E., Choguill, C., and Jia, S. (2015) "The new urbanization policy in China: Which way forward?" *Habitat International*, 47: 279–284.

Wang, Y. and Minzner, C. (2015) "The rise of the Chinese security state," *China Quarterly*, 222: 339–359.

Wang, Y., Gao, Q., and Yang, S. (2019) "Prioritising health and food: Social assistance and family consumption in rural China," *China: An International Journal*, 17(1): 48–75.

Waqar, S., Ahmed, S., and Badshah, I. (2021) "Chinese FDI for infrastructure development in Africa – Assessing the impact of cooperation," *Studies of Applied Economics*, 39(3).

Watts, J. (2005) "In China's richest village, peasants are all shareholders now – by order of the party."

Weber, I. (2021) *How China Escaped Shock Therapy: The Market Reform Debate*. Routledge.

Weber, M. (1951) *The Religion of China*. The Free Press.

Weber, M. (2001) *The Protestant Ethic and the Spirit of Capitalism*, trans. Stephen Kalberg. Los Angeles: Roxbury Publishing Company.

Wei, Q., Luo, J., and Huang, X. (2020) "Influence of social identity on family firms' FDI decisions: The moderating role of internal capital markets," *Management International Review*, 60(5): 651–693.

Wei, Y. (2002) "Beyond the Sunan model: Trajectory and underlying factors of development in Kunshan, China," *Environment and Planning*, 34(10): 1725–1747.

Wei, Y. and Liu, X. (2006) "Productivity spillovers from R&D, exports and FDI in China's manufacturing sector," *Journal of International Business Studies*, 37(4): 544–557.

Wei, Y., Ang, Y., and Jia, N. (2023) "The promise and pitfalls of government guidance funds in China," *China Quarterly*, 256: 939–959.

Wei, Y., Li, W., and Wang, C. (2007) "Restructuring industrial districts, scaling up regional development: a study of the Wenzhou model, China," *Economic Geography*, 83(4): 421–444.

Wen, J. (2009) "Full text of Chinese premier's press conference in Egypt," November 10.

Westney, D. (1987) *Imitation and Innovation: The Transfer of Western Organizational Patterns to Meiji Japan*. Harvard University Press.

Whiteford, P. (2003) "From enterprise protection to social protection: Pension reform in China," *Global Social Policy*, 3(1): 45–77.

WHO (1983) *Public Health Care: The Chinese Experience*. Geneva: World Health Organization.

WHO (n.d.) "Aging and Health in China."

Wike, R. and Parker, B. (2015) "Corruption, pollution, inequality are top concerns in China."

Williamson, J. (2014) "Beijing consensus versus Washington consensus," *Handbook of Emerging Economies*, ed. R.E. Looney, Routledge, pp. 177–184.

Williamson, J., Fang, L. and Calvo, E. (2017) "Rural pension reform in China: A critical analysis," *Journal of Aging Studies*, 41: 67–74.

Wilson, M., Li, X., Ma, Y., Smith, A., and Wu, J. (2017) "A review of the economic, social, and environmental impacts of China's South–North water transfer project: A sustainability perspective," *Sustainability*, 9(8): 1489.

Wines, M., Bradsher, K., and Landler, M. (2009) "China's leader says he is 'worried' Over U.S. Treasuries."

Wingender, M. (2018) *Intergovernmental Fiscal Reform in China*. International Monetary Fund.

Wong, C. (2000) "Central–local relations revisited: The 1994 tax-sharing reform and public expenditure management in China," *China Perspectives*, September 1:52–63.

Wong, C. (2009) "Rebuilding government for the 21st century: Can China incrementally reform the public sector?" *China Quarterly*, 200: 929–952.

Wong, C. (2018) "An update on fiscal reform," in Garnaut, R., Song, L., and Cai, F. eds., *China's Forty Years of Reform and Development: 1978–2018*. Canberra: ANU Press, pp. 271–290.

Wong, D., Li, C., and Song, H. (2007) "Rural migrant workers in urban China: Living a marginalised life," *International Journal of Social Welfare*, 16(1): 32–40.

Woo, J. (1991) *Race to the Swift: State and Finance in Korean Industrialization*. Columbia University Press.

World Bank (1993) *The East Asian Miracle: Economic Growth and Public Policy*. Oxford University Press.

World Bank (n.d.) "Gini Index."

World Economic Forum. (2023) "Ranked: The largest bond markets in the world."

Wright, T. (2010) *Accepting Authoritarianism: State–Society Relations in China's Reform Era*. Stanford University Press.

Wright, T. (2015) *Party and State in Post-Mao China*. Polity.

Wrigley, E. (1988) *Continuity, Chance, and Change: The Character of the Industrial Revolution in England*. Cambridge University Press.

Wu, H. and Ye, J. (2016) "Hollow lives: Women left behind in rural China," *Journal of Agrarian Change*, 16(1): 50–69.

Wu, S., Zhu, W., Li, H., Lin, S., Chai, W., and Wang, X. (2012) "Workplace violence and influencing factors among medical professionals in China," *American Journal of Industrial Medicine*, 55(11): 1000–1008.

Wu, X., Yan, H., and Jiang, Y. (2018) "How are new community governance structures formed in urban China?: A case study of two cities, Wuhan and Guangzhou," *Asian Survey*, 58(5): 942–965.

Wu, Y. (2005) *Political Explanation of Economic Growth: State Survival, Bureaucratic Politics, and Private Enterprises in the Making of Taiwan's Economy, 1950–1985*. Harvard University Asia Center.

Wu, Y. (2024) "China's outbound investment: Recent developments, opportunities, and challenges."

Wu, Y. and Chen, C. (2016) "The impact of foreign direct investment on urbanization in China," *Journal of the Asia Pacific Economy*, 21(3): 339–56.

Wu, Y., Li, X., Yu, L., Wang, T., Wang, J. and Liu, T. (2022) "Review of soil heavy metal pollution in China: Spatial distribution, primary sources, and remediation alternatives," *Resources, Conservation and Recycling*, 181: 106261.

Xia, Y., and Wang, Y. (2023) "An unlikely duet: Public–private interaction in China's Environmental Public Interest Litigation," *Transnational Environmental Law*, 12(2): 396–423.

Xiao, H., Wang Z., Liu F., and Unger J. (2023) "Excess all-cause mortality in China after ending the zero COVID policy," *JAMA Network Open*, 6(8): e2330877.

Xiao, Q. (2019) "President XI's surveillance state," *Journal of Democracy*, 30(1): 53–67.

Xie, P. (1995) "Guanyu woguo zhongyang yinhang de dulixing wenti" ["Analysis of central bank independence in China"], *Jinrong yu jingji [Journal of Finance and Economics]* 6: 6–7.

Xie, Y. and Wu, X. (2008) "Danwei profitability and earnings inequality in urban China," *China Quarterly*, 195: 558–581.

Xing, C. and Zhang, R. (2021) "COVID-19 in China: Responses, challenges and implications for the health system," *Healthcare*, 9(1): 82, MDPI.

Xinhua (2004) "Some 10% migrant children drop out of school."

Xinhua (2014) "China's forex reserves rise to $4 trillion."

Xinhua (2021a) "Xi Focus: Green growth generates gold as Xi's iconic words on ecology put into practice."

Xinhua (2021b) "Full text: Xi Jinping's speech at the COP15 leaders' summit."

Xinhua (2022) "China registers 415 million motor vehicles, 500 million drivers," December 8.

Xinhua (2022) "China's steadfast economic growth in past decade boon to world."

Xinhua (2024) "China's bond market issuances total 71 trillion yuan in 2023."

Xinhua (2024) "Number of listed companies in China reaches 5,346 by end of 2023."

Xiong, Y. (2015) "The broken ladder: Why education provides no upward mobility for migrant children in China," *China Quarterly*, 221: 161–184.

Xu, J. (2022) "Developments and implications of central bank digital currency: The case of China e-CNY," *Asian Economic Policy Review*, 17(2): 235–250.

Xu, M. (2004) *Jiangnan shishen yu Jiangnan shehui, 1368–1911* (Gentry and Society in Jiangnan, 1368–1911). Beijing: Shangwu yishuguan.

Xu, Y. (2013) "Labor non-governmental organizations in China: Mobilizing rural migrant workers," *Journal of Industrial Relations*, 55(2): 243–259.

Xu, Y. (2017) *Sinews of Power: The Politics of the State Grid Corporation of China*. Oxford University Press.

Xu, Y. (2018) "China's giant state-owned enterprises as policy advocates: The case of the state grid corporation of China," *China Journal*, 79(1): 21–39.

Xu, Y. and Yu, L. (2019) "The unification of rural and urban dibao in China: A case study," *China: An International Journal*, 17(1): 109–129.

Xue, L. (2014) "China's foreign aid policy and architecture," *IDS Bulletin*, 45(4): 36–45.

Xun, P. and Shuai, W. (2018) "The international political significance of Chinese and US foreign aid: As seen in United Nations General Assembly voting," *Social Sciences in China*, 39(1): 5–33.

Yang, C., (2012) "Restructuring the export-oriented industrialization in the Pearl River Delta, China: Institutional evolution and emerging tension," *Applied Geography*, 32(1): 143–157.

Yang, D. (1996) *Calamity and Reform in China: State, Rural Society, and Institutional Change since the Great Leap Famine*. Stanford University Press.

Yang, D. (2004) *Remaking the Chinese Leviathan: Market Transition and the Politics of Governance in China*. Stanford University Press.

Yang, D. (2012) *Beyond Beijing: Liberalization and the Regions in China*. Routledge.

Yang, G. (2005) "Environmental NGOs and institutional dynamics in China," *China Quarterly*, 181: 46–66.

Yang, G. and Calhoun, C. (2007) "Media, civil society, and the rise of a green public sphere in China," *China Information*, 21(2): 211–236.

Yang, J. (2012) *Tombstone: The Untold Story of Mao's Great Famine*. London: Penguin UK.

Yang, J., Huang, X. and Liu, X. (2014) "An analysis of education inequality in China," *International Journal of Educational Development*, 37: 2–10.

Yang, L., Walker, R., and Xie, J. (2020) "Shame, face and social relations in northern China: ramifications for social assistance provision," *China Quarterly*, 243: 655–675.

Yang, N., Hong, J., Wang, H., and Liu, Q. (2020) "Global value chain, industrial agglomeration, and innovation performance in developing countries: Insights from China's manufacturing industries," *Technology Analysis & Strategic Management*, 32(11): 1307–1321.

Yao, S. (2006) "On economic growth, FDI and exports in China," *Applied Economics*, 38(3): 339–351.

Yao, Y. 2010. "The end of the Beijing consensus," *Foreign Affairs*, 2(2).

Ye, J. (2018) "Stayers in China's "hollowed-out" villages: A counter narrative on massive rural–urban migration," *Population, Space and Place*, 24(4): e2128.

Ye, J. and Lu, P. (2011) "Differentiated childhoods: Impacts of rural labor migration on left-behind children in China," *Journal of Peasant Studies*, 38(2): 355–377.

Yi, W., Qin, G., and Sui, Y. (2019) "Prioritising health and food: Social assistance and family consumption in Rural China," *China: An International Journal*, 17(1): 48–75.

Yin, P., Brauer, M., Cohen, A., Wang, H., Li, J., Burnett, R., Stanaway, J. et al. (2020) "The effect of air pollution on deaths, disease burden, and life expectancy across China and its provinces, 1990–2017: An analysis for the Global Burden of Disease Study 2017," *Lancet Planetary Health*, 4(9): e386–e398.

Yin, T., De Propris, L., and Jabbour, L. (2021) "Assessing the effects of policies on China's outward foreign direct investment," *International Business Review*, 30(5): 101818.

Yip, W. and Hsiao, W. (2008) "The Chinese health system at a crossroads," *Health Affairs*, 27(2): 460–468.

Yip, W., Fu, H., Chen, A.T., Zhai, T., Jian, W., Xu, R., Pan, J., Hu, M., Zhou, Z., Chen, Q., and Mao, W. (2019) "10 years of health-care reform in China: Progress and gaps in universal health coverage," *Lancet*, 394(10204): 1192–1204.

You, K. and Solomon, O. (2015) "China's outward foreign direct investment and domestic investment: An industrial level analysis," *China Economic Review*, 34: 249–260.

Yu, H. (2014) "The ascendency of state-owned enterprises in China: Development, controversy and problems," *Journal of Contemporary China*, 23(85): 161–182.

Yu, S. (2023) "Millions drop out of China's state health insurance system," *Financial Times*, December 9.

Yu, Y. (2012) "Rebalancing the Chinese economy," *Oxford Review of Economic Policy*, 28(3): 551–568.

Yu, Y. (2015) "Macroeconomic management of the Chinese economy since the 1990s," in Chow, G.C. and Perkins, D.H. eds., *Routledge Handbook of the Chinese Economy*. Routledge, pp. 138–156.

Yuan, D. (2023) "Cujin minying qiye pingdeng zhunru de sikao he jianyi (Thoughts and Suggestions on Promoting Equal Entries for Private Enterprises)," Zhongguo Jingji Shibao, *China Economic Times*, August 9.

Yuan, F., Wei, Y., and Chen, W. (2014) "Economic transition, industrial location and corporate networks: Remaking the Sunan Model in Wuxi City, China," *Habitat International*, 42: 58–68.

Yusuf, S. (1994) "China's macroeconomic performance and management during transition," *Journal of Economic Perspectives*, 8(2): 71–92.

Zhan, J. (2011) "Explaining central intervention in local extra-budgetary practices in China," *Asian Survey*, 51(3): 497–519.

Zhang, C. (2017) "Reexamining the electoral connection in authoritarian China: The local People's Congress and its private entrepreneur deputies," *China Review*, 17(1): 1–27.

Zhang, C. (2020) "Clans, entrepreneurship, and development of the private sector in China," *Journal of Comparative Economics*, 48(1): 100–123.

Zhang, H. (2019) "Stuck between the idea of philanthropy and social right: dilemma of social assistance in China," *Journal of Social Service Research*, 45(5): 673–683.

Zhang, J., Mauzerall, D., Zhu, T., Liang, S., Ezzati, M., and Remais, J. (2010) "Environmental health in China: challenges to achieving clean air and safe water," *Lancet*, 375: 1110–19.

Zhang, K. (2005) "Why does so much FDI from Hong Kong and Taiwan go to Mainland China?" *China Economic Review*, 16(3): 293–307.

Zhang, K. and Song, S. (2003) "Rural–urban migration and urbanization in China: Evidence from time-series and cross-section analysis," *China Economic Review*, 14: 386–400.

Zhang, L. (1999) "Chinese central-provincial fiscal relationships, budgetary decline and the impact of the 1994 fiscal reform: An evaluation," *China Quarterly*, 157: 115–141.

Zhang, L. (2002). *Strangers in the City: Reconfigurations of Space, Power and Social Networks within China's Floating Population*. Stanford University Press.

Zhang, L. (2012) "The stages of political innovation in rural China's local democratisation: four cases of villagers' political innovations," *China Report*, 48(4): 427–448.

Zhang, L. (2015) *Inside China's Automobile Factories: The Politics of Labor and Worker Resistance*. Cambridge University Press.

Zhang, L. (2017) "The paradox of labor force dualism and state-labor-capital relations in the Chinese automobile industry," in Kuruvilla, S., Lee, C.K., and Gallagher, M.E. eds., *From Iron Rice Bowl to Informalization: Markets, Workers, and the State in a Changing China*. Cornell University Press, pp. 107–137.

Zhang, L., Brooks, R., Ding, D., Ding, H., He, H., Lu, J., and Mano, R. (2018) "China's high savings: Drivers, prospects, and policies," IMF Working Papers.

Zhang, Q. (2003) "The people's court in transition: The prospects of the Chinese judicial reform," *Journal of Contemporary China*, 12(34): 69–101.

Zhang, Q. (2022) "Sectoral and country-origin dynamics of FDI in China in 1997–2020," *The Chinese Economy*, 1–15.

Zhang, Q. and Liu, M. (2013) "The political economy of private sector development in communist China: Evidence from Zhejiang province," *Studies in Comparative International Development*, 48(2): 196–216.

Zhang, S. (2018) "Wind and solar power in China," *China's Electricity Sector*. Singapore: Palgrave Pivot, pp. 83–105.

Zhang, S. (2020) *Villagers' Life Transformation and Community Governance in China's Land Expropriation-Induced Resettlement Neighborhoods: A Shanghai Case Study*. University of Waterloo.

Zhang, Y., Chen, Y., Wang, Y., Li, F., Pender, M., Wang, N., Yan, F., Ying, X., Tang, S., and Fu, C. (2020) "Reduction in healthcare services during the COVID-19 pandemic in China," *British Medical Journal Global Health*, 5(11): e003421.

Zhao, C. (2022) "Foreign Assets for Chinese Control: Capital Filtration, New Triple Alliance, and the Global Political Economy of China's Information Industry (1995–2020)," PhD dissertation, University of Victoria, Canada.

Zhao, F., Ma, Y., Zhu, Y., Tang, Z., and McGrath, S. (2015) "Soil contamination in China: Current status and mitigation strategies," *Environmental Science & Technology*, 49(2): 750–759.

Zhao, S. (1993) "Deng Xiaoping's southern tour: Elite politics in post-Tiananmen China," *Asian Survey*, 33(8): 739–756.

Zhao, S. (2010) "The China model: Can it replace the Western model of modernization?" *Journal of Contemporary China*, 19(65): 419–436.

Zhao, S. (2017) "Whither the China model: Revisiting the debate," *Journal of Contemporary China*, 26(103): 1–17.

Zhao, W. (2023) "Qian san jidu quanguo xinshe minying qiye 706.5 wanhu fazhan renxing chixu xianxian (7.065 million new private enterprises in the first three quarters, continuing to show developmental resilience)."

Zhao, W., Liu, L., and Zhao, T. (2010) "The contribution of outward direct investment to productivity changes within China, 1991–2007," *Journal of International Management*, 16(2): 121–130.

Zhao, X. and Xie, Y. (2022). "The effect of land expropriation on local political trust in China," *Land Use Policy*, 114: 105966.

Zheng, L. and Wang, H. (2021) "Authority and autonomy without independence: The gradual institutional change of the Chinese central bank," *Journal of Contemporary China*, 30(129): 349–367.

Zheng, Y. (2007) *De Facto Federalism in China: Reforms and Dynamics of Central–Local Relations*. Singapore: World Scientific.

Zhou, C., Sylvia, S., Zhang, L., Luo, R., Yi, H., Liu, C., Shi, Y., Loyalka, P., Chu, J., Medina, A., and Rozelle, S. (2015) "China's left-behind children: Impact of parental migration on health, nutrition, and educational outcomes," *Health Affairs*, 34(11): 1964–1971.

Zhou, H., Liu, J., He, J., and Cheng, J. (2021) "Conditional justice: Evaluating the judicial centralization reform in China," *Journal of Contemporary China*, 30(129): 434–450.

Zhou, K. (1996) *How the Farmers Changed China: Power of the People*. Westview Press.

Zhou, S. and Cheung, M. (2017) "Hukou system effects on migrant children's education in China: Learning from past disparities," *International Social Work*, 60(6): 1327–1342.

Zhou, Y. (2022) "Trapped in the platform: Migration and precarity in China's platform-based gig economy," *Environment and Planning A: Economy and Space*: 0308518X221119196.

Zhu, H. and Lu, J. (2022) "The crackdown on rights-advocacy NGOs in Xi's China: politicizing the law and legalizing the repression," *Journal of Contemporary China*, 31(136): 518–538.

Zhu, H. and Walker, A. (2018) "Pension system reform in China: Who gets what pensions?" *Social Policy & Administration*, 52(7): 1410–1424.

Zhu, J. and Wu, Y. (2014) "Who pays more "tributes" to the government? Sectoral corruption of China's private enterprises," *Crime, Law, and Social Change*, 61(3): 309–333.

Zhuang, H., Zinda, J., and Lassoie, J. (2022) "'Crouching tiger, hidden power': A 25-year strategic advocacy voyage of an environmental NGO in China," *Journal of Environment & Development*, 31(4): 331–351.

Zuo, X., Peng, X., Yang, X., Adams, P., and Wang, M. (2023) "Pension module and its application – Population ageing and the impacts of retirement age extension on the economy and pension system in China," in Peng, X. ed., *CHINAGEM – A Dynamic General Equilibrium Model of China: Theory, Data and Applications. Advances in Applied General Equilibrium Modeling*. Springer.

Zweig, D. (1997) *Freeing China's Farmers: Rural Restructuring in the Reform Era*. Routledge.

Index

Page numbers in italic indicate maps

"advancement of the state, and the retreat of the private," 83, 95
Agricultural Bank of China (ABC), 162, 165
Agricultural Development Bank of China, 163
Agricultural Producers' Cooperatives (APCs), 19–21, 53
agriculture: bureaucratic state and, 5; collectivization of, 19–20, 53; de-collectivization of, 52, 54–55, 58–59, 140; efficiency of, 11; expropriation of land, 65, 69; fertilizer consumption, 56; grain production quotas, 55, 56; impact on environment, 197; incentive problem, 53; in late imperial period, 11; per capita output, 21; productivity of, 11, 53–54, 55–56; share in GDP, 56; state subsidies to, 56; taxation, 68, 192. *See also* peasants
air pollution, 197–200, 204, 208
Alibaba, 104, 125
All-China Federation of Trade Unions (ACFTU), 127–128, 133, 275
Anhui Province: entrepreneurial elite in, 7; household farming in, 54, 55, *40*; in Qing period, 7
Ant Group, 104
Asian Financial Crisis (AFC), 164, 182, 186, 216, 275

Asian Infrastructure Investment Bank (AIIB), 219–220, 251, 275
authoritarian environmentalism, 206, 214

Bank of China (BOC), 162, 165
Bank of Communications, 163
Bank of Taiwan, 173
banks: Big Four, 163, 164; crisis of, 80; expansion of, 163; foreign, 165; government bailout of, 164; lending to private businesses, 98–99; loans to green energy projects, 174; non-performing loans in, 164; reform of, 162–165; state control of, 173, 176; structures and functions of, 162, 173
"barefoot doctors," 140, 275
Basic Plan for Old Age Social Insurance in the Countryside, 136
"Beijing Consensus," 259, 260, 272, 275
Beijing municipality, *40*, 44
Beijing Olympics (2008), 197–198, 260
Beijing Stock Exchange, 166
Belt and Road Initiative, 87, 196, 215, 218–220, 241, 243, 246, 275
Biden, Joe, 194
Blair, Tony, 214
Bo Xilai, 31
bond market, 169–170, 171
boom-and-bust cycles, 179, 180–182, 275
Boxer Rebellion, 16
Bretton Woods Conference, 230

British Virgin Islands (BVI), 235
Brown, Lester: *Who Will Feed China*, 65
Budget Law, 160
building materials industry, 84
business associations, 107, 108

"cancer villages," 197, 202, 276
capital: types of, 249
capital market, 162, 165–166, 171
capitalism, 3, 8
Cayman Islands, 235
Center for International Knowledge on
  Development, 272–273
Center for Legal Assistance to Pollution
  Victims (CLAPV), 211, 213
central bank. *See* People's Bank of
  China (PBC)
central bank digital currency (CBDC),
  189
central bank independence (CBI), 185,
  186, 276
Central Commission for Discipline
  Inspection (CCDI), 27, 31, 32–33, 86
Central Committee of CCP: annual
  meetings of, 28–29; authority of, 32;
  economic policies, 81; election of
  members of, 27, 33; tasks of, 27–28
Central Economic Work Conference,
  191
Central Huijin fund, 164, 165
Central Organization Department
  (COD) of CCP, 28, 29, 32, 43–44
central-local relationships, 41, 42, 43
"century of humiliation," xviii, 19, 276
Chen Yuan, 30
Chen Yun, 24, 30
Chiang Kai-shek, 18
China, People's Republic of (PRC):
  administrative units of, 39, *40*; aid
  to North Korea, 30; autonomous
  regions, 39; central-local relations
  in, 39, 41–45; climate change
  initiatives, 216–217; comparison
  with Europe and Japan, 26; debt
  accumulation, xvi; "democratic"
  parties in, 33; demographics, 130,

270; as developmental state, 90, 174,
  175, 176; economic liberalization
  of, xviii; election system in, 46–47;
  employment protection in, 126;
  energy consumption in, 198;
  establishment of, xix, 18–19, 52;
  foreign relations, 49–50, 251–252,
  270–271; foreign-exchange reserves,
  191, 242; imports of goods and
  services from, 190; industrialization
  of, 72; internal migration, 62–64;
  labor's rights in, 127; life expectancy
  in, 270; major cities, 39; Maoist
  reforms, 19–23, *40*; modernization
  of, 251; open policy, 222, 241; as
  paternalistic state, 152; political
  system of, 4–5, 26, 30–31, 50, 76,
  77, 80–81, 273; rural-urban divide,
  61–62; Soviet aid to, 72; state–society
  relations in, 45–50; stratification of
  society, 150; as surveillance state, 48;
  territory of, 39; urbanization in, 52,
  64–66; U.S. relations with, 72, 194;
  WTO membership, 81–82, 230
China, Republic of (ROC): currency
  reform, 19; era of warlords,
  18; establishment of, 17–18;
  participation in Bretton Woods
  Conference, 230. *See also* Taiwan
China Aeronautics and Space
  Corporation, 36
China Banking Regulatory Commission
  (CBRC), 186
"China Circle," 234
China Construction Bank (CCB), 83,
  162–163, 165, 174
China Democratic League, 33
China Development Bank (CDB), 163
"China Dream," xviii
China Interbank Offered Rate
  (CHIBOR), 189
China Investment Corporation, 242
China Mobile Communications, 83
China Model (CM) for development:
  challenges of, 270–272; complexity
  of, 263; debates over, 272–273;

China Model (CM) for development (*cont.*)

different versions of, 261–263; *vs.* East Asian model, 262; elements of, 259–260; environmental problems and, 271–272; incremental process of, 262; limitations of, 267–271, 273; pragmatic experimentalism of, 263–264, 265–266; promotion of, 260–261; role of state, 262–263; success of, 261–262; variation across sectors, 264–265

China National Democratic Construction Association, 33

China National Petroleum Corporation, 88

China Overseas Engineering Group Co. Ltd. (COVEC), 250

China Post Group, 83

China Power Investment Corporation, 88

China Railway Engineering Group, 83

China Resources, 86

China Securities Finance Corporation (CSF), 170

China Securities Regulatory Commission (CSRC), 166, 170, 171

China Southern Airlines, 86

China State Construction Engineering, 83

China Unicom, 239

China-Angola bilateral co-operation agreements, 255

China-China-Foreign (CCF) scheme, 239

Chinese Banking and Insurance Regulatory Commission, 219

Chinese Civil War, 18–19, 22

Chinese Communist Party (CCP): 15th National Congress, 237; 17th National Congress, 207–208; 18th National Congress, 196; 20th National Congress, 195; adaptiveness of, 47, 50; control of economy, 48, 49, 50–51; criticism of, 29, 47; "Decision on Issues Concerning the Establishment of a Socialist Market Economic Structure," 78; "Decision to Strengthen Rule of Law," 38; Department of Propaganda of, 31; Department of United Front Work of, 31; economic reforms of, 20, 23, 24, 27; environmental concerns of, 197, 205, 207–208; establishment of, 18, 26–27; first five-year plan, 20; foreign policy of, 31–32; General Secretary of, 28; hierarchical system of, 27, 30; ideology of, 27; legitimacy of, 23, 27, 32; membership trends, 27, 33, 46; personnel control, 31, 43–44; policies on private enterprises, 91, 92–93, 94, 100–101, 106, 269; political monopoly of, 26–27, 31, 45; price stabilization, 181; principle of "democratic centralism," 27; relationship between state sector and, 85; reliance on rural population, 61; rise to power, 18–19, 224, 259; Standing Committee of, 28; state–society relations under, 45–46

Chinese constitution, 92, 93, 94

Chinese Labor Law, 122

Chongqing municipality, 39

Christian missionary, 6, 13

city banks, 165

civil society, 211–214

Cixi, Empress dowager of China, 15–16, 25

climate change, 200–201, 215–217

Clinton, Bill, 214

coal: air pollution and, 198; China's consumption of, 198, 208, 217; as energy source, 198, 208

"Coastal Development Strategy," 225

collectively owned enterprises (COEs), 75, 92, 96, 105, 113, 135, 264

Columbus, Christopher, 3

command-and-control state, 80

Committee of Financial and Economic Affairs, 32

Committee of Political and Legal Affairs, 32

"common prosperity," 193

communes, 20–21, 46, 47, 52, 53, 55, 57, 61, 66, 276
comprador bourgeoisie, 20, 91, 276
Confucianism, 5, 6, 8, 13–14, 276
construction industry, 58
Cooperative Medical System (CMS), 140, 276
corporate governance, 168–169
corporate savings, 192
corruption, 32, 86, 110, 160
courts, 37–38
Covid-19 pandemic: control over the population during, 44, 49, 145; death toll, 145; government response to, 144–146, 261; impact on economy, 184; impact on migrant workers, 63, 121; lockdowns, 145; outbreak of, 144
"crossing the river by groping the stones" approach, 23, 266, 276
Cultural Revolution: attacks of state institutions during, 37; impact on private sector, 97; impact on rural China, 57, 69; launch of, 21–22; opposition to, 22; outcomes of, 22–24, 27; suspension of trade unions during, 133
cultural triumphalism, 9

Daoism, 9
debt securities, 169
"debt trap," 257, 276
"debt-swap" program, 161
deforestation, 200, 203, 215
Deng Pufang, 22
Deng Xiaoping: appeal to the army, 156; economic policies, 21, 23–24, 30, 42, 54, 73, 77–78, 93, 156, 207, 266; on inequality, 150; Mao's persecution of, 22, 30; political career of, 22, 23, 29; pragmatism of, 23, 265–266; rise to power, 23, 30; Southern tour of, 78, 93, 94, 180, 247; speech to the 12th CCP National Congress, 102
dependence ratio, 112, 277
Description of the World or *The Travels of Marco Polo, A* (Polo), 1–2

desertification, 203
development aid: to Africa, 251, 255, 260; Chinese characteristics of, 252–255; economic impact of, 256; expansion of, 258; focus on extraction and infrastructure, 253; impact on OFDI, 256; political effect of, 253–254, 256–257; positive and negative reactions to, 254, 257; promotion of economic interests and, 254; size of, 253; standards for, 252; types of, 252, *253*
Development Assistance Committee (DAC), 252, 254–255, 258, 277
developmental state, 91, 277
dibao. See Urban Minimum Living Guarantee System (UMLGS)
Didi Chuxing, 125
doctors: attacks on, 141, 142. *See also* barefoot doctors
dual pricing system, 42, 74, 76, 77, 229, 262, 264–265
Dulles, John Foster, 77

East Asian model of economic development, 227, 262, 263, 277
"ecological civilization," 196, 206, 216, 277
economy: boom-and-bust cycles, 179, 180–182; CCP control of, 48, 49, 50–51, 71–72; challenges of, xvi; command model of, 72–73; environment and, 197, 220; global economic system and, 82–83, 265, 273; governance of, 26, 30; growth of, 184, 191, 259, 269–270; imbalance of, 190–195; impact of the AFC on, 182; industrial over-production, 87; internationalization of, 37, 270–271; liberalization of, 77, 95, 179, 261; Maoist approach to, 20–21, 23, 30, 73; marketization of, 24, 35–36, 37, 42–43, 45, 188, 264; opening of, 240; politics and, 26, 36, 48, 50; public and non-public sectors of, 92; reforms of, 21, 23–24, 30, 42, 54,

322 Index

economy (*cont.*)
76, 77, 81; relationship between the state and, 89–90; resilience of, 267; restructuring of, 73–74, 192; socialist planning system in, 20, 24, 35, 41; state sector in, 86–87; stimulus package, 183, 193, 226, 281
"efficiency first and equity second" approach, 151
elections, 46–47, 66–67
electric vehicles (EVs), xvii
electronic industry, 84, 118–119
energy sector, 173–174
entrepreneurs, 7, 105, 106
environment: Belt and Road Initiative and, 219; civil society and, 211–214; degradation of, 197–200, 205, 207, 220; economic growth and, 205, 207–208, 220; enforcement of policy on, 107, 210; foreign relations and, 215–220; fragmented authoritarianism and, 209–210; international agreements, 206, 215–217; international organizations, 213–214; laws and regulations, 206; local governments policy, 209–210; Maoist policies and, 197; national government policy, 43, 196, 205–206; political economy and, 205–214; public concern about, 208, 211–213; water shortage and pollution, 200–203
environmental Kuznets Curve (EKC), 205
Environmental NGOs, 211–213, 214
environmental public interest litigation (EPIL), 212, 213
European Industrial Revolution, 1, 3, 4, 11–12, 24
European Union (EU): Chinese infrastructure projects in, 250; green energy in, 218
Everbright Bank, 163
exchange rate regime, 229
export: of commodities, 118; of electronics, 118–119; evolution of, 118; global financial crisis' impact on, 63; manufacturing and, 228; positive impact of, 228; productivity level and, 228; sectors with overcapacity to, 243; share of private enterprises in, 96; SOEs contribution to, 96; of solar panels, 217–218; to-GDP ratio, 222, *226*, 227
Export– Import Bank of China, 163, 248
export-led development model, 227–228
export-processing trade, 225, 226, 229, 234, 265, 277
extra-budgetary finance (EBF), 159, 160, 176, 277

Financial Regulatory Coordination Joint Ministerial Committee (JMC), 186
Financial Stability and Development Committee (FSDC), 186
financial system: evolution of, 176; industrial policy and, 176; major players in, 162; "National Team," 170; ranking of, 161; reform of, 165; state control of, 171–172, 173
First Auto Works, 86
fiscal system: crisis of, 155–156; decentralization of, 43, 155, 176, 277; decline of revenue, 155–156; definition of, 154; evolution of, 176; in planned economy, 154; post-recentralization problems, 158–161; recentralization of, 157–158, 278; reform of, 81, 156–158, 160; spending priorities, 154; transfers to provinces, 158
Five Anti campaign, 97
Five-Guarantees program, 133, 147
five-year plans, 20, 24, 35, 173, 205, 208, 212, 241, 244, 269
floating population, 62, 278
foreign direct investment (FDI): benefits of, 231–232, 236; definition of, 278; economic development

and, 235–236, 239–240; evolution of, 232–235; global financial crisis and, 234; government policy on, 75, 103–104, 126, 238; joint ventures and, 278; legislation on, 232; negative effects of, 238; political economy of, 236–238; ratio in GDP, 236–237; share in China's exports, 235; sources of, 233–234; statistics of inflow of, 222, *232*, 233, 234; studies of, 242

foreign reserves, 191, 242, 245

foreign trade: balancing of, 226; economic development and, 227–228; in Maoist era, 224; in the reform era, 225; restructuring of, 228–231; with the Soviet Union, 224; state monopoly of, 225

foreign-invested enterprises (FIEs), 75, 80, 92, 96, 105, 126, 130, 237

foreign-trade companies (FTCs), 225, 278

Forum of China-Africa Cooperation, 260

"four cardinal principles," 101–102

Foxconn Technology Group, 122, 123

fragmented authoritarianism, 41, 209–210, 278

Friends of Nature (FON), 211, 213, 214

Fujian Province, *40*; special economic zone, 116, 232, 266; strategic location of, 44

Gama, Vasco da, 3

gaming industry, 103

Gang of Four, 23

"gangster capitalism," 70

GDP (gross domestic product): annual growth rate, 49; decline of, 194; environmental cost of, 206–207, 208; growth of, xvii, xviii, 157, 182–183, 191, 235; per capita, *xvii*, 138, 278; in premodern era, 3; private sector contribution to, 95; ratio between government revenue and, 155, 156; state sector contribution to, 73

General Agreement on Tariffs and Trade (GATT), 230

George III, King of Great Britain, 9, 10

gig economy, 125

Gini Index in China, *134*

global financial crisis (GFC): Chinese investment in Western economies and, 244; impact on China's economy, 63, 82, 95, 160, 165, 183–184, 264, 267; impact on global economy, 186, 273

global photovoltaic (PV) module market, 217–218

global value chains (GVCs), 235–236

Global Village Beijing, 211

Gorbachev, Mikhail, 77

government bonds, 171

government industrial guidance funds, 174

Government Insurance Scheme (GIS), 139, 278

government revenue: ratio between GDP and, 155, 156, 157

government-organized NGOs (GONGOs), 211, 213

"grain first" agricultural policy, 53–54

Grain-for-Green program, 204

"grasping the big and letting go the small" policy, 79–80, 93, 182, 265, 278

Great Britain: embassy to Qing court, 9, 13; industrialization in, 3, 12

"great divergence" between China and Europe, 1, 4

Great Green Wall of China project, 203–204

Great Leap Forward (GLF) campaign, 20, 21, 23, 24, 27, 30, 53

green development conception, 220

Green GDP, 206, 207, 209–210, 278

greenhouse gas (GHS) emission, 199, *199*, 205, 215, 219

Greenpeace, 214

gross domestic savings, 190

"growing out of the plan" strategy, 229, 278

Guangdong Province: GDP of, 44; *40*; migrant workers in, 62, 135; population of, 44; special economic zones, 116, 232, 266; TVEs in, 59
Guangxi election experiment, 46
Guangxu, Emperor of China, 15–16, 25

Hainan Province: *40*; strategic location of, 44
Han Dynasty, 6, 8, 13–14, 276
health insurance schemes, 139–140, 141, 143–144, 146
healthcare system: cost of, 141; Covid-19 pandemic and, 146–147; deterioration of, 140, 141, 143; facilities, 146; funding of, 139, 141, 143, 144, 146; for government employees, 268; investment in, 151; Maoist, 139; out-of-pocket spending on, *146*; reform of, 139, 144; in rural and urban areas, 140, 141
healthcare utilization, 145
"Healthy China 2030," 144
Henan Province, *40*, 44, 200
high-level equilibrium trap, 11
homeowners' associations, 47
Hon Hai Precision Industry, 122
Honda Strike, 129
Hong Kong: British rule of, 13, 59; CCP influence in, 31; investment in China, 233–235; labor costs, 116; as manufacturing powerhouse, 225, *40*; multinational corporations from, 117
Hong Kong exchange (HKEX), 167
Hong Xiuquan, 14, 25
hospitals, 141
household businesses, 75
household farming, 52, 53, 54–55, 57, 66, 115
household income, 151, 192
household responsibility system, 54, 55–56, 114, 266, 279
Hu Jintao, 80, 136–137, 158, 191, 205–206, 263, 264
Hua Guofeng, 23, 30
Huawei, 122

Huaxi Village, 59, 60
Huaxia Bank, 163
hukou (household registration system), 61–62, 70, 113, 116, 123, 279
"Hundred Flowers" campaign, 34

Illustrated Gazetteer of the Countries Overseas (Wei), 13–14
imperial China: 1911 revolution, 17; attitude toward foreigners, 9, 14, 17; barriers to non-agricultural activities, 13; bureaucracy, 5, 6, 7; cities, 2; commercial activities in, 6–7; communication system, 2; comparison with Europe, 12, 12–13; comparison with Japan, 16–17; Confucian ethics of, 6, 8–9; cultural triumphalism of, 8–9; decline of, 3–4, 5–6, 8; diplomatic relations, 9; dynasties, 25; economic and demographic conditions, 10–13; epidemics, 11; GDP per capita, 3; industrial development of, 6, 12, 15, 24; infrastructure, 2; inventions, 3; labor, 11; medieval descriptions of, 1–2; Mongol conquest of, 1–2; obstacle to capitalism in, 6; opening of, 3; opium trade, 3; political system, 4–7, 16; population growth, 10–11; rebellions in, 14, 16; reforms in, 13–16; science and technology in, 2–3, 5, 6, 9, 24; size of economy, 2; upward mobility, 6; Western conquest of, 3, 13, 17
Imperial Summer Palace, 13
income-per-capita level, 228
incomplete urbanization, 63
individual enterprises, 92–93, 94, 95, 96, 105, 133
Industrial and Commercial Bank of China (ICBC), 83, 163, 165
Industrial and Commercial Federation, 107
industrial enterprises, 229
industrialization, 73
infant mortality, 139

inflation, 24, *180*, 181
informal financing, 101
initial public offerings (IPOs), 166, 167, 170
interbank market, 171
International Aid Transparency Initiative, 252
International Monetary Fund (IMF), 49, 161, 230, 260
international trade, 223–224, 227, 231
International Trade Organization (ITO), 230
"iron rice bowl," 117, 237, 268, 279
Ito, Hirobumi, 15

Janus-faced business associations, 107, 279
Japan: attitude toward foreign cultures, 17; comparison with China, 16–17; DAC framework, 254–255; foreign direct investment, 236, 238; modernization of, 17, 227, 236; political system of, 16–17; savings rate, 190; Western powers and, 16
Jiang Qing (Madame Mao), 21–22, 23
Jiang Zeming, 81, 100, 136, 157, 187, 241, 263
Jiangsu Province, *40*, 44, 59, 62, 202
Jiangxi Province, 22, *40*
joint ventures, 60–61, 238, 240, 279

Kang Youwei, 15, 25
Khrushchev, Nikita, 224
Kowloon Peninsula, 13
kuaikuai (pieces) authority relationships, 39, 41, 279
Kublai Khan, Emperor of China, 2, 25
Kuomintang (KMT), 18, 33, 72, 173, 181, 230
Kyoto Protocol, 215

labor: aging, 119; bureaucracy and, 128; conditions of, 119–125; cost of, 116, 119; lack of independent unions, 128; law on, 126, 128; management of, 114–115; mass organization

of, 127; mobility of, 113–114; non-agricultural, 114; in non-state enterprises, 115; productivity of, 56, 114; supply of, 129–130; transfer of, 119; unrest, 123; wages, 114
Labor Insurance Scheme (LIS), 139, 140, 279
labor market: formation of, 112, 113–119; *hukou* system in, 116; precarious employment in, 124–125; reform of, 114, 117; segregation of, 121; state regulations of, 115
land: degradation of, 203–204, 215; redistribution of, 53; tenure, 55–56
Land Reform Law, 19
Landesa Rural Development Institute, 68
Law on Joint Ventures Using Chinese and Foreign Investment, 232
"laying eggs with borrowed hens" policy, 222
Leading Group of Environmental Protection, 205
legal system, 38–39
Legalism, 9
Li Hongzhang, 14–15, 25
Liang Qichao, 214
Liang Sicheng, 214
Liaoning Province, *40*, 44
life expectancy, 139
"lifeline industries," 172
limited liability companies, 79, 95
Lin, Justin Yifu, 5, 6, 53
Lin Huiyin, 214
Lin Zexu, 3, 25
Liu Shaoqi, 21, 22, 30, 54
local government financing vehicles (LGFVs), 159, 161, 175
local governments: autonomy of, 44–45; borrowing practices, 160–161, 175–176; corruption of, 107, 160; debt of, 176; "debt-swap" program, 161; elections of, 46–47; environmental policies and, 209–210; fiscal conditions of, 158–159, 160; incentives to develop TVEs, 59,

Index

local governments (*cont.*)
194; lobbying efforts, 44; national leadership and, 41, 43, 44–45, 47; popular protests against, 47–48, 68; private enterprises and, 101, 107; revenue of, 158, 175; social policy experiments, 150; SOEs and, 41–42; tasks of, 47
Lou Jiwei, 160
Luckin Coffee, 167

Ma, Jack (Ma Yun), 104
Macao, 31, 39, *40*
Macartney, George, 9, 10, 13
macroeconomic management, 178–179, 182–184
"Made in China 2025" program, 174, 175, 279
mafia-like business systems, 109, 110
manufacturing products, 174, 175
Mao Zedong: approach to nature, 197; authority of, 29, 34; China's development strategy, 73; death of, xviii, 27, 52; Deng Xiaoping and, 22; economic policy, xviii, 20–23, 27, 30; foreign policy, 42; industrial output under, 71; as leader of CCP, 18; on local governments, 41; purges, 21–22; "Third Front" campaign 42; sent down youth movement and, 113
Marx, Karl: *Das Kapital*, 93
medical disturbance, 141, 282
medical savings accounts (MSAs), 141
Medium-and-Long-Term Program of Science and Technology, 88
mega-cities, 122
Meiji, Emperor of Japan, 17
"middle income trap," 243
"Middle Kingdom," 1, 13, 24
migrant workers: benefits for local communities, 64; children of, 63–64; Covid-19 pandemic and, 121; delayed payments, 121; destinations of, 62; dream for upward mobility, 120; education level, 120, 130; employment opportunities for,

52, 62–63, 267–268; generational transition of, 130; health insurance, 121; housing, 121–122; labor activism of, 130; life beyond work, 121; marginalization of, 122, 124–125, 130; mass eviction of, 122; mental health problems, 122, 123; pension plans, 121; self-employment of, 120; social insurance coverage, 124; sources of, 119; statistics of, 62, 119–120, 124–125; wages, 121; working conditions of, 112
military spending, 156, 158
military-run farms, 156
Ming Dynasty, 2, 6, 16
Ministry of Environmental Protection, 205
Ministry of Labor and Social Security, 36
Minsheng Bank, 163
"mixed ownership" enterprises, 83–84, 92, 103
Mohism, 9
monetary policy, 188
Moore, Barrington, 102
MSCI Emerging Market Index, 168–169
multinational corporations (MNCs), 117, 231, 233, 234, 235, 240, 242

Nanjing, Treaty of, 13
National Audit Bureau, 160
National Audit Office, 35
national bourgeoisie, 20, 91, 279
national champions: international operations of, 83, 88; political connections of, 88; preferential policies for, 82, 83, 264, 279; SASAC supervision of, 82, 85–86
National Conferences on Environmental Protection, 205
National Data Bureau, 36
National Development and Reform Commission (NDRC), 35, 80–81, 87, 128, 187, 192–193, 247
National Financial Work Conference, 186

National Health Commission, 35
national income identity, 190
national interbank market, 189
National New-Type Urbanization Plan, 121
National Party Congress: annual meetings of, 28–29; authority of, 27, *28*; Congresses, 29, 79, 92, 102; election of delegates of, 28, 29
National People's Congress (NPC), 33–34, 35, 92, 94, 280
national savings, 192
national security, 50
National Social Security Fund, 136
"National Team," 170, 280
Nationalist Party (KMT), 18, 77, 156
Needham, Joseph, 5, 12, 280
Needham puzzle, 5, 280
neo-Confucianism, 13–14
new Chinese proletariat, 119
New Development Bank (NDB), 251, 280
New Left, 273, 280
New Orient Education and Technology (*Xindongfang*), 103
New Rural Cooperative Medical Scheme (NCMS), 143
New Rural Pension Scheme (NRPS), 137
newly industrialized economies (NIEs), 227
Nian Guangjiu, 94
Nixon, Richard, 72
nomenklatura system, 85–86
non-bank financial institutions, 165
non-public economic sector, 81
non-state enterprises, 75
Nu River Dam Project, 212

official development assistance (ODA), 252
open market operations (OMO), 189
"Opinions on Deepening Health System Reform," 144
Opium Wars, 3, 13, 18, 276, 277
ordinary trade, 225, 226

Organic Law on Village Self-Governance, 46
Organization of Economic Cooperation and Development (OECD) countries, 126, 146, 252, 254, 277
outward foreign direct investment (OFDI): actors of, 244; annual flow of, 247; banking system and, 100, 248–249; evolution of, 243–244; geographic distribution of, 244; impact on domestic economy, 245, 246; impact on innovation and technology, 245–246; motivations for, 242–243, 258; political economy of, 247–250; private sector and, 96, 244; regulations of, 247, 248, 249; state sector and, 244; statistics of, 247, *248*; studies of, 249; traditional theories of, 248; unfavorable factors for, 247

Pan family, 7
Paris Climate Agreement, 206, 216–217
Park Chung-hee, 172
Party state: capitalism and, 90, 91, 263; concept of, 27, 50, 280; control of banks, 193; control of state sector, 88; flow of authority in, *28*; focus on development, 193; governance of the private sector, 108; personnel control in, 43–44; resilience of regime of, 108; social contract with the Chinese people, 48
Pearl River Delta: floating population in, 62; model of TVEs in, 59; soil quality, 204; trade in, 225
peasants: financial burden of, 67–68, 73; land expropriation from, 65–66, 67, 68–69; non-agricultural work, 12, 57, 114; organization into collectives, 113; productivity of, 267; protests of, 68, 69–70; urban migration, 62
Peng Dehuai, 30
Peng Lifa, 29
Peng Zhen, 66

pension system: administrators of, 134–135; debt accumulation, 138; for enterprise workers, 138; fragmentation and inequality of, 135, 136, 138; funding of, 133, 135, 136, 137; individual contributions, 137; investment in, 151; local programs, 136; pay-as-you-go (PAYG) principle, 135, 136; for public sector employees, 137–138, 268; reform of, 134, 135, 138; for rural residents, 136, 137, 150; unsustainability of, 138; for urban residents, 136, 137

people-oriented development approach, 151

People's Bank of China (PBC): autonomy and authority of, 162, 187, 188, 189, 195; establishment of, 181; evolution of, 185–186; function of, 187–189, 280; implications of financial technology, 189; legislature on, 185–186; lending activities, 163; macroeconomic management, 178–179, 184–185; monetary policy, 188–189; professionalism and expertise, 187; reorganization of, 43; state apparatus and, 35, 36, 128, 187

People's Daily, 95

People's Liberation Army (PLA), 156

permanent migrants, 120, 280

Perry, Matthew, 17

PetroChina, 86

pharmaceutical companies, 141

Poland fiasco, 250

Political bureau (Politburo) of the CCP, 27–28, 194–195, 280

political participation, 46, 50

political systems: economy and, 50; Europe *vs.* China, 4–5

Polo, Marco, 1–2, 25

popular protests, 47–48, 67, 69–70, 150–151. *See also* Tiananmen movement

precariat, 124, 125, 267–268, 281

price liberalization, 76

private enterprises: associations of, 107–108; banks and, 98; charitable contributions, 106–107; contribution to economy, 110; Covid pandemic and, 103; discrimination against, 109–110; diversity of, 108–109; efficiency of, 95, 97, 99; employment opportunities in, 95–96, 105; expansion of, 91–96, 115; financing of, 98, 99–100, 101; institution-bending strategies of, 110; lack of unity for collective action, 109; local governments and, 101, 107; mafia-like, 109, 110; management of, 100–101; "mixed ownership" of, 92; nationalization of, 91, 97; overseas investments, 96, 244, 258; Party control of, 92–93, 94, 102, 103; public relations fees, 99; registration of, 106; regulations of, 103; relations with the government, 106, 109; return on assets, 96, 97; share in exports, 96; State Council's policies on, 97–98; statistics of, 92, 95; types of payments of, 98–99; unfavorable environment, 20, 96; "wearing a red hat" practice, 106, 107; during Xi era, 102

Private Entrepreneurs' Association, 107

private property, 94–95, 98

private sector, 90, 92, 97–105, 108

Protestantism, 8–9

Provisional Act of Private Enterprises of the People's Republic of China, 93

public economic sector, 81

public service organizations, 133, 159

Qianlong, Emperor of China, 9, 10

Qin Dynasty, 4

Qing Dynasty, xix, 1, 9, 13–17, 34, 277

R&D resources, 119

real estate industry, 84, 180

red capitalists, 281

"Re-employment Projects," 123

Regulations on Labor Insurance, 133

regulatory state, 36, 80

"releasing authority and sharing benefits" policy, 74
Renminbi (RMB), 225
retirement age, 138
Revolutionary Committee of the Chinese Kuomintang, 33
Ricardo, David, 223
"rightful resistance," 68, 281
Rio Convention, 215
rural China: collective economic organization, 61, 67; cooperative welfare, 132; de-collectivization, 55; economic transformation of, 19, 66, 70; elections in, 66–67; industrial activities in, 57–59, 60, 92; labor statistics, 114; migrant workers in, 116; population decline, 140; protests, 67, 69–70; self-governance in, 66–67; transformation of, 52, 54, 67, 69; *vs.* urban China, 61–62. *See also* agriculture; peasants
rural-urban divide, 62–64, 68, 69, 113, 116

Samoa, 235
"scientific outlook on development," 206
Securities Finance Corporation (CSF), 170
securities industry, 166, 170
security apparatus, 48
Self-Employed Laborers' Association, 107
Self-Strengthening Movement (a.k.a. Westernization Movement), 1, 14–15, 17, 24, 281
sent-down youth movement, 113
Severe Acute Respiratory Syndrome (SARS), 142–143
Shandong Province, *40*, 44
Shanghai municipality, *40*, 44, 62, 165
Shanghai Stock Exchange (SSE), 166, 170
Shanghai-Hong Kong Stock Connect, 166
Shanxi Province, *40*, 44

"Shazi Guazi (Fool's Sunflower Seeds)" trademark, 94
Shenzhen Development Bank, 163
Shenzhen Stock Exchange (SZSE), 166, 170
Shenzhen-Hong Kong Stock Connect, 166
Shimonoseki, Treaty of, 15
shipbuilding industry, 173
"shock therapy," 76, 77, 262, 281
Sichuan Province, *40*, 55
"Silk Road Economic Belt," 218–219, 241, 275
Sino capitalism, 265
Sino-Japanese wars, 15, 18
Sinopec Group, 83, 86
Smith, Adam: *Wealth of Nations*, 3
social assistance, 147–149
social inequality, 77, 133–134
Social Insurance Agencies, 134
social organizations, 211, 213
social pooling account (SPA), 141, 142
soft budget constraints, 74, 182, 281
soil erosion and pollution, 203, 204, 215
solar power, 198, 206, 217, 218
Song Dynasty, 10, 13
South Korea: democratic movements, 45; economic development, 45, 105, 172; financial policy, 172; foreign direct investment, 236; savings rate, 190
sovereign bonds, 169
sovereign wealth funds (SWFs), 242
Soviet Union: industrialization of, 20; support of China, 20, 72
special economic zones (SEZs): benefits of, 59; definition of, 281; establishment of, 75, 116, 225, 240, 266; multinational corporations in, 116–117
Spring-and-Autumn period, 8
Sri Lanka's Hambantota Port project, 257
State Administration of Foreign Exchange (SAFE), 242

state apparatus: economic reform and, 36; executive branch of, 35–36; judicial branch, 37; legislative branch of, 34; regulatory agencies, 36–37

State Council: investments regulations, 102, 247; macroeconomic policies, 181, 183, 186; pension reform, 135; Premier of, 73; promotion of international capacity cooperation, 243; reform of, 80, 81; securities regulation, 166; support of non-state-owned enterprises, 97–98; tasks of, 33, 35

State Development Planning Commission, 35

State Environmental Protection Administration (SEPA), 205

State Grid Corporation of China, 83, 88, 249

State Planning Commission (SPC), 35, 73, 80, 181

State Power Corporation of China, 88

state sector: bifurcation of, 79; economic development and, 86; employees statistics, 96; evolution of, 72; government protection of, 102; market mechanisms in, 90; Party state's control of, 80, 81–84, 85, 87, 88; reform of, 72–76, 84, 85, 89–90; restructuring of, 74–75, 125

State Taxation Administration, 35, 36

state-invested enterprises (SIEs), 84

State-owned Assets Supervision and Administration Commission (SASAC), 82, 85–86, 219

state-owned commercial banks (SOCBs), 163–164, 168

state-owned enterprises (SOEs): abandonment of small and medium, 79–80, 81; access to credit, 181–182; benefits of, 73; borrowing practices, 159, 163–164; as bureaucratic agencies, 73; business opportunities, 74; competitiveness of, 58, 74, 265; contract management responsibility system, 74; contribution to exports, 96; corporatization of, 79, 81; employment security, 73; expansion of, 82–83; foreign investments of, 244; formation of, 36, 41; government subsidies to, 71, 76, 82, 83–84, 89, 263, 264; groups of, 81, 86; impact of economic reform on, 117; industrial output of, 71, 75; inefficiency of, 71, 72–73, 89; legislation on, 84; local governments and, 41–42; managerial positions in, 85–86; negative effect of state control of, 88–89; overseas investments, 88; political economy of, 85–89; private investments in, 84, 89; privatization of, 79, 100; procurement contracts, 98; productivity of, 75, 97, 155, 264; profitability of, 81, 82, 134; reforms of, 74–75, 84, 85, 87, 124; return on assets, 96, 97; SASAC-controlled, 86; share in urban economy, 154; state support of, 79, 83, 95, 182; statistics of, 79–80; taxation of, 155; as total institutions, 73; welfare system, 133, 135. *See also* national champions

state–society relations, 45–50

stimulus package, 183, 193, 226, 281

stock exchanges, 166, 167, 168, 171

stock market, 99, 168, 169

Sun Yat-sen, 17–18

"supply-side" structural reform, 87, 183

Supreme People's Court (SPC), 33, 37

Supreme People's Precuratory, 33

surveillance instruments, 48–49

System of Environmental-Economic Accounting (SEEA), 207

Taiping Rebellion, 14

Taiwan: banks, 173; CCP United Front Work regarding, 31; democratic movement, 45; economic development of, 105, 172–173; foreign direct investment, 233–235, 236; Japanese rule of, 15; labor costs,

116, *40*; multinational corporations, 117; seat at UN Security Council, 251

Tang Dynasty, 8
tax sharing system (TSS), 157, 158
taxation: of businesses, 233; control of, 65; reform of, 68, 151, 156–157; of rural population, 67, 68; transformation of, 43, 59
telecommunication infrastructure, 239
temporary migrants, 120, 281
"Temporary Regulations on the Use of Labor Contracts in State-Run Enterprises," 115
Third Plenum of the 14th CCP Congress, 78
Third Plenum of the 18th National Party Congress, 95
Three Gorges Project, 34
"Three Represents" theory, 100, 282
Three-Withouts, 133, 147, 148
Tiananmen movement, 30–31, 47, 77, 85, 93, 100, 230, 270–271, 282
Tianjin municipality, 2, *40*
tiaotiao (strips) authority relationships, 39
Tibet Autonomous Region, *40*, 44
tied aid, 282
Tokugawa Shogunate, 17
Tongren Hospital incident, 142
tourism, 196
township and village enterprises (TVEs): competitiveness of, 58, 59, 75, 264; conversion to joint-stock cooperatives, 60–61; decline of, 59–60, 67; definition of, 282; emergence of, 265; employment opportunities in, 57; export-processing (EP) operations, 225; foreign trade, 58; models of, 59, 60; in the Pearl River Delta, 265; share in industrial output of, 57–58, 71; spread of, 42, 52, 75
Trump, Donald, 194

21st Century Maritime Silk Road, 219, 241, 275

UN Climate Change Conference in Durban, 215
UN Conference on Human Environment, 205
UN Convention to Combat Desertification (UNCCD), 203
UN Framework Convention on Climate Change (UNFCCC), 215
UN Industrial Development Organization, 227
UN Security Council, 251
UN Sustainable Development Summit, 272
unemployment, xvii, 80, 85, 117, *118*, 119, 123, 147, 268
United States: Chinese investment in, 245, 250; greenhouse gas emission of, 199, *199*; Paris Agreement and, 216; relations with China, 72, 194, 216; relations with Japan, 17; solar energy in, 218
"upper levels policies, lower levels counter-policies" phenomenon, 39
urban China: economic liberalization in, 20, 69, 114–115; employment in, 113; healthcare in, 141; social welfare in, 113
Urban Employee Basic Medical Insurance (UEBMI), 141, 144
urban industrial economy, 71, 73–74
Urban Minimum Living Guarantee System (UMLGS), 147, 148, 149, 277
urban population: middle class, 102; statistics, *64*, 64–65, 199
Urban Resident Basic Medical Insurance (URBMI), 143
Urban Residents Pension Plan (URPP), 137
urbanization, 64–66, 130
Urban-Rural Resident Basic Medical Insurance (URRBMI) program, 143–144

value-added tax (VAT), 156, 157
villagers' committees, 46–47, 66–67, 69, 148

Wan Li, 54, 55
Wang, Canfa, 211
"Washington Consensus," 260, 263, 272, 282
water shortage and pollution, 201–203
Wealth of Nations (Smith), 3
"wearing a red hat" practice, 106, 107, 269, 282
Weber, Max, 8
Wei, Yuan, 25; *Illustrated Gazetteer of the Countries Overseas*, 13–14
welfare system: comparative studies of, 151; economic modernization and, 132, 133, 150; future of, 153; impact of political system on, 152; level of protection provided by, 151; neoliberalism in, 268; political economy of, 149–152; reform of, 151, 153; in rural areas, 158; transformation of, 132–133, 149–150, 153, 158; types of, 151–152; urban-rural divide and, 134; work units in, 47
Wen Jiabao, 80, 136–137, 158, 191, 205–206, 212, 228, 260, 263, 264
White Paper on China's Population, Environment, and Development in the Twenty-first Century, 205
Who Will Feed China (Brown), 65
Williamson, John, 260
wind power, 198, 206, 217
work units *(danwei)*, 47, 61, 73, 113, 140, 282
World Bank, 173, 230, 260, 263, 264, 269
World Health Organization (WHO), 139
World Trade Organization (WTO):

China's membership in, 81–82, 157, 164, 192, 226, 228, 230–231, 247
Wu, Emperor of Han Dynasty (personal name Liu Che), 25
Wu Renbao, 60

Xi Jinping: anti-corruption campaigns, 32, 86; authoritarian power of, 29, 273; Belt and Road Initiative, 87, 218–219; "China Dream" slogan promoted by, xviii; consolidation of state security, 48; criticism of, 29; economic policy of, 95, 260–261, 272; environmental policy of, 196, 206, 216, 277; "holistic national security concept," 50; Jack Ma and, 104; political career of, 29, 43, 260; punishment of party officials, 32–33; visit to Yucun, 196
Xiaogang Village household farming experiment, 54
Xiaomi, 122
Xie Yang, 49
Xinjian Village fire, 122
Xinjiang Uygur Autonomous Region, 38, *40*, 44

Yangtze River: trade operations, 225; water diversion project on, 201
Yuan Dynasty, 1
Yunnan Province, *40*

Zeng Guofan, 14, 25
Zhao Ziyang, 31, 54, 55, 73, 85
Zhejiang Province, *40*, 59, 62, 100, 101, 105, 135
Zheng He, 2–3, 25
Zhou Dynasty, 8
Zhou Xiaochuan, 187
Zhu Rongji, 80, 81, 136, 156, 157, 181, 230, 263
zombie enterprises, 87